W9-CRH-518

THE TITLE OF TOTONICAPÁN

THE TITLE OF
TOTONICAPÁN

Transcription, Translation, and Commentary by

Allen J. Christenson

UNIVERSITY PRESS OF COLORADO
Louisville

Published by University Press of Colorado
245 Century Circle, Suite 202
Louisville, Colorado 80027

 The University Press of Colorado is a proud member of
the Association of University Presses.

The University Press of Colorado is a cooperative publishing enterprise supported, in part, by Adams State University, Colorado State University, Fort Lewis College, Metropolitan State University of Denver, Regis University, University of Alaska Fairbanks, University of Colorado, University of Denver, University of Northern Colorado, University of Wyoming, Utah State University, and Western Colorado University.

∞ This paper meets the requirements of the ANSI/NISO Z39.48-1992 (Permanence of Paper).

ISBN: 978-1-64642-263-0 (hardcover)
ISBN: 978-1-64642-265-4 (paperback)
ISBN: 978-1-64642-264-7 (ebook)
https://doi.org/10.5876/9781646422647

Library of Congress Cataloging-in-Publication Data

Names: Christenson, Allen J., 1957– transcriber, translator, writer of added commentary.
Title: The title of Totonicapan / transcription, translation, and commentary by Allen J. Christenson.
Other titles: Titulo de Totonicapan. English (Christenson) | Titulo de Totonicapan. Quiche (Christenson)
Description: Louisville, Colorado : University Press of Colorado, [2022] | Includes bibliographical references and index. | English and Quiche. |
Identifiers: LCCN 2022030972 (print) | LCCN 2022030973 (ebook) | ISBN 9781646422647 (ebook) | ISBN 9781646422630 (hardcover) | ISBN 9781646422654 (paperback)
Subjects: LCSH: Quiche Indians—Social life and customs. | Quiche Indians—History. | Quiche language—Texts. | Totonicapan (Guatemala)—History.
Classification: LCC F1465.2.Q5 (ebook) | LCC F1465.2.Q5 T55 2022 (print) | DDC 305.897/4230728181 23/eng/20220—dc16
LC record available at https://lccn.loc.gov/2022030972

Cover illustration: *Baile de la Conquista*, Santiago Atitlán, 2019. Mask and costume made in Totonicapán. Photo by Allen J. Christenson

To my wife, Janet

Xa at ayaom uki'il uqusil uk'ok'al qachoch

Contents

Illustrations and Maps

ILLUSTRATIONS

(All photographs are by the author unless otherwise noted on the captions.)

MAPS

Foreword

Motion Capture

STEPHEN HOUSTON

Long ago, my mother, a brave soul, crossed the Atlantic from Sweden to settle with her American husband in the woods of Pennsylvania. I can only imagine the trauma. She had left her family behind. Parents and siblings were distant, phone calls were costly, and letters from relatives arrived in small batches at best. Her long-term future: a new people, language, and land. But it was ever thus for most people. By now, genetic studies confirm that in broadest scope, humans do move around if having to adjust, as my mother did, to novel settings. The early Americas attest to such migrations, some possibly from an Australasian route (the so-called Population Y pattern; Skoglund et al. 2015), others going *back* to Eurasia after sojourns in North America (Flegontov et al. 2019). Yet there is also a pronounced tendency to stay put, to find comfort in the familiar (Lindo et al. 2017; Posth et al. 2019). With air travel, my mother returned yearly to the beaches and glowing summer nights of her youth. Time and place—journeys started and reversed, then started again—marked her identity. In so doing, they marked mine.

In this book, Allen Christenson says many useful things about place, time, and the meaning of movement in establishing and affirming identity. By translating the *Título de Totonicapán* (*Title of Totonicapán*), a document in K'iche' Maya from about AD 1554, he shows what it takes to transpose the words and thoughts of a far language into our own. In *Errata: An Examined Life*, the belletrist George Steiner (1998, 107) tells us what is at stake. Without these labors "we would inhabit parishes bordering on silence." Can anyone doubt that to thrive, the world needs

https://doi.org/10.5876/9781646422647.c000a

more communication, not less, and from times both far and near? Allen has done his part to ensure that we know of the historical claims and links to the landscape of the highland Maya of Guatemala. He makes mountains and valleys talk; he invites luxuriant, coupletted metaphors to settle into the cadence of our own thought. This is his gift and his hard work, honed from close knowledge of the K'iche' language, a superlative translation of the *Popol Vuh*, a K'iche' epic, and many days of asking questions of the indigenous, still active keepers of time, the *ajq'ijab'*.

A second virtue of this book is that he reminds us of the importance of place but, above all, the predicaments of movement: when to set down roots, when to relocate, and how to record those migrations in the face of existential challenges posed by the Spanish empire (Matsumoto 2017, 5–7). It is not, perhaps, for us to say whether these journeys occurred in fact. They were thought vitally important, validating history by referring to a visible, treadable landscape, one that might be revisited and ritually venerated. Of course, Mesoamerica is not the only region to be understood in this way, to judge from the manifold accounts of emergence, movement, splitting apart, conjoining, and settling in Native North America. There was a continual state of becoming, a kind of "process philosophy" in which there were waypoints and paths that became like "umbilical" cords, a living part of the self (Preucel and Duwe 2019, 13–19). Other accounts refer to special "runners" carrying messages along routes, organized as "fraternities" bound by rules of behavior and guided by dreams; well-attested examples include the Mesquackie of Iowa, the Chemehuevi of California, and the Iroquois Confederacy of New York (Nabokov 1981, 14–18). More than conveying messages, such motion might re-create, to local belief, the Milky Way, waterways, cardinal directions, and seasons and tie together different states of being. Indeed, among the Hopi of Arizona, to sprint was to summon rain clouds for agriculture, the swift runner becoming "rain-cloud-blown-by-wind, or sun-on-his-path" (23, 26–27). It appears likely that similar marvels were facilitated by the Maya roads and causeways, the *sak bih*, or "white roads," of Classic Maya times (Houston 2013).

The Classic Maya that I study had profound interest in primordial movement and ritual motion. Many things and people were said to "go up" or "rise" (*t'abayi*), either in raising a stela or a chocolate cup but also in a reference to political exile, perhaps up to some high refuge. Individuals might exit or "leave" (*lok'oyi*), conceptualized as a snake slithering out of a split opening. Others could "arrive" (*huli*), or they might stand in place (*wal*), "return" (*pakxi*), an expression applied at times to supernatural brides; then there were those who might "run" or "walk briskly" (*ahni*) or "go" (*bixniiy*). A vase found at Baking Pot, Belize, lays out many verbs of motion as components of an intricate narrative of regional conflict (Helmke et al. 2018, fig. 12). These readings result from the work of several scholars, but they all point to two features: first, everyday movements found added nuance in dynastic or supernatural contexts; and, second, they appeared always to concern individuals, somewhat like the heroic figures described in the *Títulos*. Foundations are known in Classic Maya sources as well, hinting equally at the concerns of the *Títulos*. First studied by David Stuart, these glyphic references have been compiled in a number of sources (e.g., Tokovinine 2013, 79–81). On occasion, as on Throne 1 at Piedras Negras, Guatemala, such events marked a change in dynasty. The movements or the deities, bundles, or ritual effigies —called a "luminous image" or "body" at Piedras Negras— recall similar practices in the *Títulos*. There must have been more to these shifts and resets than simply a shuffling of legs in swinging gait or a burden on the back (Oudijk 2002; Olivier 2007). Central Mexican sources, some from about the same time as the composition of the *Títulos*, mention purification, music, fire and fire drilling, sacrifice, measurements, metaphors of rising and bleeding suns (a new dawn), and the building of essential temples (Codex Vienna f. 20). Visions and portents decided where to settle. These actions are likely to have accompanied the events in the more terse passages of the T*ítulos*.

Pictorial documents that package origins, motion, identities, and motion occur with some frequency in colonial Mexico. Doubtless, they had Pre-Columbian roots. A copy of what may be an event-laden map of Teotihuacan origin even appears, rather surprisingly, in a mural at La Sufricaya, Guatemala, that dates to ca. AD 400 (Tokovinine 2013, fig. 33). In Western thought, maps tend to operate as synchronous displays. What is depicted exists at the same time. Indigenous maps, by contrast, place events in sequence by means of connecting paths with images nearby of people, buildings, and actions. Elizabeth H. Boone (2000, 163, 165) calls these documents "itineraries," albeit ones that record relative rather than absolute space. The *Títulos* must have had some visual precursors, and perhaps they had sonic or kinetic ones as well. In the early 1990s, David Stuart and I considered that a historical anniversary on a Classic-era monument, Hieroglyphic Stairway 4 of Dos Pilas, Guatemala, involved dance and song or oratory. One can imagine the same for Highland Guatemala. In a sense, the *Títulos* can be seen as an example of ekphrasis, in which a visual display and oral performance were distilled into a paginated record in Roman script. To be sure, the accounts of the *Títulos* must be a composite. Patched from multiple sources, they are fixedly local in intent despite their couching in primordial time and creation. Ultimately, as Allen points out, the work confronted a difficult task: to acknowledge a past full of "miraculous" events and ancestors—the motherless, those possessed of perfect sight, glorious people yet ones dressed in wild skins and rags—yet still recognize a new reality of Christian faith and imperial rule.

Intriguing kernels of cultural detail can be retrieved in the pages that follow. There is the news (to me) that the *Títulos* were used in arguing land disputes as late as 1834. This was truly a manuscript with an afterlife. I was struck personally that the quadripartition of the layout in the K'iche' capital of Q'umarkaj resembles to eerie extent Felipe Guaman Poma de Ayala's *El primer nueva corónica y buen gobierno*, from 1615 (folio 42; http://www5.kb.dk/permalink/2006/poma/42/en/text/?open=idm46287306358272). Also beginning with an abbreviated account of creation (with Old and New Testament inflections), that manuscript presents a four-part model of imperial quadrants in Castile and in the Inka empire, each exemplified by a city laid out around a central square. (Guaman Poma conceded, it seems, that the Spanish cities were larger, yet he managed to highlight the Andean peaks, over which the sun shone merrily; in a dig at the *conquistadores*, Castile was given a dull, featureless plain.) The *Títulos* offer other riches: there are the seven caves common to origin accounts linked to the Tower of Babel—before was harmonious, easy communication; afterward, dissension and difference. Then there is the allusion to vessels of stinging insects on defensive palisades or to smoke signals as a method of coordinated communication. The minute description of how to use a sweatbath with fragrant plants will guide me in future use of this most excellent aspect of Maya life. And finally, in sumptuous array, Allen unveils the insignia of royal office: the canopies of precious bird feathers, the jaguar and puma throne, deer heads and hooves, talons of eagles, egret feathers, and the stone ornaments that signaled high status. There is wonder in these descriptions. With his sensitive translation Allen has retrieved, to our gratitude, the beauty and narrative genius of the K'iche' Maya. He has recaptured the adventurous motions that structured their origin and mapped out how they came to be.

Translator's Preface

ALLEN J. CHRISTENSON

This work is the first English translation of the complete text of the *Title of Totonicapán*, one of the most important documents composed by the K'iche' Maya in the highlands of Guatemala, second only to the *Popol Vuh*. The original document was completed in 1554, only a few decades after the Spanish invasion of the K'iche' region in 1524. This volume contains a wholly new translation from the original K'iche' language text. It is based on the oldest known manuscript copy, rediscovered by Robert Carmack in 1973. Included are extensive footnotes aimed at elucidating the meaning of the text in light of contemporary highland Maya speech and practices, as well as current scholarship in Maya linguistics, archaeology, ethnography, and art historical iconography. No work of literature can be translated from one language into another without losing a certain amount of the beauty and nuance of the original. The turn of the last century symbolist poet Stéphane Mallarmé felt that his poetry should never be translated because the metaphors, flow, and sound of the words were so closely bound to the French language. To convey even a portion of the associated meaning that colored his poems would require extensive explanatory notes, and for Mallarmé "to name an object is to suppress three-quarters of the enjoyment to be found in the poem, which consists in the pleasure of discovering things little by little: suggestion, that is the dream" (in Lucie-Smith 1972, 54).

To a great extent, this is also true of the *Title of Totonicapán*, which is replete with esoteric language, plays on words, and phrases chosen for their sound and

https://doi.org/10.5876/9781646422647.c000b

rhythm as much as for their meaning. I've tried to adhere as closely as possible to the tone and syntax, or word order, of the K'iche' text. However, certain liberties are unavoidable to make the narrative understandable in the English language. For example, the K'iche' language stresses passive verb constructions that when translated into European languages are difficult to follow. The authors of the *Title of Totonicapán* also routinely used passive forms to create gerunds that are hopelessly awkward in English.

To compensate in part for the inadequacy of a grammatical English version to adhere precisely to the wording of the original, I have also included a "literal" word-for-word translation of the text. I have chosen to use this arrangement because I believe language is reflective of the flavor of the culture that created it. When the original phraseology and grammatical construction of the ancient text are preserved, subtle nuances of meaning become evident.

One of my hopes for this project was to make the original K'iche' text of the *Title of Totonicapán* available to the K'iche' people themselves in a form that is consistent with the modern script taught in the Guatemalan school system. I have therefore utilized in the literal translation an entirely new transcription of the K'iche' text using modern orthography. I have also included a transcription of the original modified-Latin orthographic version of the text as it was written by its K'iche' authors in the sixteenth century for comparative purposes.

The translation contained in this book would not have been possible if it were not for the numerous dictionaries, grammars, and theological treatises compiled during the Early Colonial period that are an invaluable source for archaic and non-Maya loanwords that are no longer used by modern K'iche'. These include works attributed to Bishop Francisco Marroquín and Fr. Domingo de Vico, O.P., as well as the dictionaries and grammars compiled by Fr. Alonso de Molina (2001 [1571]), Fr. Marcos Martínez (ca. 1575), Fr. Antonio de Ciudad Real (1929 [ca. 1590]), Fr. Thomás de Coto (1983 [ca. 1656]), Fr. Bartolomé de Anleo (ca. 1660), Fr. Tomás de Santo Domingo (ca. 1690), Fr. Benito de Villacañas (1692), Fr. Domingo de Basseta (1921 [ca. 1698]), Fr. Francisco de Vare[l]a (1929 [1699]), Fr. Francisco Ximénez (ca. 1701), Fr. Pantaleón de Guzmán (1984 [1704]), Fr. Francisco Herrera (1745), and Fr. Ángel (ca. 1775).

The K'iche' language has changed surprisingly little in the centuries since the *Title of Totonicapán* was composed. With important exceptions, most of the vocabulary is still understandable to modern K'iche' speakers. It is therefore fortunate that a number of dictionaries in modern K'iche' have been compiled in the last century, particularly the work of Manuel García Elgueta (1892, ca. 1900), Carmelo Sáenz de Santa María (1940), Juan de León (1954), Munro S. Edmonson (1965), Miguel Alvarado López (1975), James L. Mondloch and Eugene P. Hruska (1975), Rémi

Siméon (1977), Abraham García Hernández and Santiago Yac Sam (1980), my own dictionary of the K'iche' language compiled in Totonicapán and Momostenango (Christenson 1978–1985), Candelaria Dominga López Ixcoy (1997), Francisco Pérez Mendoza and Miguel Hernández Mendoza (1996), María Beatriz Par Sapón and Telma Angelina Can Pixabaj (2000), and the magnificent monolingual K'iche' dictionary compiled by Don Florentino Pedro Ajpacaja Tum (2001).

I have also relied on consultations with native K'iche' speakers in the highland Guatemalan towns of Momostenango (and the surrounding *aldeas* of Santa Ana, Canquixaja, Nimsitu, and Panca), Totonicapán (and its *aldeas* of Nimasak, Chuxchimal, and Cerro de Oro), Nahuala', Cunén (and its *aldeas* of Los Trigales, Xesacmalha, Xetzak, Las Grutas, Chitu, and Xepom), and Chihul.

For terms and phrases associated with Maya religion and ritual, I have also collaborated with several K'iche' *ajq'ijab'*, traditional Maya priests, since I began work as an ethnographer and translator in Guatemala in 1976. These women and men continue to carry out traditional calendric and divinatory ceremonies in a manner similar to those practiced at the time the *Title of Totonicapán* was compiled. I am particularly indebted to Don Vicente de León Abac for his wisdom and patience with me in unraveling the mysteries of Maya ceremonialism when I lived in Momostenango from 1978 to 1979.

When I published a translation of the *Popol Vuh* in 2003, I wrote that "translation is an art whose cloth is woven from a variety of threads. Any defects are solely the fault of the weaver. Its beauty is solely dependent on the threads themselves." Since that time, I've learned that many K'iche' have come up with a word for computers in their own language—*kemb'al tz'ib'* ("word loom"). Fortunately, the threads of highland Maya literature are surpassingly beautiful, despite the limitations of our modern word looms and the dusty old academics who use them.

Acknowledgments

This volume is the culmination of many years of collaboration with friends and colleagues who have been more than generous with their time, expertise, encouragement, and, at times, sympathy. It has become a somewhat clichéd and expected thing to claim that a work would not be possible without such support. It is nonetheless true, at least from my experience, and I am indebted to all those who helped move the process along.

First and foremost, I would like to express my sincerest gratitude to my Maya teachers, colleagues, and friends who have selflessly devoted their time and knowledge to help carry out this project. Without their efforts, none of it would have ever gotten off the ground. I would like to particularly recognize in this regard Don Vicente de León Abac, who, with patience and kindness, guided me through the complexity and poetry of K'iche' theology and ceremonialism. Without his wisdom, I would have missed much of the beauty of ancestral vision that is woven into the very fabric of highland Maya literature. I dearly miss him. I would also like to acknowledge the profound influence Antonio Ajtujal Vásquez had on this work. It was his kind and gentle voice that I often heard when I struggled at times to understand the ancient words of this text. Others who have aided this work include Diego Chávez Petzey, Nicolás Chávez Sojuel, Felix Choy, Gregorio Chuc, Juan Mendoza, Francisco Mendoza, and Juan Zárate.

I especially recognize the kind mentorship, support, and unfailing encouragement of Robert Carmack. He is truly one of the giants in our field, and it is an honor to have worked with him. He has been unfailingly generous not only in supporting this project but in making his work accessible to anyone who shares his love for K'iche' literature and culture. His presence runs deeply through nearly all work in this field for the past half century.

I am sincerely grateful for my friends and colleagues in the field of highland Maya literature. We are a rather small community, and I am grateful that we support one another with patience and genuine kindness—something that has become all too rare in the academic world. I am indebted most especially to Steve Houston, Kerry Hull, Mallory Matsumoto, Frauke Sachse, Garry Sparks, and Andrew Weeks, who have undergone deep dives into this project at various stages. Their wise influence can be seen on every page.

Among the many who have contributed to this project in invaluable ways, I would like to recognize with my sincerest thanks the following individuals: Karen Bassie, Iyaxel Cojti Ren, Garrett Cook, John Fox, Nicholas Hellmuth, Jesper Nielsen, and Ruud van Akkeren.

I am fortunate to have an office literally next door to outstanding scholars in the field of Arabic studies. I am grateful for the time I was able to spend with Kevin Blankenship, Spencer Scoville, and James A. Toronto, who helped me through the intricacies of the Arabic alphabet, elements of which the K'iche' used in composing the *Title of Totonicapán*. Our department also includes scholars in the Classics, and I am grateful to Mike Pope and Seth Jeppesen for their invaluable help with Latin grammar and orthography.

I would also like to thank my graduate students who keep me constantly on my toes and challenged with their curiosity and energy. Among these students, Karen Fuhriman and Marie Bardsley helped with the initial transcription of the text used in this volume.

Finally, I thank my genius son, David Christenson, for his unfailing willingness to help his luddite dad negotiate the troubled waters of modern computers, as well as his work in modifying the maps found at the end of this volume and many of the images that illustrate the text.

THE TITLE OF TOTONICAPÁN

Introduction

Highland Maya Land Titles

The *Title of Totonicapán* was completed in 1554 as a land title written by surviving members of the K'iche' nobility, a branch of the Maya that dominated the highlands of western Guatemala prior to the arrival of the Spanish conquerors in 1524. Titles of this kind were relatively common for Maya communities in the Guatemalan highlands in the first century after the Spanish Conquest as a means of asserting land rights and privileges for its leaders. Such claims were often recognized by the Spanish Crown, particularly in the mid-sixteenth century when indigenous rulers were supported by the Dominican clergy who administered the K'iche' region of Guatemala (Sparks 2017, 214). It was in the interest of Spanish authorities to maintain a vigorous indigenous upper class with vassal lords to stabilize society, maintain control, and ensure the regular collection of taxes and tribute (Matsumoto 2017, 20). Yet Colonial-era highland Maya land titles, particularly the earliest ones such as the *Title of Totonicapán*, were not limited to elite claims for territorial boundaries, tribute rights, or status. They were often assertions of national identity, containing significant passages describing the creation of the world, the origin and migrations of their first ancestors, their religious beliefs, their relationship with the gods, their sociopolitical organization, and the source—often supernatural—of their right to rule. The *Title of Totonicapán* is among the richest of the highland Maya texts in this kind of cultural detail, far exceeding the background that would have been necessary to assert land claims in court. Matsumoto (6) suggests that documents such as the *Title of Totonicapán* may never have played a significant role in Spanish courts,

https://doi.org/10.5876/9781646422647.c000c

particularly considering the "ambiguous territorial boundaries and inexact measurements they often cited in defining indigenous land claims." Indeed, the *Title of Totonicapán* contains numerous passages that show reverence for the ancient gods and unapologetic descriptions of ceremonial practices such as human sacrifice and bloodletting that would have offended Spanish authorities. This suggests that the document may have been written primarily for use by the authors' own indigenous community.

The *Title of Totonicapán* was written in the K'iche' language utilizing a modified Latin script developed by Spanish missionaries soon after the Conquest (see pp. 49–52). As an official document, it was duly signed by the ruling lords of all three major K'iche' lineages—the Kaweqib', Nijayib', and Ajaw K'iche'—as a testament to its veracity. The names of the signatories appear at the end of the document, although being a later copy, it does not display any actual signatures (p. 185–186). The final page of the document declares that it is the "Act" of K'iq'ab' Nima Yax, the ruler of Chuwi' Miq'ina', an important fortified citadel also known by its Tlaxcalan name of Totonicapán.[1] K'iq'ab' Nima Yax was the K'iche' nobleman who conquered the Totonicapán region on behalf of the ruling K'iche' lords in the mid-fifteenth century (pp. 173–177). He would have long since died, but the document served as a legal land title based on right of conquest.

The composition of the Totonicapán document most likely took place slightly before that of the *Popol Vuh*, the more famous contemporary K'iche' text, which is dated to approximately 1554–1558 (see figure 1). Like the *Popol Vuh*, the *Title of Totonicapán* is written in the elevated court language of the Early Colonial period and eloquently describes the mythic origins and history of the K'iche' people. For the most part, the *Title of Totonicapán* agrees with the *Popol Vuh*'s version of K'iche' history and cosmology, providing a complementary account that attests traditions that must have been widely known and understood. But in many instances, the Totonicapán document is richer in detail and departs from the *Popol Vuh*'s more cursory description of history, genealogy, and political organization. In other instances, it contradicts assertions made by the authors of the *Popol Vuh*, perhaps a reflection of internal dissent and jealousy between rival lineages within the K'iche' hierarchy. It also contains significant passages of cosmology and history that do not appear in any other highland Maya text.

The authors of the *Title of Totonicapán* chose to begin their account with a lengthy description of Old Testament theology and history harmonized with their own uniquely Maya worldview. This section of the text is based to a large degree on

---

[1]   Totonicapán is the name recognized by Spanish authorities in Guatemala. As with many major highland Maya cities, Chuwi' Miq'ina' was given the new name of Totonicapán by the Tlaxcalan allies of the Spaniards during the Conquest period.

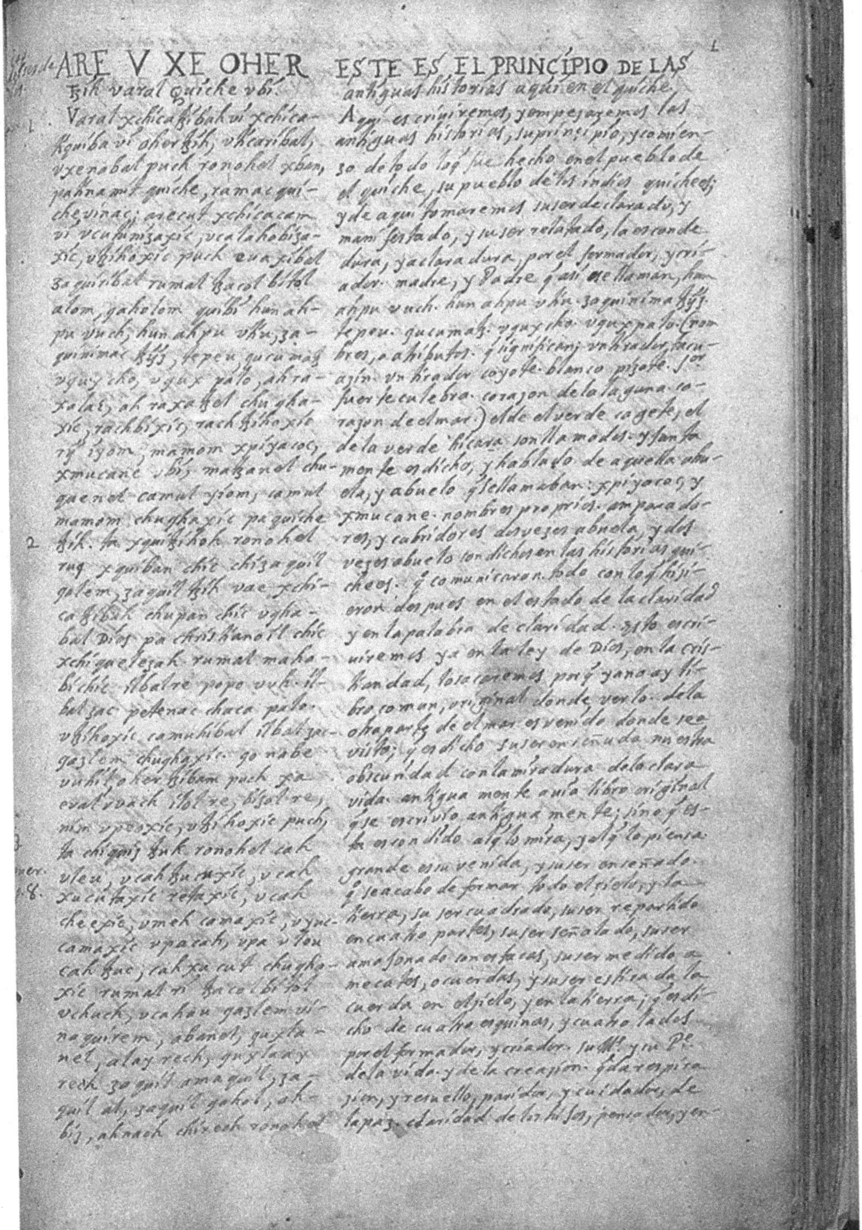

ARE V XE OHER

ESTE ES EL PRINCIPIO DE LAS

Tzih varal quiché ubi.

antiguas historias aqui en el quiché.

Figure 1. Initial page of the *Popol Vuh*. *Courtesy*, Newberry Library, Chicago, IL.

a contemporary treatise, the first volume of the *Theologia Indorum*, composed in K'iche' between 1551 and 1553 by a Dominican priest named Domingo de Vico in collaboration with K'iche' advisers (Carmack and Mondloch 1983, 13; Sparks 2019, 149, 239). But the Totonicapán version is replete with variants that modify, alter, and even directly contradict Vico's writings. The *Title of Totonicapán*, the *Theologia Indorum*, and the *Popol Vuh* were all written within a few brief years of each other and can best be seen as literary arguments among Maya and Spanish Christian intellectuals with very different beliefs regarding the nature of deity and how the world of the sacred interacts with that of humankind.

Unlike the *Popol Vuh*, which was written anonymously and apparently not intended for non-Maya eyes (Christenson 2007, 64), the *Title of Totonicapán* was written as a legal document and signed by the most important K'iche' rulers of the time. The latter portion of the text focuses on the boundaries of the K'iche' realm, particularly those established by K'iq'ab' Nima Yax, the K'iche' lord who conquered the Totonicapán valley in the mid-fifteenth century (figure 2).

We do not know whether the Totonicapán document was used in any specific court case in the Early Colonial period; however, the principal signatory, Don Juan de Rojas, was involved in a land dispute in 1550 in which he asserted his right to collect tribute from merchants in the Q'umarkaj area based on the claim that he was the rightful lord of that region (Lutz 1994, 25–26, n. 28). This is just the type of legal claim for which a land title would have been valuable. In his mature years as a *cacique* (an indigenous ruler), he collected tribute, carried out censuses, provided labor to his Spanish overlords, enforced Christian church attendance and instruction, and acted as the principal judge in local disputes (Carmack 1981, 313). He would have come into frequent contact with both secular and ecclesiastical Spanish authorities. According to Ximénez, Juan de Rojas was given a special hall at the Royal Palace of Guatemala next to the king's representative. Here, he administered the affairs of the Maya as the vassal lord of the Spaniards (Ximénez 1929–1931, I.xxviii.79). I think it is highly probable that Rojas would have used the Totonicapán document as a testament to his territorial and sovereignty rights not only before Spanish officials but in disputes with fellow highland Maya as well. He was the principal signatory of the document and no doubt recognized its potential benefits as a bolster to his own authority based on historical precedent.

If the *Title of Totonicapán* was ever used to defend land and tribute claims in Spanish courts, the authors of the text would have had to walk a very fine line. To assert territorial rights and privileges, Pre-Columbian history and practices had to be laid out to document the K'iche' elite's right to rule. At the same time, descriptions of the ancient gods and ceremonialism of their Pre-Columbian ancestors, which were so closely woven into the fabric of their society, had to be handled

Figure 2. The valley of Totonicapán. The modern city can be seen in the distance.

cautiously so as not to offend the sensibilities of their Christian overlords or raise questions concerning their conversion to the new faith. This inevitably led to contradictions where the authors tried to express reverence for their ancestors and at the same time condemn them for their idolatry should the document ever be seen by Spanish authorities. In the following passage, the progenitors of the K'iche' people are described as powerful, wise, and honorable:

> Then the enchanted people contemplated their journey. From far away they arrived in their obscurity in the sky and on the land. There are none to equal them. They saw everything beneath the sky. They were great sages. They led all of the Seven Nations as well as the tribes. (p. 92–93)

The authors used the term *nawal winaq* ("enchanted, wondrous, magical, or miraculous people") to describe the first K'iche' ancestors. Previously, they had used the same term *nawal* to describe the power of God to create the world and to perform miracles in Egypt (p. 81, n. 118). There is no hint of condemnation in this description. On the contrary, their very natures bear a patina of sanctity otherwise ascribed to the Christian God, then only recently introduced among the K'iche' following the Spanish invasion of their lands.

Tulan, the mythic place of origin for K'iche' power and authority, is at times equated with the Paradisiacal Garden of Eden (p. 89) and at other times with Egypt or Babylonia, thus identifying the ancient K'iche' with the Israelites fleeing bondage in the time of Moses (pp. 83, n. 123; 89, n. 173) or returning to the Promised Land from exile in Babylon (pp. 88, 184). In this example, the journey from Tulan is described as sanctioned by God himself, linking the Christian deity with the Pre-Columbian creator gods Tz'aqol and B'itol:

> Surely this was the love of God for them because there was only one, Tz'aqol B'itol, that they called upon in the center of the sky and the earth they say. (p. 97)

Tz'aqol ("Framer") and B'itol ("Shaper") are paired creator deities in ancient K'iche' tradition. In other indigenous K'iche' texts, they are listed as two among many Pre-Columbian Maya deities venerated by the K'iche' (Christenson 2007, 60–63; Maxwell and Hill 2006, 11–12). In the *Popol Vuh*, they are described as the first of several luminous beings who initiated the creation of the world:

> All alone are Tz'aqol [Framer] and B'itol [Shaper], Sovereign and Quetzal Serpent, They Who Have Borne Children and They Who Have Begotten Sons. Luminous they are in the water, wrapped in quetzal feathers and cotinga feathers. Thus they are called Quetzal Serpent. In their essence, they are great sages, great possessors of knowledge. (Christenson 2007, 68–69)

Despite the nature of Tz'aqol and B'itol as a pair of deities, one female and the other male, Domingo de Vico and other Dominican missionaries used their names as equivalents for the one Christian God, perhaps in an effort to make the newly introduced deity more understandable to the K'iche' (Sparks 2017, 13, 112; 2019, 155). On this point the Dominicans differed sharply from the Franciscan order, which insisted that the Spanish word Dios ("God") should be used to avoid the taint of Pre-Columbian religious practices. In the *Theologia Indorum*, composed by the Dominican priest Domingo de Vico, Tz'aqol B'itol are frequently equated with God as the only true deity: *xa tuqel tçakol bitol Dios nimahau ubi* ("merely alone Tz'akol B'itol are God, Great Lord is his name") (Vico 1605 [1553], folio 98r); *xahûtçakol bitol. kachuch kakahau. xbano cah xbano vleu* ("only one, Tz'aqol B'itol, our mother and our father, made the heavens and made the earth") (folio 168r).

The K'iche' Maya authors of the *Title of Totonicapán* are less consistent in their references to Tz'aqol and B'itol. The passage cited above is the last appearance of Tz'aqol B'itol in the text as monotheistic. After this, the authors transition toward a more consistently indigenous view of K'iche' history, and Tz'aqol and B'itol appear as two separate deities alongside other indigenous gods (see pp. 125, 140).

In contrast to this positive view of their ancestors and gods, in other sections the authors of the *Title of Totonicapán* describe their forebears as idolators and sinners justly condemned for their excesses (pp. 86, 88, 143). Immediately after describing their departure from Tulan, they felt it necessary to add that their ancestors were condemned for worshipping the ancient gods:

> It was then that they festered in lies. They spoke to the sun and to the moon. They called the one "Young Boy," and they called the other "Maiden." Junajpu they called the sun; Xb'alankej was called the moon by them. "Cigars of K'iq'ab'" the stars were called. (p. 91)

The *Title of Totonicapán* claims territorial rights based on right of conquest, and much of the latter part of the text describes the various campaigns made by the K'iche', particularly in the valley of Totonicapán (pp. 168–177). Again, this presents a dilemma. The authors must accurately document these wars of conquest to establish their claims, but they also wish to convey to the Spanish authorities that they are now opposed to war and are a peaceful people. Perhaps this explains why the military campaigns that began soon after their ancestors' arrival from Tulan are preceded by a reminder that they were also God's chosen people, that war was wrong, and God justly punished them for it:

> These, therefore, are our roots, our existence, our journey here from the the place where the sun emerges.
>
> Hear ye therefore, give heed to me, and I shall declare it to you all. It was in war that they were lost, they, our grandfathers and our fathers. We are their grandsons, the sons of Adam and Eve, Enoch, Abraham, Isaac, and Jacob. This was because they forgot their God. Therefore, they were abandoned by God, the Great Lord. (p. 87–88)

There are no claims of descent from biblical figures in any of the more traditional texts such as the *Popol Vuh*, the *Annals of the Kaqchikels*, or the *Título K'oyoy*. A few early Spanish missionaries taught this idea as an aid to their evangelization efforts, including Father Domingo de Vico. In chapter 101 of the *Theologia Indorum*, Vico (1605 [1553], folio 168r) writes, *ahisrael yx petinak ui yxcamic umam vȝahol Abram. Ysaac. Jacob* ("you are Israelites, you have come; this day you are the grandsons and the sons of Abraham, Isaac, and Jacob"), specifically descendants of the lost ten tribes of Israel.

No doubt some Maya, including the authors of this section of the *Title of Totonicapán*, saw the claim that they were descendents of Israel as a means of avoiding persecution during the post-Conquest period or of demonstrating the sincerity of their conversion to Christianity. But subsequent to the passage cited above, the wars waged by the K'iche' in the Guatemalan highlands are described as glorious and with no suggestion of condemnation, including the attendant practices of bloodletting, prayer to the ancient gods, veneration of Pre-Columbian deities and their images, and human sacrifice:

Armed, then, were the men in the buildings of the bloodletters and the sacrificers, they who were our grandfathers and our fathers; of we, the Kaweqib', the Nijayib', and the Ajaw K'iche'. Ik'i B'alam had died in his youth.

Tojil was the god of B'alam K'itze'. Awilix was the god of B'alam Aq'ab'. Jaqawitz was the god of Majukotaj. It was at K'wal Ab'aj that the Bundled Glory, which had come from the place where the sun emerges, was unbound on Jaqawitz. Glory and sovereignty came to be theirs over the Seven Nations and the tribes. (p. 104–105)

There is no evidence as to whether the *Title of Totonicapán* was actually used within the Spanish Colonial legal system in the sixteenth century. If it was, it would have been fascinating to be a fly on the wall of the court chambers to hear how this intricate dance of simultaneously condemning their ancestors and glorifying them played out.

The authors of the *Title of Totonicapán* chose to include mostly passages from the *Theologia* that focus on the creation of the world (pp. 61–69)—Adam and Eve as the first people (pp. 70–77), Moses as the founder of Israelite society (pp. 80–83), and the migration of the Israelites out of Egypt toward the Promised Land (pp. 84–89). This follows the highland Maya precedent of beginning major works of literature with the creative actions carried out by the ancient gods, the creation of the founders of the major K'iche' lineages, and their migration from their mythic origins in Tulan until they established their centers of power. The best example of this pattern is seen in the *Popol Vuh*, which begins with a lengthy account of the creation of the world (Christenson 2007, 59–90), the work of the gods in establishing the order of the seasons and the life cycle of humankind (91–191), the creation of the first human beings who founded K'iche' society and political power (192–208), and the migration from their mythic place of origin, Tulan, into the Guatemalan highlands (209–222).

The *Title of Totonicapán* follows this traditional highland Maya precedent, but repeated twice—first in a modified Christian version based on the *Theologia Indorum* and then again according to their own highland Maya traditions beginning on folio page 7r (p. 90). But unlike the *Theologia Indorum*, which was composed as a theological interpretation of the Bible, here the authors of the Totonicapán document use relevant elements of the *Theologia* to bolster their own claims of authority, extending back to the creation of the world. What mattered most was not to produce a facsimile of Catholic doctrine as taught to them by Father Vico and other Christian missionaries but to present the Christian version of the world's history in a way that would best resonate with uniquely Maya traditions. This is no doubt why the authors of the Totonicapán document claimed descent from biblical figures such as Abraham, Jacob, Moses, and the exiled Israelites coming out of Babylon, interwoven with references to their own purely indigenous mythic sources of power—Tulan and its ruler Nakxik:

These then were their residences, their abodes, because of God, the Great Lord. These were the conquests of the Canaanites, the Hebrews, and the Israelites. Three, then, were their names: Israelites, Canaanites, and Hebrews they were called. They are our grandfathers and our fathers . . .

Within the Earthly Paradise we were framed and we were shaped by God, the Great Lord . . .

In this division of the word I shall speak of the establishment of lordship and the root as well of authority—the account of the Very Abundant Mountain, the Very Verdant Mountain. This was at Pa Sewan and Pa Tulan, as told in the writings of Pek, the writings of Sewan Tulan, as they said . . .

We are the grandsons, we are the sons, of the Israelites and of Saint Moses. From the lands of the Israelites departed our grandfathers and our fathers. They came from the place where the sun emerges, there in Babylonia. The powerful Lord Nakxik was the root of our ancestry, of our parentage. (pp. 87–92)

As direct descendants of the ancient chosen people of the Christian God, the K'iche' could claim co-inheritance with the Spanish Christians for God's divine favor and authority. The authors' choice to include the Christian version of the creation may be a genuine expression of their religious conversion, but it may also represent the appropriation of Christian doctrine to use as a weapon in defending their own indigenous rights and legitimacy as rulers. It allowed them to claim the religious underpinnings of Spanish domination and superiority as equally their own. This strategy was used in other areas of the Maya world as well. The indigenous authors of the various *Books of Chilam Balam* and the *Teabo Manuscript* used the creation account in Genesis to explain and validate the spiritual and political authority of their community leaders (Christensen 2016, 11–26). The relationship between the Maya and their Spanish-Christian overlords was complex and dynamic, a constant negotiation between resistance and conformity.

K'ICHE' HISTORY

The present population of K'iche' people in Guatemala who speak the language and maintain traditional clothing and customs to one degree or another is nearly 2 million, although many more have intermarried over the centuries with other Maya groups or with those of Spanish descent. Many have also emigrated to other countries, particularly Mexico, Belize, and the United States. They are the most numerous of the twenty-two major highland Maya groups in Guatemala, and in many communities they comprise the majority of the population. The K'iche' people live primarily in a series of market towns and smaller agricultural villages in the modern Guatemalan states of Quiché, Totonicapán, and Quetzaltenango.

Figure 3. K'iche' women in traditional dress, Totonicapán, 1977

Their homeland is some of the most beautiful country in the world, dominated by a range of high mountains, volcanoes, and steep-walled plateaus blanketed with green pine forests and watered by numerous rivers and waterfalls. Its high elevation keeps the climate comfortably cool in the summer, while its location in the tropics prevents the extreme cold temperatures usually associated with mountainous environments. Guatemala's boast of being the "Land of Eternal Spring" is no exaggeration.

Although the highland Maya have lived in this area for thousands of years, post-Conquest K'iche'an texts—including the *Title of Totonicapán*, the *Popol Vuh*, the *Annals of the Kaqchikels*, the Nijayib' documents, and the *Título K'oyoy*—are united in their assertion that the region came to be dominated by a militaristic confederation, led by the four progenitors of the principal K'iche' lineages. The first was B'alam K'itze', founder of the ruling Kaweq lineage; second was B'alam Aq'ab', founder of the Nijayib' lineage; and third was Majukotaj, founder of the Ajaw K'iche'. Together, these three lineages comprised the Nima K'iche' ("Great K'iche'"). The fourth progenitor was Ik'i B'alam who died in his youth and thus did not found a lineage. These four ancestors are described in the *Popol Vuh* as the first men created by the gods, endowed with great power and magical abilities:

> It is said that they were merely given frame and shape. They had no mother. They had no father. They were merely lone men, as we would say. No woman gave them

Figure 4. Highlands above Cunén, Guatemala

birth. Nor were they begotten by the Framer or the Shaper, by She Who Has Borne Childen or He Who Has Begotten Sons. Their frame and shape were merely brought about by the miraculous power, and the spirit essence of the Framer and the Shaper, of She Who Has Borne Children and He Who Has Begotten Sons, of Sovereign and Quetzal Serpent . . . Perfect was their sight, and perfect was their knowledge of everything beneath the sky. (Christenson 2007, 197)

The *Title of Totonicapán* also describes the four K'iche' progenitors as wise and magical beings:

They did great wonders and demonstrations of strength. There they showed their stride, their miraculous power, and their spirit essence . . . Truly this was also the origin of the manifestation of glory and sovereignty by the K'iche' people before all of the warriors. Their greatness came forth. (pp. 108–109)

Despite their miraculous power, the first ancestors of the K'iche' were described as poor, pitifully exposed to the elements, and bordering on starvation before they arrived in the Guatemalan highlands:

When they came here they were uncovered. They were naked when they came. They only had their spears and their leafy tunics when they arrived at the shore of the sea . . . There was no food, no water. They would merely sniff the heads of their staffs to console their hearts. (p. 96–97)

The *Title of Totonicapán* and other highland Maya texts claim that the first ancestors of the K'iche' people received their authority to rule at a great city called Tulan, located "across the sea" in the East where the sun emerges (pp. 90, 93–96). Tulan is a Nahuatl word, the language of central Mexico, meaning "place of reeds." According to these texts, Tulan was ruled by a king called Nakxit (or Nakxik in the *Title of Totonicapán*) (p. 92, n. 185). In the *Popol Vuh*, Nakxit gave the four K'iche' progenitors their gods and their political legitimacy:

> Then they passed over the sea, arriving there in the East. They went there to receive their lordship. This, then, is the name of the lord, the lord of the East, when they arrived: Then they arrived before the face of the lord, whose name was Nakxit. He was the only judge over a great dominion. He then gave to them the signs and symbols of their lordship. (Christenson 2007, 256–257)

The *Annals of the Kaqchikels* give a similar description:

> They [the K'iche'an progenitors] came before Mevac and Nacxit, who was a great king … Then they dressed them, they pierced their noses, and they gave them their offices and the flowers called *Cinpual.* Truly he made himself beloved by all the warriors. And turning to all of them, the Lord Naxcit said: "Climb up to these columns of stone, enter into my house. I will give you sovereignty." (Recinos and Goetz 1953, 64–65; see also Maxwell and Hill 2006, 67–69)

The name Nakxit is derived from the Nahuatl words *nawi* ("four") and *ikxit* ("foot") (Campbell 1983, 84), perhaps referring to the extent of his power, extending to the four cardinal directions of the earth. Nakxit is also one of the titles for the feathered serpent deity known as Kukulcan in the Maya lowlands and as Quetzalcoatl in central Mexico (Recinos and Goetz 1950, 207, n. 3; Roys 1967, 83; Edmonson 1982 16, n. 220; Nicholson 2001, 228). Nakxit was apparently one of the titles used by Maya rulers at both Chichen Itza and Mayapan, indicating their attempts to claim central Mexican authority as an important component of their own right to rule (Nicholson 2001, 228–229).

Tulan is a common term for Mexican-influenced centers of power. It is therefore difficult to identify which Tulan the K'iche' saw as the origin of their authority, although it may have been linked to one of the major lowland Maya centers on the Yucatán Peninsula (Carmack 1981, 481; Akkeren 2003). Chichen Itza or its successor, Mayapan, are good possibilities for this Tulan.

Tulan may have been an actual location that held prestige as a pilgrimage center for Maya groups aspiring to political power at a time of social unrest, but it may also have been a purely mythic place of origin. Tulan's location "across the sea" where "the sun emerges" places it within the realm of otherworldly time and space.

Figure 5. View of the Castillo, Chichen Itza

Figure 6. View of Mayapan

Frauke Sachse (2008; Sachse and Christenson 2005) has written convincingly that the description of Tulan is consistent with metaphors for supernatural places of origin that appear throughout Mesoamerica. Even Carmack (1981, 44), who asserts that at least some aspects of the migration stories in K'iche' texts are historical, cautions that highland Maya migration tales often "turn out to be myths that serve to rationalize the occupation of a territory or a connection with some prestigious authority source." In the *Title of Totonicapán* and other highland Maya texts, "dawn" and the "emergence of the sun" are not merely celestial events but rather are indicative of the establishment of political sovereignty (Chinchilla Mazariegos 2013, 694; Christenson 2016, 116–127; Cojti Ren 2021). Thus the "first" dawn for the K'iche' took place atop the mountain Jaqawitz, where they had established their fortified citadel after defeating their enemies in the region (see pp. 123–127). Immediately following this first dawn of the sun, the ancestors of the K'iche' address their children, describing the event in terms of political and military power:

> You, our sons, you have achieved completion. You have multiplied. Receive then this Bundled Glory. Watch over and keep it. We have not yet found our mountain place. You will achieve glory and sovereignty there and then you will open this as a sign of your lordship. It came from the place where the sun emerges. You will engender the [titles of rulership] Ajpop, Ajpop K'amja, and Q'alel Atzij Winaq. You will attain glory; sovereignty will come to be. (p. 128)

Carmack (1981, 46–48, 121–123) suggests that the founders of the K'iche' ruling lineages first established their centers of power in highland Guatemala about the time of Chichen Itza's collapse, which Yucatec Maya histories date around 1220–1225 CE. More recent archaeological evidence suggests that the final downfall of Chichen Itza was preceded by a long period of decline after the tenth century (Morley et al. 1983, 167; Schele and Mathews 1998, 197–255; Akkeren 2000, 314–315), although it may have maintained its prestige as a pilgrimage center for many centuries afterward. Chichen Itza had been the dominant force in the lowland Maya world. Its collapse disrupted the political alliances and interregional trade in the area, resulting in the displacement of numerous groups of people seeking new power bases and economic opportunities (Fox 1978, 1–2). Many of these groups claimed authority based on Mexican-influenced symbols of power and prestige (Roys 1967, 88–98; Schele and Mathews 1998). It is possible that elements of what would become the K'iche' and related highland Maya groups were part of this human wave.

Archaeologically, there is evidence in the K'iche' region of architectural and cultural changes that may correspond to the apex of this "migration" during the transition between the Early and Late Postclassic phase, ca. 1200 CE (Rands and Smith 1965; Fox 1978, 270–275; Carmack 1981, 48–49). At this time, many of the most important Maya ruling lineages in the region were heavily influenced by ideas from beyond their borders, particularly the people of the Maya lowlands to the north and east and Nahuatl speakers from Mexico. According to Bernardino de Sahagún

(1950–1963, X.170), a Spanish priest who worked among the Mexica soon after the Spanish Conquest, the lowland Maya area was known as Nonoualcat ("Land of the Dumb") because it was occupied by non-Nahuatl speakers, although he acknowledged that many could speak Nahuatl as a second language.

The highland Maya in particular remembered the legendary Toltecs, the ruling class of central Mexico in the Early Postclassic period, as the greatest artists and sages. The *Popol Vuh* claims that the divine creators who formed the first ancestors of the K'iche' were *Aj Toltecat* ("Toltecs") (Christenson 2007, 80, n. 102) and emphasized that the K'iche' people were "brothers" with the Yaki, the K'iche' term for groups of Mexican descent who spoke Nahuatl (231). The *Popol Vuh* goes as far as to say that the principal god of the K'iche', Tojil, was equivalent to the Mexican god Quetzalcoatl (Nahuatl: "Feathered Serpent") (231). By the time of the Spanish Invasion, the K'iche' had allied themselves with a number of Nahuatl-speaking Yaki groups along the Pacific Coast who established military outposts to guard the southwestern borders of K'iche' territory (pp. 105, n. 507; 180, n. 687; 182, n. 690).

This affinity for foreign Mexican culture helps explain the numerous Nahuatl loanwords in the *Title of Totonicapán* and other highland Maya texts (Carmack and Mondloch 1983, 17–18; Campbell 1970, 8). These include personal names, toponyms, and objects linked to political power and authority, reflective of the prestige of Mexican and Mexican-influenced institutions in the eyes of the K'iche' hierarchy. At least twenty-seven such loanwords from the Nahuatl language appear in the Totonicapán text. For example, the K'iche' used the word *tepew* for "sovereignty," derived from the Nahuatl term *tepehualiztli* ("to conquer; to cast down") (see p. 105, n. 247). Nevertheless, this does not mean that the K'iche' could speak Nahuatl fluently. The Nahuatl loanwords that appear in the *Title of Totonicapán* and other early K'iche' texts are heavily "Mayanized," altering spelling to conform to the K'iche' language. The authors of the *Popol Vuh* acknowledge that after they left Tulan, they could no longer speak the language of the Yaquis, their name for Nahuatl speakers:

> Then all the nations entered therein—the Rabinals, the Cakchiquels, and the Ah Tziquinahas, along with the Yaqui people, as they are called today. It was there that the languages of the nations were changed. Their languages came to be different. They did not hear each other clearly when they came from Tulan, thus they split apart. (Christenson 2007, 213; see also 230–231)

In a later passage from the *Popol Vuh*, the founders of the K'iche' hegemony lamented that they had become separated from their Yaqui "brothers":

> "We were separated there at Tulan Zuyva. We left them to come here. But we were complete before we came here."

> This they said among themselves when they remembered their older brothers
> and their younger brothers, the Yaqui people. These dawned there in Mexico, as it is
> called today. (Christenson 2007, 230–231)

As described in the *Title of Totonicapán*, the K'iche' forefathers were gradually able to dominate most of western Guatemala and set up their own militaristic kingdom that ultimately extended from the Pacific Coast in the west to the borders of the Petén rainforest in the east. K'iche' accounts of a simultaneous mass migration of all the major K'iche'an lineage groups into the Guatemalan highlands should not be taken literally. Rather, this was more likely a slow process carried out over a period of several centuries involving a complex series of historical and social interactions (Carmack 1981, 43–74). Indeed, many of these lineages had always lived in the highlands, although the symbols of their authority to exercise military or political authority during the Late Postclassic period may have been obtained from outside centers of power, exemplified by the legendary Tulan. The confederation of people known as the K'iche' was more likely a complex and linguistically diverse group of lineages composed of native highland Maya, Mexicanized clans from nearby Pacific Coastal areas, and immigrants from the Maya lowlands (Akkeren 2000). The interrelationship between these groups was dynamic and changed significantly over time.

The *Title of Totonicapán* does not contain what we might call "objective history" (if such a thing is possible). It is instead a collection of traditions, based in part in historical fact and in part on mythic interpretation. It describes the rise to power of their ancestral lineages, specifically that of the ruling Kaweq lineage of the K'iche' who came to dominate the highland Maya region in the centuries prior to the Spanish Conquest. By ca. 1250 CE, the K'iche' confederation under the leadership of the Kaweq lineage had established strongholds within the central and western highlands of Guatemala, slowly expanding their territory by means of conquest and strategic alliances. By ca. 1450, Lord K'iq'ab' had extended K'iche' control throughout the highlands as well as the Pacific Coast near the present-day border with Chiapas.

Soon after K'iq'ab''s successes in a series of campaigns described in detail in the *Title of Totonicapán*, K'iche' control of its newly won territories began to weaken. During the annual rites honoring the god Tojil at the K'iche' capital Q'umarkaj (ca. 1470), an attempted coup directed at K'iq'ab' was carried out by rebel K'iche' factions including two of K'iq'ab''s sons, supported by the Ajtz'ikinaja and other rival lineages (Recinos and Goetz 1953, 94–97; Maxwell and Hill 2006, 166–180). Although K'iq'ab' survived, the incident severely weakened the K'iche' and inaugurated a prolonged series of disastrous wars. The Kaqchikel, who had been allied with the K'iche' for generations, broke away and established a new center at Iximche'.

Figure 7. The site of Iximche'

The ensuing conflict involved nearly all the highland Maya in a tangled web of rapidly shifting alliances and betrayals.

Weakened by decades of internecine conflict, plague, and unusually poor harvests and drought, the kingdoms of highland Guatemala were reduced to a shadow of their former strength; this was the state of affairs the Spanish invaders encountered when they initiated a war of conquest against them in 1524. After the Mexica capital Tenochtitlan fell to Spanish forces led by Hernán Cortés in 1521, the major ruling lineages in the Guatemalan highlands sent envoys to Cortés offering fealty to the new ruler of Mexico. In his fourth letter to the Spanish Crown, Cortés wrote:

> While returning from the province of Pánuco, in a city called Tuzapan, two Spaniards arrived whom I had sent with some of the natives of the city of Temixtitan and others from the province of Soconusco (which lies up the coast on the shores of the Southern Sea, toward where Pedro Arias de Ávila resides as your Highness's governor, two hundred leagues from this great city of Temixtitan) to two cities, called Uclaclán [Utatlan, the capital of the K'iche'] and Guatemala [the capital of the rival Kaqchikel], of which I had known for some while and which lie another seventy leagues from this province of

Soconusco. With these Spaniards there came some hundred natives of those cities sent by their lords to offer themselves as the subjects and vassals of Your Caesarean Majesty. I received them in Your Royal name and assured them that if they remained true to their promise they would be very well treated and honored by me and all my company in Your Highness's Royal name. (Cortés 1986, 301)

No doubt, both the K'iche' and the Kaqchikel sought to gain advantage in their ongoing war with one another by securing the alliance of the Spaniards following their military successes in central Mexico. Cortés came to doubt these envoys' sincerity, however. In the same letter, Cortés (1986, 301) wrote that soon after the arrival of the highland Maya envoys, he was informed that they had "not maintained that goodwill which they showed at first; on the contrary, they are said to have harassed those villages of Soconusco because they are our allies."

Once he had consolidated his victories in central Mexico, Cortés sent one of his captains, Pedro de Alvarado, to subdue any potential resistance from the Maya highlands and to claim the area for the Spanish Crown. In his first letter to Cortés, Alvarado (1979, 105, author translation) described Guatemala as "the wildest land and people that has ever been seen ... We are so far from help that if Our Lady does not aid us, no one can." The K'iche' tried to arrange a hasty alliance with other highland Maya groups to meet the Spanish threat, but they were rebuffed. The Kaqchikel ultimately allied themselves to the Spaniards, whereas the Ajtz'ikinaja replied that they could defend themselves without help. Following a brief yet bloody battle in the valley of Quetzaltenango near present-day Olintepeque (see figure 8), Alvarado entered the K'iche' capital of Q'umarkaj (also known by its Nahuatl name, Utatlán) without resistance on March 7, 1524, at the invitation of the K'iche' rulers Oxib' Kej and B'elejeb' Tz'i'.

Once inside the city, Alvarado suspected a trap and ordered the arrest and execution of its lords:

As I knew them [the K'iche' lords] to have such ill will toward the service of His Majesty, and for the good and tranquility of the land, I burned them, and I commanded to be burned the town of Utatlan to its foundations, for it was dangerous and strong ... All they that were taken prisoners of war were branded and made slaves. (Alvarado 1979, 102–103)

The Kaqchikel version of this incident, as recorded in the *Annals of the Kaqchikels*, confirms that the K'iche' lords were burned: "Then [the Spaniards] went forth to the city of Gumarcaah, where they were received by the kings, the Ahpop and the Ahpop Qamahay, and the Quichés paid them tribute. Soon the kings were tortured by Tunatiuh. On the day 4 Qat [March 7, 1524] the kings Ahpop and Ahpop

Figure 8. Spanish battle against highland Maya. From Diego Muñoz Camargo, "Historia de Tlaxcala." By permission of University of Glasgow Library, Archives Special Collections, Glasgow, Scotland.

Qamahay were burned by Tunatiuh [Alvarado]. The heart of Tunatiuh was without compassion for the people during the war" (Recinos and Goetz 1953, 120).

It is unclear whether Alvarado's suspicion of treachery was well-founded; however, Fray Bartolomé de las Casas believed the K'iche' lords were executed for failing to satisfy Alvarado's demand for gold, which is rare in Guatemala: "Guiltless of other fault and without trial or sentence, he immediately ordered them to be burned alive. They killed all the others with lances and knives; they threw them to savage dogs, that tore them to pieces and ate them; and when they came across some lord, they accorded him the honour of burning in live flames. This butchery lasted about seven years from 1524 to 1531. From this may be judged what numbers of people they destroyed" (in MacNutt 1909, 352–353). This version of events is supported by the sixteenth-century account of the trip to Spain by Don Juan Cortés in 1557, in which Alvarado is accused of burning Don Juan's grandfather because he "did not give him gold" (in Carrasco 1967, 253).

The authors of the *Popol Vuh* wrote that Alvarado hanged the K'iche' rulers (Christenson 2007, 295). This "hanging" refers not to the execution of the lords, which was by flame, but rather to the torture and elicitation of confessions mentioned by both Alvarado and the Kaqchikel document. Dennis E. Tedlock (1996, 334, n. 195) notes that the method for obtaining such confessions, according to the Spanish methods of the time, was to hang a prisoner by the wrists while inflicting various types of torture. Undoubtedly, this must have been done in a very public way to have impressed the authors of the *Popol Vuh* writing decades after the event.

It is estimated that there were approximately 2 million Maya inhabitants in Guatemala at the time of the Spanish Invasion. By 1595, less than a century later, the population had fallen to 133,280, a decline of more than 93 percent as a result of war, forced labor, and disease (Early 2006, 148–150). Fortunately, Alonso López de Cerrato, a successor to Pedro de Alvarado, was more tolerant and somewhat eased the burdens of the highland Maya as described in the *Annals of the Kaqchikels*:

> During this year [1549] the Lord President Cerrado [*sic*] arrived . . . When he arrived, he condemned the Spaniards, he liberated the slaves and vassals of the Spaniards, he cut the taxes in two, he suspended forced labor and made the Spaniards pay all men, great and small. The Lord Cerrado truly alleviated the sufferings of the people. I myself saw him, oh, my sons! (Recinos and Goetz 1953, 137)

Christianity was formally established in Guatemala in 1534 under Bishop Francisco Marroquín, who sent priests with portable altars to the various highland towns and villages to baptize the Maya and destroy any remnants of "idolatry" and "paganism" that might have survived the Spanish Invasion. To aid in the process of conversion, missionary priests gathered the Maya into towns, each with a church to administer Catholic rites and instruct them in the Christian faith. Because Q'umarkaj had been all but destroyed during the war, the remnants of its population were moved to a new settlement nearby in ca. 1555, which the Spanish authorities called Santa Cruz del Quiché ("Holy Cross of the K'iche'").

AUTHORSHIP OF THE *TITLE OF TOTONICAPÁN*

The *Title of Totonicapán* appears to have been composed by multiple authors. Although the core elements of K'iche' history outlined in the text are consistent with other highland Maya documents, minor historical inconsistencies even within the document itself suggest that individuals with different perspectives and perhaps agendas contributed to the text as we now have it.

It is unclear if any of the lords who signed the *Title of Totonicapán* participated in the composition of the text or if they merely appended their names to verify its contents. The first of these signatories was Don Juan de Rojas, the son of Tekum Belejeb' B'alam and the fourteenth successor to the founding ancestor, B'alam K'itze', of the ruling Kaweq lineage. His father had been hanged in 1540 for sedition, although by the time he signed the Totonicapán manuscript in 1554, Don Juan de Rojas had established the right to receive tribute payments and was recognized as the Ajpop, or ruling lord, of the K'iche'. He certainly would have been an authoritative source for genealogical information regarding the dynastic line of the Kaweq lineage. A certain Don Cristobal appears among the list of signatories who identifies himself as the *escr[ibano] cabilto* ("scribe of the town hall") (p. 186). He may have contributed to the contents of the document, although it is more likely that he only acted as scribe or counter-signed the document as an important town official, something like a notary.

Only one author is clearly identified by name in the *Title of Totonicapán* (see p. 117), Don Diego Reynoso, a K'iche' nobleman who accepted Christianity and worked closely with the Spanish clergy a decade or so after the destruction of the K'iche' capital of Q'umarkaj in 1524 (Akkeren 2011, 104–106; Sparks 2019, 100, 273). Reynoso was the son of Lajuj No'j, who served at the K'iche' royal court at Q'umarkaj (Carmack and Mondloch 2007, 94–95). We do not know his indigenous Maya name. Diego Reynoso was the name he adopted following baptism. Bishop Marroquín brought Reynoso to the Spanish administrative capital of Santiago de Guatemala in 1539 where he was "taught to read and write" (Ximénez 1929, I. xl.119; Anonymous 1935 [ca. 1700], II.iv.191). We do not know how old he was at the time, however the anonymous Dominican author of the *Isagoge Histórica Apologética* (1700–1711) writes that he was already an *indio principal* (an indigenous leader) when he arrived in Santiago de Guatemala, so he must have been a person of sufficient maturity to warrant a position among the K'iche' nobility (Anonymous 1935 [ca. 1700], II.iv.191). He was undoubtedly born prior to the Spanish Conquest of 1524 and could recall the major ceremonial practices in his home city of Q'umarkaj, the royal capital, that he witnessed growing up. Reynoso at some point prior to the 1550s received the title Popol Winaq, an honorific given to members of the K'iche' governing council (Carmack and Mondloch 1983, 182).

Soon after he arrived at the Spanish capital under the auspices of Bishop Marroquín, Reynoso began to work with Roman Catholic missionaries from Spain, helping them compose religious tracts in the K'iche' language for use in their evangelization efforts. One of these is a now-lost manuscript on the Passion of Christ and a history of the Spanish Conquest that was quoted by both the anonymous author of the *Isagoge* as well as Francisco Ximénez more than a century later (Anonymous 1935 [ca. 1700], 2.4.191; Christenson 2016, 114).

In the section of the *Title of Totonicapán* written by Diego Reynoso, he describes the second generation of K'iche' lords making a pilgrimage to Tulan in the East to obtain tokens of power and sovereignty. Reynoso's contribution immediately follows an account of the same event by the principal authors of the text that differs significantly from his. In Reynoso's version, the twin sons of the first progenitor

B'alam K'itze', K'oka'ib' and K'okawib', returned to Tulan to obtain titles and symbols of authority that legitimized their right to rule. Reynoso's account is consistent
with that of the *Popol Vuh* in that the two conducted themselves honorably, completed their journey to Tulan by crossing the sea in the East, and subsequently held
the two highest positions of rulership with no question of their legitimacy:

> Then they arrived before Lord Nakxik. They pleaded for their authority from Lord
> Nakxik. Thus they were given lordship by Lord Nakxik. And so K'oka'ib' and
> K'okawib' returned. Along with the Nim Ch'okoj Kaweq they arrived here. They
> delivered their authority. "It has been accomplished. We have done it. They have
> come; these signs of authority have come," they said. Then they delivered their
> authority. (p. 118)

Yet in the section immediately preceding Reynoso's account, the Totonicapán
text contradicts this version of events:

> And so they were sent, the two sons of B'alam K'itze'. These, then are the names of the
> two sons of B'alam K'itze', they who were given their task—K'oka'ib' and K'okawib'.
> They went to the place where the sun emerges to obtain lordship. One went under
> orders to the place where the sun emerges. The other went to the place where the sun
> sets. K'oka'ib' went to the place where the sun emerges. K'okawib' went to the place
> where the sun sets. K'oka'ib' quickly went straight to the place where the sun emerges.
> But he, K'okawib', merely returned from the sea. He did not cross the sea, but returned
> from Mexico. Then he diminished his heart. He lay in secret with his sister-in-law, the
> wife of K'oka'ib'. He engendered a son. Surely it was he, B'alam K'okawib'. (p. 113)

In this version of events, the illegitimate son of K'okawib' and the wife of K'oka'ib',
B'alam K'onache, held the secondary office of Ajpop K'amja, a claim made both
before (p. 116–117) and after (p. 154) the chapter composed by Diego Reynoso. In
Diego Reynoso's account, there is no hint of K'okawib's adulterous affair, and it
does not appear in the *Popol Vuh*. The *Popol Vuh* also insists that B'alam K'onache
held the highest ruling office among the K'iche', that of Ajpop (Christenson 2007,
262). The *Popol Vuh* was written by court noblemen who would understandably
have avoided any hint of scandal that would have challenged the legitimacy of one
of their ancestors and their own right to rule.

It is curious that the same text would give two radically different versions of
such an important event in the founding of K'iche' sovereignty. Reynoso's version
of events may have been a deliberate attempt to "correct" the record and assert
the legitimacy of the K'iche' rulers within the Kaweq lineage. This would explain
Reynoso's pointed assertion that his was a truthful version of events, emphasizing
that he would speak with "esteem" about the character of the persons involved,

including K'okawib'. Perhaps to establish his credentials as a qualified source, he also declared his own parentage and title as a Kaweq nobleman:

> Hear ye the straightforward truth. The account shall be told. I shall speak with esteem of their natures. I shall write then, I Diego Reynoso, Popol Winaq, son of Laju No'j. We shall begin now the tale of their journey, they the three enchanted people. For a second time they went to the place where the sun emerges. These were their names—K'oka'ib', K'okawib', and K'o'akul Akutaq'. These went to the place where the sun emerges before the face of Lord Nakxik. They received their lordship. (p. 117)

Although we may never know, I suggest that Reynoso's account was inserted by officials at some later date to refute the assertions of the main body of the text, which taints the memory of one of their founding dynasts and may even question the legitimacy of that branch of the Kaweq lineage's right to rule. It is therefore clear that Diego Reynoso did not compose the entire document and probably only had a hand in the brief section that specifically bears his name. The authorship of the bulk of the text therefore remains a mystery.

There are good reasons to believe that the contemporary *Popol Vuh* was composed by anonymous noblemen from the three highest K'iche' lineages who held the title Nim Ch'okoj ("Great Steward"). The *Popol Vuh* refers to them as the "mothers of the word, and the fathers of the word" (Christenson 2007, 305). "The word" is used in the text to describe the *Popol Vuh* itself (59), indicating that the Nim Ch'okoj were most likely the authors of the book (D. Tedlock 1996, 56–57; Akkeren 2003; Christenson 2007, 36–37).

Nim Ch'okoj was an important position within the K'iche' nobility, charged with certain duties at royal banquets—perhaps including the recitation of tales dealing with the gods, heroes, and past rulers of the K'iche' nation. The *Title of Totonicapán* also singles out the Nim Ch'okoj for their importance. They are the only class of noblemen identified as having accompanied the brothers K'oka'ib' and K'okawib' in their pilgrimage to Tulan, and they are said to have received their authority directly from Nakxik himself (p. 118), an extraordinary claim for a titled class of noblemen that did not have sovereign power.

The Ximénez dictionary (1985 [1701], 201) glosses *chocol* as "to put in order or to seat someone." In the same dictionary, the related verbal form *chocola* is to "gather food or drink for consumption among many people" (201) In the Sáenz de Santa María (1940, 97) dictionary, the equivalent term *choqola* refers to a "popular banquet in which each one contributes 20 grains of cacao," and *choqolaaj* is to "invite people to a banquet or to community work." Ritual feasting is a major component of Maya ceremonialism as a symbol of unity between participants and their gods (Christenson 2010; see figure 9). The places where invited persons sit are determined

Figure 9. Oration at a ceremonial meal, Santiago Atitlán, Guatemala, 2010

by their position within the social hierarchy. This is why thrones and benches often function as a metaphor for the position of those who sit on them (see pp. 121-122, 135, 167, 169). The Nim Ch'okoj held important positions within the K'iche' hierarchy, organizing feasts and determining the seating order of invited dignitaries. In the *Popol Vuh*, they are described as "great," but in "a small way": "These three stewards [Nim Ch'okojs] gathered together as the givers of birth, the mothers of the word, and the fathers of the word. Great, in a small way, is the essence of these three stewards" (Christenson 2007, 305).

One of the signatories of the *Title of Totonicapán* identifies himself as Don Cristóbal Velasco, Nim Ch'okoj Kaweq (p. 186). This same Don Cristóbal Velasco was probably one of the unnamed authors of the *Popol Vuh*, specifically the Nim Chokoj of the ruling Kaweq lineage who held this title in the mid-sixteenth century (D. Tedlock 1985, 61; Christenson 2007, 47). It may be that Don Cristóbal Velasco had a hand in writing the Totonicapán document as well, although there is no explicit evidence to prove it conclusively. In stark contrast, the section composed by Diego Reynoso goes out of its way to demean and even insult the Nim Ch'okoj. On page 118, he refers to them as "mere bench sitters, (a play on words referring to the meaning of *ch'okoj* as 'to seat')" who were not considered "leaders, or great fasters or penitents. Neither did they have their lordship." Perhaps Reynoso is engaging in a bit of ill-tempered rivalry with the principal authors of the *Title of Totonicapán*. Certainly, he goes out of his way to distinguish his view of history from that of the other authors of the Totonicapán text.

Whoever they may have been, the authors of the *Title of Totonicapán* manuscript were trained in the use of European letters. Soon after the formal establishment of Christianity in highland Guatemala, Roman Catholic missionaries began to teach representatives of the various Maya lineages of Guatemala to read and write their languages using a modified Latin script developed by Fr. Francisco de la Parra (Campbell 1971; Álvarez Sánchez 2014). The first bishop of Guatemala, Francisco Marroquín, strongly advocated this policy as a means of aiding the conversion effort to Christianity. The authors of the *Title of Totonicapán* undoubtedly learned to read and write with the Latin alphabet under the direction of Christian missionaries who were actively establishing schools for this purpose in major Maya towns.

HISTORY OF THE *TITLE OF TOTONICAPÁN* MANUSCRIPT

The final folio page of the *Title of Totonicapán* as it exists today is missing its upper section and is heavily damaged along its right edge. A fragmentary phrase at the beginning of the remaining portion of the page can be read "today . . . in the year 155 . . ." Fortunately, a copy of the text was made in 1834 either from this same manuscript before the damage occurred or from an intact copy, allowing the missing date to be recovered as September 28, 1554 (Recinos and Goetz 1953, 194).

The original mid-sixteenth-century manuscript is lost. The oldest known copy is privately owned by a prominent K'iche' family in the Totonicapán area. In 1973, the family allowed Robert Carmack to view the contents of their lineage chest, and he found that it held at least seven Colonial-era texts, including a copy of the *Title of Totonicapán* (Carmack and Mondloch 1983, 9). The manuscript was in good condition, with few tears and with the text intact other than the final page.[2] The tears that did appear on other folio pages were apparently present at the time the copy was made, as the scribe avoided those areas when writing the text (10).

Carmack was allowed to photocopy all thirty-one folios of the Totonicapán document front and back using an old machine in the town (sixty-four pages in all). He subsequently returned three times to consult the manuscript, to transcribe areas missed by the first photocopies, and to take photographs. On his third visit,

---

[2] Garry Sparks (personal communication, 2020) suggests that there may have been one or more pages missing at the beginning of the text as it seems to be lacking an opening statement, commonly seen in other K'iche' notarial documents.

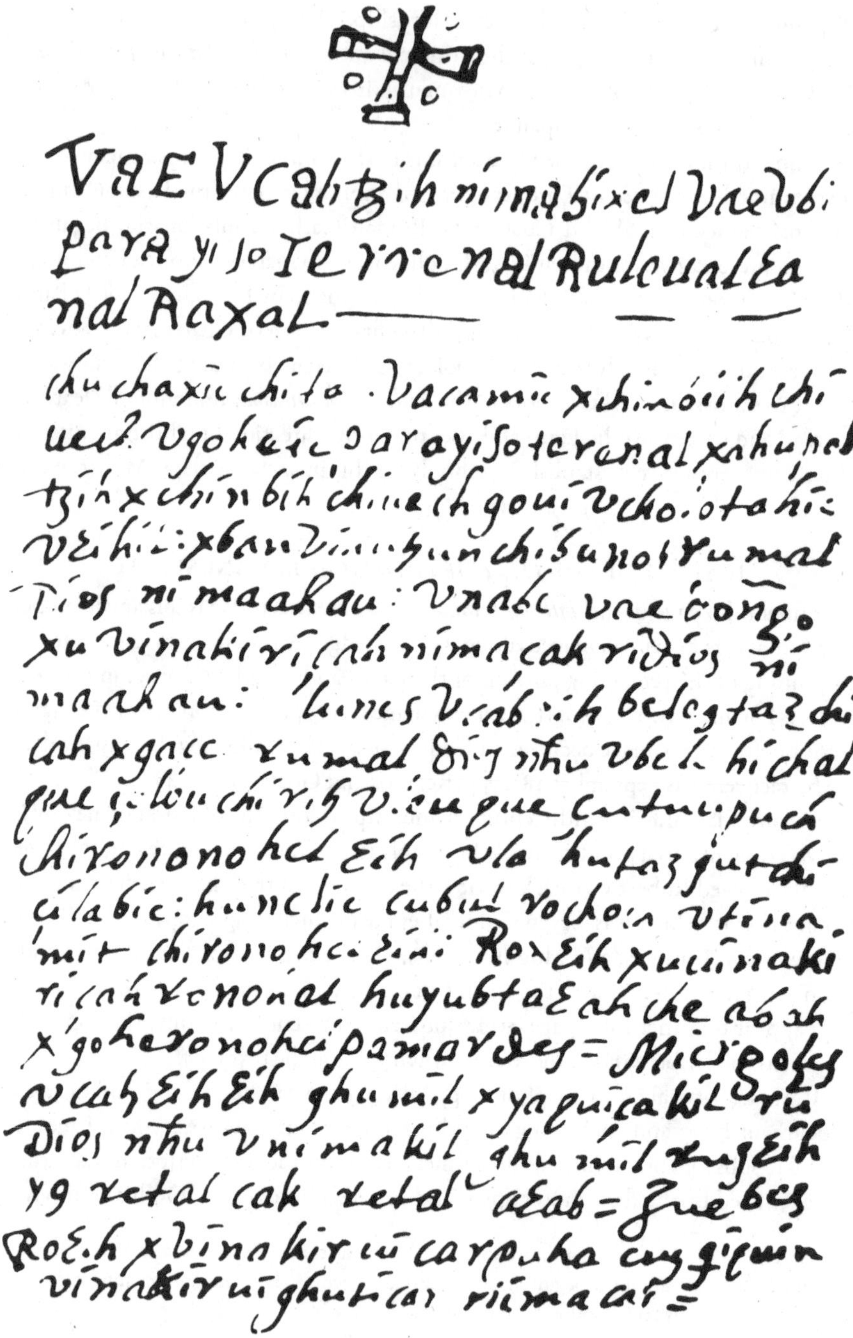

VRE V cah tzih nima bixel vae vbi
Para yi so Terrenal Ruleual Ea
nal Aaxal———

chu chaxie chi lo . Vacamu xchinoeih chi
ueel vgokaie oarayi so terenal xahupch
tzih xchin bih chinach goui vcho oto hi
vei hi xbau linepun chisunol vu mal
Tios ni maahau: vnabe vae tong
xu vinakiri cah nima cak vidios S:
ni
ma ahau: lunes vrabih beles taz chi
cah xgaee vu mal Dig nhu vbeh hi chal
que ci lou chi rih view que cutu pucu
Mivonono hel Eih vla hutaz jut chi
elabie: hune lie cubui vochoin vtina
mit chivono he cini RoEih xueinaki
vi cah venonal huyubtaE ah che ao xi
xgovevonohei pamarJes = Miceoles
vcah Eih Eih ghu mil x yaquica kil ru
Dios nhu vni ma kil thu mil xugEih
yg vetal cak vetal aEab = Juebeg
RoEh x bina kir u carpuho cug ji uin
vinakir u ghuti cai riima cai =

Figure 10. First page (folio 1r) of the *Title of Totonicapán*. *Courtesy*, Robert M. Carmack.

he was allowed to photocopy the manuscript again in its entirety using a newer machine. This later copy was subsequently published in 1983 as a facsimile[3] under the title *El Título de Totonicapán*, along with a transcription of the K'iche' text and a Spanish translation prepared in collaboration with James L. Mondloch (Carmack and Mondloch 1983, 2007).

Carmack made drawings of several of the watermarks from the manuscript and showed them to the Guatemalan historian René Acuña, who concluded that at least one of the marks could not have belonged to the sixteenth century and likely dated to between 1650 and 1725 (Carmack and Mondloch 1983, 11). The location of the original sixteenth-century document, if it still exists, is unknown. It is also unknown how many stages of copying separate this manuscript from the original. Numerous examples of scribal errors are apparent throughout the manuscript. Where these affect the translation of the text, they have been marked with a footnote in the modern orthographic transcription. These errors might have resulted from inconsistencies in applying an alphabetic script to the K'iche' language by the original sixteenth-century authors. They may also have been the result of errors creeping into the text by later copyists. Without the original manuscript for comparison, it is impossible to know.

Little is known of the history of the Totonicapán document until 1834, when it was presented before a municipal judge in Totonicapán as evidence in a land dispute. This was only thirteen years after Guatemala declared its independence from Spain, and territorial claims were no doubt common throughout the country. The judge asked a local priest, Father Dionisio Chonay, to translate the text from K'iche' to Spanish so it could be used in court. Chonay described the document as consisting of thirty-one folio pages. This is the same length as the manuscript shown to Robert Carmack, and it is very likely that it is the same document translated by Chonay 150 years earlier (Carmack and Mondloch 1983, 9–10).

Father Chonay completed his translation in three weeks, although he noted that it was not an easy task:

> By this date I have been able to finish the commission you made me in your letter of August 21 [1834]. I should have liked to serve you and the interested parties in two or three days; but despite this desire I have spent three entire weeks, because of the difficulty of understanding a thing so full of words or terms that are no longer used and of things we do not know. I hope that it will be of some use to the interested parties, and that you will have the goodness to overlook and correct the defects. (Recinos and Goetz 1953, 166)

---

3   The only exception was folio page 14v, which didn't come out when photocopied the second time. The earlier photocopy of the page was published in its place.

Figure 11. K'iche' confraternity leaders, Totonicapán, 1902. Photograph by Gustavus A. Eisen.

Chonay chose not to include the first seven folios because they had no bearing on the court case, containing as he described it an account of "the creation of the world, of Adam, the Earthly Paradise in which Eve was deceived not by a serpent but by Lucifer himself, as an Angel of Light. It deals with the posterity of Adam, following in every respect the same order as in Genesis and the sacred books as far as the captivity of Babylonia" (Recinos and Goetz 1953, 166–167).

Father Chonay did a remarkable job of translating the text in such a short time, although when one compares it with the original manuscript, there are numerous errors in both transcription and translation. These errors would have had little bearing on the court case. Chonay is also likely responsible for numbering many of the pages and for writing *Capítulo 2°* ("Chapter 2nd" in Spanish) in the left margin of page 101, continuing into the space between lines two and three. This is written in a distinct hand, and it is the only place in the document that is marked as a "*Capítulo*" in Spanish. It appears at the point where Chonay apparently believed a new section began.

Following the legal proceeding, the original K'iche' manuscript was presumably returned to its K'iche' owners, and Father Chonay's translation remained in the municipal archives. Chonay's abbreviated translation was discovered in 1860 by the antiquarian Abbé Charles Étienne Brasseur de Bourbourg,[4] who copied the Spanish translation and took it with him to Paris. Following his death in 1874, Brasseur's copy of the Chonay Spanish translation came into the possession of Charles-Félix-Hyacinthe Gouhier, comte de Charencey, who translated it into French and published the text in both French and Spanish under the title *Título de los señores de Totonicapán* in 1885. Brasseur's copy of the Chonay translation was eventually acquired by the Bibliothèque nationale de France (BnF), where it resides today as Manuscrit Américain 77. The location of the Spanish manuscript written in Chonay's hand is unknown.

Adrián Recinos published a Spanish translation of the *Annals of the Kaqchikels* in 1950 and included Brasseur de Bourbourg's copy (now at the BnF) of Chonay's Spanish text of the Totonicapán document. In 1953, Recinos published an English translation of this compilation prepared by Delia Goetz titled *The Annals of the Cakchiquels and the Title of the Lords of Totonicapán*.

FR. DOMINGO DE VICO AND THE *THEOLOGIA INDORUM*

The first fourteen pages of the *Title of Totonicapán* manuscript are based to one degree or another on a fascinating text, the *Theologia Indorum* (Latin for "Theology of/for the Indians"), composed in the K'iche' language by the Dominican missionary Domingo de Vico, most likely with the collaboration of early K'iche' converts to the Roman Catholic faith (Akkeren 2011, 95–97; Sparks 2017, 32; 2019, 4). The *Theologia Indorum* is a massive theological text written in the K'iche' Maya language between 1551 and 1554. Part one was completed in February 1553, a little over a year before the signing of the *Title of Totonicapán*. It consists of a redaction of Old Testament history and doctrine from the creation of the world until the coming of Christ. According to Garry Sparks (2017, 30; 2019, 309–312), the first volume of the *Theologia Indorum*, specifically chapters 1–24, align very closely with St. Thomas Aquinas's *Summa Theologica*. The second part was completed the following year, in 1554, and outlines doctrines from the *Summa Theologica* as well as treatises on the sacraments and prayer, New Testament history, the Last Judgment, and the lives of various saints (Sparks 2019, 117). The full text of the *Theologia Indorum* has never been published and only exists today in the form of handwritten copies.

---

[4] Brasseur also collected the oldest known copy of the *Popol Vuh*, the *Rabinal Achi*, and numerous other important documents during his travels in Guatemala.

Figure 12. Fr. Domingo de Vico. Dominican Convent, Guatemala City. Photograph by Ruud van Akkeren.

The original manuscript of the *Theologia Indorum* is lost; however, numerous copies were made, and many of these have survived. Sparks (2019, 118, table 3.2) has identified at least eighteen partial copies of the *Theologia Indorum*. These were mostly composed in K'iche', although there are also translations in other highland Maya languages such as Kaqchikel, Tz'utujil, and Q'eqchi' scattered in various archives in Europe and the United States (Sparks 2017, 31). Although no single manuscript contains the entire text, enough is accessible in the various copies to reconstruct the contents and organization of the original with some confidence.

The *Theologia Indorum* was highly influential in highland Guatemala during the Early Colonial period and was widely used by Christian missionaries in their evangelization efforts. It can be assumed that the authors of the *Title of Totonicapán* had

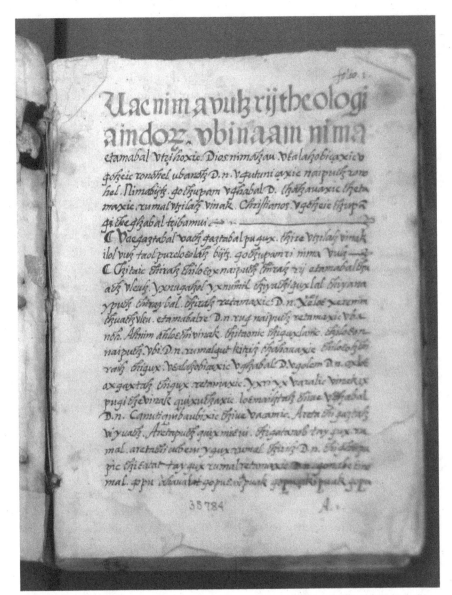

Figure 13. First page of the *Theologia Indorum*. *Courtesy*, American Philosophical Society, Philadelphia, PA.

at least a partial copy to work from when they composed the first section of their work. I think it is very likely that one or more of the authors of the Totonicapán text also worked with Vico in the preparation of his *Theologia*. Diego Reynoso is known to have aided early Christian missionaries in highland Guatemala in their efforts and must have known Father Vico well (Akkeren 2011, 106; Sparks 2019, 100).

Although the biblical narratives serve as the foundation for the *Theologia Indorum*, Vico goes well beyond this to interpret the Old Testament through the lens of sixteenth-century Roman Catholicism. This was an ambitious undertaking that most likely began in the late 1540s and ultimately resulted in nearly 900 manuscript pages of text. Sparks (2017, 32; 2019, 117–119) characterizes it as a *Summa*, akin to the *Summa Theologica* by St. Thomas Aquinas, in that it is intended to be "a systematic theological summary or compendium." It is the first original work of Christian theology written in the Americas and the longest single text of any kind written in an indigenous language during the Colonial era (Sparks 2019, 4).

In some cases, the authors of the Totonicapán document quote the *Theologia Indorum* nearly word for word, but more often they paraphrase or modify the text to better reflect K'iche' cosmology. They also ignore large sections of the *Theologia Indorum*, particularly the passages of doctrinal interpretation. In other passages, the *Title of Totonicapán* uses the *Theologia* merely as a springboard to introduce material that is entirely unique and not found in any other known text. In other words, the authors of the Totonicapán text did not simply copy directly from the *Theologia Indorum*. Rather, it is a synthesis of the Christian narrative contained in the *Theologia* harmonized by K'iche' Maya intellectuals with their own distinctive worldview. Elements of Christian doctrine that did not resonate were ignored or altered. Where consistency of belief could be found, the K'iche' authors dovetailed these passages with their own traditions. The *Title of Totonicapán* is a window into the minds of literate K'iche' Maya noblemen grappling with the tenets of the newly introduced Christian theology and attempting to fit them into their own centuries-old beliefs.

Vico studied theology at the University of Salamanca and the Dominican Convent of San Esteban while residing in the adjacent Convent of Santo Domingo de la Cruz in Salamanca, Spain. At that time, the chair of theology was Francisco de Vitoria, who introduced the scholasticism of St. Thomas Aquinas blended with a humanistic understanding of the inherent dignity of all people, both Christian and non-Christian (Sparks 2017, 25–27; 2019, 13). Vitoria asserted that the indigenous people of the New World were free individuals who could not be legally forced to submit to the Spanish Crown:

> The conclusion of all that has been said is that the barbarians undoubtedly possessed as true dominion, both public and private, as any Christians. That is to say, they could not be robbed of their property either as private citizens or as princes, on the grounds that they were not true masters (*ueri domini*). It would be harsh to deny to them,

Figure 14. Monument to Francisco de Vitoria, Convent of San Esteban, Salamanca, Spain

who have never done us any wrong, the rights we concede to Saracens and Jews, who have been continual enemies of the Christian religion. (Vitoria 1991 [1539], 250–251)

Under Vitoria's influence, missionaries trained in the philosophy of the "School of Salamanca" believed that evangelization efforts should be made through persuasion and rational argumentation rather than compulsion:

> My fourth conclusion is that if the Christian faith is set before the barbarians in a probable fashion, that is with provable and rational arguments and accompanied by manners both decent and observant of the law of nature, such as are themselves a great argument for the truth of the faith, and if this is done not once or in a perfunctory way, but diligently and observantly, then the barbarians are obliged to accept the faith of Christ. (Vitoria 1991 [1539], 271)

Vico's *Theologia Indorum* was written with just this kind of "rational argument" in mind. Bartolomé de Las Casas recruited Domingo de Vico as a missionary to the Maya of Guatemala. Las Casas had been appointed the "Protector of the Indians" in 1516, and in March 1544 he was consecrated as the first resident bishop of Chiapas and northern Guatemala. Vico was one of forty-six Dominican missionaries to leave for New Spain with Las Casas soon thereafter (Torre 1985, 22, 59–60; Sparks

2019, 96–97). This was the largest contingent of Dominicans to sail to the New World in the sixteenth century. Las Casas agreed fully with Vitoria's approach to the evangelization of indigenous people. In his defense of the Indians presented at the Council of Valladolid in 1550, Las Casas (1992 [1552], 40) echoed Vitoria's assertion that the indigenous people of the New World were free citizens, and if they are sought out "gently, mildly, quietly, humanely, and in a Christian manner you may instruct them in the word of God and by our labor bring them to Christ's flock, imprinting the gentle Christ on their minds."

By 1545, Vico had arrived in western Guatemala. Late in his ministry, he was among the first of the Dominican missionaries to undertake the peaceful evangelization of the Verapaz region. In other words, he came into contact with highland Maya communities that were still governed by indigenous rulers and practiced ancient Pre-Columbian ceremonies before the region was converted to Christianity. Vico's linguistic skills were extraordinary. According to Fr. Antonio de Remesal, O.P., who published a history of the early missionary efforts of the Dominican order in Guatemala and Chiapas in 1619, Vico dedicated himself to learning the languages of indigenous people wherever he went and spoke seven Maya languages:

> He came to Guatemala and became a teacher in that province. He hadn't set foot in a town more than three or four days before he knew their language as well as if it were his first and mother tongue, even though it was a rare and unusual language. And with this perfection he came to know seven different languages. (Remesal 1966, X.viii.2.297; see also X.vi.1.289, author translation)

Despite Remesal's obvious exaggerations, Vico's language abilities were unquestionable. Fr. Francisco Ximénez (1929–1932, I. xxiii.57–58) noted that Vico had written treatises on Christian doctrine in Kaqchikel, K'iche', Tz'utujil, Q'eqchi', Pokomam, and Lacandon that were still used in various communities in his day, at the beginning of the eighteenth century.

From 1551 through 1554, Father Vico served as the prior of the Dominican Convent in the Spanish administrative capital city of Santiago de Guatemala. In this capacity, he was tasked by Bishop Marroquín to teach the children of Maya lords Christian doctrine as well as how to read and write using Latin characters. Vico was not the first such teacher. Bishop Marroquín himself brought Diego Reynoso, the son of a K'iche' lord from Q'umarkaj, to Santiago de Guatemala to teach him to read and write (Ximénez 1999, I.171). At least two Franciscan priests, Fr. Pedro de Betanzos and Fr. Francisco de la Parra, also taught highland Maya youths in the years that followed, the latter adapting the Latin alphabet for use in writing highland Maya languages—a system followed by Maya scribes for centuries (Álvarez Sánchez 2014). This modified-Latin script was used with some variation to

Figure 15. Dominican Monastery of Santiago de Guatemala, now Antigua, where Domingo de Vico taught

compose all the known indigenous Maya texts of the Early Colonial period, including the *Popol Vuh* and the *Title of Totonicapán*.

Vico's school followed the established policy of Spanish authorities to teach the youths of highland Maya nobility not only Christian doctrine but also literacy in European modes of writing. Among those who attended the school in the Dominican convent were undoubtedly some of the future authors of such important early K'iche' texts as the *Popol Vuh* and the *Title of Totonicapán*. The *Annals of the Kaqchikels*, composed by members of the Kaqchikel nobility, noted the death of Vico in 1555 and asserted that *qitzij chi nima ajtij qatata'* ("truly a great teacher [was] our father") (Maxwell and Hill 2006, 301, author translation).

Alonso de Zorita, judge of the Audiencia of Mexico, was particularly impressed with Vico's character and determination to teach the Maya in their own language:

> In the monastery of Santo Domingo de Guatimala, I particularly worked with Fray Domingo de Bico while I was *Oidor*, a man highly esteemed by all for his devotion and exemplary life even though he was continually ill from the great acts of penitence he performed and his tireless work in preaching to the Spaniards and in teaching and converting the indigenous people of that land . . . Because he never wished to be idle, he had the habitual custom of writing three sheets of paper [daily] of doctrine and

sermons in the language of the Indians to be used in preaching to them. (Zorita 1999, 708, author translation)

At the beginning of 1553, there was a major struggle between the Franciscan and Dominican orders over ecclesiastical control of the provinces in highland Guatemala. The Dominicans had planned to found monasteries in the territories of both Quetzaltenango and Sacapulas in that year, but the Franciscans claimed that because they had arrived first as missionaries, the Dominicans had no authority to expand into their areas of influence. Ultimately, the Dominicans yielded to the Franciscans with regard to Quetzaltenango and the Franciscans acquiesced to the Dominican claims on the territory of Sacapulas. In effect, this gave the Dominicans control of the central region of the old K'iche' kingdom, including the ancient capital city of Q'umarkaj, Totonicapán, and Chichicastenango where many of the surviving members of the K'iche' nobility came to reside. In the remaining year of his service, Vico would have been intimately involved in the ecclesiastical affairs of the central K'iche' area, giving him ample opportunities to further his collaboration with indigenous K'iche' noblemen.

Sections of the *Theologia Indorum* contain a wealth of information on K'iche' Maya cosmology, including references to deities and myths that do not appear in any other known K'iche' text. This suggests that Vico collaborated closely with living K'iche' sources or had access to texts that are now lost. Chapter 25 of the *Theologia Indorum* concerns the "idolatry" of the highland Maya. In this chapter Vico lists the denizens of Xib'alb'a, the K'iche' otherworld, which Vico associated with the Christian hell:

nim chi 4ux xibalba nim chi 4ux = hunahpu xbalanqueh. taçul hurakan εeteb pubaix. Hun hunahpu. vukub hunahpu hun came vukub came qui4 re. qui4 r'ix4ak. mam y3 choa. voc hunahpu. Are xicabauilaj oher.

Great in your hearts was Xib'alb'a and great in your hearts were Junajpu, Xb'alankej, Tasul, Juraqan, Q'eteb' Pub'a'ix, Jun Junajpu, Wuqub' Junajpu, Jun Kame, Wuqub' Kame, Kik' Re', Kik' Rixk'aq, Mam, Ik' Choa, Wok, and Junajpu. These you venerated anciently. (Vico 1605 [1553] XXV, folio 33r lines 20–23, author translation)

Some of the gods listed here also appear in indigenous K'iche' texts, particularly the *Title of Totonicapán* and the *Popol Vuh*. These include Tojil (patron god of the Kaweq K'iche' lineage), Q'eteb' Pub'a'ix, Junajpu, and Xb'alankej. In K'iche' tradition, Junajpu and Xb'alankej defeated the lords of death in Xib'alb'a prior to being apotheosed as the sun and moon (see p. 91, Christenson 2007, 158–191). Xb'alankej appears in the *Title of Totonicapán* with the same spelling as in the *Theologia Indorum*, suggesting a common source (p. 91), whereas the *Popol Vuh* consistently spells the name Xb'alanke, without the final j. Other gods listed in chapter 25 of Vico's text do not appear in the *Title of Totonicapán* but are listed in the *Popol Vuh*. These include Jun Junajpu ("One Junajpu"), Wuqub' Junajpu ("Seven Junajpu"), Jun Kame ("One Death"), Wuqub' Kame ("Seven Death"), Kik' Re' ("Bloody Teeth"), and Kik' Rixk'aq ("Bloody Claws").

There are four other lists of ancient K'iche' gods in the *Theologia Indorum*. Most of these deities are otherwise known only from the *Popol Vuh*, although Ch'ipi Kaqulja and Raxa Kaqulja also appear in the *Title of Totonicapán* (p. 184, n. 698). In addition to the gods listed above, Vico (1605 [1553]) mentions Juraqan (chapter 25, folio 33v, line 19; chapter 82, folio 127v, line 17), one of the deities the ancient K'iche' venerated under the name "Heart of Sky" (Christenson 2007, 70); Ch'amiya B'aq ("Bone Staff") (chapter 48, folio 70r, line 14); Ch'amiya Jolom ("Skull Staff") (line 15); Ch'ipi Kaqulja ("Littlest Thunderbolt") (chapter 72, folio 109r, line 16; chapter 82, folio 127v, lines 18–19); Raxa Kaqulja ("Sudden Thunderbolt") (chapter 82, folio 127v, lines 18–19); Tepew ("Sovereign") (chapter 72, folio 109r, lines 17–18); and Q'ukumatz ("Quetzal Serpent") (line 18). Although most of these gods only appear in the *Theologia Indorum* and the *Popol Vuh*, this does not mean Vico had access to the text of the *Popol Vuh* itself, at least not in the form that survives today. Based on internal evidence, the *Popol Vuh* was compiled sometime between 1554 and 1558 (D. Tedlock 1996, 56; Christenson 2003, 37–38). Vico completed this portion of the *Theologia Indorum* by 1553. He subsequently left Santiago de Guatemala for the Alta Verapaz region in 1554 and was martyred the following year at the hands of the Ch'ol while working in the Lacandon region. He could not, therefore, have seen the completed manuscript of the *Popol Vuh* text.

There are also deity names that appear in Vico's *Theologia* that do not appear in any known indigenous K'iche' text. These include Tasul in chapter 25, folio 33r, line 21, folio 33v, line 19, chapter 72, folio 109r, line 16, and chapter 82, folio 127v, line 17; Mam ("Grandfather or Ancient One") in chapter 25, folio 33r, line 23, chapter 25, folio 33v, line 22, and chapter 48, folio 70r, line 14 (the god Mam is also mentioned as a deity in Yucatán [López de Cogolludo 1957 (1688), IV.5.185]); Ik' Chuaj (most likely a variant of Ek' Chuaj, a Yucatec Maya merchant deity) in chapter 25, folio 33r, line 23, chapter 25, folio 33v, line 23, and chapter 48, folio 70r, line 14; Wok ("Falcon") in chapter 25, folio 33r, line 23, chapter 25, folio 33v, line 20, chapter 48, folio 70r, line 12, and chapter 82, folio 127v, line 17; Kab'lajuj Kame ("Twelve Death") in chapter 48, folio 70r, line 13; Oyayax Meb'a (an unknown deity) in chapter 72, folio 109r, line 17; Tzitzimit, a female central Mexican deity who early Christian missionaries linked with the devil (Sahagún 1950–1963, 6.14.vii.163, 8.14. ix.34; Chimalpahin Quahtlehuanitzin 1997, 82–83; Molina 2001 [1571]) in chapter 82, folio 127v, line 18; and K'ulel ("Enemy," a K'iche' word that was chosen by early

Christian missionaries as one of the principal names for the devil; Sparks [personal communication, 2020] suggests that it may have been an attempt to literally translate "Satan," which means "adversary" in Hebrew) in chapter 82, folio 127v, line 18.

Because these gods appear only in the *Theologia Indorum*, Vico's Maya theogony could not have been based entirely on knowledge gleaned from any known highland Maya text. Further, this would not have been necessary to account for the deity names in Vico's manuscript. In addition to Reynoso, Vico undoubtedly consulted a number of K'iche' noblemen in his school or as part of his ministerial work on points of K'iche' religious belief. Among the noble class, this type of knowledge would have been common knowledge.

THE POETIC STRUCTURE OF THE *TITLE OF TOTONICAPÁN*

K'iche' poetry is not based on rhyme or metric rhythms but rather on the arrangement of concepts into innovative and even ornate parallel structures. Seldom are the authors content with expressing a single idea without embellishing it with synonymous concepts, metaphors, or descriptive epithets. The K'iche' poet is much like the composer of classical music who begins with a simple melody and then weaves into it both complementary and contrasting harmonies to give it interest and depth. Thus endless variations on a given theme are possible.

I have arranged the literal translation of the *Title of Totonicapán* according to its poetic structure beginning on p. 187. Lines that are parallel in form or concept have been indented an equal number of spaces from the left margin of the page.

TYPES OF PARALLELISM IN THE *TITLE OF TOTONICAPÁN*

1. *Identical Parallelism:* The repetition of identical elements. Example, p. 229, lines 1189–1190:

| xa raqan b'alam | only its pawprints jaguar |
| xa raqan utiw | only its pawprints coyote |

2. *Synonymous Parallelism:* The repetition of elements that are similar in meaning or significance. Example, p. 297, lines 3218–3219:

| wa'e **loq'olaj** tinamit | this **esteemed** citadel |
| **mayjalaj** tinamit | **admirable** citadel |

3. *Antithetic Parallelism:* The contrast of one element with an opposite or antithetical element. Example, p. 243, lines 1630–1631:

| jun xb'e chikej **chi relib'al q'ij** | one went by order **to its coming out place sun** |
| jun k'ut xb'e **chuqajib'al q'ij** | one thus went **to its setting place sun** |

4. *Associative Parallelism:* The correlation of elements that are complementary to one another. This association may be material, familial, functional, gender-based, or color-based.

a. Material association, in which the substance of the elements is similar in nature. Example, p. 290, lines 2995–2996:

| ajuwa **cho** | they of its shore **lake** |
| ajuwa **palo** | they of its shore **sea** |

b. Familial association, in which elements are related by kinship. Example, p. 229, lines 1195–1196:

| e **qamam** | they **their grandfathers** |
| **qaqajaw** | **their fathers** |

c. Functional association, in which two elements act in a similar manner. Example, p. 223, lines 1020–1021:

| e **ajk'ix** | they **bloodletters** |
| e **ajkaj** | they **sacrificers** |

d. Gender association, in which two elements are paired based on gender. Example, p. 280, lines 2705–2706:

| chaya' ta **qami'al** | give then **our daughters** |
| **qak'ajol** | **our sons** |

e. Color association, in which two elements are paired based on color. Example, p. 260, lines 2102–2103:

| **q'analaj** juyub' | **very yellow** mountain |
| **raxalaj** juyub' | **very green** mountain |

f. Quantitative association, in which two elements are paired based on numbers. Example, p. 250, lines 1826–1827:

| **b'elej** winaq | **nine** periods of twenty days |
| **oxlaju** winaq | **thirteen** periods of twenty days |

5. **Augmentive Parallelism:** Parallel elements in which one word or phrase clarifies or augments the meaning of another. Example, p. 268, lines 2339–2340:

xawi chiri' xkisik'ij [j]un ab'aj	merely there they called on a **stone**
xkik'ab'awilaj **k'wal ab'aj**	they venerated **precious stone**

6. **Causative Parallelism:** Parallel elements in which the first word or phrase directly affects or precipitates the associated words or phrases. Example, p. 287, lines 2904–2905:

chulk'ama' ri alit	**may they arrive to take** the girl
chipe k'amol re	**may they come as takers** of her

7. **Epithetic Parallelism:** The association of an element with a complementary noun or adjective that serves to define the nature of that element. Example, p. 225, lines 1083–1084:

kich'akatajik **ri e wuq amaq'**	their being defeated **the seven nations**
ajlab'a[l]	**warriors**

8. **Alliterative Parallelism:** Elements that parallel one another in sound when read aloud. On p. 290, lines 3017–3018, the nouns *achib'al* and *wachib'al* were apparently chosen for their similar sounds:

kumal **qachib'al**	by them **our image**
qawachib'al	**our visage**

9. **Grammatical Parallelism:** Elements that are grammatically parallel in construction, such as the following example from p. 255, lines 1963–1964, in which the same concept is expressed using transitive and intransitive verb forms, respectively:

xkik'ajolaj	**they engendered [transitive] sons**
xek'ajolan	**they engendered [intransitive] sons**

10. **Clarifying Parallelism:** A couplet in which the second line clarifies or defines the previous line. Example, p. 240, lines 1513–1514:

chikech	**to them**
wa'e q'apojib'	**these maidens**

11. **Agentive Parallelism:** A couplet in which an action is described in the first line, followed by the agent who carried out that action in the second line. Example, p. 234, lines 1340–1341:

k'ate k'ut **xjaqataj sokob'**	then thus **were opened great pots**
kumal **xoq'ojawab' rixoqil**	by them **esteemed their wives**

12. **Translation Parallelism:** A couplet in which an element is given in one language and then translated into another. In the following example on p. 210, lines 647–648, *marakow* is a toponym borrowed from the *Theologia Indorum*, the biblical Mara, which means "bitter water" in Hebrew. In the second line, the word is translated into K'iche' as *k'aylaj ja'* ("bitter water").

chi **marakow**	at **marakow**
k'aylaj ja'	**bitter water**

13. **Toponymic Parallism:** A couplet in which a single toponym, or place name, is identified by its original name, followed by the name by which it is known by another group. In the following example on p. 187, Q'umarkaaj is the capital of the K'iche' as it was known prior to the Spanish Conquest. Santa Cruz is the name given to the same place by the Spaniards:

chi **q'u[m]arkaj,**	chi **q'u[m]arkaj,**
Santa Cruz kuchax kamik	**Santa Cruz** it is called today

14. **Merismus:** The expression of a broad concept by a pair of complementary elements that are narrower in meaning. Thus on p. 217, lines 851–852, "**sky-earth**" represents the world as a whole; on p. 190, lines 35–36, "**mountain-valley**" refers to the face of the earth; on p. 222, lines 976–977, "**trees-bushes**" refers to all plants; on p. 222, lines 978–979, "**food-water**" refers to all consumables; on p. 213, lines 716–717, "**wood-stone**" refers to all sculpted images of deities; on p. 228, lines 1176–1176, "**daughters-sons**" refers to all children; on p. 214, lines 756–757, "**grandfathers-fathers**" refers to all ancestors.

STROPHIC ARRANGEMENTS IN THE *TITLE OF TOTONICAPÁN*

1. **Alternative Parallelism:** Parallelism in which elements appear in an alternating arrangement, such as the following example from p. 270, lines 2399–2404, with the first three lines listing the major lineages of the K'iche' hierarchy, followed by the founders of those lineages in the same order, giving the arrangement ABCA'B'C':

xawi kuk'am kib' chi **kaweq**	merely they united themselves **kaweq**
chi **nijayib'**	and **nijayib'**
chi **ajaw k'iche'**	and **ajaw k'iche'**
ri **B'alam k'itze'**	the **B'alam k'itze'**

b'alam aq'ab'	b'alam aq'ab'
majukotaj	majukotaj

2. **Chiasmus, or Reverse Parallelism:** Parallelism in which the first element of a strophe parallels the last, the second element parallels the next to last, and so on. These may be simple four-line chiasms or may extend over an entire section. On p. 264, lines 2217–2220 is an example of the simpler type, arranged in the form ABB'A':

chi **ma wi wa**	now **not food**
chi **ma wi ja'**	now **not water**
ta xe'opan **chi kak**	then they arrived **in thirst**
chi **wa'ij**	**in hunger**

The first chiasm I was able to identify in highland Maya literature appears in lines 32–35 of the *Popol Vuh*:

I'yom,	Midwife,
Mamom,	Patriarch,
Xpiyakok,	Xpiyacoc,
Xmucane, ub'i',	Xmuqane, their names,

(Christenson 2003, 14)

The name of the "Midwife" in line 32 is Xmucane, which appears in line 35. The name of the "Patriarch" in line 33 is Xpiyacoc, which appears in line 34. The descriptions and proper names of this couple thus appear in a chiastic arrangement. Munro S. Edmonson (1971, 5n35), who believed the *Popol Vuh* is arranged entirely in paired couplets, was confused by the order of the names Xpiyacoc and Xmucane: "It is odd that this frequent couplet places the male first, the reverse of the usual K'iche' order; indeed, if the reconstructed forms are correct, they would make better sense reversed." Recognition of the chiasmus in this passage clears up the confusion. This example from the *Popol Vuh* also elucidates a tendency in the *Title of Totonicapán* to list paired deities or ancestors with their associated epithets given in reverse order, as on pp. 216-217, lines 823–828:

ta **xecha'**	then **they said**
chirech ri **q'ij**	to the **sun**
ik'	to the **moon**
jun **q'apoj**	one **maiden**

jun **k'ajol**	one **young boy**
xecha'	**they said**

In K'iche' literature and discourse, female names and titles appear before their male counterparts when paired in parallel couplets. The major exception is where they appear in chiastic form, as here where the male sun precedes the female moon and their titles as maiden and young boy are given in reverse order.

Chiasms may extend for several lines, as in the following seven-line example on pp. 222–223, lines 999–1005, which is arranged in the form ABCDC'B'A':

ta xe'ul chi k'u chiri' chi xpa'ch	**then they arrived again thus there** chi xpa'ch
xkiya'	**they gave**
retal	**its sign**
pa ja ayin ab'aj	pa ja ayin ab'aj
retal	**its sign**
xkiya'o	**they gave**
ta kipetik chi k'ut chila'	**then their coming again thus there**

Chiasmus is a rather common poetic form in sixteenth-century Maya literature, particularly in the Guatemalan highlands. However, none of the known documents composed after 1580 contain passages of chiasmus (Christenson 2012, 330–334). Several of these later texts might otherwise be expected to contain ancient poetic forms, since they include significant sections of Pre-Columbian history and culture. Among them are the *Título Zapotitlan*, the *Título Santa Clara*, the *Título Chauchituj*, and the *Título Uchabaja*. By 1580, however, the older poetic literary forms utilized in Early Colonial indigenous texts were already forgotten or had fallen into disuse.

3. **Envelope Parallelism:** The repetition of parallel elements at the beginning and end of a long stanza or section of poetry. This has the effect of tying together the introduction and conclusion of a passage to set it apart from that which precedes and follows it. Example, p. 250, lines 1811–1820 which begins and ends a section with the couplet "they delivered it/their authority":

xkimolob'a' k'ut	**they delivered it** thus
kitaqikil	**their authority**

xb'anataj	it has been done
xqab'ano	we did it

xpe	it has come
wa'e ajawarem	this lordship
retal	its sign
xpetik xecha'	it has come they said

ta **xkimolob'a'**	then **they delivered it**
kitaqikil	**their authority**

4. **Monocolon**: An isolated line that does not parallel any associated line, thus standing on its own. Because monocolons are relatively rare in the *Title of Totonicapán*, they are all the more powerful when they do occur. In general, they are used when the authors desire to give extra emphasis to a passage. In this example on p. 288, line 2925, the authors give the terse statement that their ruler's bride arrived at their capital, further emphasizing the singularity of the phrase by adding two slash marks, used in the text to mark the end of a section.

ta xulik //	then she arrived //

STROPHIC LENGTHS

The various types of parallelism in the *Title of Totonicapán* may appear within a pair of lines, or they may extend through multiple lines of text. While the parallel couplet is the standard poetic form in the *Title of Totonicapán*, it is by no means the only one. Dennis E. Tedlock (1983, 230) recognized this in his work with highland Maya literature: "To measure all Mayan texts by the single standard of the couplet is to miss the very essence of Mayan verse rhythms, which move in twos, and sometimes threes, and once in a while arch over to produce a four." I would only add that such verse rhythms may also extend beyond four lines to form cinquains, sestets, septets, and even longer arrangements.

The following are examples of the various strophic types in terms of length found in the *Title of Totonicapán*:

1. **Parallel Couplets:** By far the most common strophic length in the *Title*

of Totonicapán is the couplet, consisting of two parallel lines. Example, p. 281, lines 2713–2714:

| at relib'al q'ij | you its coming out place sun |
| at raq'anib'al q'ij | you its rising up place sun |

In modern K'iche' speech, formal prayers and discourses also tend to utilize parallel couplets. The following selection is from a prayer made by a K'iche' priest-shaman in Momostenango as recorded by Barbara Tedlock (1982, 197). The translation, orthography, and punctuation have not been altered from Tedlock's transcription, although I have arranged the prayer into couplet form:

Pardon my sin God.	Sachaj la numac Tiox.
Pardon my sin Earth.	Sachaj la numac Mundo.
I am giving my fine,	Quinya'o ri numulta,
my present	nu presenta
before you God,	chiwäch la Tiox,
before you Earth.	chiwäch la Mundo.
I am giving my wax candle,	Quinya'o wa' jun nuceracandela,
my stake	nu tac'alibal
toward the legs	pa ri akän
arms of God	k'äb la Tiox
at the rising of the sun,	chirelebal k'ij,
at the setting of the sun	chukajibal k'ij
the four corners of sky,	cajxucut kaj,
the four corners of earth.	cajxucut ulew.
Come here then my work,	Sa'j la rech c'ut nuchac,
my service.	nupatan.

2. **Parallel Tercets:** Three parallel lines of text. Example, p. 224, lines

1054–1056:

ta xkich'ak kitzij	then they achieved their lighting fire
ta xkitikib'a' k'ut ub'aqik kiq'aq'	then they began thus its igniting their fire
nab'e k'ut xel kiq'aq'	first thus it came forth their fire

3. **Parallel Quatrains:** Four parallel lines of text. Example, p. 232, lines 1293–1296

jun sokob' q'awonon:	one great pot bumblebees:
jun sokob' sital	one great pot wasps
jun sokob' q'atz'itij:	one great pot hornets:
jun sokob' wonon ——	one great pot bees ——

4. **Longer Parallel Series:** The following is an example of a parallel cinquain on p. 253, lines 1892–1896:

ta xulik q'alelay tem	then arrived q'alelay bench
atzij winaqil tem	atzij winaqil bench
nim ch'okojil tem	nim ch'okojil bench
q'ale k'amja'il tem	q'ale k'amja'il bench
nima k'amja'il tem	nima k'amja'il bench

The *Title of Totonicapán* is fundamentally based on these various forms of parallelism. Recognition of the presence of parallelism in a given text helps focus attention on what the authors feel is important. By pairing each thought with complementary ones, the authors are able to develop their ideas with greater clarity. They may compare elements, contrast them, elaborate on their significance, or add layers of meaning that would not otherwise be obvious.

Parallelism is also the primary means used by K'iche' authors to give order to their thoughts. The words of the *Title of Totonicapán* were not arranged into sentences and paragraphs as in modern literature. They seldom use periods, commas, or capitalization to separate independent concepts. When they do appear, they are inconsistent in purpose, reflecting the authors' lack of familiarity with European devices for punctuation. Parallelism provided a means of structuring the book's ideas into distinct and coherent entities.

Much of K'iche' literature was based in whole or in part on oral tradition. Parallelism is a common mnemonic device used in many ancient cultures to help narrators remember the flow and direction of their tale. This is particularly true of the chiastic type of parallelism, which may give order to large sections of a story. It also gives listeners an opportunity to hear a recapitulation in reverse order of what had been said while reminding them of the central themes that are of special importance. The presence of parallelism in the *Title of Totonicapán* is also a tremendous, though unintended, boon to modern translators. By comparing an ambiguous word or passage with its associated line, its general meaning is often clarified. This is especially important when interpreting a word that has more than one possible meaning or is poorly transcribed through scribal error.

Perhaps the most important reason I have stressed the poetic nature of the *Title of Totonicapán* in this translation is for the insight it gives into the mind of the ancient K'iche' authors. We can see how they organized their thoughts as they took pen or brush in hand to set them down in permanent form. Far from the random musings of unlearned storytellers, the *Title of Totonicapán* can be appreciated as the eloquent creation of master poets with a sophisticated literary heritage.

ORTHOGRAPHY AND PRONUNCIATION GUIDE

The *Title of Totonicapán* was written using a modified Latin alphabet to represent K'iche' sounds that was first developed by the Franciscan mendicant friar Francisco de la Parra ca. 1545. The orthography is therefore consistent with the writing system taught by Christian missionaries during the Early Spanish Colonial period. Although most of the characters used in the script developed by Parra to write K'iche'an languages were based on the Latin alphabet, two characters were borrowed from Arabic. The glottalized palatal (4 in the sixteenth-century manuscript of the *Title of Totonicapán*, and k' in modern K'iche' orthography) is derived from the Arabic letter ﺝ (*waw*), and the glottalized uvular (ε in the manuscript, and q' in modern K'iche') is derived from the Arabic letter ع (*ayn* or *a'yn*) (Chinchilla Mazariegos and Helena 1993, xii). Neither of these Arabic characters bears any relationship to the phonetic sound of the K'iche' letters for which they substitute, and thus they may have been chosen arbitrarily to represent K'iche' sounds with which the early Spanish missionaries were unfamiliar. It is possible, however, that the choice was less arbitrary than it would appear at first glance. The Arabic letter ﻕ (*qaf*) has the same basic shape as *waw* but with two dots over the primary symbol. There is no equivalent to this sound in the English or Latin languages. It is similar to the initial k in *karma* or *kayak* but pronounced from further back in the soft palatal area. Similarly, the Arabic letter غ (*ghayn*) follows the same basic shape as the ع (*ayn*) but with a single dot on top. This letter is similar to the sound of the g in *ghost* or *gift* but pronounced from further back in the throat, something like a more guttural pronunciation of the Parisian French

r. In both cases, the Arabic characters chosen by Francisco de la Parra represent non-Latin consonants, like their K'iche' counterparts, when the dots above the letters are added. Since none of the characters used by Parra for his K'iche' alphabet utilize dots or other diacritical marks, it is entirely possible that he removed them for convenience of use.

Father Parra came from the Andalucía region of southern Spain where the Iberian Muslim presence was strong. He would have been intimately acquainted with Arabic characters and their pronunciation. Unfortunately, Parra's original writings concerning the alphabet he constructed to record highland Maya languages have not survived, making it difficult to reconstruct his thoughts on the matter.

The K'iche' authors who composed the *Title of Totonicapán* in the sixteenth century were pioneers in the use of a foreign alphabet to represent their language in written form. They did not have the luxury of officially recognized dictionaries with standardized spellings, and they did not have computers to scan for errors. In light of the enormous difficulties involved in its composition, the orthography of the *Title of Totonicapán* is remarkably consistent, although scribal errors and discrepancies in spelling inevitably appear in the text. Variant spellings of words occur throughout the manuscript, and glottalized sounds in particular are haphazardly distinguished at best. Nevertheless, the Totonicapán document is more consistent in its use of the Parra alphabet than many other texts composed afterward, including the *Popol Vuh* (Christenson 2007, 53).

The K'iche' language utilizes both a palatal stop (k) and a uvular stop (q). The authors of the *Title of Totonicapán* tended to overuse the glottalized q' form in words that should have carried the un-glottalized form q. They also often substituted s for x, although these generally appear in both forms as variant spellings. This may reflect the fact that there was a sound shift in the Spanish language such that these same letters are often interchanged in contemporary Spanish documents as well. In the Parra alphabet transcription, I have preserved the original spellings, including variants and apparent scribal errors. In the modern orthographic transcription, these spellings have been standardized and corrected to be consistent with modern usage where appropriate.

Glottalized vowels, common in the K'iche' language, are rarely distinguished in any Colonial-era texts. Thus there is no difference between the written form of *che* ("toward him/her") and *che'* ("tree"). Long and short vowels are treated as separate letters in K'iche' but are generally not distinguished in this text. For example, the word transcribed as *vach* might be read with a long vowel *vaach* ("my companion") or with a short vowel *vach* ("my face").

For the most part, the writing in the original manuscript is clear, and there are few lacunae until the final page. There are always the inherent difficulties in reading a handwritten text, particularly one that is hundreds of years old, and this manuscript is no exception. The letters a and e may not have a completely closed loop at the top, making them appear as a u or a c. The tail on the letter ç can be left off by mistake or it can be masked by a tall letter beneath it, making it appear as a c. The neck of an h may be a bit short, making it appear to be an n. All these are rather frequent annoyances; however, context usually helps make the interpretation clear.

It is impossible to know how many errors may have crept into the text when its contents were copied by scribes after its original composition in the mid-sixteenth century. The extant manuscript appears to have been written sometime between 1650 and 1725 based on the type of paper used and the form of its watermarks (Carmack and Mondloch 1983, 11). It is unknown if this copy was based on the original or on another copy. Without the original document, a perfect reading of the text is impossible to verify.

Since the sixteenth century, a number of writing systems have been invented for K'iche'an languages in an attempt to avoid the confusion inherent in the Parra alphabet. In 1986 the Guatemalan Ministry of Public Education set up a commission to standardize alphabets for the twenty-two recognized highland Maya languages. This standardization effort had become particularly important due to the Guatemalan government's proposed "Program of Bilingual Education" in Maya communities, designed to improve literacy and promote Native American cultures and languages. This program included the publication of bilingual dictionaries, school textbooks, and official translations of the Guatemalan Constitution in the various highland Maya languages. The results of this commission were officially endorsed by the Guatemalan government and signed into law as Governmental Decree Number 1046-87 by President Marco Vinicio Cerezo Arévalo on November 23, 1987.

The following is a list of the modified Latin letters developed by Parra as used in the *Title of Totonicapán* text, along with the modern orthographic equivalents and a guide to pronunciation.

Parra	Modern	
a, aa	a	As in the *a* of "father."
a	ä	As in the *o* of "mother."
b	b'	Similar to the English *b*, but pronounced with the lips tightly closed before the air is more forcefully expelled.
c, qu	k	Palatal stop, as in the *k* of "king."
4	k'	Pronounced with the back of the tongue in the same position as for the *k*, but the air is more forcefully expelled.
ç, s, z	s	As in the *s* of "same."

continued on next page

Parra	Modern	
ch	ch	As in the *ch* of "child."
ɉh	ch'	Pronounced with the tongue placed against the roof of the mouth in the same position as for *ch*, but the air is more forcefully expelled.
e, ee	e	As in the *a* of "late."
h, j	j	Pronounced like the English *h*, but further back in the throat. Similar to the Spanish *j* or the German *ch* (as in the proper name "Bach").
i, ii	i	As in the *ee* of "eel."
k	q	Uvular stop, pronounced from further back in the throat than the letter *k*, similar to the *kh* in the Egyptian word *ankh*.
ɛ	q'	Pronounced the same as the *q*, but the throat is closed and air forcefully expelled.
l, ll	l	As in the *l* of "linger."
m	m	As in the *m* of "mat."
n	n	As in the *n* of "net."
o, oo	o	As in the *o* of "home."
p	p	Pronounced like the English *p* but shortened in length.
r	r	Similar to the Spanish *r*, pronounced with a brief tap of the tongue against the roof of the mouth.
t	t	Similar to the English *t* but shortened in length.
tt	t'	Pronounced with the tongue in the same position as for the *t*, but the tongue is pressed more tightly against the palate and air forcefully expelled.
tz	tz	As in the *ts* of "mats."
g	tz'	Pronounced with the tongue in the same position as for the *tz*, but the tongue is pressed more tightly against the palate and air forcefully expelled.
u, uu	u	As in the *oo* of "root."
v	w	As in the *w* of "wind."
x	x	Pronounced like the *sh* in "shy."
y	y	When preceding a vowel, it is pronounced like the *y* of "yellow." Otherwise it is pronounced like the i (see above).
	'	Glottalization mark for vowels. For example, *a'* would be similar to the pronunciation of the *ott* in the Scottish pronunciation of "bottle." There is no equivalent for glottalized vowels in the *Title of Totonicapán*.

When pronouncing Maya words, the emphasis is always on the final syllable. When pronouncing Nahuatl words, the emphasis is always on the next to last syllable.

The Title of Totonicapán

https://doi.org/10.5876/9781646422647.p001

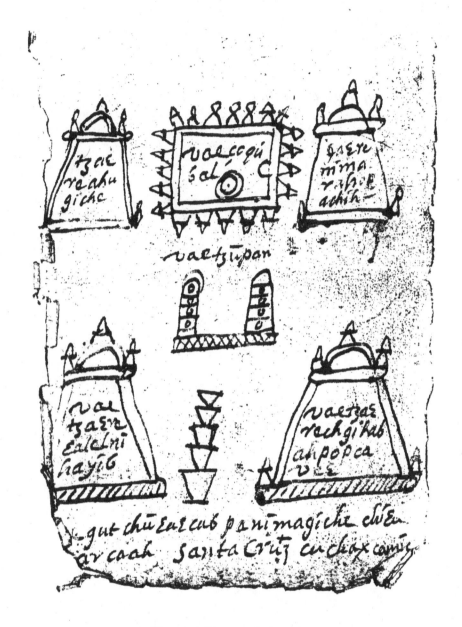

Figure 16. Diagram of Q'umarkaj.
Folio i, *Title of Totonicapán*. Courtesy Robert M. Carmack.

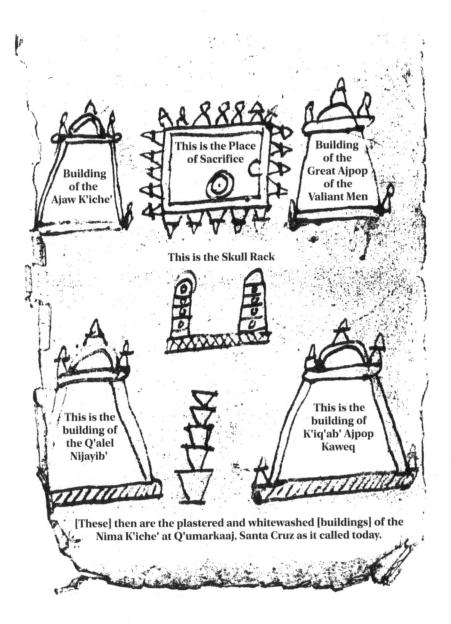

Figure 16a. Folio i, *Title of Totonicapán* with English translation

Building of the Ajaw K'iche'[5]
This is the Place of Sacrifice[6]
Building of the Great Ajpop of the Valiant Men[7]
This is the Skull Rack[8]
This is the building of the Q'alel Nijayib'[9]
This is the building of K'iq'ab' Ajpop Kaweq[10]

---

[5] Ajaw K'iche' ("Lord K'iche'"): One of three ruling lineages at the K'iche' capital of Chi Q'umarkaj. The Ajaw K'iche' were founded by the progenitor Majukotaj. This lineage is the third-ranked of the three and had the least power and influence. Structures labeled as *tz'aq* appear in each corner of the "map," likely corresponding to the Great Houses, or administrative buildings, for each of the three major lineages plus the residence of the Ajpop, or head of the ruling Kaweq lineage, at the lower right.

[6] Sokib'al ("Place of Sacrifice"). Derived from *sok* ("to cut or wound with a knife").

[7] Nima Rajpop Kaweq Achij (Great Ajpop of the Kaweq Valiant Men). Highland Maya documents list numerous offices among the ruling aristocracy who bear titles including Ajpop. The dictionary compiled by Fr. Thomás de Coto (1983 [ca. 1656]) gives various definitions for the term, including "constable, chief, counselor, dignitary, and lord." *Ajpop* is therefore a title that refers to anyone who rules or administers. This title specifically refers to a leader of the warriors at Chi Q'umarkaj that belong to the Kaweq lineage.

[8] In the drawing, the altar is labeled *tzumpan*, a K'iche' spelling of the Nahuatl word *tzompantli* ("skull rack"). The *tzumpan* is shown in profile with four vertical posts supporting eight horizontal poles on which the skulls of sacrificial victims were hung. Las Casas (1958 [ca. 1550], 177.152, author translation) wrote that this type of structure was used to display sacrificial victims: "They placed the heads of the sacrificed victims on wooden poles above a certain altar that was dedicated solely for this purpose, and there they kept them a certain time, after which they buried them."

[9] Q'alel Nijayib'. *Q'alel* is the highest office in the Nijayib' lineage, the second-ranked of the ruling K'iche' lineages. The Nijayib' were descended from the progenitor B'alam Aq'ab'. The name is a contracted form of *nimajayib'* ("they of the Great House"). Q'alel Nijayib' is the third highest office in the K'iche' kingdom, after Ajpop and Ajpop K'amja, the titles for the two principal rulers of the K'iche' (Christenson 2007, 262–263, n. 718). Colonial dictionaries give a variety of descriptive meanings for *q'alel*, including *cacique* (Taino for a native chief, a term adopted by the Spaniards to refer to all indigenous leaders), "generous person, prince" (Coto), or simply an "important person" (Vare[l]a). The Basseta dictionary defines *calel achi* as a "captain of soldiers." In modern K'iche', the title is given to judges, and some early dictionaries suggest that this office may have included judicial functions. The title is something akin to "magistrate," with duties that include administrative, judicial, peacekeeping, and military activity.

[10] This is the residence of the Ajpop Kaweq, the highest ruling office among the K'iche'. The Kaweq were the preeminent K'iche' lineage, descendants of the first progenitor, B'alam K'itze'. They were the first-ranked of the three K'iche' lineages at Chi Q'umarkaj (see note 12). *Ajpop* means literally "she/he/they of the mat." The ancient lords of the Maya sat on mat thrones, which became symbolic of lordship and authority itself. The mat represented the power not only of the ruler but also of his subjects. In this sense, the interlaced reeds of the

[These], then, are the plastered and whitewashed[11] [buildings] of the Nima K'iche'[12] at Q'umarkaj,[13] Santa Cruz[14] as it is called today.

---

mat represent the members of the community, linked in a common purpose. Thus Francisco Ximénez, the first translator of the *Popol Vuh*, translated *popol* as "community." This office might then be translated "she/he/they of the community" or "master of the community." K'iq'ab' ("Many Hands") was the name or possibly title of one of the most powerful of the Kaweq K'iche' lords (see pp. 157–184).

[11] *chun q'aq'kab'* ("plastered fire earth"?). I agree with Carmack and Mondloch (1983, 204, n. 4) who suggest that this is an example of scribal error and should read *chun saqkab'* ("plastered white earth"). The same phrase appears in the *Annals of the Kaqchikels* describing the great buildings of the Kaqchikel capital at Iximche': "See the buildings! [With] *chun saqkab'*" ("lime [with] white earth") (Maxwell and Hill 2006, 209). *Chun* ("lime, plaster"). Lime is derived from limestone and was used extensively by the ancient Maya as cement, mortar, and plaster. The etymology of the word *saqkab'* is a bit complex. *Saq* is white, but *kab'* is understood as "earth" only in lowland Maya languages. Diego de Landa (1941, 18, 171) wrote concerning the Maya of Yucatán: "and in each town they built a temple, seeing that there is an extraordinary abundance of stone, lime and a certain *sac cab* ('white earth')." In K'iche' and other highland Maya languages, however, *kab'* means not "earth" but "honey." In this context, the authors either borrowed the term *saq kab'* from the lowland area, or they may also have had in mind the widespread practice among the Maya of using honey as a binder in lime plaster (Villaseñor Alonso 2010; Dezso 2015). In the *Popol Vuh*, the use of lime and whitewash in K'iche' Maya construction was an indicator of power: "Then their glory and their sovereignty were increased in K'iche'. The grandeur and importance of the K'iche' were glorified and made sovereign. Then as well the canyon-citadel was whitewashed and plastered. The nations came there, the small and the great" (Christenson 2007, 274; see also 262).

[12] Nima K'iche' ("Great K'iche'") refers to the three principal K'iche' lineages: Kaweqib', Nijayib', and Nima Ajaw, who jointly ruled at the capital city of Chi Q'umarkaj.

[13] Chi Q'umarkaj ("At Ancient/Rotten Canes/Reeds"). The name of this citadel has generally been translated "Place of Rotten Canes" (Recinos and Goetz 1950, 215; D. Tedlock 1996, 183). *Q'umarik*, however, also refers to something ancient, while *aj* can be used for a wide variety of reeds. The more likely translation of the citadel is "Place of Ancient Reeds." This ties the city figuratively with the ancient place of their origin at Tulan (Nahuatl for "Place of Reeds"). Following the Spanish Invasion, Chi Q'umarkaj was renamed Utatlán by the Tlaxcalan allies of the Spaniards. In the Tlaxcalan dialect of Nahuatl, this name means "among the reeds," a close translation of the K'iche' name. Chi Q'umarkaj was the capital of the Nima K'iche' at the time of the Spanish Conquest.

[14] The ancient capital of the K'iche', Chi Q'umarkaj, was renamed Santa Cruz (Spanish for "Holy Cross") soon after the conquest of the city by Spanish forces. The name was chosen because the fall of Chi Q'umarkaj took place on or near Easter Sunday: "And in another place [Diego Reynoso] notes that it was in the month of April, in the final days of Lent and the beginning of Easter, that this took place [the conquest of the K'iche']. And it appears that because this took place in those days of Holy Week, they gave the new city of Quiché the name of Santa Cruz, and with this Santa Cruz they extinguished the rage of that nation" (Anonymous 1935 [ca. 1700], II, iv, 191).

Figure 17. Folio ii, *Title of Totonicapán. Courtesy*, Robert M. Carmack.

Coat of Arms of Señor Don Juan de Aguilar, conqueror.[15]

[15] This is a variant of the royal coat of arms of Charles V (1500–1558), emperor of the Holy Roman Empire, although modified by the K'iche'. The lions on the escutcheon (representing the Spanish state of León) are depicted as striding rather than rampant, and they display rather prominent penises. They are also more reminiscent of jaguars than of Old World lions. B'alam ("jaguar") was the name of the founding ancestor of the ruling Kaweq lineage of the K'iche', and jaguars are often associated with royal power among the ancient Maya. The castles, representing the state of Castile, have crosses added to make them churches, a common motif in indigenous lienzos and texts where they symbolize towns rather than royal residences. The vertical stripes of Aragón are present without modification. The supporting eagle rests on a mat, a symbol for royal power in K'iche' society (Andrew Weeks, personal

Figure 18. Coat of Arms of Charles V, Holy Roman emperor

communication, 2020). The Habsburg double eagle heads are crowned, and the right head has droplets dripping from its beak, possibly blood. The double-headed eagle is still a common motif in art and oral traditions in a number of highland communities, symbolizing miraculous power and protection (Christenson 2001, 138–141). According to Carmack and Mondloch (1983, 164, n. 6), the Habsburg Royal Coat of Arms was granted to the ruling lineage of Totonicapán. Carmack was unable to locate the name of Juan de Aguilar in any of the lists of soldiers who participated in the conquest of Guatemala. He notes, however, that a prominent family bearing the name Aguilar lives in the Chiyax area of Totonicapán where the manuscript of the *Title of Totonicapán* was discovered. It is possible that the founder of this lineage was a K'iche' nobleman who adopted the name Aguilar from an unknown Spanish conqueror.

Section 1

Maya Synthesis of the *Theologia Indorum*

THE CREATION OF THE EARTH[16]

This is the fourth word[17] of the great song.[18] This is its name: Earthly Paradise,[19] the

---

[16] lines 1–87.

[17] *ukaj tzij* ("fourth word"). *Tzij* is literally "word" but also "story, tale." This section is taken from the fourth major theme of the *Theologia Indorum*. The K'iche' authors chose not to include most of the contents of the previous three themes, which deal primarily with the nature of God and the Trinity, and begin their account with the creation of the Earthly Paradise, corresponding to chapter 30 of the *Theologia* (Vico 1605 [1553], folios 44r–45v; see Sparks 2017, 219).

[18] *nima b'ixel* ("great account/song"). *B'ixel* does not appear in any known dictionaries from the Early Colonial period, and it is also not found in the *Theologia Indorum* from which much of this section of the Totonicapán document derives. The word appears to be unique to this document. It is possible that it could be an odd grammatic construction based on the passive form of the verb *b'ij* ("that which has been said"), although this is unlikely. Instead, it appears to be based on the verb *b'ix* ("to sing"), indicating that the text is meant to be sung or at least recited with a rhythmic cadence, such as a poem. This is akin to the Western tradition of dividing epic poems such as Dante's *Divine Comedy* and Lord Byron's *Don Juan* into cantos ("songs") rather than chapters.

[19] Parayiso Terrenal (Spanish for "Earthly Paradise"). The K'iche' authors of the text used the Spanish phrase, perhaps because there was no K'iche' language equivalent that conveyed the same concept.

---

https://doi.org/10.5876/9781646422647.c001

Land of Abundance[20] and New Life[21] it is called. Hear me this day and understand. I shall tell you of the nature of the Earthly Paradise.

In the first division of the word[22] I shall tell you of the ordering of times in which were done each of the works of God, the Great Lord.[23]

On the first of these, Sunday, He conceived the great light,[24] He, the Great Lord. On Monday, the second day, the nine divisions[25] of the sky were raised up by God,

---

[20] *q'anal*. Literally, "yellowness," but with the implication of "richness, abundance, ripeness." Here the K'iche' authors describe the Earthly Paradise in uniquely Maya terms. They are meant to be read as proper nouns rather than adjectives, and they are capitalized in the text. In Maya languages, yellow and orange are shades of the same color, *q'an*. When used in this form, *q'anal*, it means "yellowness/orangeness." This is specifically the abundance of ripe yellow maize; however, it is used by the K'iche' to refer to abundance or wealth of any kind (B. Tedlock 1982, 114), a metaphor that appears in various Maya languages (Houston et al. 2006, 25). According to Ruth Bunzel (1952, 282), it may also refer to rebirth and regeneration.

[21] *raxal*. Literally, "greenness," but with the implication of "vitality, newness, rebirth, freshness, fertility." The highland Maya consider green and blue to be shades of the same color, *rax*. The couplet *q'anal raxal* ("yellowness greenness") is used frequently in early highland Maya literature to refer to abundance and new life, as in a ripening maize field. Karen Bassie (personal communication, 2019) suggests that the authors of the text are describing the Earthly Paradise as a cultivated field with both immature green maize (*raxal*) and mature yellow maize (*q'anal*), comprising the entire life cycle of maize. This pairing of youth and maturity is also used in the *Popol Vuh* to refer to the life cycle of humans, as can be seen in this prayer to the ancient K'iche' gods: "Pleasing is the day, you, Huracan, and you, Heart of Sky and Earth, you who give abundance [*q'anal*] and new life [*raxal*], and you who give daughters and sons. Be at peace, scatter your abundance [*q'anal*] and new life [*raxal*]. May life and creation be given. May my daughters and my sons be multiplied and created, that they may provide for you, sustain you, and call upon you on the roads, on the cleared pathways, along the courses of the rivers, in the canyons, beneath the trees and the bushes" (Christenson 2007, 289). In the Basseta dictionary, the pairing of *q'anal raxal* is defined as "blessedness" and in the Coto dictionary as "glory." Early Christian missionary sources often translate the couplet *q'anal raxal* as "glory" or the "glory of God" (Sachse 2016, 104–105).

[22] *paj tzij* ("division word"). This is a phrase, first used in the *Theologia Indorum*, that utilizes K'iche' words to describe the non-Maya concept of a book chapter as a "word/story division."

[23] Dios Nima Ajaw. The authors chose to use the Spanish word *Dios* ("God") paired with the K'iche' terms *Nima Ajaw* ("Great Lord"), thus blending Christian and Maya theologies.

[24] *xuwinaqirisaj nima saq* ("he conceived/created great light"). The verb *winaqirisaj* can be translated "to conceive, to create, or to generate." The root, *winaq*, means "people"; a more literal translation would be "to people." The creation is thus seen as similar to the way people come to be, a natural process of conceiving and giving birth. The same verb may be used for the concept of "to plan" or "to think of something," similar to the English meaning of "conceive."

[25] *tas* ("division, layer, tier, stratum"). *Tas* is used to describe horizontal divisions, such as the courses of adobe for a house or layers of sheets and blankets on a bed. Here the K'iche' authors of the text follow closely Domingo de Vico's *Theologia Indorum*, which describes

the Great Lord. Each of the nine encircles the earth, rotating every day. Each thus moves, forever adorning their homes and their towns every day.

On the third day he conceived all the mountains and the valleys,[26] the wood and the stones.[27] These all came to be on Tuesday.

On Wednesday, the fourth day, the sun and stars were given their light by God, the Great Lord. The stars received their greatness, along with the sun and moon; the one the sign for brightness and the other the sign for night.

On Thursday, the fifth day, were conceived the fish in the water along with the birds. The small fish and the large fish were conceived.

On Friday, the sixth day, were conceived the small serpents and the large serpents. All animals of the earth were conceived by God, the Great Lord. They were conceived on Friday.

Thus the works of God were given life on each of the days. "Propagate yourselves, increase yourselves, multiply yourselves," said God, the Great Lord, to that which he had made. Thus they were counseled, all his works, by Tz'aqol B'itol.[28]

---

nine concentric spheres of heaven encircling the earth. The nine levels of heaven are not based on biblical tradition but rather on the writings of Pseudo-Dionysius the Areopagite, a Christian theologian of the late fifth to early sixth centuries. His works were highly influential in later Christian tradition. Pseudo-Dionysius's ordering of the heavens into nine hierarchies, each assigned to an order of angels, was cited at length in St. Thomas Aquinas's *Summa Theologica* and probably served as the basis of Dante's nine levels of heaven in the *Divina Commedia*. In K'iche' tradition, the number nine is also significant as a symbol for completion or bringing any major period of training or work to a close. For example, the training of *ajq'ijab'* (K'iche' religious specialists) is traditionally a period of nine months, based on the period of human gestation in which the fetus is formed, as well as a full count of days on the 260-day traditional Maya calendar. Here the authors use the number nine as a symbol for completeness or perfection.

[26] This is an example of a common K'iche' literary device, merismus, in which a broad concept is expressed by a pair of complementary elements that are narrower in meaning. Thus *juyub'-taq'aj* ("mountain-valley") is used to describe the face of the earth as a whole. The same pairing appears often in early highland Maya literature, such as the *Popol Vuh* (Christenson 2007, 71–72).

[27] *che'* ("tree/wood") and *ab'aj* ("stone") is another example of merismus, although not an obvious one outside of K'iche' tradition. In Colonial-era K'iche' literature, the pairing of *che'* and *ab'aj* specifically refers to the carved images of Pre-Columbian gods. Thus in the *Popol Vuh*, the earliest K'iche' people lamented that they did not yet have gods to watch over them: "There did not exist then wood or stone to watch over our first mothers and fathers" (Christenson 2007, 207; see also 206). In the *Theologia Indorum*, the reason given for the confounding of the languages at the Tower of Babel is that the people began to "call upon *che' ab'aj* ('wood stone')." The choice of the pairing here appears to be purposeful and perhaps subversive to the overall Christian message of this section, indicating that the ancient K'iche' gods, formed of wood and stone, are as old as creation itself.

[28] Here, God is equated with the ancient K'iche' creator deities, Tz'aqol ("Framer") and B'itol ("Shaper"). In the *Popol Vuh* they are described as a pair of deities, female and male, who are

This day we shall begin[29] the story, the account of the Earthly Paradise; of the care[30] of the earth and the completion of Paradise we shall speak. Thus I shall begin the account.

THE ORGANIZATION OF THE HEAVENS[31]

Fourth division of the word.[32] This is the account of the nine assemblies, the nine divisions of angels.[33] Truly good and beautiful are the formation and the creation of

---

responsible for the creation of all things: "Thus were established the four corners, the four sides, as it is said, by Tz'aqol ('Framer') and B'itol ('Shaper'), the Mother and the Father of life and all creation, the givers of breath and the givers of heart, they who give birth and give heart to the light everlasting, the child of light born of woman and the son of light born of man, they who are compassionate and wise in all things—all that exists in the sky and on the earth, in the lakes and in the sea" (Christenson 2007, 65–66). Dominican missionaries, including Fr. Domingo de Vico who composed the *Theologia Indorum*, often used Tz'aqol B'itol to refer to the God of the Old Testament in their missionary efforts to make Christianity more understandable to the K'iche'. Franciscan missionaries believed this practice perpetuated pagan beliefs and insisted on using the Spanish word Dios ("God") for deity. This was a major point of conflict between the two orders. Tz'aqol refers to one who makes something by putting things together (i.e., a building from stone or adobe, a meal from various ingredients, or a woven cloth from individual threads). B'itol refers to one who makes something by modeling (i.e., pottery from clay or a sculpture from carved stone), thus giving shape to an otherwise amorphous substance. Together, the two deities represent the two principal means of creation. Following K'iche' convention, the first of the deities would be female, the goddess who actually "frames, builds" all things like a mother forms a human infant in the womb, while the male contributes to its form or appearance.

29 *xchintiqikib'a'* literally means "I shall plant/sow." The subsequent narrative is thus seen as growing, like a field of plants sown by the author.

30 *rachb'anik* means "to care for, to tend, to take care of something."

31 lines 88–151.

32 This section on the organization of the angels in heaven is taken from the fourth division of the third major theme in the *Theologia Indorum*, corresponding to chapter 29 of that work (Vico 1605 [1553], folios 42v–44r). The previous section was based on chapter 30 of the *Theologia Indorum*. It is not known why the authors of the *Title of Totonicapán* chose to alter the order, but the very fact that they did further illustrates the extent to which the authors of this text are not merely copying the contents of the *Theologia* but rather redacting it for their own purposes.

33 The following list of the "divisions" of angels is heavily dependent on the *Theologia Indorum*, although the spelling of each division differs: "These are the names of the assemblies: *Angeles* is the name of the first, *Archangeles* is the name of the second order; *Prinçipados* is the name of the third order; *Potestates* is the name of the fourth level; *Virtutes* is the name of the fifth level; *Dominationes* is the name of the sixth level; *Tronus* is the name of the seventh level; *Cherubines* is the name of the eighth level; *Seraphinis* is the name of the ninth level" (Vico 1605 [1553], folio 42v, author translation). The order of the names is nearly the same in the

Figure 19. "Truly good and beautiful are the formation and the creation of the angels by God, the Great Lord, in their nine levels." Antonio Campi, detail from *Mysteries of the Passion of Christ*, 1569, showing the nine circles of heaven. Louvre, Paris.

Title of Totonicapán, although "Angels" are listed first in the *Theologia Indorum* and last in the *Title of Totonicapán*. The organization of angels into nine divisions appears to be derived from the writings of Pseudo-Dionysius (1987, 156–174), particularly *De Coelesti Hierarchia* ("The Celestial Hierarchy") which divides the heavens into a hierarchy (a term apparently coined by Pseudo-Dionysius) of three types of angels, each with three orders, giving a total of nine: "The word of God has provided nine explanatory designations for the heavenly beings, and my own sacred-initiator has divided these into three threefold groups. According to him, the first group is forever around God and is said to be permanently united with him ahead of any of the others and with no intermediary. Here, then, are the most holy 'thrones' and the orders said to possess many eyes and many wings, called in Hebrew the 'cherubim' and 'seraphim.' Following the tradition of scripture, he says that they are found immediately around God and in a proximity enjoyed by no other. This threefold group, says my famous teacher, forms a single hierarchy which is truly first and whose members are of equal status. No other is more like the divine or receives more directly the first enlightenments from the Deity. The second group, he says, is made up of 'authorities,' 'dominions,' and 'powers.' And the third, at the end of the heavenly hierarchies, is the group of 'angels,' 'archangels,' and 'principalities.'" St. Gregory the Great also lists the same nine, although the position of Virtues and Princi-palities is reversed: "We speak of nine choirs of Angels, because we know, by the testimony of the angels by God, the Great Lord, in their nine levels, in their nine orders, and in their nine divisions. Truly good and beautiful are their arrangement and their order, each having been divided. At the beginning, all the angels were named; each was given a name according to their order. To each was given their order, to each their level. Surely there was a name for each assembly of angels.

This is the first division, the first order: Archangels[34]

The second order are the Principalities.[35]

The third order are the Powers.[36]

The fourth order are the Virtues.[37] This is their name.

The fifth order are the Dominions.[38]

The sixth order are the Thrones.[39]

Holy Scripture, that there are the following: Angels, Archangels, Virtues, Powers, Principalities, Dominations, Thrones, Cherubim, and Seraphim" (Hom. 34, In Evang. in Pope 1907). St. Thomas Aquinas (1952, I, q.108, a.3, ad 2, 552–562) cites Pseudo-Dionysius as the principal authority on the order of the angels in his *Summa Theologica*, Question CVIII "Of the Angelic Degrees of Hierarchies and Orders," which also follows this same basic outline of the hierarchy of angels into nine orders.

[34] *Arcangeles* (Spanish for "Archangels" from the Greek ἀρχάγγελος [*archangelos*], meaning "chief angel"). This is the second order of angels in the *Theologia Indorum* and the eighth in Pseudo-Dionysius. They are possibly listed first here because in the same section, San Miguel Arcangel is described as first in authority and power of all the angels (see n. 44). In biblical tradition, the word *archangel* appears only twice (1 Thessalonians 4:16 and Jude 1:9) and always in the singular, referring to Michael the Archangel.

[35] *Principados* (Spanish for "Principalities"; derived from the Latin *principatus*—"Princedom" or "Rulers," a translation in the Vulgate from the Greek ἀρχαί [*archai*] where it appears in Ephesians 3:10: "To the intent that now unto the principalities and powers in heavenly places might be known by the church the manifold wisdom of God" [see also Ephesians 1:20–21]). In the *Theologia Indorum* it is the third order, and in Pseudo-Dionysius it is the ninth.

[36] *Podestades* (Spanish for "Powers," from the Latin *potestates*). In Greek it appears as ἐξουσίαι (*exousiai*) in Ephesians 3:10. It is the fifth order of angels in the *Theologia Indorum* and the sixth in the list composed by Pseudo-Dionysius.

[37] *Virtudes* (Spanish for "Virtues"). Virtues appear in the *Theologia Indorum* as the fifth order of angels. This order of angels is the only one that does not appear in Pseudo-Dionysius, where it is substituted with "Authorities" as the fourth order of angels. Virtues is included, however, as one of the nine orders of angels in Thomas Aquinas's *Summa Theologica*, probably based on Ephesians 1:21, where it appears as the Greek δύναμις (*dynamis*), generally translated as "Virtue" or "Power."

[38] *Dominaçiones* (Spanish for "Dominions," from the Latin *dominationes*, or the Greek κυριότης [*kuriotés*], meaning "dominions" or "lordships"). It is the fifth order in Pseudo-Dionysius and the seventh order in the *Theologia Indorum*. This order is mentioned in both Ephesians 1:21 and Colossians 1:16.

[39] *Dronos* (variant of *Tronos*, Spanish for "Thrones"), from the Greek θρόνοι (*thronoi*).

The seventh level are the Cherubim.[40]
The eighth order are the Seraphim.[41]
The ninth level are the Angelic Spirits.[42]
These, then, are the names for each assembly, for each citadel, that occupies each level, each division. Ninth is the throne of the Great Lord God there in the sky. These are the names for each of the angels,[43] but there are only one or two who are

---

[40] *Herubines* (variant of Jerubines, Spanish for "Cherubim," from the Hebrew בּוּרְכ [*kerub*]). They are the second order of angels in Pseudo-Dionysius and the eighth in the *Theologia Indorum*. Cherubim are frequently mentioned in the Old Testament where they "keep the way of the tree of life" in the Garden of Eden (Genesis 3:24) as well as protect the throne of God (Ezekiel 28:14–16).

[41] *Serafines* (Spanish for "Seraphim" from the Hebrew שׂפָרִים [*seraphim*], meaning "burning, or fiery ones"). In Pseudo-Dionysius, they are the third order of angels, and in the *Theologia Indorum*, they are the ninth and final order. In the Old Testament, the seraphim are winged beings who guard the throne of God (Isaiah 6:2).

[42] *Angelicos espiritus* (Spanish for "Angelic Spirits"). Only the Totonicapán document describes these as spirits. Pseudo-Dionysus lists them simply as "angels," and they occupy the first order. The *Theologia Indorum* also lists them first and names them as *angeles* ("angels").

[43] The following list of thirteen angels (or archangels) appears to be unique to the Totonicapán document. It is not taken from the *Theologia Indorum* (which only lists the first three—Michael, Gabriel and Raphael) or from any other Christian source. There are numerous texts in the Judaeo-Christian tradition that list angels and archangels. In the *Book of Tobit*, the Archangel Raphael appears to Tobit (Tobias) and declares that he is "one of the seven who stand before the Lord" (Tobit 12:15), which is the foundation for the widespread belief that there are seven archangels. Pseudo-Dionysius lists the seven as Michael, Gabriel, Raphael, Uriel, Camael, Jophiel, and Zadkiel. Other variant lists name ten or fifteen archangels. None list thirteen other than the *Title of Totonicapán*. The number thirteen is significant in Maya cosmology as an indication of completeness or as an ideal number. In the sacred highland Maya calendar, or *cholq'ij*, each of the 20 named days occurs thirteen times, giving a total of 260 days. In highland Maya prayers, saints, culture heroes, and sacred places often have many manifestations, referred to in multiples of thirteen. In Santiago Atitlán, there are thirteen Virgin Marys, thirteen San Martíns, thirteen sacred mountains, thirteen mountain shrines, and so on. Although there are twenty confraternities in the K'iche' community of Momostenango, they are collectively called the *oxlajuj ch'ob'* ("thirteen groups") (B. Tedlock 1982, 36). In the *Chilam Balam* texts, the principal groupings of ancient gods are said to number either nine (consistent with the number of orders of angels in this text) or thirteen (Roys 1967, 99; Craine and Reindorp 1979, 65, 113, 118–121; Edmonson 1982, 34, 46; 1986, 154).

Figure 20.
"Saint Michael
Archangel with
the burden
of authority."
St. Michael
Archangel
carried in
procession,
Totonicapán,
1978.

clearly the greatest: Saint Michael Archangel[44] with the burden of authority;[45] and Gabriel[46] is the name of the other.

Saint Raphael[47] is the name of the third.

Saint Uriel[48] is the fourth.

---

[44] San Miguel Arcangel (Spanish for Saint Michael Archangel), from the Hebrew לְאָכִימ (Mikhael, "Who Is Like God?"). He is the only archangel mentioned in the Bible (Daniel 10:13–21, 12:1; I Thessalonians 4:16; Jude 1:9; Revelation 12:7–9). He is the first archangel in the lists compiled by Pseudo-Dionysius and St. Gregory the Great. He also appears in the *Book of Enoch* (I Enoch 9:1–3).

[45] *reqale'n* ("his power/authority"). The root, *eqale'n*, means literally "a burden borne on one's back." This can refer to power or authority but also implies that St. Michael bears the greatest burden of responsibility among the angels. St. Michael the Archangel was adopted as the patron saint of Totonicapán when it was re-christened after the Spanish Conquest. Perhaps this is another reason to emphasize his power and authority in this text (see figure 20).

[46] Cabriel (K'iche' spelling for Gabriel—the K'iche' language has no equivalent for the *g* sound of English or Spanish), from the Hebrew לְאָרְבַּ (*Gavri'el*, "God is my Strength"). In Judaeo-Christian tradition as well as Islam, Gabriel is recognized as an archangel, although only Michael is explicitly identified as such in the Bible. Gabriel is mentioned in both the Old Testament (Daniel 8:15–26, 9:21–27) and the New Testament (Luke 1:11–38), as well as the *Book of Enoch* (I Enoch 9:1–3).

[47] San Rafael (Spanish for Saint Raphael, from the Hebrew לְאָפֵר [*Rafael*, "God Heals"]). Raphael appears as an archangel in the *Book of Tobit*, which is considered deuterocanonical by Roman Catholics, Eastern Orthodox Christians, and Anglicans. He also appears as one of the four archangels in the *Book of Enoch* (I Enoch 9:1–3).

[48] Uriel (from the Hebrew לְאִירוּא [*Uri'el*, "God Is My Light"]). Uriel is the fourth archangel listed by Pseudo-Dionysius. The *Theologia Indorum* only lists the previous three, suggesting that the authors of the *Title of Totonicapán* used other sources in addition to the *Theologia Indorum* in compiling their synthesis of Christianity and Maya cosmology, or more likely they based this

Jeremia[49] is the fifth.

Others are Numiel,[50] Pamiel,[51] Romiel,[52] Samiel,[53] Asael,[54] Sejutiel,[55] Jorchiel,[56] and Escaltiel.[57] Clearly then, these are their names and these are the places of the honored angels behind God, the Great Lord.

list on discussions with missionary priests such as Domingo de Vico. The latter possibility may account for the variant spellings for many of the angels, which might easily occur when writing from memory or from inaccurate notes rather than copying from primary written sources. Uriel is mentioned as an archangel in the *Fourth Book of Esdras* in the Latin Vulgate (IV Esdras 4:1, 5:20, 10:28), as well as in the *Book of Enoch* (I Enoch 9:1–3, 10:1, 20:7, 40:9).

[49] The name Jeremia does not appear in either the *Theologia Indorum* or in the writings of Pseudo-Dionysius, suggesting another source. It is probably a variant spelling of Jeremiel, from the Hebrew לָאֲמְחֲרִי (*Jerahmeel*, "May God Have Compassion"), listed as one of the seven archangels in IV Esdras 4:36.

[50] Numiel. Possibly a variant spelling of Nuriel (Hebrew for "Fire of the Lord"), an angel that appears in Jewish legend linked to the ascension of Moses, where he rules the second level of heaven (Ginzberg 1948, 306–307). He is also mentioned in the *Zohar* (Zohar 23b, in Sperling and Simon 1984, 97, 103). To my knowledge, this name does not appear in the better-known canonical or non-canonical sources. Undoubtedly, either Domingo de Vico or another of the early Christian missionaries who interracted with the K'iche' was familiar with alternative sources available in the archives of the University of Salamanca, where many of the early Dominican missionaries who worked in the K'iche' region received their training.

[51] Pamiel. Possibly a variant spelling of Phanuel (Hebrew for "Face of God." There is no *ph* or *f* sound in the K'iche' language). Phanuel is the fourth angel that stands before God in the *Book of Enoch* (I Enoch 40:9, 53:6; 71:7–12).

[52] Romiel. Possibly a variant spelling of Ramiel (Hebrew לאימער for "Thunder of God"). Ramiel (sometimes written as Remiel) is listed as one of the primary archangels in I Enoch 20:8 and II Baruch 55:3.

[53] Samiel. Possible variant spelling of Camael, the fifth archangel in the list compiled by Pseudo-Dionysius; or Sariel (Hebrew לאירש for "Prince of God"), the last of the seven archangels listed in the *Book of Enoch* (I Enoch 20:6); or Samael (Hebrew for "Venom of God"), an important archangel in Talmudic and post-Talmudic sources as a destroying angel. In the "Ascension of Moses," Samael occupies the seventh heaven (Ginzberg 1948, 308; see also Ginzberg 1939, 449, 467–479). St. Gregory listed Samael as the sixth of the seven archangels (Hom. 32, 8–9).

[54] Asael (Hebrew לאהשע "Made by God"). The *Book of Enoch* lists Asael as the ninth of twenty leading angels (I Enoch 6:8).

[55] Sejutiel. Possible variant of the Hebrew לאיתלאש Shealtiel "Prayer of God" (also spelled Selaphiel or Salathiel). He is one of the seven archangels in the Byzantine Catholic and Eastern Orthodox traditions and is mentioned as a comforting angel in the Pseudepigraphal *The Conflict of Adam and Eve* (31:6, in Platt 1976, 22).

[56] Jorchiel. Possible variant of Jophiel, from the Hebrew לָאיפוֹי "Beauty of God." Jophiel is the sixth of the seven archangels listed by Pseudo-Dionysius.

[57] Escaltiel. Possible variant of Zadkiel (Hebrew לָאיקָדצ Tsadqiel, "Righteousness of God"), the seventh of the archangels listed by Pseudo-Dionysius, or Zerachiel ("God's Command"), the seventh archangel in I Enoch 20:6 and seventh in the list of archangels composed by St. Gregory the Great (Hom. 32, 8–9).

THE CREATION OF ADAM[58]

We shall now give the names of Adam and Eve in this fifth division[59] of the word.

Their names are Adam and Eve, the first man and the first woman, our mother and our father. They were ensouled[60] people. They were given form. They were people framed and shaped in the heart of God, the Great Lord, because the heavens were left desolate. They were desolated by Lucifer when he aggrandized himself,[61] along with his companions, the malevolent ones.[62]

It was said then by God, the Great Lord: "The desolation of the heavenly house shall not be remedied until I shall make replacements[63] to inhabit the heavenly house," said the Great Lord, God.

Then was the framing of a person by God, the Great Lord. Earth was put into him by God, the Great Lord. From the surface of the earth came forth the soft

---

[58] Lines 152–249.

[59] The "fifth division" refers to the fifth major theme of the *Theologia Indorum*, corresponding mostly to chapter 31 of that text (Vico 1605 [1553], folios 45v–46v), although portions of other chapters in the *Theologia* are included as well that deal with Lucifer and the nature of the devil in chapters 27, 28, and 38 (Sparks 2017, 223).

[60] *uk'u'xlaxik.* This is literally "ensouled," but with the connotation of something that is planned out or conceptualized. In this case, the first man and woman are "planned out" prior to being given physical form.

[61] *xunimarisaj rib'* ("he aggrandized himself"). This is a common K'iche' expression for pride or boastfulness. The *Popol Vuh* repeatedly describes pridefulness as forbidden or evil (Christenson 2007, 91–100), and those who are guilty of it, particularly the boastful deity Wuqub' Kaqix ("Seven Macaw"), were severely punished under the direction of the god Ruk'u'x Kaj ("Heart of Sky"): "For they saw pride as evil and went to do these things according to the word of Heart of Sky" (100).

[62] *ajmak.* It is difficult to discern how this word was understood prior to the Spanish Conquest. Ecclesiastical authorities, including Vico, chose it to signify "sinner," and this is perhaps the connotation here. This interpretation has Spanish Christian influences, however, that did not exist in Pre-Columbian K'iche' culture. As used in other highland Maya texts, such as the *Popol Vuh*, the root word, *mak*, signifies "malevolence, impurity, flaw, error, offense, imperfection, fault, or defect."

[63] In the parallel text in the *Theologia Indorum* (Vico 1605 [1553], folio 45v), the phrase is *chinban chic v4ixel xibalba* ("I shall make now replacements for Xib'alb'a—or the residents of Xib'alb'a"). In K'iche' belief, Xib'alb'a is the otherworld place where the lords of death and disease reside and where even deities die (Christenson 2007, 160–179). It is also the place where life deities such as Jun Junajpu, Junajpu, and Xb'alankej are reborn (179–191). It is therefore both tomb and womb. Vico and other early missionaries often equated Xib'alb'a with the Christian concept of hell. In this passage, the K'iche' authors of the Totonicapán document purposely leave out the reference to Xib'alb'a, most likely because their conception of Xib'alb'a did not match the Christian hell.

maize flesh[64] of the person, along with his firm flesh.[65] In an instant his arms and legs were given shape. The placement of his mouth and his face was perfected, along with his ears and his nose. His bones and tendons[66] were placed within him. Added to his legs and his arms were his feet and hands.[67] These came to be. Placed within him were his great muscles and his skin, his teeth and his nails. Thus he was adorned with humanity; his flesh came to be.

Four [things] were combined and entered into his flesh—earth, fire, water, and wind.[68] Earth entered into his body;[69] water entered into his fluids[70] and into his blood as well. Fire came to be his warmth, his heat. Wind then became his breath. Thus four classes [of things] were placed into the flesh of humanity. Beautiful he came to be because of God.

---

[64] *uq'oral* ("his soft flesh"). Although this may simply refer to human flesh, the root of the word, *q'or*, means "cooked maize dough" or "atole," a drink made from maize (Sáenz de Santa María 1940, 225). This passage is consistent with K'iche' tradition that the flesh of the first humans was made from ground maize dough as described in the *Popol Vuh*: "The yellow ears of maize and the white ears of maize were then ground fine with nine grindings by Xmucane. Food entered their flesh along with water to give them strength. Thus was created the fatness of their arms. The yellowness of humanity came to be when they were made by they who are called She Who Has Borne Children and He Who Has Begotten Sons, by Sovereign and Quetzal Serpent. Thus their frame and shape were given expression by our first Mother and our first Father. Their flesh was merely yellow ears of maize and white ears of maize" (Christenson 2007, 195). This contradicts the biblical tradition that Adam was formed out of earth (Genesis 2:7) as asserted in the following paragraph as well as in the *Theologia Indorum* (Carmack and Mondloch 1983, 207, n. 21).

[65] *uti'ojil* ("firm flesh/muscles"). Together *uq'oral* ("his soft flesh") and *uti'ojil* ("his firm flesh") form a merismus that describes all of a human being's flesh.

[66] *ib'och'il* ("tendons, nerves, blood vessels"). The reference could be to any or all of these possibilities.

[67] *uwi'*. Literally, the "ends" or "heads" of his legs and arms.

[68] These are the four components that in the Old World were believed to be the fundamental elements that give substance to the universe. The theory was first proposed by the Persian philosopher Zoroaster in the early sixth century. Empedocles (ca. 494–ca. 434 BCE) of Sicily was the earliest of the pre-Socratic philosophers to promulgate the idea in the Greek world. The four classical "elements" were also included in the writings of Plato (*Timaeus*) and Aristotle (*On Generation and Corruption*) and continued to be a major influence on European thought. This concept is entirely a European introduction and is foreign to Maya cosmology.

[69] *unima ti'ojil*. Literally, "his great flesh."

[70] *uq'anal*. Literally, "his yellowness." In physical terms this refers to fluids in the body other than blood—plasma, lymph, synovial fluid, as well as the liquid in blisters or liquids that "weep" from burns.

Figure 21. "Then was the framing of a person by God, the Great Lord." God the Father wearing a traditional Maya headdress. Church, Santiago Atitlán.

Then he gave thanks to Tz'aqol B'itol: "Thanks to thee,[71] my mother and to thee, my father.[72] Thou framed me; thou shaped me," he said to God.

---

[71] *k'amo chech la* ("thanks to thee"). The K'iche' language has both formal and familiar second-person singular and plural address. The formal terms are used when speaking to deities or persons on a higher social scale such as rulers or the elderly (see p. 100–101, n. 230). Here, Adam addresses God using the formal *la* ("thee"), but when God speaks to Adam or Eve he uses the familiar *at* ("you").

[72] Here Adam recognizes Tz'aqol and B'itol as separate female and male deities. The gratitude of Adam is not found in the Bible but parallels the Maya version of the creation as recorded in the *Popol Vuh*, in which the first four human creations thanked the Framer and the Shaper for their existence: "And they gave thanks to Tz'aqol ['Framer'] and B'itol ['Shaper']: 'Truly we thank you doubly, triply that we were created, that we were given our mouths and our faces. We are able to speak and to listen. We are able to ponder and to move about. We know much, for we have learned that which is far and near. We have seen the great and the small, all that exists in the sky and on the earth. We thank you, therefore, that we were created, that we were given frame and shape. We became because of you, our Grandmother, and you, our

Figure 22. "Then was the formation of two great zapote trees." Zapote tree and fruit.

Then was the formation of two great zapote trees.[73] This he did, God the Great Lord, in the center of the Earthly Paradise. One zapote tree was the Life Zapote Tree. "Whoever eats its fruit will live forever because of it," said God, the Great Lord. The other zapote tree was the Knowledge Zapote Tree. This was its name. It was named Knowledge Zapote Tree. Whoever would eat it would know good; they would come to know the good and they would come to know the not good.[74] This, then, was the placement of these two zapote trees.

Grandfather," they said when they gave thanks for their frame and shape" (Christenson 2007, 199). Note that the same phraseology is used here, whereby God gives to the first human being his "frame and shape."

[73] *tulul* ("zapote"). The zapote (*Lucuma mammosa*) is a sweet tropical fruit that grows in warm, lowland areas of southeastern Mexico and Guatemala. It is oblong in shape, measuring 10–15 cm in length. Its skin is tough and brownish-red, while its meat varies from dark red to brown and has a delicious, aromatic flavor. In the *Popol Vuh*, the zapote was one of the fruits found within the mountain of creation along with the maize used to form the flesh of the first men (Christenson 2007, 194). Perhaps because of its close connection with K'iche' traditions related to the creation and because of its abundant fruit, Father Domingo de Vico chose the zapote to represent both the paradisiacal Tree of Life and the Tree of Knowledge of Good and Evil in the creation section of the *Theologia Indorum* (chapter 30, folio 45r; chapters 34–35).

[74] *ma wi utz* ("not good"). There is no equivalent in the K'iche' language for the Christian concept of "evil." The K'iche' authors therefore chose to describe it as the opposite of good.

ADAM AND EVE IN THE EARTHLY PARADISE[75]

Fourth division[76] of the word: The placement[77] of Adam within the Earthly Paradise by God, the Great Lord.

"Here you shall make your home," said God, the Great Lord. "Here as well you shall remain forever."[78] Thus he was told by God, the Great Lord.

Then were gathered the small animals and the large animals before him by God, the Great Lord. "Name them. Place upon each of them their names," he was told by God, the Great Lord.

In solitude was Adam framed and shaped by God. Great was his joy; great was his state of glory[79] there. Great joy, peace, purity, and a state of brilliant glory[80] were given to him by God. Then was completed for him all of its sweetness, its deliciousness, its sweet fragrance within the Earthly Paradise.

There were two birds, doves,[81] with him that drank sweet nectar. They consoled him in his heart.

Then Adam considered within his heart.[82] He said to God, the Great Lord: "Thou God, Great Lord, provide for me a giver of joy, one with whom I may speak, one with whom I may converse,[83] I who was framed by thee, I who was shaped by thee," he said to God, the Great Lord.

Thus God heard the plea of Adam's heart. Then He gave to him his companion. Adam was put to sleep by God, the Great Lord. He was sleeping, therefore, when a

---

75 lines 250–416.
76 The "fourth division" refers to the fourth division of the fifth major theme in the *Theologia Indorum*, corresponding to chapter 34 of that work (Vico 1605 [1553], folios 50r–51v).
77 *wab'axik* ("placement"). The K'iche' word carries the implication of placing a living thing wihin an enclosed space, such as turkeys in a pen. This choice of words suggests that the Earthly Paradise is conceived as an enclosed garden.
78 *amaq'elab'* ("remain forever"). The root of the K'iche' term is *amaq'el*, meaning "always" or "forever."
79 *saq amaq'* ("white/pure nation/state"). The Coto dictionary defines *saq amaq'* as "state of glory."
80 *saqil amaq'* ("light nation/state"). The text modifies *saq* ("white, clear, pure") to *saqil* ("light, brightness"), intensifying the description of the "glorious" state of the first man.
81 *paloma* (Spanish "dove"). This is one of the rare instances where a Spanish word appears in the text other than for proper names. In this case it is used to clarify the type of bird that was a companion to Adam. The writers perhaps wish to emphasize that this was a type of dove foreign to their region, appearing as it does in a biblical account.
82 *xuk'u'xlaj*. Literally, to "heartify." It means "to think, consider, contemplate, plan, conjure, or plot." In K'iche' belief, these are all functions of the heart, not the brain.
83 According to the *Popol Vuh*, the ability to speak with knowledge is the primary characteristic of the first created beings in K'iche' tradition. It is what distinguishes humans from all other living things and gives them the ability to perpetuate the world through ritual speech (Christenson 2007, 80–85, 197; Watanabe 1992, 82). It is also the first gift mentioned by the first men when they thanked the creators for their existence (see Christenson 2007, 199, n. 487).

rib was taken from his left side.[84] It was taken from him—his bone, his rib. Woman she came to be in a moment; she was completed by the Great Lord, God. In an instant her soul[85] entered into her. She was completed already when Adam awoke.

Then he was awakened by an angel of God: "Adam, Adam awake. Speak to your bride,[86] your beloved one,[87] your cherished one," said the angel of God to Adam.

Then he gave thanks to God: "Thanks to thee, thou Tz'aqol B'itol. [She is] mine. Thou hast given to me my companion," he said to God, the Great Lord.

Immediately Adam spoke to the woman. Adam said to the woman: "You are my bones; you are my flesh. You came out from within my body," he said to the woman.

Then they were joined together[88] by God, the Great Lord: "He is your husband, and she is your wife. Love each other; cherish[89] each other; take care of each other. Have daughters and have sons," they were told.

Thus they were commanded, Adam and Eve. Eve came to be the wife of Adam because of God, the Great Lord.

Then they were commanded concerning the forbidden zapote tree: "I leave with you my inviolable[90] word, my inviolable commandment to you. Do not eat the fruit of the forbidden zapote tree, the Knowledge Zapote Tree. Do not die because of it. Eat only from the Life Zapote Tree and you will live forever because of it," Adam and Eve were told by God, the Great Lord.

---

[84] In K'iche' belief, the left side is female and the right side is male in ritual practice. The K'iche' authors thus specify that Eve came from Adam's left side. The Old Testament does not specify which side the rib came from.

[85] *ranima'* ("her soul"). *Anima'* is derived from the Latin word for "soul." In modern K'iche' speech, *anima'* is commonly used for both "heart" and "soul" and is often paired with the analogous K'iche' word *k'u'x* (also referring to both "heart" and "soul") as a couplet. This may be the earliest appearance of this important loan word in an indigenous K'iche' text. *Anima'* does not appear in the *Popol Vuh* where *k'u'x* is used exclusively for the concept of heart or soul.

[86] *ak'ulil* ("your joined one"). The root of this word is *k'ul*, meaning "to join together" or "to encounter," a common term for "to marry."

[87] *aloq'* ("your beloved"). The word implies not only romantic love but also esteem for a revered person.

[88] *xek'ulub'ax* ("they were joined together"). The word is commonly used in the Colonial period to refer to a marriage, but the root, *k'ul*, also means to "bring together" or "join together."

[89] *chik'axk'omaj iwib'* ("cherish each other"). According to the Bassetta dictionary, *k'axk'omaj* is "to love tenderly."

[90] *awas*. This is a word that is difficult to translate into English. When used in conjunction with the Knowledge Zapote Tree, it means "forbidden, prohibited, taboo, ceremonially restricted." But it is also used, as here, in reference to the word *deity* to describe something "sacred, set apart, inviolable, hallowed, sacrosanct." Ceremonial shrines carry the name *awas* in K'iche' areas, as they are not only sacred but are also prohibited from use other than for rituals conducted at the proper time and the proper place.

Figure 23. "Then they began to be deceived by the devil, by the demon." Dance mask with the face of the devil adorned with a snake and frogs, Cobán. National Museum of Archaeology and Ethnology, Guatemala City.

Then they began to be deceived[91] by the devil,[92] by the demon.[93] Because of him their hearts were pained. For Adam and Eve had been given a gift, a heavenly house. So then he arrived to deceive Eve to eat the forbidden zapote fruit.

The devil transformed into an angel, although his tail was that of a serpent. "Eat thou the fruit of the Knowledge Zapote Tree, thou Eve," he said to her.

"I do not want to because of the inviolable commandment left to us by God," Eve said.

"Do not reject, do not mock his messenger. He does not wish thee to be perfected. For God is hiding and he does not wish you to complete your knowledge. Eat," he said.

And so, then was eaten the forbidden zapote fruit by Eve. Thus was conceived malevolence and enmity[94] by them. Therefore, they were banished from within the

---

[91] *kikawachixik*. Literally, "they were two faced" by the devil.

[92] *diablo*. The authors here use the Spanish word for "devil."

[93] *k'axtok'*. In the Early Colonial period, *k'axtok'* was chosen by Spanish missionaries to refer to the devil. In the Coto dictionary, it is defined as "demon, devil, enemy, deceiver, liar, false." In the *Popol Vuh*, the word appears frequently to refer to a person or supernatural being accused of deception, lies, or treachery (Christenson 2007, 97, n. 183, 246, 249).

[94] *lab'al*. According to Coto, the word includes the concept of "sin, fault, corruption, or defect" but also "war, enmity, conflict, combat." It is unclear which emphasis is meant here. The

Earthly Paradise. Then they fell here on the face of the earth in suffering and in pain, in hunger and in thirst, in the place of tears and in the place of wailing.

Then they pleaded for children to God, the Great Lord. Their hearts lamented.[95] They wept and they wailed. They pleaded for children: "Give thou our daughters and our sons," they said. "Perhaps a boy, perhaps a girl," they said to God, the Great Lord.

Then was the giving of children. God heard the lament of their hearts, the lament of their bowels.

THE STORY OF CAIN AND ABEL[96]

The next division of the word in which is the telling of the three names: Cain, Abel, and Seth.

Adam had not yet engendered[97] sons when he left the Earthly Paradise. Soon, God gave them. Cain was born and soon after was born Abel. Two young boys, brothers to one another, were the sons of Adam. They were his children. But afterward they committed offenses.

First was Cain, the firstborn. He was truly poor. But Abel was given abundance and riches by God. Cain saw evil[98] in this. Then he killed his younger brother in secret. True was the love of God for Abel because he gave the best of his harvest, of his maize field.[99] But he, Cain, only gave rejected ears of maize to God.[100]

Basseta dictionary lists only "war or combat." *Lab'al* is used frequently in the *Popol Vuh* for warfare with no negative connotations. In fact, the K'iche' were proud of their warriors and their successful conquests in the highland Maya region. This section of the Totonicapán text may reflect attempts by early Christian missionaries to equate warfare with sin, at least when waged against Spanish forces.

[95] *xoq' kik'u'x.* Literally, "their hearts wept."

[96] lines 417–473.

[97] *jayoq,* literally, "housed." In other words, he had not yet founded a house or lineage.

[98] *itzel.* Colonial dictionaries associate this word with witchcraft and evil, and this is still a major connotation of the word in modern K'iche' usage. But this interpretation has Spanish Christian influences that did not exist in Pre-Columbian K'iche' culture. Coto glosses *itzel* as "falseness, filth, ugliness, error, perversion, and worthlessness." Basseta simply interprets it as "bad."

[99] In the biblical account, Abel was a "keeper of sheep" and "brought of the firstlings of his flock and of the fat thereof," while Cain was a "tiller of the ground" and "brought of the fruit of the ground" (Genesis 4:2–4). Other than dogs, the Maya did not have domesticated mammals prior to the Spanish Conquest; thus this biblical account did not resonate with their experience. Both brothers are described here as "maize farmers." This modification of the narrative does not appear in the *Theologia Indorum* and is purely the invention of the K'iche' authors of this text.

[100] *upich'olil.* Literally, "rejected, forgotten, abandoned."

Figure 24. "True was the love of God for Abel because he gave the best of his harvest, of his maize field." Maize fields in the valley of Totonicapán, 1978.

Then the blood of Abel cried out before the face of God. Then, therefore, was given the punishment for Cain's offense. His was not a very good death. He was merely shot by a hunter.[101]

He was in his maize field when he was seen by the blowgunner[102] Turnio.[103] It

---

[101]   *casador* (derived from the Spanish *cazador*, "hunter"). This is another rare example of a Spanish loan word in the body of the text.

[102]   *wub'anel*. The hunter is specifically referred to as a "blowgunner," the archetypal Maya weapon used for hunting birds and other small animals. Although the Bible does not record the death of Cain, there is a common tradition that he was killed by his descendant Lamech, who mistook him for a wild beast because of his poor eyesight and shot him with an arrow (Jasher 2:26–30; *Second Book of Adam and Eve* 13:5–12). The *Theologia Indorum* records that Lamech killed Cain but does not describe how this happened (chapter 47, folio 68v); therefore the authors of the *Title of Totonicapán* are adapting their account of the death of Cain from Judaeo-Christian traditions other than those available in the Bible or the *Theologia Indorum*. In addition, this passage may indirectly reference a well-known Maya tradition that pre-dates the Spanish Conquest. It would be difficult to hunt a human or a deer with a blowgun, as the Maya used small stones or clay pellets in their blowguns. For hunting larger animals or in warfare, the K'iche' typically used arrows. In the *Popol Vuh*, the twin deities Junajpu and Xb'alankej used blowguns to hunt birds (Christenson 2007, 141–143). They defeated the first great deceiver, Seven Macaw, with their blowguns under the direction of the principal creator god, Heart of Sky (97–100). The blowgunning of this primordial bird deity was a common theme in Maya art dating back more than a thousand years.

[103]   According to the syntax of the sentence, Turnio should be a proper name. It is probably a play on words, however, as *turnio* means "cross-eyed or squint-eyed" in Spanish, making it

was dark[104] when he was blowgunned. He [thought] he saw a deer,[105] so his offense was forgiven by God. It was not an offense what the blowgunner did. Understand, therefore, that the first offense committed by the children of Adam and Eve was rectified.[106]

These, then, are the sons of Adam—Cain and Abel. The sons of Cain and Abel are these—Enoch, Noah, and Methuselah. The sons of Noah are these—Shem, Ham, and Japheth.

THE CHANGING OF THE LANGUAGES AT THE GREAT TOWER[107]

This, now, is the division of the word that tells of the change of languages by God. This was done to the children of Noah after the first flood in the time of Noah.

Noah was already dead when the children of Noah planned the construction of a great building. "A great tower [rising] into the womb and the face of the sky," they said. "Should a flood occur again, there we will be saved," they said.

Then they were stopped by God, the Great Lord. He pronounced judgment on their heads. Then God, the Great Lord, changed[108] their language. Thirteen[109] kinds of spoken languages came to be. They did not understand the languages spoken among themselves. Thus was their division by God, the Great Lord.

difficult for him to see properly. This would account for his mistaking Cain for a deer and follows the story that Cain was killed by a hunter with poor eyesight. The *Theologia Indorum* identifies the hunter as Lamech rather than Turnio, indicating that the K'iche' authors derive this story from some other source.

104 *chimoymot*, meaning "obscured, blinded, cloudy, dark." In other words, it was difficult to see.

105 *masat* (Nahuatl "deer"). The K'iche' word for deer is *kej*, which is used throughout the *Popol Vuh* and periodically in this text. *Masat* is the usual term for deer in modern K'iche', and *kej* is generally used for "horse." This is an early instance of the transposition of usage from K'iche' to Nahuatl.

106 *suk'ulikil*. Literally, "making straight."

107 lines 474–520.

108 *jalk'atij*, "changed, disguised." The Coto dictionary includes the gloss that this word is used when someone speaks a foreign language, disguising their words to make them unintelligible.

109 Neither the Bible nor the *Theologia Indorum* records the number of languages that resulted from the confusion of tongues, so the thirteen languages appear to be based on K'iche' tradition. In the *Popol Vuh*, the progenitors of the highland Maya people are said to have gathered in the East, where the sun emerges, at a place called Tulan. The text records that thirteen nations gathered at Tulan and that they all spoke the same language. But when they migrated to the Guatemalan highlands, their languages changed and they could no longer understand one another (Christenson 2007, 204–215). The *Annals of the Kaqchikels* also describe the thirteen allied groups who came to Tulan (Recinos and Goetz 1953, 50–51; Maxwell and Hill 2006, 14, 22–23).

These are the sons of Shem, Ham, and Japheth—Abraham, Isaac, Esau, and Jacob. These, then, are the sons of Jacob—Reuben, Simeon, Levi, Judah, Issachar, Zebulun, Samin, Dan, Gad, Betalen, Asher, and Joseph.[110] These, then, are the grandsons of Adam. They are the sons of Noah, Abraham, and Jacob as well.

This therefore is the name of the mountain—Canaan. There lived Jacob, with his children as well. Then they entered Egypt. Four hundred[111] years they worked there, they the grandsons of Jacob.

THE STORY OF MOSES IN EGYPT[112]

Then was born Moses. Among the Hebrews was born Moses. Moses was tending sheep when he was called by God, the Great Lord. He was in a blackberry bush.[113] It was not burned, although the leaves of the blackberry bush were on fire. There God, the Great Lord, was when he called Moses:

"Moses, Moses, come then with me. Come to see me. Come to hear my word," said God, the Great Lord, to him. Then Moses came. There was the blackberry bush, burning with fire. He saw it.

"Take off your sandals. Come here with me," said God to Moses. Then was his message to Moses: "Go to Egypt with Pharoah. May they be taken out, they, my beloved and cherished people of Israel," Moses was told.

Moses responded: "I am not worthy of being spoken to by the Lord Pharoah. I am merely of poor relations.[114] Perhaps one of the great prophets[115] should go, thou Lord," said Moses to the Great Lord, God.

---

[110] The original text lists the sons of Jacob as Ruben, Simon, Leui, Jutas, Ysacab, Çabulen, Samin, Dan, Cat, Betalen, Asset, and Joseph. Most of these are K'iche' variants of the Spanish spelling for biblical names, other than Samin, which should be Neftalí (English Naphtali). In the *Theologia Indorum*, Benjamin comes after Zebulun, so it is possible that Samin is an altered spelling of Benjamin and the authors repeated the name with the variant spelling of Betalen in the tenth position, omitting Naphtali altogether. The order of the sons also differs from both the biblical account and the *Theologia Indorum*, suggesting that either the authors of the Totonicapán document did not have a text to copy from directly or they purposely chose to alter the order.

[111] *o'much*. Literally "five eighties," the standard way of writing 400 in the vigesimal (base 20) mathematical system of the K'iche'.

[112] lines 521–640.

[113] *tukan*. This word refers to brambles or thorned berry bushes, particularly blackberries. Vico used the same word to refer to the burning bush in the *Theologia Indorum* (Sparks 2019, 255).

[114] *uk'ïal*. According to the Coto dictionary, *uk'ïal* is "friend, or related by blood."

[115] *propetas* (Spanish, "prophets"). There is no equivalent word in K'iche' for the Old World concept of "prophets," and both the *Theologia Indorum* and this text leave the Spanish word untranslated.

"Surely you will go. Speak my word to Pharoah. Do not be afraid. I am with you," said God, the Great Lord, to Moses.

Then Moses left to go to Pharoah, accompanied by his younger brother Aaron. They did not bring weapons, only his staff for keeping sheep. Then Moses arrived with Pharoah. He spoke the word of the Great Lord, God, to him.

Moses said: "Thou Lord Pharoah, I am the companion of the beloved, the cherished of God, they, the people of Israel. For this is the task[116] given to me by the Great Lord, God," said Moses to Pharoah.

Pharoah did not obey the word of Moses. So then was the making of seven[117] great wonders and spirit essences,[118] manifestations of his greatness. Great wonders and spirit essences were made by God (miracles[119] they are called) before the faces of the Egyptians and before the face of Pharoah as well.

Then was the transformation of the staff of Aaron into a serpent.

On the second day was transformed water into blood.

On the third day were conceived toads and frogs, along with other kinds of frogs.[120]

The fourth time were conceived mosquitos, horseflies, moths, flies, and all biting insects.

---

[116] *taqikil* ("task, errand, authority"). This is a commonly used term for a task, but with the implication that it is carried out under the authority of someone in a position of power.

[117] In the biblical tradition, there were ten plagues or miracles sent by God against the Egyptians (Exodus 7–11); therefore, this appears to be a purposeful choice to modify the story to fit K'iche' tradition. The number seven is an important ritual number in highland Maya ceremonialism, symbolizing the seven directions of the universe—the four cardinal directions plus center, sky, and underworld. In other contemporary K'iche' texts, the number seven often appears in the names of sacred localities such as Wuqub' Pek Wuqub' Siwan ("Seven Caves, Seven Ravines"), linked to the place of origin for the K'iche' people (see p. 88, n. 168).

[118] *pus nawal*. *Pus* refers to the cutting of flesh, specifically to the practice of human sacrifice. In Colonial period K'iche' texts, the word is often paired with the word *nawal* to describe the supernatural power of deities to accomplish what ordinary humans cannot. In the *Popol Vuh*, the creation of the first four human beings from maize dough was accomplished by the "*pus nawal*" of the creator deities (Christenson 2003, 156, lines 4959–4960). In the first decades after the Spanish Conquest, Roman Catholic missionaries adopted the phrase to describe the power of the Christian God to forgive sins and offer His body as a sacrament (Coto 1983 [ca. 1656], 424). Although *nawal* is borrowed from the Nahuatl language, where it means "to transform" (Campbell 1983, 84), the K'iche' interpretation of the word also includes the root *na'*, meaning "to feel" or "to know." Thus the creation took place by means of the power of the gods' spirit essence or divine knowledge rather than by physical action.

[119] *milagro* (Spanish for "miracle"). The authors use the Spanish word here to ensure that the reader understands that the K'iche' phrase *pus nawal* is analogous to the Spanish concept of "miracle."

[120] *kalat*. According to Coto, this is a term for frog borrowed from the central Mexican Nahuatl language.

Figure 25. "Among the Hebrews was born Moses." Sculpture of Moses, 1550–1600. Museum of Colonial Art, Antigua, Guatemala.

The fifth time, then were conceived biting flies and other kinds of flies.

The sixth time was conceived a great hailstorm with great lightning, along with a great serpent that wound around a tree.[121]

Then was conceived a great darkness, sent by God, the Great Lord; and they died, the firstborn of the Egyptians.

Thus they, the Israelites, were freed by Pharoah: "They must go so that we do not die because of thee, Moses and Aaron," said Pharoah.

Thus was the departure of the children of Israel, they of the citadel of God. In great affliction departed the children and the sons of Israel. Canaanites are we and Hebrews as well, who were taken away by Moses to the sea.[122]

---

[121] There is no mention of a great serpent wound around a tree in the account of the plagues of Egypt. This is apparently a reference to the brazen serpent raised up by Moses when the Israelites were plagued by "fiery serpents" in the wilderness after they left Egypt (Numbers 21:6–9). The highland Maya associate lightning with a serpent of fire, which is the probable reason the authors linked the two events here.

[122] In chapter 99 of the *Theologia Indorum*, Vico wrote that the K'iche's are descendants of the lost ten nations of Israel and are therefore "the grandsons and sons of Abraham, Isaac, and

Then spoke God to Moses: "Throw twelve stones into the sea;[123] twelve therefore cast forth."

Then the sea became dry because of God, the Great Lord. Twelve great pathways came to be within the sea. Then we passed through it. Only a little remained to complete four great multitudes of people.[124] We are the children and sons of Israel, the people of Canaan. We are Hebrews as well.

Jacob" (chapter 99, folio 168r). Some early Christian missionaries in the Guatemalan highlands, including Father Vico, apparently taught this concept as part of their evangelization efforts. Thus the K'iche' authors of the *Historia Quiché de Don Juan de Torres (Título Tamub I)*, dated ca. 1580, and the *Título de Pedro Velasco (Título Tamub III)*, dated 1592, wrote that their ancestors originally came from "Babilonia" and were the descendants of Hebrew patriarchs: "We are the grandsons and we are the sons of Adam; we are the grandsons of Jacob, Moses, Abraham, Isaac, and Jacob" (Recinos 1957, 24–25). In the *Historia de los Xpantzay de Tecpan Guatemala (Xpantzay I)*, dated as early as 1552 and perhaps the earliest indigenous text from the post-Conquest period in highland Guatemala, the authors assert: "We are the grandsons of the grandfathers Abraham, Isaac, and Jacob. Our grandfathers and fathers lived in Canaan, in that land that God, our Lord, gave to Abraham" (120–121). This tradition continued throughout the second half of the sixteenth century, as can be seen in the *Título de los Ilokab*, dated ca. 1592: "We are the children of Jacob and Moses when we came from Babylon. We are Israelites and thus sons of Jacob" (Sparks 2017, 269). There are no such claims in the more traditionalist early highland Maya texts, including the *Popol Vuh*, the *Annals of the Kaqchikels*, and the *Título K'oyoy*.

[123] No stones are mentioned in the biblical account of Moses crossing the Red Sea. This appears to be a conflation with K'iche' traditions. In the *Popol Vuh*, the progenitors of the K'iche' people received their gods and tokens of authority at Tulan, located in the East where "the sun emerges." When they left Tulan and migrated toward the Guatemalan highlands, they miraculously crossed a sea of water over a series of stones: "It was not clear how they passed over the sea to come here. It was as if there were no sea that they had to pass over. They merely passed over on the tops of stones for there were stones on the sand. Thus they named it 'Lined up Stones'; and 'Piled up Sand' was also its name. Over these they made their passage here from within the sea. The water divided itself and through it they made their passage here" (Christenson 2007, 221). It is also possible that this account may be conflated with the later crossing of the Jordan, in which twelve stones were taken out of the river as a memorial to the miraculous passage of the Israelites through the water (Joshua 4:1–9).

[124] Here the K'iche' insinuate their own tradition. Rather than twelve nations or lineages, the K'iche' were descended from four progenitors, the first four humans created by the gods— B'alam K'itze', B'alam Aq'ab', Majukotaj, and Ik'i B'alam (see pp. 94–95). In K'iche' tradition, only three of the four progenitors actually founded major lineages (Ik'i B'alam died in his youth—see p. 104). This may explain the following line in which the authors claim descent from only three groups—Israelites, Canaanites, and Hebrews. This triad of ancestral nations does not appear in the *Theologia Indorum* and is apparently an attempt by the authors of the Totonicapán text to harmonize biblical and K'iche' traditions.

THE STORY OF THE MIGRATIONS OF ISRAEL[125]

This, then, is our departure from the place where the sun emerges.[126] I shall now describe their passage here through the grasslands and through the forests.[127] Next they [came to] Xelimkutz and Marakow,[128] or "Bitter Water."[129]

Then they left from there. They arrived at Xim,[130] this was its name.

Then they left there and came to Papitin.[131] There the Hebrews suffered, and there they defeated Amalech.

---

[125] lines 641–672.

[126] *relib'al q'ij* ("its emergence/coming out place sun"). This may simply refer to the direction east; however, throughout the text, the emergence of the sun is linked with the concepts of creation and the establishment of political authority. I have therefore chosen to leave the phrase translated in its most literal form to avoid the more limited interpretation of directionality.

[127] *pa k'im pa k'echelaj* ("in grasslands, in forest"). This is a common phrase that is used in highland Maya literature to refer to wild, uncultivated, or unpopulated areas. Thus in the *Popol Vuh*, the twins Junajpu and Xb'alankej complain that the wild beasts used their magic to revert cultivated maize fields back to grasslands and forest overnight (Christenson 2003, 104, lines 3140–3141). The same paired words appear in the creation account, before the formation of people to cultivate the land (lines 116–117, 308–310). Here the paired terms are used as a synonym for the biblical term *wilderness*, meaning an unpopulated or wild territory (Exodus 15:22–18:27).

[128] What follows are a series of four paired toponyms, or places along the migration route of the Israelites through the wilderness. The first pair, Xelimkutz and Marakow, also appears in the *Theologia Indorum* as Elim (folio 101v) and Mara (folio 101r). Elim is mentioned in the Bible as a place of "twelve springs and seventy palm trees, and they camped there near the water" (Exodus 15:27; see also Numbers 33:9–10). Mara is the biblical Marah: "And when they came to Marah, they could not drink of the waters of Marah, for they were bitter: therefore, the name of it was called Marah [Hebrew for 'bitter']" (Exodus 15:23; see also Numbers 33:8–9).

[129] *k'aylaj ja'* ("bitter water"). I do not interpret this as a separate place name but rather as a translation of Marakow into the K'iche' language, as Vico also did in the *Theologia Indorum*: "They arrived there at Mara, its name. There was no water on the road. They were thirsty at this first watered place, there at Mara because merely bitter water (*4ailah ha*) was there" (chapter 65, folio 101r, author translation). In the *Popol Vuh*, the place where the first humans were formed from maize dough was called K'ayala' ("Bitter Water") (Christenson 2007, 193, n. 455). The emphasis placed on this toponym by translating the name into K'iche' may reflect the importance of the "Bitter Water" place in K'iche' tradition. Another early K'iche' document, *The Historia Quiché de Don Juan de Torres*, also mentions a place of origin called Mamah, the only biblical name that is included in a long list of toponyms linked to the migrations of the ancestral K'iche' (Recinos 1957, 36–37)—an indication of the importance of this place among the post-Conquest K'iche'.

[130] Xim, a variant of Sin (or Zin), mentioned in the *Theologia Indorum*, folios 102v–103v, where manna was given and where Moses struck a rock to provide water for the Israelites (Exodus 16:1, 17:1; Numbers 33:11–12). The place is more accurately named Sin on p. 87.

[131] Rephidim, where the Israelites defeated the Amalekites (Exodus 17:1–13, 19:2; Numbers 33:14–15), mentioned in the next sentence.

Then the children of Jacob arrived there at Chi K'ates.[132] There died María,[133] the sister of Saint Moses.

Then they arrived there at Hor,[134] where Moses died; it was there at Moab, near Canaan.

Then they crossed over Jordan, and there Jericho was defeated when Joseph[135] reigned over them.

Then Joshua died, and there was the division[136] of the land, in the land of Canaan.

The twenty[-fifth] great name is Samuel.

THE LATER PROPHETS[137]

The second word[138] is the raising up of Saul in lordship.

The twenty-sixth great name is the young boy David.

The twenty-seventh great name is Solomon.

There are many names more than these twenty-eight great names of the prophets as well as the patriarchs.[139] They are: Elijah the prophet is his name; Elisha the

---

[132] Kadesh (Numbers 20:1, 22, 33:36–37).

[133] Miriam in the biblical account (Numbers 20:1). Both the *Title of Totonicapán* and the *Theologia Indorum* name her as María (folio 99v).

[134] Hor is the mountain where Aaron, the brother of Moses, died in the biblical account (Numbers 20:23–29). Moses was said to have died on Mount Nebo (Deuteronomy 34:1–8).

[135] Scribal error for Joshua (Josué in Spanish, which is close to José—"Joseph" in English), who is named correctly in the next line.

[136] *ujachik* ("its division, distribution"). The term does not imply conflict but rather refers to the distribution of land among the Israelites that took place under Joshua (Joshua 13–14).

[137] lines 673–685.

[138] The story of Saul is found in chapter 88 of the *Theologia Indorum*, which is the second division of the theme concerning the early prophets of Israel (Vico 1605 [1553], folio 138r; see Sparks 2019, 253).

[139] No twenty-eighth "great name" is listed in the text. This is due to a difference in interpretation between the *Theologia Indorum* and the Totonicapán text. In the *Theologia Indorum*, there is a chapter devoted to each of the previously named prophets headed by a statement that it is the such-and-such numbered *b'ij* ("narrative, story"), which is then given a title, often the name of the prophet whose life and works are described—for example, *juwinaq wuqub' nima b'ij ub'i' Salomon* ("twenty-seventh great narrative, its name/title Solomon"). But the authors of the *Title of Totonicapán* summarize this list as names, not narrative chapters: *juwinaq wuqub' nima b'i' ub'i' Salomon* ("twenty-seventh great name, his name Solomon"). The confusion comes in the twenty-eighth narrative of the *Theologia Indorum* (chapter 91), as it describes a set of several prophets, not one. The authors of the Totonicapán document follow the same convention of the previous lines and list a twenty-eighth unidentified great name (singular), then give an abbreviated list of some of the names of the prophets who are mentioned in this and subsequent chapters of the *Theologia Indorum*.

prophet is his name; Daniel the prophet is his name; Isaiah the prophet is his name; along with Jonah the prophet.

THE RETURN FROM BABYLONIA[140]

In the tenth division of the word[141] is the return of the Jews to their mountain place, named Jerusalem. They came from there in Babylonia and Assyria.

In the eleventh division[142] of the word there were ten tribes of Israel that did not arrive at their mountain place.

To their mountain place the Jews came from Babylonia. They arrived to possess again their habitations, their homeland.[143] Only one tribe, one lineage; only one group and lineage of the sons of Jacob; only they alone of his sons came to occupy Jerusalem again.

They of the other ten tribes[144] went to Assyria because of Shalmaneser.[145] They did not return again. Those who could speak of them were lost. There were not any who could give an account of them.[146] It is true that many arrived there, but they did not return. Only wood, only stone, they called upon[147] when they arrived there. It was merely their offenses, merely their wrongdoing, that caused them to be banished[148] by God, the Great Lord.

---

[140] lines 686–810.

[141] The account of the return of the Jews from Babylon comes from chapter 100 of the *Theologia Indorum*, which is the tenth subsection of the twenty-eighth set of great names (Vico 1605 [1553], folios 166v–167v; see Sparks 2019, 253).

[142] The reference to the ten tribes of Israel taken by Assyria is based on chapter 101 of the *Theologia Indorum*, which is the eleventh section of the twenty-eighth set of great names (Vico 1605 [1533], folios 167v–170r; see Sparks 2019, 253).

[143] *kamaq'* ("their homeland/dwellings"). In its possessed form, *amaq'* refers to a principal dwelling or homeland.

[144] *chinamital* ("lineages"). In this context, the authors use this term to refer to the "tribes" of Israel.

[145] *salmanasar*. A reference to Shalmaneser V, king of Assyria and Babylon from 727 to 722 BCE, who conquered the kingdom of Israel and deported the survivors to various regions of the Assyrian empire in 722 BCE (II Kings 17–18).

[146] *xek'utun uwi'*. Literally, "they [who] indicate their heads."

[147] *che' ab'aj* ("wood stone") refers to images of gods carved in wood or stone, a common metaphor used in Early Colonial highland Maya texts for the sculpted images of their gods (see n. 27). The text suggests that the ten nations of Israel that did not return were punished for their "idolatry."

[148] *xe'oq'otax uwi'*. Literally, "dismiss/reject/say goodbye to their heads." According to Coto, this carries the implied meaning of "to be banished," which is the likely interpretation in this context.

This is the name of the mountain that was previously mentioned;[149] it was told previously where they passed through. Mara is the name of the first mountain where we crossed over from the other side of the sea. The second was Xelimkutz;[150] the third was Sin;[151] the fourth was Rabitin;[152] the fifth was Xiney;[153] the sixth was Kaxerot;[154] the seventh was Chi K'ates;[155] the eighth was Eton;[156] the ninth was Jor;[157] the tenth was Chi B'och;[158] the eleventh was Chi Ab'atin;[159] the twelfth was Saret;[160] the thirteenth was Arnon,[161] the fourteenth was Matan;[162] the fifteenth was Xchamel;[163] the sixteenth was Bemot;[164] the seventeenth was Chi Moab.[165]

These, then, were their residences, their abodes, because of God, the Great Lord. These were the conquests of the Canaanites, the Hebrews, and the Israelites. Three, then, were their names: Israelites, Canaanites, and Hebrews they were called. They are our grandfathers and our fathers.

These, therefore, are our roots, our existence, our journey here from the place where the sun emerges.

Hear ye therefore, give heed to me,[166] and I shall declare it to you all. It was in war

---

[149] Rather than describe the journey from Babylonia by the Jews, this section repeats the list of the stations of the exodus from Egypt given before in the account of Moses in the wilderness, although in greater detail (see p. 84–85). Here there are seventeen named stops in their migration toward Canaan, each with a modified K'iche' spelling. In the previous account, only six stations were recorded and they appear in a slightly different order than they are here, beginning with Xelimkutz rather than Marah. Marah is the first major stop listed in the biblical account after crossing the Red Sea (Exodus 15:23; Numbers 33:8–9). See also n. 129 on the significance of Marah in K'iche' traditions. The two accounts were most likely written by different authors. In addition to being in a slightly different order, the spellings are also different—Marakow instead of Mara, Xim instead of Sin, and Papitin instead of Rabitin.

[150] Elim (Exodus 15:27, 16:1; Numbers 33:9–10).

[151] Sin or Zin (Exodus 16:1, 17:1; Numbers 33:11–12).

[152] Rephidim (Exodus 17:1, 19:2; Numbers 33:14–15).

[153] Sinai (Exodus 19:1–2; Numbers 10:12, 33:15–16).

[154] Hazeroth (Numbers 11:35, 12:16, 33:17–18).

[155] Kadesh (Numbers 20:1, 22, 33:36–37). The prefix *chi-* means "at" in K'iche'.

[156] Possibly Ezion-Geber, the stop just prior to Kadesh (Numbers 33:35–36).

[157] Hor (Numbers 20:22, 21:4, 33:37–41).

[158] Oboth (Numbers 21:10–11, 33:43–44).

[159] Abarim (Numbers 21:11, 33:44–45).

[160] unknown location.

[161] Almon (Numbers 33:46–47).

[162] unknown location.

[163] unknown location.

[164] unknown location.

[165] Moab (Numbers 22:1, 33:48–50).

[166] This passage of the text is explicitly the work of a single author, as evidenced by the use of a first-person singular discourse. While it is probable that the *Title of Totonicapán* was the

that they were lost, they, our grandfathers and our fathers. We are their grandsons, the sons of Adam and Eve, Enoch, Abraham, Isaac, and Jacob. This was because they forgot their God. Therefore, they were abandoned by God, the Great Lord.

This, therefore, is the declaration. They corrupted and changed their language[167] at Wuqub' Pek, Wuqub' Siwan,[168] Sewan Tulan,[169] they said; "[It was] at Pan Parar,[170]

---

work of many authors, this declaration may be evidence that some authors worked individu-
ally on specific sections that were later compiled into one text. This is certainly evident in
the chapter composed by Diego Reynoso where he identifies himself as the sole author (see
p. 117).

[167] Here the author asserts that their language was changed at Wuqub' Pek ("Seven Caves"),
Wuqub' Siwan ("Seven Ravines"), and Sewan Tulan ("Ravine Tulan"), not at the Tower of
Babel. This follows K'iche' tradition as recorded in the *Popol Vuh* that it was at Tulan that
the languages of the various K'iche'an groups became altered so they could not be understood clearly: "'Alas, is our language now abandoned? What have we done? We are lost.
Where were we deceived? We had but one language when we came from Tulan. We had but
one origin and creation. It is not good what we have done,' said all the nations beneath the
trees and beneath the bushes" (Christenson 2007, 215).

[168] Wuqub' Pek ("Seven Caves"), Wuqub' Siwan ("Seven Ravines"). At this point in the text, the
authors transition away from the Judaeo-Christian narrative contained in the *Theologia Indorum* and begin the account of their own K'iche' Maya traditions of their origin. In the *Popol
Vuh*, Wuqub' Pek and Wuqub' Siwan are the legendary places where the progenitors of the
K'iche' people began their journeys in the East, where the sun emerges (Christenson 2007,
210; see also *Historia de los Xpantzay de Tecpan Guatemala*, in Recinos 1957, 123). The
equivalent place of origin in central Mexican mythology is Chicomoztoc ("Seven Caves")
(Torquemada 1969, I.xiv.36–38; Tezozomoc 1975, 14-15; Davies 1977, 35–37).

[169] Sewan Tulan ("Ravine Tulan"). Tulan is derived from the Nahuatl Tullan or Tollan ("Place of
Cattail Reeds"). In the *Popol Vuh*, Tulan is the place where the progenitors of the K'iche' first
gathered and where they received their titular gods: "This, then, is the name of the mountain
that they went to . . . they arrived at Tulan Zuyva, Wuqub' Pek and Wuqub' Siwan was the
name of the citadel. There they arrived to obtain their gods. They arrived there at Tulan, all
of them. Innumerable people they were when they arrived. They walked in crowds when
the gods came out to them in succession" (Christenson 2007, 210–211). In the *Annals of the
Kaqchikels*, Tulan was the place where the seven lineages of the K'iche'an people began: "I
shall write the stories of our first fathers and grandfathers, one of whom was called Gagavitz,
the other Zactecauh; the stories that they told to us; that from the other side of the sea we
came to the place called Tulan, where we were begotten and given birth by our mothers and
our fathers, oh, our sons . . . Then we were commanded by our mothers and our fathers to
come, we the thirteen clans of the Seven Nations, the thirteen groups of warriors. Then we
arrived at Tulan in the darkness and in the night. Then we gave the tribute, when the Seven
Nations and the warriors carried the tribute. We took our places in order at the left part of
Tulan. There were the Seven Nations" (Recinos and Goetz 1953, 43, 48; see also Maxwell and
Hill 2006, 1–15). In the *Theologia Indorum*, Tulan Çuyuua is linked with the Garden of Eden,
or the *Parayso Terrenal* ("Earthly Paradise") (Vico 1605 [1553], chapter 42, folio 62v).

[170] Pan Parar ("At Waterfall"). According to the Coto dictionary, *parar* is water that falls from

Pan Paxil,[171] Pan K'ayela',"[172] they said. "[It was] there at Pan Paxil, Pan K'ayela',"
they said.

Within the Earthly Paradise we were framed and we were shaped by God, the
Great Lord. But his name was not honored by them because of their offenses. It
was at Sewan Tulan, they say; this is what it is called in its straightness: Sineyeton.[173]
This, therefore, was Wuqub' Pek, Wuqub' Siwan. True it is that in caves, in ravines,
they slept there in the place where the sun emerges. They were united there, and as
one they were lost. They were lost there in Assyria because of Shalmaneser.

---

a great height or from a cliff. The triad of Pan Parar, Pan Paxil, and Pan K'ayela' as places
of origin for the K'iche' is purely indigenous. There are no references to these places in the
Theologia Indorum.

[171] Pan Paxil ("At Cleft"). *Paxil* means "broken, split, or cleft." The Coto dictionary glosses *paxil*
as the breaking in two of an ear of maize. *Paxil* is described in the *Popol Vuh* as an "excellent
mountain" filled with the maize that would eventually be used to form the flesh of humanity
(Christenson 2007, 193–194).

[172] Pan K'ayela' ("At Bitter Water"). This is perhaps related to the widespread concept of the
primordial waters of creation that the highland Maya often associate with seawater or brack-
ish ponds, out of which the first mountains emerged. Paxil and K'ayela' are often paired in
post-Conquest K'iche' literature to refer to the place where the first human beings were
created from maize dough. The authors of the *Popol Vuh* write: "It was from within the
places called Paxil and Cayala that the yellow ears of ripe maize and the white ears of ripe
maize came ... Thus was found the food that would become the flesh of the newly framed
and shaped people. Water was their blood. It became the blood of humanity. The ears of
maize entered into their flesh by means of She Who Has Borne Children and He Who
Has Begotten Sons. Thus they rejoiced over the discovery of that excellent mountain that
was filled with delicious things, crowded with yellow ears of maize and white ears of maize"
(Christenson 2007, 193–194). Paxil is also mentioned as the place where the maize dough
used to make the flesh of humankind was first found in the *Annals of the Kaqchikels*: "They
did not know what should enter [into the man]. But at length they found whereof to make
it. Only two animals knew that there was food in Paxil ... And the animal called Tiuh-tiuh,
searching for the dough of the corn, brought from out of the sea the blood of the tapir and
the serpent, and with it the maize was kneaded. With this dough the flesh of man was made
by the Creator and the Maker. Thus the Creator, the Maker, the Progenitors knew how to
make man complete, so they tell" (Recinos and Goetz 1953, 46–47).

[173] The authors of the text here equate their legendary places of origin with Sineyeton, a variant
spelling of the biblical Sinai, making it sound more like Sewan Tulan, the legendary K'iche'
place of origin.

Section 2

The History and Traditions of the K'iche' People

THE ORIGINS IN THE PLACE WHERE THE SUN EMERGES[174]

In this division of the word[175] I shall speak of the establishment of lordship and the root of authority as well—the account of the Very Abundant Mountain, the Very Verdant Mountain.[176] This was at Pa Sewan and Pa Tulan, as told in the writings of Pek, the writings of Sewan Tulan,[177] as they said.

---

[174] lines 811–929.

[175] *Wa'e ju paj tzij* ("This one division word"). The authors of the Totonicapán text now transition away from dependence on the *Theologia Indorum*. To emphasize that this phrase marks the beginning of an independent section, the line is preceded by a symbol that indicates a new thought (¶), the first letter of *Wa'e* is capitalized, and there is no reference to a specific chapter in the *Theologia Indorum*. This phrase also follows the convention of indigenous texts rather than the *Theologia Indorum*. For example, the *Popol Vuh* begins with the phrase *are' uxe' ojer tzij* ("this is the root of the ancient word") (Christenson 2003, 13).

[176] *q'analaj juyub' raxalaj juyub'* ("very yellow mountain, very green/blue mountain"). Yellow and green are frequently combined as a couplet to indicate abundance (yellow) and fecundity (green/blue). This is a reference to the first mountain of creation in Maya cosmology (see n. 20–21).

[177] *utz'ib'al pek utz'ib'al Sewan Tulan* ("its writings Caves, its writings Ravines Tulan"). According to the authors of the *Popol Vuh*, the ancient progenitors of the K'iche' people brought "writings" with them when they left Tulan, possibly one or more painted Pre-Columbian codices: "They also brought the writings of Tulan from the other side of the sea. These were the writings, as they were called, that contained the many things with which they had been invested" (Christenson 2007, 259). The same authors wrote that the *Popol Vuh* itself was based on one of these books: "We shall bring it [their book] forth because there is no longer

---

https://doi.org/10.5876/9781646422647.c002

It was then that they festered[178] in lies. They spoke to the sun and to the moon. They called the one "Young Boy,"[179] and they called the other "Maiden."[180] Junajpu[181] they called the sun; Xb'alankej[182] was called the moon by them. "Cigars of K'iq'ab' "[183] the stars were called.

the means whereby the *Popol Vuh* may be seen, the means of seeing clearly that had come from across the sea—the account of our obscurity, and the means of seeing life clearly, as it is said. The original book exists that was written anciently, but its witnesses and those who ponder it hide their faces" (64). Alonso de Zorita (1963, 272) visited the capital of the K'iche' at Chi Q'umarkaj soon after the Spanish Conquest and was shown certain "paintings that they had which recorded their history for more than eight hundred years back, and which were interpreted for me by very ancient Indians."

[178] *xenimataj*, literally, "fester, or become gravely ill."

[179] *k'ajol* ("son of a man"). In the K'iche' language, the male child of a man is *k'ajol*. A woman's child of either sex is *al*.

[180] *q'apoj* ("virgin, or young woman"). This is the only reference in Early Colonial highland Maya texts that clearly identifies the moon as female (making the deity Xb'alankej a female lunar deity). In the *Popol Vuh* these twin gods are always referred to collectively as twin "boys, or sons"; however, in the K'iche' language, twins of different genders would be referred to collectively as males.

[181] Here we are introduced for the first time to the twin deities, Junajpu and Xb'alankej, who are the central focus of much of the mythic section of the *Popol Vuh* (Christenson 2007, 94–191). Junajpu has generally been translated as "One Master of the Blowgun" or "One Blowgun Hunter" on the assumption that *pu* is a shortened version of *[p]ub'* ("blowgun") (Recinos and Goetz 1950, 94, n. 1; Edmonson 1971, 34; D. Tedlock 1996, 238, n. 77; Sam Colop 2008, 45 n. 51). This may well be the original etymology of the name. Junajpu is described as a great "blowgun hunter" in the *Popol Vuh* text (Christenson 2007, 95–97). However, the authors of the *Popol Vuh* consistently wrote the word for blowgun as *ub'* or *wub'*, not *pub'*. It is therefore unlikely that the K'iche' authors of this text had "blowgun" in mind when they wrote the name of this deity. If the K'iche' scribes had meant to make it clear that he was a "blowgunner," they would have used the word in use at the time. I believe they remembered the name as it was handed down to them over the generations and preserved the archaic spelling because that was simply his proper name. The father of the culture hero Junajpu is named Jun Junajpu in the *Popol Vuh* (113), which if translated literally would mean "One One Master of the Blowgun," a needlessly redundant reading unless Junajpu were meant to be read as a single untranslated name.

[182] The derivation of the name Xb'alankej is problematic. The prefix *x-* is a diminutive as well as a feminine indicator. Thus, depending on the context, it may mean "young, small, little," or it may be used as a female title, such as "lady." The latter usage supports the statement in the previous line that Xb'alankej is a female lunar deity. *B'alan* is undoubtedly an archaic spelling of *b'alam* ("jaguar"), m/n letter substitutions being fairly common in K'iche'. The terminal *-kej* is more difficult to interpret. The most likely derivations are *kej* ("deer") or *q'ij* ("sun or day"). The *Popol Vuh* also links the twins Junajpu and Xb'alankej with the sun and the moon: "Then they arose as the central lights. They [Junajpu and Xb'alanke] arose straight into the sky. One of them arose as the sun, and the other as the moon. Thus the womb of the sky was illuminated over the face of the earth, for they came to dwell in the sky" (Christenson 2007, 191).

[183] Usik' K'iq'ab' ("his cigars K'iq'ab' "). Carmack and Mondloch (1983 22) identify this constellation as the Pleiades. K'iq'ab' was a prominent ruler of the K'iche' prior to the Spanish

We are the grandsons, we are the sons, of the Israelites and of Saint Moses. From the lands of the Israelites departed our grandfathers and our fathers. They came from the place where the sun emerges, there in Babylonia.[184] The powerful Lord Nakxik[185] was the root of our ancestry, of our parentage.[186]

Then the enchanted people[187] contemplated their journey. From far away they arrived in their obscurity[188] in the sky and on the land. There are none to equal

---

Conquest (Christenson 2007, 277–283). Many traditionalist K'iche' still interpret stars as cigars being smoked by deities or ancestors. Shooting stars occur when a spent cigar is tossed away, replaced immediately by another. This explains why there is always the same number of stars in the sky despite the occasional "falling" star.

[184] Pabelonia. In previous sections based on the *Theologia Indorum*, Babylonia was consistently spelled *babilonia*. It is perhaps significant that as the authors move away from this Christian source, Babylonia is spelled differently and in a manner consistent with K'iche' toponyms, which often begin with the prefix *pa* ("at"). This may indicate a different author or a move away from dependence on Christian sources.

[185] Nakxik, a variant spelling for the legendary ruler Nakxit (Carmack and Mondloch 2007, 65, n. 75). Nakxit is derived from the Nahuatl words *nawi* ("four") and *ikxit* ("foot") (Campbell 1983, 84), perhaps referring to the extent of his power to the four cardinal directions of the earth. In the *Popol Vuh*, Nakxit is the name or title of the ruler of Tulan, the mythic place of origin where the progenitors of the K'iche' people received their gods and political legitimacy: "Then they passed over the sea, arriving there in the East. They went there to receive their lordship. This, then, is the name of the lord, the lord of the East, when they arrived: Then they arrived before the face of the lord, whose name was Nakxit. He was the only judge over a great dominion. He then gave to them the signs and symbols of their lordship" (Christenson 2007, 256–257). *The Annals of the Kaqchikels* give a similar description: "They [the K'iche'an progenitors] came before Mevac and Nacxit, who was a great king ... Then they dressed them, they pierced their noses, and they gave them their offices and the flowers called *Cinpual*. Truly he made himself beloved by all the warriors. And turning to all of them, the Lord Naxcit said: 'Climb up to these columns of stone, enter into my house. I will give you sovereignty'" (Recinos and Goetz 1953, 64–65; Maxwell and Hill 2006, 67–69). Nakxit is also one of the titles for the feathered serpent deity known as Kukulcan in the Maya lowlands and as Quetzalcoatl in central Mexico (Recinos and Goetz 1950, 207, n. 3; Roys 1967, 83; Edmonson 1982, 16, n. 220; Nicholson 2001, 228). Nakxit was one of the titles used by Maya rulers at both Chichen Itza and Mayapan, thus claiming central Mexican authority as an important component of their own right to rule (Nicholson 2001, 228–229).

[186] *qamamaxik qak'ajolaxik*, literally, "our being grandfathered, our being fathered."

[187] *nawal winaq* ("enchanted/wondrous people"). The authors of the Totonicapán document appear conflicted in their loyalties in this transitional section between the Judaeo-Christian–influenced history of the Israelites and their own indigenous Maya traditions. They condemn in some passages the "idolatry" of their ancestors, yet here they describe them as revered persons with wondrous or miraculous powers. From this point on, there are few overt Christian influences in the text.

[188] *kimuqub'al* ("their obscurity"). The root of the word, *muquj*, is a verb that means "to cover, hide, bury, or obscure something," such as a cloud that obscures the sun, or burying something so it cannot be seen.

them. They saw everything beneath the sky. They were great sages. They led all of the Seven Nations[189] as well as the tribes.[190]

Then they came from the other side of the lake, from the other side of the sea;[191] from Tulan and from Sewan.

These, then, are the names of the first people. These are the first of the K'iche'.

---

[189] Wuq Amaq' ("Seven Nations"). *Amaq'* may refer to a group of allied lineages that live dispersed throughout a region, as well as to the communities in which they live. Hill and Monaghan (1987, 74) identify the *amaq'* as an alliance of confederated lineage groups. It may also describe a group of people unified by a common language or ethnic origin, such as a lineage, clan, or tribe (Hill 1996, 64; Akkeren 2000, 24). I have chosen to use the word *nation*, as this is the currently preferred term for Native American groups with common language, social, and territorial ties. In Early Colonial K'iche' texts, the "Seven Nations" appear to represent highland Maya groups that opposed the hegemony of the Nima K'iche'.

[190] Tlekpan. Tlekpan, or Tekpan, is derived from the Nahuatl language, meaning "royal house or palace." In this text, however, the word does not apply to a structure but rather to a group of people. Ximénez (1985 [1701], 527) defines *tekpan* as a "*chinamital* or *calpul* with many people." *Chinamital* is a "lineage or confederation" (195). Coto (1983 [ca. 1656], cxix) agrees, defining *chinamital* as "caste, lineage, district, generation." Carmack interprets the *chinamit* as a territorial organization in which a group of people are subject to the same lord or chief. Citing an early K'iche' dictionary that defines the members of a *chinamit* as those "called by the name and under (the authority) of one chief, so that anyone who might like to [could] join this lineage and brotherhood of people," Carmack (1981, 164) characterizes this sociopolitical organization as an "estate" led by a principal patrilineage of lords, similar to "similarly structured estates of feudal Europe." In Early Colonial documents, *chinamit* and *calpul* are used interchangeably to refer to a territorial unit that is ruled by an aristocratic core family, aided by a council of elders, and occupied by vassals "burdened with a high degree of corporate control and numerous obligations" (Hill 1992, 38–39). I have chosen the term *tribe*, as it comes closest to this concept in its original meaning. Derived from the Latin *tribus*, it refers to a division of people of a particular lineage, including their dependents, vassals, and adopted strangers.

[191] *ch'aqa palo* ("other side sea"). The authors assert that Tulan, where their founding ancestors received their right to rule, was located on the "other side of the sea" in the East. In both the *Annals of the Kaqchikels* and the *Popol Vuh*, Tulan is linked with a placed called Zuyua (Maxwell and Hill 2006, 615, 656, 657; Christenson 2007, 210, 213, 218, 227, 231). In the Yucatec Maya *Books of Chilam Balam*, Zuyua is a place of origin and power located in the Maya lowlands (Roys 1967, 88–91, 192; Craine and Reindorp 1979, 138). Based on linguistic and geographic evidence, Zuyua is linked with the area of Xicalanco, an ancient port city on the shores of the Laguna de Términos in the Mexican state of Tabasco (Recinos and Goetz 1953, 53, 216; Campbell 1970, 7; Carmack 1981, 46). The sea referred to in the highland Maya documents is probably the Laguna de Términos itself or possibly the Gulf of Mexico that feeds into it. This is consistent with the route of migration recorded later in this text, which describes a general movement from the Maya lowlands to the Alta Verapaz, ultimately settling in the K'iche' highlands of western Guatemala. Alternatively, Frauke Sachse (2008, 155) argues convincingly that the concepts of Tulan and "the other side of the sea" should not be taken literally but rather should serve as mythic places of "creation, rebirth, and human origin, which is meaningful within the context of Mesoamerican cosmology, political rhetoric, and cultural practice alike."

There were four of them. The first lord was B'alam K'itze',[192] our grandfather and our father; we, the Kaweqib'.

He, the second lord, was B'alam Aq'ab',[193] the grandfather and father of the Nijayib' lords.

The third lord, then, was Majukotaj,[194] the grandfather and father of the Ajaw K'iche'.

The fourth lord, then, was Ik'i B'alam.[195]

These, then, were the first K'iche'. B'alam K'itze' was the first lord; Kaqapaluma[196] was the name of his wife.

B'alam Aq'ab' was the second lord; Sunija[197] was the name of his wife.

---

[192] B'alam K'itze'. Founder of the ruling Kaweq lineage of the K'iche'. *B'alam* is a relatively common Maya name, even today. In its most literal sense, *b'alam* means "jaguar"; however, when used as a title, it carries with it a host of implicit meanings. Because of the nature of the jaguar as the largest and fiercest animal in the Guatemalan jungle, *b'alam* is used to refer to anything powerful or mighty. In addition, *b'alam* is sometimes used to refer to shamans or rulers with unusual spiritual or magical powers. *K'itze'* appears to be the Mam form of *k'iche'*, meaning "forest" (Akkeren 2000, 155). Thus the name of this progenitor may mean something like "Jaguar Forest," "Jaguar K'iche'," or "Mighty K'iche'." The etymology of all the progenitors' names is obscure, however, and they have therefore been left untranslated.

[193] B'alam Aq'ab'. "Jaguar Night" or "Mighty Night." Ancestor of the Nijayib' lineage of the K'iche'.

[194] Majukotaj. Founder of the Ajaw K'iche' lineage. Together, these three brothers were revered as the progenitors of the principal three K'iche' lineages that comprise the Nima K'iche' ("Great K'iche'"). The meaning of the name of this progenitor is problematic. Carmack (1981, 49) believes it is derived from the lowland Maya word for "Traveler," or "One Who Does Not Stay." Akkeren (personal communication, 2002) suggests that the name is derived from the Mam *jukotaj* ("elder, eminent one"). Coto (1983 [ca. 1656], 474) lists *hu cotah* as "one crown, ring, or similar round object." In many highland Maya languages, such as Tz'utujil, the prefix *Ma* may be honorific, meaning something like "mister, or sir."

[195] Ik'i B'alam. If this name is derived from lowland Maya languages, which is probable, it would be read as "Black/Dark Jaguar." If it is derived from K'iche', it can be read as either Iq'i B'alam ("Wind Jaguar") or Ik'i B'alam ("Moon Jaguar"). No lineage was founded by this progenitor. In the following passage, the authors note that he had no wife because he was too young when he left Tulan and he died without heirs.

[196] Kaqapaluma (possible variant of Kaqa Palu Na, "Red Sea House"). In the *Popol Vuh*, the wife of B'alam K'itze' is written as Kajapaluna ("Sky Sea House") (Christenson 2007, 202, n. 497). This is either an alternative spelling by the authors of the Totonicapán document or the result of scribal error. Each of the wives of the progenitors includes the word for "house" in her name, indicating that the wives are founders of a lineage group or "house." Kajapaluna uses the lowland Maya spelling of the word for house, *na*, rather than the K'iche' form of the word, *ja*. The preservation of this form of the word may indicate the dimly recalled memory of a royal marriage of their most important K'iche' ancestor to a royal princess from the Maya lowlands.

[197] Sunija. In the *Popol Vuh*, the third woman created was Tz'ununija ("Hummingbird House"), which is the un-contracted form of her name, although in that text she was the wife of Majukotaj (Christenson 2007, 202).

Majukotaj was the third lord; Kaqixaja[198] was the name of his wife. Ik'i B'alam was only a boy when he came from the place where the sun emerges. These, then, are the secondary K'iche', named the Tamub'.[199] These were their first lords—K'opichoch and K'ochojlan,[200] Majk'inalom and K'oq'anawil. Only four people were truly the founders[201] of the Tamub' lords. K'aqoj and Eq'omaq'[202] are their witnesses within this book.

Merely as one they came here from the other side of the lake, from the other side of the sea, from the place where the sun emerges; from Tulan and from Sewan.

And along with them there were the Ilokab'.[203] They were the third K'iche'. There were only four [Ilokab'] people then,[204] and these are the names of their first lords—Chiya' Toj and Chiya' Tz'ikin, Yol Chitum and Yol Chiramaq', Ch'ipel Kan and Muq'el [Kan].[205] These were their grandfathers and their fathers. They were lords—Q'ale, Sik'a, and Juwanija.[206] These were the Ilokab'.

---

[198] Kaqixaja ("Macaw House"). The name is the same in the *Popol Vuh*, although there she appears as the wife of Ik'i B'alam (Christenson 2007, 202).

[199] The Tamub' K'iche' were a subsidiary K'iche' lineage who lived in the areas of present-day Chiquimula, Santa Lucía la Reforma, Patzité, and northwestern San Pedro Jocopilas. Their main center at the time of the Spanish Invasion was at Chi Ismachi' (Fox 1978, 36; Carmack 1981, 167).

[200] K'opichoch and K'ochojlan. *K'o* is a prefix indicating respect or honor.

[201] *uxe'* (literally, "their root").

[202] K'aqoj and Eq'omaq' are the two principal lineages of the Tamub' K'iche'.

[203] The Ilokab' were the third of the main lineages of the K'iche' after the Nima K'iche' and the Tamub'. They lived in the area near present-day San Antonio Ilotenango and western San Pedro Jocopilas. Their principal capital was at Chisalin (Fox 1978, 36; Carmack 1981, 167–178).

[204] Although the authors state that there were only four founders of the Ilokab' lineage, they give six names. It is possible that four is used here as an ideal or symbolic number, paralleling the four named progenitors of the Nima K'iche' and of the Tamub' K'iche' listed previously. The *Title of the Ilokab'* also lists six progenitors for the Ilokab' lineage, although the lists differ slightly: Moqel Kan, Ch'ipil Kan, Jal Chi Tun, Jal Chi Ramaq', Chi Ya' Toj, and Chi Ya' Tz'ikin (Sparks 2017, 279).

[205] Later in the text, this lord's name is given as Muq'el Kan, paralleling the name of Ch'ipel Kan (p. 119). The six Ilokab' lords are arranged as three paired couplets, based on the form of their names.

[206] Q'ale, Sik'a, and Juwanija are the three principal lineages of the Ilokab' K'iche'. Q'ale[l] is a significant position of authority in the K'iche' hierarchy (see n. 325). The root of Sik'a is *sik'* ("tobacco"). A receptacle of sacred tobacco was one of the tokens of power and authority brought from Tulan by the founders of the K'iche' lineages (Christenson 2007, 258). Tobacco plays a major role in Maya ceremonies, both ancient and modern. Deities, rulers, and priests are often depicted wearing a tobacco pouch in Pre-Columbian art. Juwanija is likely a hispanicized spelling of *wanija*. According to Bassetta, *wanij* is to place a crown on one's head, suggesting that this title may have been an important courtier or adviser who oversees coronation ceremonies. In the same dictionary, *wanic* is listed as "the art of playing an instrument," particularly one that involves percussion. This office therefore may have involved arranging for or actually playing musical instruments, an important part of ceremonies among the ancient Maya.

These were the three nations of the K'iche'. They had but one language. Unified[207] were the three nations of the K'iche'. Children and sons of Israel are we, the K'iche' people, when we came from Babylonia where the sun emerges.

THE JOURNEY FROM THE PLACE WHERE THE SUN EMERGES[208]

This, then, is their journey from the place where the sun emerges. They were raised up, they the leaders B'alam K'itze', with B'alam Aq'ab', Majukotaj, and Ik'i B'alam. This therefore is their journey. They were given the Bundled Glory[209] by Lord Nakxik. When they came here they were uncovered. They were naked when they came. They only had their spears and their leafy tunics[210] when they arrived at the shore of the sea.

---

[207] *xa jun kiwach*. Literally, "merely one their faces."

[208] lines 930–1025.

[209] *Pison K'ak'al* ("Bundled Glory/Flame"). This bundle is mentioned five times in the text and consistently with this spelling, a variant or archaic form of *Pisom Q'aq'al*, as it is spelled in analogous passages of the *Popol Vuh*. Here, the text asserts that it was given to the K'iche' progenitors by Nakxik, lord of Tulan in the East. If Tulan is located in the lowland Maya region, the archaic spelling may be due to the fact that lowland Maya languages do not have a glottalized q sound and the word for "glory/flame" is pronounced *k'ak'*. The authors of the *Popol Vuh* describe the *Pisom Q'aq'al* as a token of power left behind by B'alam K'itze' as a memorial: " 'This is the token of my memory that I shall leave with you. This is your glory. These are my instructions, the result of what I have pondered,' he said when he left behind the sign of his existence. Bundled Glory it was called. Its contents were not clear for it was truly bundled. They did not unwrap it, nor was its stitching clear. No one had seen it when it was bundled . . . Thus the Bundle came to be precious to them as a memorial to their father. Straightaway they burned offerings before it as a memorial to their father" (Christenson 2007, 254–255). In a later passage of the *Title of Totonicapán*, the bundle is said to have been left wrapped for many years, until the K'iche' established their first permanent settlement on the mountain of Jaqawitz. It was the presence of this bundle that gave the K'iche' their "glory and sovereignty" before the other lineages (p. 105). Bundling an object separates it from the mundane world. It thus becomes liminal, existing in the world and yet unseen by the living. The Maya often reinforce this effect by keeping sacred bundles in wooden chests, removing them only on special days when they might be venerated more directly. This practice continues in traditional Maya communities today (Mendelson 1958; Carlsen 1997, 80–81; Christenson 2001, 157–167; 2006, 226–246; see figure 26).

[210] *xa kixaq po't* ("only their leafy shirts/mantles/tunics"). The authors describe their first ancestors as poor, naked, or clothed only in leaves. This is similar to the description of the progenitors' poverty in the *Popol Vuh*: "They were alike in the hides that they wore as coverings, for their dress was very poor. They had nothing of their own, but they were enchanted people in their essence when they came from Tulan Zuyva" (Christenson 2007, 213). Alternatively, this may be scribal error for *xajpo't*, which is defined by Coto as *cota de malla* (Spanish, "coat of mail"). This would be the type of armor worn by the ancient Maya that was padded with thick layers of cotton and perhaps reinforced with harder materials for protection in battle.

Figure 26. "They were given the Bundled Glory by lord Nakxik." Sacred Bundle, Santiago Atitlán, 2006.

Then he, Lord B'alam K'itze', took his staff. He struck[211] the sea. Immediately the sea dried up. Merely bare[212] sand it came to be. Then they passed through it, all of the three groups of the first K'iche'. Accompanying them then were the Thirteen Clans, the Seven Nations, and the tribes. They followed behind. Surely there were many who crossed over.

Then the sea closed upon itself. Surely this was the love of God for them because there was only one,[213] Tz'aqol B'itol, that they called upon in the center of the sky and the earth, they say. For surely they were the sons and grandsons of Abraham and Jacob.[214]

Then they journeyed here from the other side of the sea. They brought the roots of trees and the roots of bushes.[215] There was no food, no water. They would merely sniff the heads of their staffs to console their hearts.

---

[211] *xuq'osij* ("he struck"). This verb is usually used to describe breaking a stone or splitting wood. It would not normally be used for the act of striking water. The word choice suggests influence from the Bible in which Moses is said to have "divided" the Red Sea by striking it with his staff, leaving a wall of water on each side of the dry land (Exodus 14:16–22). The *Popol Vuh* also describes this miraculous crossing but differs in detail: "It was not clear how they passed over the sea to come here. It was if there were no sea that they had to pass over. They merely passed over on the tops of stones for there were stones on the sand. Thus they named it 'Lined up Stones'; and 'Piled up Sand' was also its name" (Christenson 2007, 221).

[212] *b'olob'ik*. The word refers to recently ploughed earth or a bare hillside with no vegetation.

[213] This phrase identifying Tz'aqol and B'itol as monotheistic is influenced by Christian teachings. Tz'aqol ("Framer") and B'itol ("Shaper") are creator deities in K'iche' tradition, but they were adopted by Domingo de Vico and other Dominican missionaries as K'iche' equivalents for the Christian God. This is the last appearance of Tz'aqol B'itol as monotheistic. After this passage, they appear alongside other indigenous gods (see pp. 125, 140).

[214] In the Bible, it is customary to list all three patriarchs, Abraham, Isaac, and Jacob. In K'iche' poetics, couplets are preferred. This may be the reason why Isaac is not mentioned in this passage.

[215] *xkik'am uloq uxe' che' uxe' k'a'm* ("they brought hither their roots trees their roots bushes").

Figure 27. "They left again, arriving there on the peak of the mountain named Jaqawitz Ch'ipaq." Hilltop ruins of Jaqawitz Ch'ipaq. Photograph by John Fox, 1971.

They then arrived at the shore of a small lake, Nimsoy Karchaj,[216] where they constructed their buildings. There were quetzals[217] and cotingas, ducks, yellow parrots and green parrots, yellow gatherer birds[218] and yellow birds.

But they did not find themselves content[219] there. They were taken away again.

This is a K'iche' expression that signifies that the K'iche' progenitors departed from a place of settlement, similar to the English expression "they pulled up roots." In the *Popol Vuh*, a similar phrase is used to describe the departure of the first K'iche' from Tulan, asserting that "they were pulled up like weeds as they came out from there, leaving the East behind" (Christenson 2007, 218). In a similar vein, the establishment of the first major K'iche' capital at Chi Ismachi' is described as "putting down roots" (265).

[216] Nimsoy Karchaj is the first settlement along the migration route that is identified by name. *Nim soy* means "great relief," no doubt related to the alleviation of hunger and thirst provided by a lakeshore settlement after a journey described as lacking food and water. Kar Chaj ("Fish Ballcourt/Ashes"). It is most likely a reference to the Q'eqchi'-Maya town now known as San Pedro Carchá located near Cobán, a city east and somewhat north of K'iche' territory in the Alta Verapaz region of Guatemala.

[217] *q'uq'* ("resplendent quetzal," *Pharomachrus mocinno*). Quetzal birds are relatively rare in Guatemala and live exclusively in tropical highland cloud forests, particularly in the Alta Verapaz region. Today, they are the national bird of Guatemala.

[218] *q'an b'ulul*. This bird does not appear in any of the early dictionaries. The verb *b'uluj* means "to hoarde, gather, or pile something up." Thus the bird's name literally means "yellow gatherer" or "yellow hoarder."

[219] *mawi xuk'an ta kiwach* (literally, "they did not find their faces"). This is a common phrase in modern K'iche' speech. When people move into a community they are often asked, *a riqom*

They brought again the roots of trees and the roots of bushes. They arrived then at Chi Xpa'ch.[220] There they gave the sign of Pa Ja Ayin Ab'aj.[221] This is the sign they gave. Then they left again. They arrived at the peak of a great mountain whose name was Chi K'iche'.[222] This is what they called it. They only tarried there.

Then they left the mountain of Chi K'iche' behind, arriving there on the peak of the mountain named Jaqawitz Ch'ipaq.[223] They settled there at the great mountain. All of them settled there, they the bloodletters[224] and the sacrificers,[225] B'alam K'itze', B'alam Aq'ab', Majukotaj, and Ik'i B'alam.

---

a wach? ("have you discovered your face?") meaning, "do you feel established, settled, or content?"

[220] Chi Xpa'ch ("At the Lizard"). Carmack and Mondloch (1983, 218, n. 96) identify this area as a small village of the same name located northeast of San Andrés Sajcabajá and suggest that the nearby ruins of Los Cimientos may be the site itself.

[221] Pa Ja Ayin Ab'aj ("At House Crocodile Stone"). This was apparently a memorial stone set up as a sign of their residence.

[222] Chi K'iche' ("At Forest"). Carmack and Mondloch (1983, 218, n. 97) identify this as a hill northeast of San Andrés Sajcabajá now called Los Achiotes, although on some older maps the original name of Chi K'iche' was still used.

[223] Jaqawitz Ch'ipaq. *Jakawitz* in Cholan Maya languages means "First/Beginning Mountain," tying it to the first mountain of creation. In K'iche' the verb *jaq* means "to open," which may recall the mountain of Paxil ("Split Mountain") that contained the maize used to create the first human beings in the *Popol Vuh* (Christenson 2007, 193–194). *Ch'ipaq* refers to natural soap, made from the roots of a variety of plants, that is used for washing. Fox and Carmack identify Jaqawitz as the hilltop ruins now called Chitinamit near the village of Santa Rosa Chujuyub', not far from the city of Santa Cruz del Quiché (Fox 1978, 57–58; Carmack 1979, 96–99; Carmack and Mondloch 1983, 218, n. 98; see map 1).

[224] *ajk'ix* can literally be translated as "she/he of the spine"; however, it refers to the practice of letting blood by auto-sacrifice, paralleling the performance of sacrifice in the next line of the couplet. This was generally accomplished with a sharp spine, such as the tip of a maguey leaf or a stingray spine. Like most Mesoamerican groups, the ancient Maya gave their own blood as an offering to the gods. They believed that by so doing, they returned a portion of their life force to the powers of the cosmos. Such auto-sacrificial acts were performed in an effort to cleanse impurities as a penitential ritual. In the *Popol Vuh*, the four K'iche' progenitors were also called bloodletters and sacrificers and were described as undergoing penitential ceremonies: "They did not sleep. They did not rest. Greatly did they weep in their hearts, in their bowels, for the dawn and for clarity. They came there surely as penitents, in great sorrow and great humility" (Christenson 2007, 225). Although auto-sacrifice is no longer performed, this concept of doing penance, confession, and pleading for cleansing of personal impurities accompanies most offerings of candles, incense, flowers, or sacrificed animals in modern-day K'iche' rituals.

[225] *ajk'aj* ("she/he of sacrifice"). *K'aj* is specifically blood sacrifice. Coto (1983 [ca. 1656], 502–503) lists the word as referring to the type of human sacrifice performed by the Maya prior to the Spanish Conquest, but it may also be a sacrifice of one's own blood. When the progenitors performed auto-sacrifice before their gods, it was by piercing their ears and their elbows (Christenson 2007, 219). Thus this term and the one that precedes it likely refer to auto-sacrificial rites whereby a person's own blood is offered to deity. Ximénez translates

THE BEGINNING OF SACRIFICES[226]

Surely, then, they all gathered again, together with the Tamub' and the Ilokab', as well as the Thirteen Clans, the Seven Nations, and the tribes. They had become a numerous people by now after many years. They were there when they planned in their hearts for the bringing forth of their fire.[227]

Said B'alam K'itze': "Surely we have also felt cold. We shall bring forth our fire," said B'alam K'itze' to the Seven Nations and the tribes.

"That's good then. What shall we give to you as reward?" asked the Seven Nations and the tribes. "Whoever will bring forth their fire first, we shall give a child of our mothers, a son of our fathers[228] to them," said the Seven Nations.

"That's good then. Then may it be so," said B'alam K'itze'.

Then they succeeded in lighting their fire. They began to ignite[229] their fire. First came forth the fire of B'alam K'itze', B'alam Aq'ab', Majukotaj, and Ik'i B'alam. But for them, the Seven Nations and the tribes, their fire did not in any way come forth. Thus they pleaded for the fire of B'alam K'itze', B'alam Aq'ab', Majukotaj, and Ik'i B'alam: "Give thou[230] to us a little fire," said the Seven Nations and the tribes.

---

k'ajb' as "punishment." The related word in Classic Maya texts, ch'ahb', has two meanings in the context of war. In one sense, it refers to the punishment of captives and at the same time to the notion that captives destined for sacrificial death represent a kind of self-sacrifice, with the sacrificial victim acting as a substitute for the captor's own blood and flesh (Taube 1994, 669–674). Thus Classic Maya lords saw in the person of the war captive their own penance and self-denial. In this way, bloodletting and sacrifice represent penitence by proxy (Stephen D. Houston, private communication, 2002).

[226] lines 1026–1088.

[227] This section on the first kindling of fire has deeper meaning in the K'iche' language. Q'aq' may simply mean "fire" or "flame"; however, it also has the larger meaning of "power, authority, glory." This section therefore is a metaphor for the establishment of authority among the principal K'iche' lineages over other groups in the highland region.

[228] jun qal qak'ajol ("one our child of our mothers, son of our fathers"). This is a play on words that creates a certain ambiguity in meaning. When taken literally, this may simply refer to marriage alliances, exchanging their sons and daughters with one another, a practice common among the ancient K'iche' (see Christenson 2007, 265). But the couplet of al and k'ajol is also a common metaphor for "vassals, or servants" (268). The ambiguity is most likely intentional in the story, masking the K'iche' progenitors' intention to subjugate and even sacrifice members of other groups while giving the impression that only intermarriage is being discussed.

[229] ub'aqik. According to Ximénez (1985 [1701], 81), this is to make fire with sticks, perhaps a twist drill, as b'aqik also has the connotation of "boring or drilling holes."

[230] The failure of the Seven Nations to produce fire has already placed them in a subservient position. Here they address B'alam K'itze' and the other K'iche' progenitors using the more formal alaq (similar to "thou, ye," used to address revered persons or deities) rather than the

"Give us then our reward," they were told.

"What, then, shall we give?" they asked.

"Perhaps you desire that we shall suck your breasts?"[231] they were asked by B'alam K'itze'.

"That's good then," they said.

So then was the suckling of their breasts, the side of their chests.[232] Thus were defeated the Seven Nations, the warriors. They gave their children and their sons as a sign of their defeat.

THE DIVISION OF THE K'ICHE' PEOPLE[233]

This day we shall begin the account of their division. Then spoke B'alam K'itze', B'alam Aq'ab', Majukotaj, and Ik'i B'alam: "Surely we shall divide ourselves, thou lords K'opichoch and K'ochojlan, K'oq'anawil and Majk'inalom;[234] and thou as well, Chiya' Toj and Chiya' Tz'ikin, Jal Chitum and Jal Chiramaq', Ch'ipel Kan and Muq'el Kan," said B'alam K'itze'.[235]

---

more familiar form, *ix* ("you"), which they had used to address the progenitors at the beginning of this section. B'alam K'itze' replies to them using the familiar *ix*, further emphasizing his superior position.

[231] Another play on words meant to trick the rivals of the K'iche' progenitors. The phrase *chiqatz'umaj uwach ik'u'x* literally means "we shall suck its face your hearts." The "face of the heart" simply means "breast or chest" in K'iche', and suckling at the breast is a metaphor for any kind of nurturing assistance. The Seven Nations may have initially understood this demand simply as a request to provide aid or sustenance, whereas the more ominous implication was that they would be sacrificed by heart extraction. In the parallel account in the *Popol Vuh*, the play on words is more straightforward, using the verb *tu'nik* ("to breast-feed, nurture") rather than *tz'umaj* ("suck, kiss") to describe the payment for giving fire as mandated by their god Tojil. In that version of the account, the play on words is emphasized more fully and explained as a masked demand for human sacrifice: "'Do they not want to give the breast (*tu'nik*) beneath their shoulders and their armpits? Do they not desire in their hearts to embrace me—I Tojil' ... This, then, was the breast-giving spoken of by Tojil—all the nations were to be sacrificed before him. Their hearts were to be carved out from beneath their shoulders and armpits" (Christenson 2007, 216, 218).

[232] *kimaske'l* ("their armpits/sides of their chests"). In K'iche' the word refers not only to the armpit but also to the space between the side of the chest and arm. The verb form of the word refers to carrying objects such as a bundle of papers wedged between the arm and the side of the chest. The suggestion is that heart extraction involved an incision on the side of the chest to avoid the sternum.

[233] lines 1089–1172.

[234] The four founding lords of the Tamub' (see p. 95)

[235] The six founding lords of the Ilokab' (see p. 95). In the earlier passage, Jal Chitum and Jal Chiramaq' were listed as Yol Chitum and Yol Chiramaq'.

Figure 28. "And so the Tamub' journeyed to the top of the mountain Amaq' Tan." Ridgetop slope of Amaq' Tan. Photograph by John Fox, 1971.

"We shall not be lost. Soon we will meet together in counsel. We have not yet found our mountain place, our valley place. Who knows how many cycles of twenty years[236] we shall tarry here on Jaqawitz Ch'ipaq?"

Then they gave names to Chi Pixab' and Chi Mamaj. They would give names to Chi Q'iyaj and Chi Qamamaj.[237]

In this way they spoke among themselves.

And so the Tamub' journeyed to the top of the mountain Amaq' Tan.[238]

Likewise, they of the Ilokab' journeyed to the top of the mountain Uk'in.[239]

---

[236] *umaytzij. May* is a period of twenty years; *maytzijol*, according to Sáenz de Santa María (1940, 258), is an expression of doubt, ex. *mai tsijol ojer* ("who knows how much time?").

[237] Carmack and Mondloch (1983, 219, n. 107) identify these as mountains to the northeast of the city of Santa Cruz del Quiché, along the border with San Andrés Sajcabajá.

[238] Amaq' Tan or Amaq' Tam ("Homeland of the Tam"—Tamub' is the pluralized form of Tam). Identified as the archaeological site known as Cruzche', located on the northeast slope of the hill Telecuche', northeast of Santa Cruz del Quiché (Fox 1978, 45–47; Carmack and Mondloch 1983, 220, n. 108). This was not a long journey. Cruzche' is approximately 3 kilometers west of Jaqawitz (the archaeological site of Chitinamit, see p. 123, n. 223).

[239] Uk'in. Now known as Oquin, a community northeast of San Pedro Jocopilas. It is located on a long ridge extending northeast from the hill Telecuche'. Carmack and Fox surveyed

Figure 29. "Likewise, they of the Ilokab' journeyed to the top of the mountain Uk'in."
Ridgetop of Uk'in with mounds. Photograph by John Fox, 1971.

Then followed the Seven Nations and the tribes behind them.
Only they alone, the bloodletters and sacrificers, B'alam Aq'ab', B'alam K'itze',
Majukotaj, and Ik'i B'alam, they remained there atop the mountain Jaqawitz
Ch'ipaq. There they engendered daughters and engendered sons. There were engendered K'oka'ib'[240] and K'okawib'[241] by Lord B'alam K'itze'.

---

the nearby archaeological site in 1973. It is only about 2 kilometers northwest of Amaq' Tan
across a narrow canyon. The two sites are visible from one another. Both are easily defensible
hilltop sites (Fox 1978, 43–45; see map 1).

[240] K'oka'ib' ("Lord Two"). The prefix *k'o-* (*qo* in the original sixteenth century orthography),
which appears often in this document in the names of K'iche' lords, is an honorific meaning
sir or lord. When used as a title, it suggests "nobility, lordship, or authority." Thus Coto lists
qo ch'u vi (literally, "it is at its head") as "to be charged, or have jurisdiction/authority"; *qo r'a*
("there is his/her breath") as "to have authority"; or *qo uɛij* ("there is his/her sun/day") as "to
have authority, a great thing, famous, or glorious." *Ka'ib'* simply means "two." Thus this name
would be something like "Lord or Sir Two." When used as a verb, *ka'ib'aj* is "to multiply or
divide." The name may refer to the fact that he had a large posterity or that his was a significant division of the lineage.

[241] K'okawib' ("Lord Adornments"). *Kawib'* is the plural form of *kaw*, meaning adornments,
such as jewelry or symbols of authority. In a military sense, the word is used to refer to armor

Figure 30. "Tojil was the god of B'alam K'itze'." A highland Maya god from a mural at Iximche'. Drawing by Linda Schele.

They also multiplied[242] there as well, the children and sons of the Seven Nations, the warriors.

Armed,[243] then, were the men in the buildings of the bloodletters and the sacrificers, they who were our grandfathers and our fathers; of we, the Kaweqib', the Nijayib', and the Ajaw K'iche'. Ik'i B'alam had died in his youth.

___

or weapons. This is a notable example, however, of word play. The verb *kawachij*, derived from the same root word, *kaw*, carries the meaning of infidelity in marriage (Ximénez 1985 [1701], 165), a foreshadowing of this lord's adultery with the wife of his brother, K'oka'ib'.

[242] *kipoq'otajik* ("their being multiplied"). Although the root verb refers to having many children, this may also be a play on words. Depending on the context, it can also mean "to be killed, tormented, tortured, or ruined," foreshadowing their defeat by the Nima K'iche'.

[243] *wiqil* ("adorned, armed"). Although the word is often used to refer to something that is adorned or decorated, the context here is that they were adorned with armor and weapons, as will be stated more directly later in the text (see p. 106).

Tojil was the god of B'alam K'itze'. Awilix was the god of B'alam Aq'ab'. Jaqawitz was the god of Majukotaj.[244] It was at K'wal Ab'aj[245] that the Bundled Glory,[246] which had come from the place where the sun emerges, was unbound on Jaqawitz. Glory and sovereignty[247] came to be theirs over the Seven Nations and the tribes. They had passed many cycles of twenty years divided among themselves.

BEGINNING OF THE DISAPPEARANCES FROM
AMONG THE SEVEN NATIONS[248]

Then began the disappearance of the daughters and the sons of the Seven Nations and the tribes. It was not clear how they disappeared. They disappeared because of the enchanted ones.[249] It was only their entrails that were left behind to be found by the Seven Nations.

"What shall we do? Perhaps it is only the mountain?"[250] they said.

They looked for the prints of what had done it but found only the pawprints of jaguars, only the pawprints of coyotes that had been left behind. But the blood was taken before the gods, before Tojil, Awilix, and Jaqawitz.

---

[244] These three gods are the patron deities of the three major lineages of the Nima K'iche'. According to the *Popol Vuh*, they were received by the progenitors at Tulan (Christenson 2007, 211–212).

[245] Chi K'wal Ab'aj ("At Precious Stone"). From the context of the sentence, this is a site somewhere on the mountain Jaqawitz.

[246] This is the bundle given to the K'iche' progenitors by Nakxik at Tulan as a token of their power and authority (see p. 96). Up until this time, it had been left wrapped in a bundle. Opening it indicates that the K'iche' now believe they are in a position to exercise authority over other lineage groups.

[247] *e q'aq' wi e tepew wi* ("glories sovereignties"). *Q'aq'* means "glory, power" in K'iche'. *Tepew* is the K'iche' spelling of *tepeuh*, the Nahuatl equivalent term, meaning "power, sovereignty." Both Nakxik and Tulan are names derived from Nahuatl, the language of central Mexico. The power and authority symbolized by the "Bundled Glory" is therefore seen as ultimately derived from the prestige of central Mexican political rule.

[248] lines 1173–1192.

[249] *chalamakat*. According to Coto (1983 [ca. 1656], cxvi), *chalamecat* is a loan word from Nahuatl that means "to enchant," or to accomplish something through supernatural means.

[250] *juyub'* ("mountain"). Although the word literally means "mountain," it also refers to dangerous untamed areas, or "the wild." Untamed animals living outside populated areas are collectively called *juyub'al chicop* ("mountain/wild animals").

THE FIRST WAR WITH THE SEVEN NATIONS[251]

And so then they planned to kill our grandfathers and our fathers,[252] B'alam K'itze', B'alam Aq'ab', Majukotaj, and Ik'i B'alam. It was they who did it, the Seven Nations, the warriors.

, Soon thereafter, this became known in secret[253] to B'alam K'itze'. Immediately he went before Tojil and Awilix and told them of the plot by the Seven Nations to kill them. Then responded Tojil:

"Do not be afraid. When it is clear what day is set for the war, you will come to tell me," said Tojil, Awilix, and Jaqawitz.

Then the day was set by the Seven Nations and the tribes when B'alam K'itze', B'alam Aq'ab', Majukotaj, and Ik'i B'alam were to be killed. They, the warriors, armed[254] themselves with slings[255] and with spears, with crowns of precious metal and with lip plugs[256] of precious metal.

Then they waged the first war there at Jaqawitz. But they were not furious men or death bats.[257] They merely slept; they were drowsy.[258] They were merely sleeping

---

[251] lines 1193–1244.

[252] It is apparent that the Seven Nations ultimately understood that it was the K'iche' progenitors who were responsible for the disappearances among their people and that the wild animal tracks were merely a ruse. The meaning of this passage is more direct in the *Popol Vuh*: "Then they [the Seven Nations] would be taken to be sacrificed before the faces of Tohil and Auilix. Afterward their blood and skulls would be placed on the road. Thus the nations would say, 'a jaguar ate them.' This they would say because only the tracks of a jaguar were left behind. They would not reveal themselves. Many were abducted from the nations until after a long time, the nations came to their senses: 'Perhaps Tohil and Auilix have come after us. We shall merely seek out the bloodletters and the sacrificers'" (Christenson 2007, 238).

[253] *nataj* ("to become known"). According to Coto, the word implies knowledge gained through prognostication or prophecy, while Sáenz includes a gloss that this is knowledge obtained in secret.

[254] *xkiwiq* ("they adorned"). The word is not exclusive to adornments. When used in the context of warriors, it can also mean "to be armed." In this passage, both meanings are implied.

[255] *tzol*. From the context of the passage, this should be a weapon, paired with the following word for spear. *Tzol* does not appear in Colonial-era dictionaries. As a verb, the word means to revolve or spin around. Carmack and Mondloch (1983, 221, n. 118) suggest that based on this root meaning, *tzol* may be a sling.

[256] *tesakaw* ("lip plug"). Lip plugs and nose plugs were worn not only as ornaments in ancient Mesoamerica but also as symbols of authority (figs. 41 and 52).

[257] *kamasotz'* ("death bats"). In the *Popol Vuh*, the death bats were denizens of the otherworld realm of Xib'alb'a. They were terrible creatures that succeeded in cutting off the head of one of the Hero Twin gods, Junajpu: "Next they were put inside Bat House, which had only bats inside. It was a house of death bats. These were great beasts with snouts like blades that they used as murderous weapons" (Christenson 2007, 172). In this context, the warriors of the Seven Nations are described as lacking ferocity or fearsomeness.

[258] *xesayab'* ("they were drowsy"). According to Ximénez, the root of this word, *say*, means *dormilón* (Spanish for "drowsy person" or "sleepyhead").

when were taken away their slings and their spears, their crowns and their bracelets, along with what was on each of their little fingers and their little toes.[259] They were simply naked when they awoke. And so there was no war waged by them. They returned again to their mountain places.

THE SECOND WAR WITH THE SEVEN NATIONS[260]

For the second time they [the Seven Nations] met together, because a multitude of their children and sons had disappeared. There was war in their hearts, but they were unable to carry it out. It hadn't been long since they had gathered together before their breasts had been sucked,[261] when they had pleaded for fire. But they had not understood this.

This, then, is the second time that the day was set for war by the Seven Nations, the warriors, in order to kill our grandfathers and our fathers—B'alam K'itze', B'alam Aq'ab', Majukotaj, and Ik'i B'alam.

And again they [our grandfathers and our fathers] were instructed by Tojil, Awilix, and Jaqawitz. B'alam K'itze' said to Tojil and Awilix: "The day has just been set again for our being killed by the Seven Nations, the warriors, you Tojil, Awilix, and Jaqawitz," he said to them.

And so Tojil said to B'alam K'itze': "You shall make twelve effigies[262] armed with the slings and spears that you took from the Seven Nations. These you shall place on the effigies of carved wood. Place them atop the palisades.[263] And with these, place four great pots at the four corners of the buildings—one great pot of bumblebees, one great pot of wasps, one great pot of hornets, and one great pot of bees."

Because surely they were not many with B'alam K'itze', B'alam Aq'ab', Majukotaj, and Ik'i B'alam, it was inevitable that they would be persecuted by the Seven Nations, the warriors. On a day Ka'oq[264] they were nearly killed, they our grandfathers and our fathers.

---

[259] The expression implies that they were deprived of everything, down to what they wore on their pinkies and little toes. The removal of symbols of status, and nakedness in general, was a gesture of humiliation among the Maya.

[260] lines 1245–1389.

[261] kitu'xtz'umaxik ("their breasts were sucked"). This phrase alludes to sacrifice (see p. 101, n. 231).

[262] poy ("effigy, scarecrow, manikin").

[263] k'ej ("palisades, fences"). A line of wooden stakes or upright logs placed around a building or settlement for defense.

[264] Ka'oq. One of the twenty named days of the cholq'ij, or 260-day highland Maya calendar. The text indicates that the Seven Nations predetermined this day for the battle, likely by divination. Among modern-day traditionalist K'iche', ajq'ijab' ("they of days" or "daykeepers") are consulted to determine the day most propitious for important events or ceremonies. Each of the twenty named days of the cholq'ij carries certain auguries that, depending on the question, can be interpreted for good or ill. In modern Momostenango, the day Ka'oq (now pronounced

But they did great wonders and demonstrations of strength. There they showed their stride, their wondrous power, and their spirit essence. They fought by means of the effigies of carved wood and braziers of hot coals,[265] the bees and the wasps, the fiery comets[266] and the phantom globes of fire,[267] the strangulations and the sudden deaths,[268] the clouds and the mist, the great hailstorms, the earthquakes, and the thunderbolts, their stride and their gait.

Then they entered into war, they the Seven Nations and the tribes. But it was only the effigies of carved wood that fought. Surely thus ended their strength.

Then were opened the great pots by the beloved[269] wives of B'alam K'itze', B'alam Aq'ab', Majukotaj, and Ik'i B'alam. The great pots were opened, releasing the bees, the wasps, and the bumblebees. Thus were conquered they that belonged to the

---

Kawoq) is linked with the concept of "setting out," in the sense of preparing an altar or placing food on a table. On the days 1, 6, 8, and 9 Kawoq, *ajq'ijab'* visit shrines to place offerings on "the table," or altar, of the mountain deity as well as "to ask that any troubles placed there by their enemies be returned to those same enemies" (B. Tedlock 1982, 123). In this sense, Ka'oq would be a propitious day for the Seven Nations to exact vengeance on the K'iche'. In a K'iche' calendar composed in 1722, the day 11 Ka'oq is accompanied by the augury "there is only deceiving on this day, because he seized the prisoner by force; an evil day" (Weeks et al. 2009, 106), reinforcing the potential for violence and retribution on this day.

[265] *uchuk saqlaq'* ("hot coals brazier"). Apparently, the K'iche' used hot coals or embers from a large brazier to pour out onto their enemies below the walls.

[266] *ch'ab'i q'aq'* ("shooting fire"). *Ch'ab'ij* is to shoot an arrow from a bow. In the Coto dictionary, the phrase refers to comets, considered by the highland Maya to be a powerful portent for death or misfortune. In Momostenango, the K'iche' identify *ch'ab'i q'aq'* as "a shooting star, falling star, or meteor . . . Obsidian points and blades found by Momostecans in their cornfields today are considered to be the remains of falling stars" (B. Tedlock 1992, 180).

[267] *kaq tijax* ("red flint knife"). This is a ghost, phantasm, or phantom. Sáenz de Santa María (1940, 184) defines the phrase as "to appear in flames and fire (it applies to those who at night take the form of globes of fire)." The K'iche' people in the area of Momostenango often claim to have seen mysterious globes of light or fire floating around the mountains at night. Similar stories are told in the Lake Atitlán region, where the globes of light are said to emerge from San Jorge cave and then move quickly across the surface of the lake (Andrew Weeks, personal communication, 2020). The same pairing of comets and phantasms appears in the list of wonders performed by the first K'iche' progenitors in their battle with the Seven Nations (see p. 184). Karen Bassie suggests that on the most basic level, the *ch'ab'i q'aq'–kaq tijax* pairing is a contrast between obsidian arrow points and flint knife weapons and thus refers to warfare in general (personal communication, 2019).

[268] *qeteb' pub'a'ix. Qeteb'* is "strangulation." *Pub'a'ix* is "to be shot by a blowgun." The two terms are often paired in Early Colonial literature and dictionaries. In Coto, the paired terms refer to a malevolent or "fateful day." In the dictionaries compiled by both Ximénez and Bassetta, *pub'a'ix* refers to "sudden death."

[269] *xoq'ojawab'.* The term means both "esteemed" and "beloved." Either would be an appropriate translation in this context.

Seven Nations, the warriors. On the ground were they. They were on the ground. They threw down their slings and their spears, even their arrows and their shields. There were those who died. There were those who fled of the Seven Nations and the tribes. They no longer waged war. In vain they had made war.

Thus was realized the greatness of the K'iche'. Their glory and sovereignty came to be.

And now, these are the names of the Seven Nations. These therefore are the names of the Seven Nations who had desired to wage war there at Jaqawitz—Rotzayib', K'ib'aja, Uxab', B'akaj, and Keb'atzunja. These are they who caused war to be waged. They were the beginning of the civil war, the beginning as well of arrows and shields. Truly this was also the origin of the manifestation of glory and sovereignty by the K'iche' people before all of the warriors. Their greatness came forth.

THE THIRD ATTEMPT TO DEFEAT THE K'ICHE'[270]

For a third time, then, war was their desire; it was plotted[271] within the hearts of the Seven Nations and the tribes. They used their deadly words[272] to defeat our grandfathers and our fathers, B'alam K'itze', B'alam Aq'ab', Majukotaj, and Ik'i B'alam.

For seven days they bathed,[273] the sacrificers and bloodletters, our grandfathers and our fathers.

Then said the Seven Nations: "It is to our victory that they go to the hot springs,[274] to their bathing place. Is it not merely because they don't see the faces of women[275]

---

[270] lines 1390–1601.

[271] k'u'xlaj ("to plot"). The term may be used in non-malevolent ways, such as "to plan, to consider, or to contemplate," but Coto also defines it as "to conjure against someone," implying a plot against the progenitors.

[272] xkikamisaj chi kitzij ("they kill with their words"). The phrase indicates that the Seven Nations intend to wage war by means of deadly curses rather than the force of arms.

[273] The seven days of consecutive bathing suggests ritual cleansing rather than simple hygiene.

[274] miq'ina' ("hot springs, hot water"). The Popol Vuh does not specify that the bathing place of the K'iche' progenitors was a hot spring. Perhaps the emphasis here is due to the fact that the manuscript was composed at Totonicapán, whose K'iche' name is Chuwi' Miq'ina' ("Above the Hot Springs").

[275] kakil uwach ixoq ("they see her face woman"). An expression that is commonly used in K'iche' to imply sexual relations. Abstention from sex as well as fasting are important components of K'iche' ritual and ceremonialism. In the Popol Vuh, abstention from sex and abstention from food were among the primary responsibilities of rulers: "Truly great was the performance of their sacred obligations. This was the sign of their essence. Neither would they sleep with their women. They would merely provide for each other, fasting in the houses of the gods. Each day they would merely worship, merely burn offerings, and merely offer sacrifices. They were there in the darkness and at dawn weeping in their hearts and in their bowels, pleading

that they are glorious, that they have sovereignty? Thus we shall adorn and ornament with jewels three beautiful[276] girls. Perhaps then they will be enamored with them, and soon the hearts of Tojil, Awilix, and Jaqawitz will be deadened[277] because of them. Thus their deaths will be accomplished. We will be the cause of it," they said.

Thus was accomplished their word. The day was set for the defeat of our grandfathers and fathers by the Seven Nations, the warriors.

Soon, however, B'alam K'itze'[278] learned of it. They went as bathers to the hot springs. The three beautiful girls went to the hot springs as well. Soon the girls arrived there.

"Honor to you, ye lords.[279] We have come to you. We are the emissaries of our fathers [who said to us]: 'Go with them, the lords B'alam K'itze', B'alam Aq'ab', Majukotaj, and Ik'i B'alam. Go to speak with them and say this: 'What shall you want to give to us? Perhaps you shall want to join with us.'[280] This is what they said,

for the light and the lives of their vassals and servants. They would lift up their faces to the sky for their lordship" (Christenson 2007, 288). Traditionalist highland Maya today abstain from sex while preparing for major ceremonies in order to conserve spiritual power (Mendelson 1957, 240; Tarn and Prechtel 1990, 73; B. Tedlock 1992, 116; Early 2006, 224). Some important positions require celibacy for as long as the office is held (Mendelson 1958, 122; Carlsen 1997, 81; Christenson 2001, 258). If the vow to abstain from sex is broken, the individual loses the ability to carry out important ceremonies or may even be cursed with illness or death. Adultery in particular was a serious offense, and K'iche' often tell stories about the horrible deaths suffered by those who violate marital vows (Tarn and Prechtel 1990, 1997).

[276] *josq'ilaj* ("very beautiful"). The word also implies "clean, thin, delicate." There are more common terms for beautiful or clean (virginal); therefore, this may be a play on words as *jox*, similar to *josq'*, means "prostitute, adulteress, fornicator." This is much more explicit in the version of the story in the *Popol Vuh*. In that account, the lords of the Seven Nations hoped the maidens would be violated sexually (*xejox*) to shame the K'iche' (Christenson 2007, 243). Thus the lords of the Seven Nations commanded the maidens to seduce them: "undress yourselves before their faces. And if their hearts should desire you, then you shall offer yourselves to them . . . If you do not give yourselves to them, then we will kill you" (241).

[277] *k'elax uk'u'x* ("deadened their hearts"). The root verb means to be "paralyzed, deadened, withered." The phrase is used to describe someone who is not "obedient, [who does not] pay attention, or [who does not] respond to another" because their hearts are dead to them. The implication is that if the K'iche' lords were to violate the rules of sexual propriety, they would be abandoned by their gods and therefore left defenseless.

[278] Only B'alam K'itze' is mentioned here; however, he is referred to consistently in the following section as "them" or "they." Apparently, the authors wished to avoid listing all four names of the progenitors repeatedly, although their involvement is implied.

[279] Throughout this section, the three maidens address the lords of the Seven Nations as well as the K'iche' progenitors with the formal *alaq* ("ye"), while the lords address the maidens with the more familiar *ix* ("you").

[280] *kixk'ule' quk'* ("you join with us"). This is also an expression that implies sexual relations or marriage.

they our fathers Rotzjayib', Uxab', K'ib'aja, B'akaj, and Keb'atzunja," said the maidens to B'alam K'itze'.

Then they reached an accord.

"That's good then, you, our daughters. Say: 'We just spoke with them, the lords. We saw their faces as well,'[281] this you shall say to your fathers, you, our daughters," said B'alam K'itze'.

"Yet this was our task, ye lords: 'Bring the sign that you truly spoke with them. If the sign is not brought by you, then we will kill you. You will be cut into pieces[282] before the face of the river, before the face of the ravine.' This is what our fathers said to us, ye lords. Favor us. Give the sign to us," said the maidens.

Then B'alam K'itze' responded with accord: "Wait. Surely we will give the sign to you," the maidens were told.

Then B'alam K'itze' went before the faces of Tojil, Awilix, and Jaqawitz. "You, Tojil and Awilix, what should be the sign of this word that we shall give to them, these maidens, the daughters of the Seven Nations?"

Said then Tojil and Awilix: "Paint[283] three robes[284] to give to them—one with wasps within, one with a jaguar within, and one with an eagle within. These will be draped around them as their gifts," said Tojil, Awilix, and Jaqawitz to B'alam K'itze'.

Then, therefore, were painted three robes by B'alam K'itze' to be given to the three maidens, the daughters of the Seven Nations. These were the names of the maidens: Jun Puch,[285] Jun Tax,[286] and Jun K'ib'atz'unja.[287]

Then they bore the three painted gifts to their fathers. They rejoiced as they went.

---

[281] *mi puch qil kiwach* ("we also just now saw their faces"). This is a play on words. For a young woman to "see the face" of a man is a euphemism for sexual relations in K'iche'. Although the three maidens did see the faces of B'alam K'itze' and his brothers, they did not succeed in seducing them as the expression might imply.

[282] Perhaps a play on words, as the names of the maidens are given later in the section as Jun Puch ("One Eviscerate"), Jun Tax ("One Slice"), and Jun K'ib'atzunja ("One Giver of Much Pain House").

[283] *chitz'ib'aj* ("paint"). The word is used for both writing and painting. Both were done with a paintbrush.

[284] *k'ul* ("robe"). It is difficult to know precisely what type of clothing this might have been in Pre-Columbian times. Basseta refers to it as a *manta*, Spanish for a large woven cloth worn wrapped around the body like a robe or cloak.

[285] Jun Puch ("One Eviscerate"). In the *Popol Vuh*, her name is Xpuch ("Lady Eviscerator").

[286] Jun Tax ("One Slice"). In the *Popol Vuh*, her name is Xtaj ("Lady Lust").

[287] Jun K'ib'atz'unja. *K'i* is "many." *B'atz'un* is "to spin thread" but with implied meanings as well of "to bind, to give pain, to arm for battle, or to marry." *Ja* is "house," often appended to women's names to indicate a female founder or leader of a lineage. Considering the context and the names of the other maidens, this woman's name may be translated as "Giver of Much Pain House" or "Much Binding House."

When they arrived, their fathers also greatly rejoiced for their gifts, they the lords of the Seven Nations.

" 'Each of these robes, then, is theirs; they belong to each of your fathers,' said the Lord B'alam K'itze'," they said to their fathers.

Immediately one of the lords took his robe, the one with the wasps inside. He put it on his back and immediately the wasps came to life and stung the flesh of the lord. Likewise, then, the eagle inside the other robe came to life. The eagle and the jaguar bit the lords, they the lords of the [Seven] Nations.

"Was it not to torment us that you have brought their gifts? You are demons,"[288] they said to their daughters.

Thus was ended the war of the nations against Jaqawitz Ch'ipaq by the greatness and glory of the K'iche'. Then was the manifestation of the glory and sovereignty of the K'iche' people before the faces of all the warriors. It came forth, the greatness of our grandfathers and our fathers, B'alam K'itze', B'alam Aq'ab', Majukotaj, and Ik'i B'alam. Here, then, they came to know the glory and sovereignty that was done at Jaqawitz Ch'ipaq.

A great many cycles of twenty years they completed there at Jaqawitz.

THE JOURNEY OF K'OKA'IB' TO THE PLACE WHERE THE SUN EMERGES[289]

This, now, is the inception[290] of lordship by B'alam K'itze'[291] over the defeated Seven Nations.

And so they [the K'iche' progenitors] said: "They shall go, our envoys, there before Lord Nakxik, to the place where the sun emerges. They did not defeat us, they, the Seven Nations, the warriors. They did not cause us to disappear or destroy us. Nor have they cast down our day, our birth,[292] our names, or our faces. May this be so henceforth," they said.

---

[288] *k'axtok'anel* ("demons, deceivers"). This is a derogatory term for harmful beings, either human or supernatural, particularly when the harm is some form of deception or trickery. In the Colonial period, Christian missionaries used the word to refer to devils, and this is still the most common usage in modern K'iche' communities. "Demon" or "rascal" is perhaps closer to the authors' intent here.

[289] lines 1602–1754.

[290] *na'oxikik* ("inception, contemplation"). This is something that has been "thought through" carefully.

[291] B'alam K'itze' is referred to as "them," implying that his three brothers are also included.

[292] *qa q'ij qalaxik* ("our day, our birth"). This pairing is commonly used to refer to the fortunes of a person or group, for good or ill. The same couplet appears in the *Popol Vuh* three times. For example, the gods of the K'iche' people declare themselves to have attained greatness: "It is here that our mountain and our plain shall be. We have come to be yours. Great is our day

And so they were sent, the two sons of B'alam K'itze'. These, then, are the names of the two sons of B'alam K'itze', they who were given their task—K'oka'ib' and K'okawib'. They went to the place where the sun emerges to obtain lordship.

One went under orders to the place where the sun emerges. The other went to the place where the sun sets. K'oka'ib' went to the place where the sun emerges. K'okawib' went to the place where the sun sets.

K'oka'ib' quickly went straight[293] to the place where the sun emerges.

But he, K'okawib', merely returned from the sea. He did not cross the sea but returned from Mexico.[294] Then he diminished his heart.[295] He lay[296] in secret with his sister-in-law, the wife of K'oka'ib'. He engendered a son. Surely it was he, B'alam K'okawib'.

The child was in a cradle when K'oka'ib' learned of it. He had gone to receive the canopy[297] and the throne, the paw of the puma and the paw of the jaguar, as well as the *titil* stone[298] and the yellow stone. This was accomplished when K'oka'ib' went there. He received also the floral vessel[299] of precious metal and the rattle of pre-

---

(*qaq'ij*). Great as well is our birth (*qalaxik*), because of all your people and all the nations. We shall surely be your companions then, your citadel. We shall give to you your knowledge" (Christenson 2007, 234).

[293] *suk'ulik* ("straightaway"). In this context, the word means to go somewhere without deviation.

[294] Xico. I agree with Carmack and Mondloch (1983, 225, n. 146) who suggest that this is a contracted form of "Mexico." Mexico is the area governed by the Mexica (otherwise known as the Aztecs) at the time of the Spanish Conquest. In the *Popol Vuh*, the progenitors of the K'iche' considered the Yaki people of Mexico to be their "brothers," although they remained behind in the East when the various lineages separated after leaving Tulan: "'We were separated there at Tulan Zuyva. We left them to come here. But we were complete before we came here.' This they said among themselves when they remembered their older brothers and their younger brothers, the Yaki people. These dawned there in Mexico, as it is called today. Thus surely a portion of them remained there in the East, they whose names are Tepeu and Oliman" (Christenson 2007, 231).

[295] *xuch'utinaj uk'u'x* ("he made small his heart"). According to Coto, the phrase means that he became "despicable." Sáenz lists the phrase as "pusillanimous, cowardly."

[296] *xjoxow*. Literally, "he plowed." "To plow" is a common euphemism for sex, which is the obvious meaning here.

[297] *muj* ("canopy"). Literally, "shade." It is used in Early Colonial highland Maya literature to refer to a canopy held or affixed over a throne.

[298] *titil* ("stone"). Derived from the Nahuatl, *tetl/tetil*, the general word for "stone," forming a couplet with *q'an ab'aj* (K'iche' for "yellow/precious stone"). Elsewhere in the text, the couplet of stone and yellow stone refers to an ornament inserted through a pierced nose as a marker of high status (see p. 164, n. 590). The type of "yellow stone" is undefined. Possibilities include agate, jasper, citrine (yellow quartz), or amber, all of which can be found in the Maya highlands.

[299] *kotz'ijab'al* ("flower place or thing"). *Kotz'ij* is "flower" but also anything that smells sweet, such as perfume. This is most likely a container or vessel for flowers or some aromatic

Figure 31. "The floral vessel of precious metal." Pots of flowers in front of an altar, Cofradía San Juan, Santiago Atitlán, 2005.

cious metal. These belonged to the Mama Ajtz'alam,[300] the Rajpop Ajtz'alam,[301] the Utza'm Chinamital.[302]

Then said K'okawib': "It is true that right away[303] I did it. I was on the road when I was nearly hanged.[304] I returned because of this."

substance. In modern highland Maya ceremonies, sacred objects as well as participants are censed with incense smoke as well as sprayed with a sweet liquid. In Santiago Atitlán, this is often men's cologne dispensed from an aerosol can. Alternatively, vessels of flowers are placed on and around the altars of ritual houses as a token of life as well as a means of scenting the air of the interior. Flowers and their aroma are said to reflect the presence of deities and ancestors.

[300] *mama ajtz'alam* ("ancestral nobleman"). According to the Ximénez dictionary, *ajtz'alam* is a "lord who has a throne." Coto glosses the word as "prince, noble."

[301] *rajpop ajtz'alam* ("Ajpop of the noblemen").

[302] *utza'm chinamital* ("its nose/leader lineage"). An honorific title for the head of a lineage.

[303] *chiyan* ("right away"). This is a play on words. According to Coto, the phrase means "right away." But as a verb, Bassetta glosses the word as "to be ashamed," and *iyan* is to "engender children."

[304] *jitz'axoq* ("hanged, bound, caught in a net"). This presages the ultimate fate of K'okawib' who, according to the *Relación de Zapotitlán*, hanged himself out of fear of the consequences of committing adultery with his sister-in-law (Acuña 1982, 60).

He arrived then, the Lord K'oka'ib'. "Who shall set aside[305] the child?" His heart despaired.

And thus he divided the lordship between themselves.

These, then, were the signs of the lordship of K'oka'ib'—truly the canopy and the throne, the puma and the jaguar, the shining image[306] and the floral vessel of precious metal. These belonged to the Mama Ajtz'alam, the Rajpop Ajtz'alam, and the Utza'm Chinamital.

These were the first chosen ones, they who paid heed to the misery of their people, their sons and their younger brothers. They were the victors in war, the conquerors of the earth—they of the Great House, the place of sacrifice.[307] They are the punishers, the captors,[308] and the chasteners. The sons and the younger brothers of the ancient lords first received their burdens of authority[309] from K'oka'ib'.

This, then, was done at Jaqawitz. And thus it will be manifested henceforth.

Three times thirteen score [days][310] K'oka'ib' journeyed before he returned from the place where the sun emerges. The child was in his cradle when he arrived.

"Who is the child?" asked K'oka'ib' of the noblewoman.[311]

---

[305] *xchijachaj* ("it shall be divided, separated, set aside"). This is another example of a play on words. The implication may be that he questions whether or not to separate or set aside the child from its mother or from the lineage. But the word is also used to refer to "betrayal." Another possibility is that the authors are playing off the similarity of the root verb with *jach'aj* ("to harvest maize"), suggesting that K'oka'ib' is wondering who had "harvested" the child from his wife. "Plowing a maize field" is a common metaphor for sex in highland Maya languages.

[306] *waqachib'al. Waq* is something shiny or brilliant. According to Coto, *chib'al* is a "figure or image."

[307] *sokb'a[l] kiwi'* ("place of sacrifice their heads"). This is one of the major structures located at the K'iche' capital at Chi Q'umarkaj. It is illustrated on the "map" on the first folio page of the Totonicapán document with the label *sokib'al* (see pp. 54, 56, n. 6).

[308] *ximonel.* Literally "binders," but commonly used to refer to the taking of captives, binding them with cords or ropes.

[309] *eqale'n* ("burden, authority"). Offices and positions of authority in K'iche' communities are often referred to as "burdens," which demand great sacrifices in time, resources, and physical health from overwork and stress.

[310] *oxmul oxlaju winaq. Winaq* is literally "person" but also the number twenty (or score). The Maya utilized a vigesimal (base twenty) rather than a decimal (base ten) numbering system. The word for twenty is *winaq* because a person has twenty fingers and toes. Thus this phrase is equivalent to "three times thirteen twenties (780)."

[311] *xoqojaw* ("female lord, noblewoman, wife of a ruler, principal wife"). This is a rarely used title in the text, and it is in the unpossessed form. *Rixoqil* ("his wife") is used consistently elsewhere and always in the possessed form. In the next sentence, she is simply referred to as *ixoq* ("woman"). The authors may have wished to use a less personal term due to her infidelity, although it is also possible that they chose to emphasize her status as a noblewoman.

"He is merely as if[312] he were of thy flesh, of thy skin. But also he, thy older brother, thy younger brother, he is the one responsible,"[313] said the woman.

"So be it then. He shall not be rejected, nor shall he be cursed. I will give to him his lordship. I will also give to him his glory and his sovereignty," said K'oka'ib'.

Then he uncovered[314] the face of the cradle. "He, then, this little boy—B'alam K'onache[315] he shall be called for as long as the sun shall move, for as long as there shall be light," said then K'oka'ib'.[316]

Thus was the advent of the first lordship, and this was because of K'oka'ib'.

It was then that K'okawib' engendered a child with his sister-in-law, and this was the conception of he whose name was K'onache Ristayul,[317] as the lord is called

---

[312] *je* ("like, as if"). The wife of K'oka'ib' suggests that the child is practically his, because it was his brother who was the father. Siblings are considered to be of the same flesh and blood in K'iche' society.

[313] *ajchoq'e* ("master, owner, responsible one").

[314] *xuk'onok'a'* ("to uncover, shave head, make bare a plot of land"). This is a play on words. K'oka'ib' uncovers the child's cradle and calls the child K'onache ("bald"), partly as a reference to the "uncovering" of his wife's adultery and perhaps because K'onache will be "bald" in later life.

[315] B'alam K'onache ("Jaguar Bald One").

[316] The *Relación de Zapotitlán*, published in 1579, includes a parallel account of this incident: "This Co Caibim [K'okawib' in the Totonicapán text], the second brother, because of the absence of his brother, who travelled away from his house, had a son by his sister-in-law. And when his brother returned, recognizing the penalty under the law that had been instituted before, out of fear he hanged himself. The son that he had engendered with his sister-in-law was hidden away by a grandmother of his. And when the child came of age, his uncle and step-father gave to him the office of his father, which was to be one of the *ajpops*. Therefore, in Co Caib [K'oka'ib' in the Totonicapán text] remained the reign and kingdom, while another person governed who was not the king ... And from the second brother who was called Co Caibim, descended all those that were called *ajpops*, until the coming of a successor who was called Co Nache, the grandfather of Don Juan Cortés who at the present time lives" (Acuña 1982, 59–60, author translation).

[317] K'onache Ristayul ("Bald One His White Heart"). Lyle R. Campbell (1983, 85–86) suggests that Istayul is derived from the Nahuatl *ista* ("white") and *yul or yullotli* ("heart"), giving a reading of "White Heart." This is the only highland Maya document to give Ristayul as one of the names of K'onache, and it is also the only text that claims he held the secondary office of Ajpop K'amja (see also p. 154). This section of the *Title of Totonicapán* casts doubt on the legitimacy of K'onache and his descendants to hold the highest office among the Nima K'iche', that of Ajpop, a clear indication that rivalry existed among the various branches of the Kaweq lineage. In the *Popol Vuh*, K'onache is named as the Ajpop with B'elejeb Kej as the secondary Ajpop K'amja (Christenson 2007, 262). The *Popol Vuh* also claims that K'onache founded the office of Ajpop and that Istayul was the Ajpop K'amja in the next generation that succeeded K'onache and B'elejeb Kej (293). The *Título Yax* repeats the same line of succession as the *Popol Vuh* (Carmack and Mondloch 1989, 51). In the *Historia Quiché de Don*

today. Then also was the conception of the Ajpo K'amjayil,[318] the second lordship, held by Lord Stayul as he is called.

He, then, the first Lord K'oka'ib', was the son of B'alam K'itze', the Lord Ajpop Kaweq.[319]

THE JOURNEY TO THE PLACE WHERE THE SUN
EMERGES AS TOLD BY DIEGO REYNOSO[320]

Hear ye now the straightforward truth.[321] The account shall be told. I shall speak with esteem[322] of their nature. I shall write then, I, Diego Reynoso, Popol Winaq,[323] son of Laju No'j. We shall begin now the tale of their journey, they the three enchanted people. For a second time they went to the place where the sun emerges. These were their names—K'oka'ib', K'okawib', and K'o'akul Akutaq'.[324] These went to the place where the sun emerges before the face of Lord Nakxik.

Juan de Torres, K'onache is described as the legitimate son of the wife of K'okawib' and is the only ruler listed in that generation, presumably the Ajpop. In the same text, K'onache is described as "illustrious" and his mother as a "princess" (Recinos 1957, 44–45). In the *Xpantzay Cartulary*, K'onache is referred to as the "leader" of the Kaweq and not a subsidiary lord (Maxwell and Hill 2006, 679, 684). The *Relación de Zapotitlán* is the only other text that claims that K'onache was the illegitimate son of K'okawib' but nevertheless agrees that he held the title of Ajpop (Acuña 1982, 60; see n. 316).

[318] Ajpo[p] K'amjayil ("He of the Mat Reception House"). This is the second highest office among the K'iche', second only to the Ajpop. "Reception House" likely refers to a reception hall for meeting with visiting dignitaries or for receiving tribute. Coto defines *k'amja* as a "messenger," perhaps referring to this official's responsibilities as an "emissary, envoy, or legate" for the Ajpop.

[319] B'alam K'itze' was thus the first to hold the title of Ajpop, the principal lord of the ruling Kaweq lineage.

[320] lines 1755–1932.

[321] *suk'ulikil*. Literally, "straightness," but with the implication of "truth."

[322] *xchinloq'bij* ("I shall speak with esteem"). *Loq'* ("esteem/respect/love/honor") is inserted into the verb to emphasize that this speech is delivered with "esteem." Reynoso then describes the honorable journey of both K'oka'ib' and K'okawib' to Tulan, contradicting the previous narrative in which K'okawib' is characterized as an adulterer who did not successfully make it to Tulan. This chapter appears to have been inserted into the narrative to assert the honorable nature of K'okawib' in the face of his slanderous treatment elsewhere in the text.

[323] Popol Winaq ("Mat Person") is the head of a ruling or deliberative council, the unity of the council symbolized by the interlaced reeds in a woven mat. Diego Reynoso was a K'iche' nobleman who accepted Christianity soon after the Spanish Invasion and subsequently worked closely with the Spanish clergy. Reynoso was the son of Laju[j] No'j, who served at the K'iche' royal court in the capital city of Q'umarkaj (see p. 23).

[324] The *Popol Vuh* also lists three lords who went to the court of Nakxik/Nakxit: K'o Ka'ib' representing the Kaweqib', K'o Akutek of the Nijayib', and K'o Ajaw of the Ajaw K'iche'

They received their lordship—the puma throne and the jaguar throne, the bone flute and the drum. These represented the authority of the lords Ajpop, Ajpop K'amja, and the Q'alel Atzij Winaq.[325]

Then came forth the Nim Ch'okoj Kaweq.[326] Mere bench sitters[327] they came to be. They were not declared to be great leaders, or great fasters, or penitents. Neither did they obtain lordship. They went to receive their authority because of B'alam K'itze'.

Then they arrived before Lord Nakxik. They pleaded for their authority from Lord Nakxik. Thus they were given lordship by Lord Nakxik.

And so K'oka'ib' and K'okawib'[328] returned. Along with the Nim Ch'okoj Kaweq they arrived here. They distributed their authority.

"It has been accomplished. We have done it. They have come; these signs of authority have come," they said.

Then they distributed their authority.

But they did not declare as great leaders the Ajtz'isomcha, Ajkuk'umam, or K'a'am.

For nine score days, for thirteen score days,[329] they would fast. They would undergo suffering, the suffering of lordship.[330]

(Christenson 2007, 256). In Reynoso's version of the story, K'okawib' of the Kaweqib' replaces K'o Ajaw, perhaps to justify having both offices—Ajpop and Ajpop K'amja—held by the Kaweq lineage.

[325] Q'alel A[j]tzij Winaq ("magistrate scribe/speaker person"). The *q'alel* title is the third highest position in the ruling Nima K'iche' line and is linked with the Nijayib' lineage.

[326] Nim Ch'okoj Kaweq ("Great Steward of the Kaweq"). See pp. 25–26 on the role of the Nim Ch'okoj in the K'iche' hierarchy.

[327] Diego Reynoso goes out of his way to denigrate the Nim Ch'okoj Kaweq, playing on the words *Nim Ch'okoj* ("Great Seater") to say that he is nothing but a "bench sitter" with no authority or important ritual responsibilities. Although only the Nim Ch'okoj of the Kaweq lineage is mentioned here, the text refers to the Nim Ch'okoj in the plural, no doubt to demean all those who hold this office. The *Popol Vuh* was most likely composed by the Nim Ch'okoj of all the three ruling K'iche' lineages soon after the Totonicapán text was signed (Christenson 2007, 36–37; D. Tedlock 1985, 60–61). The authors of the *Popol Vuh* praise the Nim Ch'okok as important lords, perhaps in part as an answer to Diego Reynoso's insulting description: "These, then, are the three Great Stewards [Nim Ch'okoj]. They are like the fathers of all the K'iche' lords. As one the three stewards gathered together as the givers of birth, the mothers of the word, and the fathers of the word" (Christenson 2007, 305).

[328] In Reynoso's version of the journey to Tulan, there is no mention of K'okawib's adulterous affair with the wife of K'oka'ib', and it also does not appear in the *Popol Vuh*.

[329] *b'elej winaq oxlaju winaq* ("nine score, thirteen score"). It is probable from the context of this passage that the authors are referring to periods of time, although they do not specify what length of period it is. For clarity of meaning I have chosen "days," which is the most likely implied meaning here.

[330] Fasting and penitential abstention practices were important responsibilities for highland

Then they distributed to B'alam K'onache these—the canopy of quetzal feathers and the canopy of cotinga feathers, the puma throne and the jaguar throne, the bone flute[331] and the drum, the *titil* stone[332] and the yellow stone, the head and the hooves of the deer,[333] the talon of the eagle and the paw of the jaguar, the shell[334] and the net of tobacco,[335] the feathers of the beautiful bird[336] and the feathers of the snowy egret,[337] the tail feather of the vulture and the bracelet of precious stones,[338]

Maya rulers, carried out on behalf of their people. A fuller description is given in the *Popol Vuh*: "They [the K'iche' lords] were great in their essence. Great as well were their fasts. In order to venerate their temples and venerate their sovereignty, they fasted for long periods of time and sacrificed before the faces of their gods. And this was their method of fasting: for nine score days they would fast, and for nine they would sacrifice and burn offerings. Then for thirteen score days they would observe a fast and for thirteen they would sacrifice and burn offerings before the face of Tohil, as well as before the faces of the other gods. They would eat only zapotes, matasanos, and jocotes. They would not eat food made from maize" (Christenson 2007, 288).

[331] *su'b'aq* ("bone flute"). Ximénez defines this as "a great flute." Sáenz lists *suibak* as a large flute used to accompany dances. Coto (1983 [ca. 1656], 234) notes that the *su'b'aq* flute is played along with the drum at dances. The flute and drum are commonly used by modern Maya to accompany important ceremonies and dances (see figure 32).

[332] *titil*. Derived from *tetl*, Nahuatl for "stone." Carmack and Mondloch (1983, 129) translate this as "black stone," although no color is referenced directly here. Alternatively, Bassetta lists *titil* as "bright powder." Ximénez (1985 [1701], 536) interprets *titil* as an "unguent with which they (K'iche') paint/smear" (see also pp. 113, n. 298; 137, n. 434).

[333] The principal symbol for the patron deity of the ruling Kaweq lineage, Tojil, was a deerskin. This may be what is referred to here, as Tojil was given to the progenitors by Nakxik at Tulan (see p. 105). In the *Popol Vuh*, the deerskin was highly venerated: "When you are asked, 'Where is Tohil?' It will be this deerskin bundle that you shall show them. But do not reveal yourselves. Do this now and your existence shall become great. You shall conquer all the nations ... They did the same [offer sacrifices] before the deerskin bundles. They would burn pine resin, pericón flowers, and stevia flowers. There was a deerskin bundle for each of them on the tops of the mountains" (Christenson 2007, 234–235).

[334] *t'ot'* ("shell"). In the *Popol Vuh*, this symbol of authority is identified as a *t'ot' tatam* ("shell rattle") (Christenson 2007, 258).

[335] *matak'us*. This is a compound word derived from *matat* (Nahuatl for "net or net pouch") and *k'utz* (Yucatec Maya for "tobacco"). A number of the names for these objects given to the progenitors by Nakxik of Tulan are borrowed from the Mexican Nahuatl language, an indication of respect for Mexican centers of power, authority, and political legitimacy. Tobacco plays a major role in Maya ceremonies, both ancient and modern.

[336] *ch'ayom*. Colonial dictionaries gloss this as an unidentified type of bird. As an adjective, it is "chosen, beautiful."

[337] *astapulul* ("snowy egret"). Derived from the Nahuatl *aztatl* ("great heron, great egret, or snowy egret") and *veypul* or *pul* ("great or large") (Campbell 1983, 84; Molina 2001 [1571], II.10, I.66).

[338] *makutax*. Derived from the Nahuatl *macuextli*, a "string of precious stones worn on the wrist" (Molina 2001 [1571], II.51).

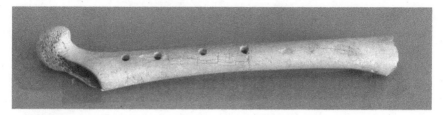

Figure 32. Bone flute, Iximche'. National Museum of Archaeology and Ethnology, Guatemala City.

the braid[339] and the ear ornament of stone.[340] These were arranged in order for the envoys there at the place where the sun emerges.

"May the lords take these as their signs," the envoys were told.

He, the Lord Ajpop, had four canopies of cotinga feathers above his throne.[341] There also were the bone flute player and the drum player.

He, the Ajpop K'amja, had three canopies above his head. He, the Great Ajpop of the Valiant Men,[342] had two canopies above his head and he, the Lesser Ajpop of the Valiant Men,[343] had one canopy above his head in the Plume House.[344] They would take these, but they did not have their bone flute or their drum because they were vassals.

Thus, this was the authority of the lords when they arrived, when they came from the place where the sun emerges—eternal authority.

---

[339] *malili.* Derived from the Nahuatl *mali* ("twisted, braided"). *Malinqui* is a twisted cord; *malichtic* is a long braid of hair. In Classic Maya art, the *jal*, or "braid," motif is a common element of royal headdresses positioned directly in front of the ear.

[340] *nakat ab'aj.* A compound word derived from the Nahuatl *nacatz* ("ear") and the K'iche' *ab'aj* ("stone"). *Nacazteyollotl* is an implement for piercing ears; *nacazticpac* is "something on the ears" (Molina 2001 [1571], II.62). This object may be an ear ornament, which I prefer in this context, or a stone implement used to pierce ears. Nose and ear ornaments are markers of high status in Mesoamerica.

[341] Alonso de Zorita (1963, 272), the judge of the Audiencia of Mexico (1556–1564), wrote that in Pre-Columbian times, the ancient K'iche' were distinguished in rank by the numbers of canopies they had over their thrones: "The principal lord had three canopies or mantles adorned with fine featherwork over his seat, the second had two, and the third one."

[342] Nima Rajpop Kaweq Achij ("Great Ajpop of Valiant Men"). Ajpop is a title given to lords or rulers, as well as to those who sit on ruling councils. Achij is derived from *achi* ("man"), but in Early Colonial highland Maya literature this form refers specifically to warriors. Coto (1983 [ca. 1656], 327) glosses the term to include "valiant, brave."

[343] Ch'uti Rajpop Achij ("Lesser Ajpop of Valiant Men"). A lesser rank of military ruler.

[344] Pa Xik'aja ("At Plume/Wing House"). Carmack (1973, 282, 340; cf. Carmack and Mondloch 1983, 229, n. 170) notes that the Plume House is also mentioned in the *Título K'oyoy* where it is specifically linked to military leaders.

Figure 33. "There also were the bone flute player and the drum player." Kaqchikel drum and flute players, Santiago Atitlán, 2002.

Then came the Q'alelay bench,[345] the Atzij Winaqil bench, the Nim Ch'okojil bench, the Q'ale K'amja'il bench, and the Nima K'amja'il bench.

There were four Ajtojil,[346] three Ch'okoj, three Utza'm Pop, three Yakol Ja,[347] and many Ajpop K'amja behind the K'iche'.

Then arrived that which belonged to the Ajaw K'iche'—then arrived the Atzij Winaqil bench, as well as those of the Lolmet Ajaw and the Nim Ch'okoj.

These belonged to the lord of Jaqawitz of the Ajaw K'iche'.

[345] Q'alelay *tem* ("Q'alel's bench"). The following four offices pertain to the Nijayib' branch of the K'iche'. Q'alel was the highest office in this lineage. Benches represent authority and status. The *Relación de Zapotitlán* describes Co Caib (K'oka'ib' in this text) as the ancestor who first established the laws and organization of the K'iche' kingdom: "Co Caib was he that inherited the reign of his father, and the first who made it a republic. This Co Caib subjected to himself eleven dominions of his ancestors, and was the first to found a town. He was the first to give seats . . . and to appoint governors and captains. He established the heads of the assemblies. He was the first to establish laws and charters and it was he who caused each of those that he had taken and conquered to pay tribute. And those who did not have to pay tribute served him in the things in which they had reached an accord" (Acuña 1982, 59–60, author translation).

[346] Ajtojil ("She/He/They of Tojil"). These are noblemen dedicated to the care of the god Tojil, the patron deity of the ruling Kaweq lineage of the K'iche'.

[347] Yakol Ja ("Builders/Patrons House").

Figure 34.
"Then came the Q'alelay bench, the Atzij Winaqil bench." Bench for indigenous authorities, Cofradía Santa Cruz, Santiago Atitlán, 2006.

There were only three Nima Ch'okoj, they who gave birth to the benches. They merely received these in company with the lords [Aj]pop and [Ajpop] K'amja at the place where the sun emerges. From there came the designations of K'iche' lordship, the K'iche' [Aj]pop and the K'iche' [Ajpop] K'amja, the lordly people.

And so their hearts were consoled—B'alam K'itze', B'alam Aq'ab', Majukotaj, and Ik'i B'alam. Their sons were invested with lordship atop the mountain Jaqawitz Ch'ipaq.

THE LINEAGE OF THE FOUNDERS OF THE K'ICHE' PEOPLE[348]

Hear ye this day of the suffering of our grandfathers and our fathers; of the fasting and affliction there on the mountain Jaqawitz. B'alam K'itze' was our grandfather, we, the Kaweqib'. Here, then, began the engendering of sons by B'alam K'itze', B'alam Aq'ab', and Majukotaj. He, Ik'i B'alam, died in his youth.

These, then, are the sons of B'alam K'itze'. His first sons were K'ok'oja and K'oraxonamaq'. These were the names of the two sons of B'alam K'itze'.

And again, K'ok'oja and K'oraxonamaq' engendered sons, E' and Tz'ikin.

And again, they engendered sons. Tz'ikin engendered Aj and Kan.[349] These, then, are the names of his engendered sons, the fourth generation of their people.

---

[348] lines 1933–1994.

[349] E' ("Tooth"), Tz'ikin ("Bird"), Aj ("Maizecob"), and Kan ("Captive") are all days from the highland Maya 260-day sacred calendar, or *cholq'ij*. It was common practice among the ancient K'iche' to name children after the day on which they were born.

The fifth generation of people, then, are K'oka'ib' and K'okawib'. Aj and Kan engendered the fifth generation of people.

Five, then, were the sons engendered by K'oka'ib'—Kejnay, K'oyoy, Xmaykej, Chokoy, and Laq'amal. These were the engendered sons of K'oka'ib'.

He, then, K'okawib', engendered K'onache, the illegitimate child of his mother, Tzipitawar.[350] This was the name of the wife [of K'oka'ib'].

Six generations were engendered, were set in order.[351]

THE ARRIVAL OF THE FIRST DAWN[352]

Then they went to receive lordship at the place where the sun emerges. And this, then, is what B'alam K'itze' and B'alam Aq'ab' were counseled by Tojil, Awilix, and Jaqawitz: "You lords: For only a little while more will there be no dawn. Therefore, prepare yourselves. Take us away from here and it will become a mercy to you. Place us, then, within hidden forests. There you will come to speak to us. For there comes a great light; there come as well the sun, moon, and stars. We, then, will be manifested again because of you," said Tojil to B'alam K'itze', B'alam Aq'ab', Majukotaj, and Ik'i B'alam.

So then B'alam K'itze' obeyed. He went to place Tojil within a great forest.

---

[350] Tzipitawar is a Nahuatl name, derived from *tzipitl*. According to the Molina (2001 [1571], 152) dictionary, this is a child who is "ill or disillusioned because her mother is pregnant." The implication is that the pregnancy is illicit. This may be her given name, but more likely it is an epithet given to her because of her adultery. Alternatively, it may suggest that her mother was also a person of questionable character.

[351] Another version of this genealogy appears on pp. 154–155. The *Relación de Zapotitlán* contains a similar genealogy for the Kaweq line: "Balam Quitze, the elder brother, had two sons: the one was called Co Coha and the other Co Rojon Amac . . . Co Coha engendered E . . . Co Rojon Amac, the second son of Balam Quitze and the brother of Co Coha, engendered Tziquin . . . E, the Indigenous king because he was the elder brother, engendered Ah . . . Tziquin engendered Can . . . Ah, an Indigenous lord, engendered Co Caib [K'oka'ib' in the *Title of Totonicapán*] and Co Caiuim [K'okawib' in the *Title of Totonicapán*] . . . This Co Caib engendered Queh Nay and another five sons . . . And from then until the arrival of the Spaniards, the kings bore this name of Queh Nay because among the Indigenous people it was like the title Caesar. And from the second brother, who was called Co Cai[u]im, descended all of those who were called *ah pops* until the arrival of a successor who was called Co Nache, the grandfather of Don Juan Cortés who lives to this day. This Co Nache died in the battle that the adelantado Don Pedro de Alvarado waged in the valley of the pueblo of Quetzaltenango, which pertains to the Royal Crown" (Acuña 1982, 59–60, author translation). According to both sources, K'oka'ib' and K'okawib' (Co Caib and Co Caiuim/Caibim in the *Relación de Zapotitlán*) were not the literal sons of B'alam K'itze' but were his great-great-grandsons (the fifth generation of K'iche' lords).

[352] lines 1995–2137.

Figure 35. "Immediately he named the forest Pa Tojil." View of the hilltop site of Jaqawitz Ch'ipaq from the forested mountain of Pa Tojil. Photograph by John Fox, 1971.

Immediately he named the forest Pa Tojil.[353] There Tojil was among the eagles and among the jaguars, among the rattlesnakes and among the pit vipers.[354] There he was, the god of B'alam K'itze'.

He that belonged to B'alam Aq'ab' went to Pa Awilix,[355] to a hidden forest.

He, then, that belonged to Majukotaj was there atop the mountain Jaqawitz.[356]

There they were when it dawned.[357] They rejoiced as they waited for the dawn there atop the mountain Jaqawitz. They continually bled themselves[358] toward the place where the sun emerges as they awaited the dawn.

[353] Pa Tojil ("At Tojil").

[354] *k'ula wi sochoj k'ula wi k'anti'* ("among the rattlesnakes among the pit vipers"). *Sochoj* is the Middle American rattlesnake (*Crotalus simus*). *K'anti'* is a name borrowed from lowland Maya languages that means "yellow mouth." It may refer to a variety of poisonous vipers, although it is most likely the *fer-de-lance* (*Bothrops asper*), which is pale yellow on its ventral side beneath the mouth. In Spanish it is known as *barba amarilla* ("yellow beard"). Together, the pairing of rattlesnake and pit viper forms a merismus referring to all poisonous serpents. Karen Bassie notes that both the rattlesnake and the fer-de-lance lunge aggressively when they attack and are therefore excellent metaphors for warriors (personal communication, 2019).

[355] Pa Awilix ("At Awilix").

[356] Jaqawitz was the god of Majukotaj.

[357] Throughout Mesoamerica the "first dawn" of the sun is a symbol not only for the birth of a new age but also for the divine sanction of power to a lineage or allied group (León-Portilla 1969, 30–31; Akkeren 2000, 164; Chinchilla Mazariegos 2013, 694; Christenson 2016, 116–127).

[358] *k'ixe'* ("to bloodlet"). The verb is derived from *k'ix* ("spine"), used to pierce the body.

Figure 36. "He that belonged to B'alam Aq'ab' went to Pa Awilix, to a hidden forest."
View of the dense forest atop the hill of Pa Awilix. Photograph by John Fox, 1971.

Then it dawned. First came forth the great star,[359] the guide for the pathway of the
sun. And then was the emergence of the sun. It dawned therefore. And then cried
out the birds. The first was the lordly parrot.[360] Thus, it was there that they saw the
sun, the light, atop the mountain Jaqawitz.

And so they rejoiced, they gave thanks, and they sang. They unwrapped their
incense that they had wrapped there at the place where the sun emerges.

Then came their vassals. Their arrival was delayed.

Then they gave thanks. They opened their incense, the means of giving thanks by
B'alam K'itze'. Kasiwastan[361] was his incense. For B'alam Aq'ab', Mixtan[362] incense
was his. For Majukotaj, K'abawil[363] incense was his. These, then, they burned.

"Twice we give thanks, thrice we give thanks, to you Tz'aqol and to you B'itol, to
you the center of the sky and earth, to you the four corners and the four sides we
give thanks. We have just seen the dawn, the brightening of the sky. Now we have

---

[359] This is the planet Venus in its appearance as the morning star.

[360] *ajpop k'eletza* ("principal lord parrot").

[361] In the *Popol Vuh*, this incense is called *cawistan* (Christenson 2007, 228), perhaps derived
from the Nahuatl *cauitl* ("time") and *istlaceltia* ("to rejoice/he that gives thanks") or "time of
rejoicing."

[362] *mixtan* is probably derived from the Nahuatl *mixtitlan* ("cloud place").

[363] *k'ab'awil* ("god, divine"). Classes of incense called K'ab'awil and Mixtam were still sold in
Chichicastenango in the mid-twentieth century (Schultze-Jena 1954, 91).

Figure 37. "They opened their incense, the means of giving thanks by B'alam K'itze'." Traditional incense burned at a ceremony above Santiago Atitlán, 2006.

seen the sun; we have seen the stars. We give thanks, then, to you our mountain, Tulan Sewan, the Very Abundant Mountain, the Very Verdant Mountain," they said.

And so then they burned their incense. The smoke of their incense rose straight into the sky.[364] Because of them, it was wondrously straight as it went to the place where the sun emerges. Then the smoke arrived within that mountain place; the crying out of their hearts arrived as well before the face of the Lord Nakxik.

"As one we have just seen the sun and the light. We were with you, our older brothers. But you, our older brothers and our younger brothers, the tribes, you were left behind at our mountain place and at our valley place," they said.[365] Their hearts cried out, they, our grandfathers and our fathers when they saw the dawn, when they gave thanks.

---

[364] In modern K'iche' ceremonies, it is considered particularly powerful when the smoke of incense or burned offerings rises straight into the sky without being blown one way or the other by the wind. If the ceremony concerns rebirth or healing, it is considered appropriate if the smoke moves toward the east, as is described in the next line. In this case, the smoke goes directly eastward to their ancient mountain place of Tulan where Lord Nakxik rules.

[365] This is a reference to the allied lineages that were left behind at Tulan. The *Popol Vuh* clarifies that these were Mexican people, known as the Yaqui (Yaki in modern orthography). In both accounts, this lament took place in conjunction with the first dawn: "Thus began their song called Our Burial. Their hearts and bowels wept as they sang. And this is what they said in their song: 'Alas, we were lost! At Tulan we split ourselves apart. We left behind our older

Figure 38. "Luminous stone images there were." Deity image in the mountains with offerings, above Chichicastenango.

Luminous stone images[366] there were; they dried themselves out in the sun above the trees and the mountains.

This, then, was the dawn and the affliction of our grandfathers and our fathers.

brothers and our younger brothers. Where did they see the sun? Where were they when it dawned?' This they sang concerning the bloodletters and sacrificers of the Yaqui people. Tohil is the god of the Yaqui people, who they call Yolcuat Quitzalcuat. 'We were separated there at Tulan Zuyva. We left them to come here. But we were complete before we came here.' This they said among themselves when they remembered their older brothers and their younger brothers the Yaqui people. These dawned there in Mexico, as it is called today. Thus surely a portion of them remained there in the East" (Christenson 2007, 230–231).

366 *k'ot saq* ("sculpted stone luminous"). *K'ot* is a sculpted stone image. *Saq* is "bright, beautiful, pure, shining, or luminous." The statement here is abbreviated but most likely refers to the drying out of the earth in the presence of the newly dawned sun, as well as to the transformation of the K'iche' gods into stone images as described in the *Popol Vuh*: "Then also the face of the earth was dried by the sun. Like a person was the sun when he revealed himself. Hot was his face and thus he dried the surface of the earth. Before the sun had come forth the face of the earth was wet; it was soggy prior to the coming forth of the sun. But when the sun ascended upward, he was like a person. His heat could not be endured . . . Then straightaway Tohil, Auilix, and Hacavitz became stone, along with the sacred images of the puma and the jaguar, the rattlesnake and the pit viper. Zaqui Coxol took them and hid himself in the trees. When the sun, moon, and stars appeared, they all turned to stone" (Christenson 2007, 229–230).

THE DISAPPEARANCE OF THE FOUR PROGENITORS[367]

This, now, is the counsel that they gave to their sons following the dawn:
"You, our sons, you have achieved completion. You have multiplied. Receive, then, this Bundled Glory.[368] Watch over and keep it. We have not yet found our mountain place. You will achieve glory and sovereignty there, and then you will open this as a sign of your lordship. It came from the place where the sun emerges. You will engender the Ajpop, Ajpop K'amja, and Q'alel Atzij Winaq. You will attain glory; sovereignty will come to be. For now we die, we shall vanish. We shall depart and go back. But we leave you in peace. There is no longer war with the Seven Nations, the warriors. Do not mourn therefore. Look after your mothers," they said.

They were not ill when they gave their counsel. They were well when the night came. But when it had again dawned they were no more. It was not long afterward that they vanished.[369] Thus do not lose heart; hear this word. Truly B'alam K'itze', along with B'alam Aq'ab', Majukotaj, and Ik'i B'alam, appointed their sons. They were called at the time of the dawning.

Now their grandsons and their sons were many—they the Kaweqib', the Nijayib', and the Ajaw K'iche'.

And so they named the mountain of the Kaweqib', Saqirib'al Tojil; Saqirib'al Awilix belonged to the Nijayib'; and Saqirib'al Jaqawitz belonged to the Ajaw K'iche'.[370]

To the Tamub' belonged Saqirib'al Maq' Tan;[371] to the K'aqoj and the Eq'omaq'[372] it belonged.

Saqirib'al Ajuk'in[373] belonged to the Ilokab', to the Sik'a'ab' and the Juwanija.[374]

---

[367] lines 2138–2202.

[368] This is the symbol of authority that the four progenitors received from Nakxik at Tulan (see pp. 96, 105).

[369] It is a common belief among the highland Maya that powerful folk heroes and sacred ancestors do not die but rather join their fellow liminal beings in the mountains or in caves (Carmack and Mondloch 1983, 234, n. 194; Christenson 2001, 210–211).

[370] Each of the five mountains in this passage bears the name *saqirib'al* ("place of the dawn") (see map 1).

[371] A contracted form of Amaq' Tan, the mountain of the Tamub' K'iche' (see p. 102, n. 238).

[372] K'aqoj and Eq'omaq' are the two lineages of the Tamub' K'iche' (see p. 95, n. 202).

[373] Uk'in was the name of the principal settlement of the Ilokab' (see p. 102, n. 239).

[374] Sik'a and Juwanija are two of the three lineages of the Ilokab' K'iche'. The third, Q'ale, is omitted here (see p. 95, n. 206).

THE FIRST TWENTY-TWO SETTLEMENTS OF THE K'ICHE' MIGRATION[375]

1. They were unified with the Nijayib' there atop Pa Tojil. Truly they named one side of the house "Kaweqib'" and the other side of the house "Nijayib'," it is said. They were equally distributed. Truly as one they constructed their buildings at the first dawn.

2. Then they abandoned their first citadel, Q'aq'awitz.[376] They abandoned [Pa] Tojil.[377] They arrived at the second citadel, Sib'aqija. There they remained for a long time. They had borne with them the Bundled Glory on their backs,[378] the sign of their lordship that came from the place where the sun emerges. They did not have maize food or water there. They arrived in thirst, in hunger.

3. The third citadel was Chi Wa'ij.[379] There they built a great dwelling. There they carved images of wood and stone in their hunger and their thirst.

4. The fourth citadel was Pakaja Xejoyan. They raised up their buildings. There they remained for a long time.

5. The fifth citadel was _____.[380]

6. The sixth citadel was B'arab'ik Chun, B'oqotajinaq Sanaylo. They remained there for a long time.

7. The seventh citadel was Pan Jilil, Pan Tz'okon. For a long time they remained there. Only the larvae of bees and wasps did they eat.[381] They only ate[382] the charred remains of wood.[383] There was the din[384] of macaws and parrots.[385]

8. The eighth citadel was this—Tikaj Ch'alib'. There they again raised up their

---

[375] lines 2203–2553.

[376] Q'aq'awitz ("Fire Mountain"). This is an alternative name for Jaqawitz, the mountain where the K'iche' gathered to witness their first dawn. In the *Título Yax*, both the god Jaqawitz and the mountain on which he was placed are called Q'aq'awitz (Carmack and Mondloch 1989, folio 21, 107, n. 135).

[377] In this context, Tojil refers to the first settlement of the Kaweq K'iche', Pa Tojil, not their patron god.

[378] *keqa'm* ("they had borne on their backs"). This verb form is used only in reference to the Bundled Glory, the principal token of power brought from Tulan. Other symbolic objects were simply "brought."

[379] Chi Wa'ij ("At Hunger"). The name recalls the hunger and thirst they suffered at this place.

[380] The name of the fifth settlement of the migration is left blank.

[381] *xkechaj* ("they ate"). This verb is used to describe eating meat, referring to the insect larvae.

[382] *xkilo'o* ("they ate"). This verb is used to describe eating fruit or plants, referring to the charred wood.

[383] *k'atib'al che'* ("charcoal, charred wood").

[384] *wajwij*. In contemporary K'iche', *wajwinik* is the sound of someone or something eating loudly, particularly animals. This passage is written in an uncharacteristically sloppy hand and with several long, blank spaces, but it appears to refer to the loud noises made by macaws and parrots while feeding, perhaps mocking the K'iche' in their hunger.

[385] *alRaj*. According to the Coto dictionary, *alaj* is a male parrot, which parallels "macaws" in the paired couplet.

buildings. They brought the sign of lordship that had come from the place where the sun emerges in hunger and in affliction.

9. The ninth citadel was Tib'atzi Rajawiche'. They again raised up their buildings there. There originated the wind that rent the peaks of Soq'oj and Uk'in. "La'e La'e,"[386] they said.

10. The tenth citadel was Job'alam Q'an Ulew. This was the name of the mountain that they passed by. They merely paused there.

11. The eleventh citadel was Chi Wa'an Chi Q'aq'. Many were the names of the mountains where they dwelled. Again, they merely paused there.

12. The twelfth citadel was this—Xech'ayab' Ximb'axuk. They merely brought the signs of lordship that had come from the place where the sun emerges. Again, they suffered hunger and thirst.

13. The thirteenth citadel was this: They arrived at last at Tz'utuja.[387] There they captured the Lord Tz'utuja. He was found at Payo Pab'aq'oj. The quail cried out. It was heard by B'alam Aq'ab', B'alam K'itze', and Majukotaj. Then he was taken in a net;[388] he was captured.

And so he spoke: "Do not take me by force, you lords. Do not kill me," he said.

Thus he was asked: "Who are you?"

"I am called Tz'utuja," he said. "I am your recompense.[389] I shall be your completion," he said.

"It is true what you have said. It is well. It shall be so. You, then, shall become as if paired with me[390] and with my word," said B'alam K'itze' to Tz'utuja. "You shall become the replacement for father Ik'i B'alam," he was told.

So thus was the discovery of Lord Tz'utuja of the Saqik. He came to be the complement[391] of Majukotaj. He came to be the replacement for Ik'i B'alam who had died in his youth. Thus was restored the first four who had come from the place where the sun emerges. He was named as the lord of the Saqik K'iche'[392] when

---

[386] In Colonial dictionaries, this is a lament or a cry for mercy.

[387] Tz'utuja ("Maize Flower House"). Located in the area of present-day Cubulco (Carmack 1981, 124–125).

[388] xuq'. According to Basseta, xuq' is a type of net used by hunters to capture birds.

[389] iwajil ("your recompense"). Ajil is "price, recompense, debt, or debtor."

[390] ulaq'el n[u]wach ("its pair my face"). The phrase implies a closer tie than merely a companion.

[391] uk'aaut ("his complement, renewal, reparation"). The word suggests that Tz'utuja "completed or repaired" Majukotaj following the loss of his brother Ik'i B'alam. This phrase also attests that the four progenitors were conceived by the K'iche' as two pairs of individuals—B'alam K'itze' was paired with B'alam Aq'ab', and Majukotaj was paired with Ik'i B'alam until he died and was replaced by Tz'utuja.

[392] The Saqik lineage, founded by Tz'utuja, now becomes the fourth major lineage of the Nima K'iche'.

[Ik'i B'alam] died there at Tz'utuja. Therefore, may our sons and our grandsons not lose heart.

There they called upon a stone. They venerated[393] a precious stone, the second to have come from the place where the sun emerges. Thus the pair of precious stones were completed there at Tz'utuja. They remained there for a long time.

14. The fourteenth citadel was this—Ub'e Chi Uk'ab'al.[394] There they raised up their homes. They paused there, having brought the signs of lordship that had come from the place where the sun emerges.

15. The fifteenth citadel was this—Yamukutu Raxaj. For a long time they remained there. Merely straw,[395] merely the larvae of bees, merely the larvae of wasps did they eat, they, our grandfathers and our fathers.

16. The sixteenth citadel was this—Chi Tzaq'eb' Chi Yaki. There they paused again. They constructed their buildings and their towers. There were great afflictions there. Every seven days they would eat a mouthful of maize to comfort their hearts. The Kaweqib' and the Nijayib' were unified.

17. The seventeenth citadel was this—Q'ale Mi'al Kukur Ab'aj. They merely paused there. They gathered together; they endured hardship in the ravines and in the forests from hunger and from thirst.

18. The eighteenth citadel was this—Pa Che' Chi Q'ojom was the name of the mountain where they abode. They remained there for a long time, our grandfathers and our fathers—B'alam Aq'ab', B'alam K'itze', and Majukotaj, the bloodletters and sacrificers.

19. The nineteenth citadel was this—Chi K'ab'awilanik.[396] There, then, they venerated the precious stone that came from the place where the sun emerges. Then they laid foundations and constructed their buildings there. They came together, they the Kaweqib', the Nijayib', and the Ajaw K'iche'. B'alam K'itze', B'alam Aq'ab', and Majukotaj joined with Tz'utuja, the replacement for Ik'i B'alam.

---

[393] *xkik'ab'awilaj* ("they venerated/worshiped"). The root of this verb, *k'ab'awil*, is a deity or the image of a deity. As a verb it means to venerate something as a god.

[394] Ub'e Chi Uk'ab'al ("its road to its drinking place"). This could be read as a toponym, or the text may simply be noting that the settlement was on the road to a source of potable water such as a freshwater spring.

[395] *tum.* It is difficult to know what type of plant is indicated here. Coto lists *tum* as "straw, palm." Basseta defines it as "a grass or weed that is stretched out, like rods or the rays of the sun." Ximénez defines it as "a fleshy leaf, such as that of the maguey; a stem, or a certain type of straw or grass."

[396] Chi K'ab'awilanik ("At Worship/Veneration"). *K'ab'awil* is a god or the image of a god. When used as a verb, it means to worship or venerate a deity. In the next paragraph, the authors list locations on this mountain where bloodletting and sacrificial offerings were carried out on behalf of the god Tojil, the patron deity of the Kaweq lineage.

There they began to hunt for deer, offering the blood before the god Tojil. Moreover they began to venerate their god at Chi K'ix[397] and Chi Ch'at.[398] They were skinners of deer before the sanctuaries.[399]

Then two forest people passed by who were with the Seven Nations. In that moment they asked, "What is it that you skin? Perhaps it is our brothers who are with us that you skin,"[400] they said therefore on behalf of the Seven Nations.

And so again was the fomenting of war by the nations. And here again they embarrassed themselves.[401] They had attempted war there at Jaqawitz.[402] And now in an instant they plotted again for war. They of the K'alaqam and they of the Tib'ilkat arrived. One of them arrived, cloaked up to his ears as a deceiver;[403] from his ears to his feet he was cloaked as a spy in order to kill our grandfathers and our fathers.

In an instant, however, it became known to our grandfathers and our fathers there at Chi K'ix and at Chi Ch'at. There the Lord Tz'utuja of the Saqik saw war. He had not seen war at Jaqawitz.[404]

In an instant they were followed by the envoy. "Fine, then. We shall die,"[405] said our grandfathers and fathers.

Then went the furious valiant men,[406] the watchers belonging to the warriors

---

[397] Chi K'ix ("At Spine"). This is a toponym for a place dedicated to the ritual practice of blood-letting, which was carried out using spines to prick the body.

[398] Chi Ch'at ("At Scaffold"). In the context of ancient ritual, *ch'at* refers to a raised platform (Coto) or scaffold (Basseta), used for offering sacrifices.

[399] *ja* ("house"). In the context of this passage, I interpret these to be the houses or sanctuaries of the god Tojil, located at Chi K'ix and Chi Ch'at, and not the houses of the K'iche' themselves.

[400] The K'iche' lords are being accused of skinning (killing) the people of the Seven Nations rather than just deer.

[401] *xkik'ut wi kib'* ("they embarrassed themselves"). Literally, the phrase means "to point at or manifest one's self." Ximénez interprets the phrase as "to embarrass or shame one's self," which appears to be the meaning in this passage.

[402] This is a reference to the previous war waged by the Seven Nations against the progenitors of the K'iche' in which the Seven Nations were soundly defeated at Jaqawitz (see pp. 106–109).

[403] *uq'um uxikin k'a[x]toq'ol* ("covered/cloaked/wrapped to their ears as deceivers"). This may be metaphoric, or they may have actually cloaked themselves from head to toe to conceal their identities or to hide themselves from detection.

[404] Lord Tz'utuja had not yet joined the K'iche' progenitors as the replacement for Ik'i B'alam when the battle of Jaqawitz took place.

[405] *kojkamoq* ("may we die" or "we shall die"). Perhaps this is meant as a taunt directed at the spy of the Seven Nations to lure him and his allied warriors into a trap.

[406] *oyew achij* ("furious valiant men"). This is a common phrase used to refer to warriors in highland Maya texts. *Oyew* means "angry, furious, ill-tempered," but when used to describe warriors it implies "fierceness, furor." *Achij* is literally "man," but it is often coupled with *oyew* in Early Colonial texts to refer to one who is "brave, valiant, courageous" in battle.

[of the K'iche']. They were there atop the mountain called Muq'b'al Sib'.[407] There smoke arose as a message.[408] The furious valiant men were naked; they were nude.

Then the fasters and the sufferers manifested their wondrous power and their spirit essence atop the mountain of Muqb'al Sib'. They called forth a gale and a whirlwind, a hailstorm and thunder; sudden death[409] fell upon the heads of the Seven Nations, the warriors. In no way were they able to make war. Merely undone were their plans for war, they of K'alaqam and they of Tib'ilkat who came to be the warriors of the Seven Nations.[410]

20. The twentieth citadel was this—they arrived again at Jume'taja. Of bark alone they built their homes. They merely venerated their gods with mushrooms, with misshapen mushrooms, and with young birds. These they offered before their gods. Great was their suffering. They gathered together and they endured hardship. In the forests and the bushes were Tojil, Awilix, and Jaqawitz, along with the Bundled Glory, the sign of lordship that came from the place where the sun emerges.

21. The twenty-first citadel was this—K'ulb'a Kawinal.[411] There they again raised up their buildings, there at K'ulb'a Kawinal. There they joined with the Aq'a'ab':[412] "Ye are our grandfathers, ye are our fathers. Ye are our leaders, ye are our heads," said the Aq'a'ab' to our grandfathers and our fathers—B'alam K'itze', B'alam Aq'ab', and Majukotaj, along with Lord Saqik Tz'utuja, the replacement for Ik'i B'alam. They gave their incense smoke and their offerings before their gods. Merely young deer snakes,[413] merely young parakeets did they offer before their gods there at K'ulb'a Kawinal.

---

[407] Muqb'a[l] Sib' ("Looking Place Smoke"). This is apparently a lookout position for sending up messages by means of smoke, as can be seen in the following sentence.

[408] *tajkil* ("message, order, commandment, authorization"). This is a unique instance in highland Maya literature where smoke was used to convey messages, in this case a sign of alert.

[409] *q'eteb' pub'a'ix*. Literally, this can be read as "lightning blowgunned." But as a phrase it is defined as "sudden death" in the Ximénez dictionary and as "fateful day" in Coto.

[410] This narrative is somewhat cryptic. I interpret it to mean that the K'iche' lords lured the spy and his allied warriors away from their homes. The "furious valiant men" of the K'iche's reinforce the subterfuge by appearing defenseless and unarmed ("naked"). The K'iche's were able to coordinate their actions with the use of smoke messages from a high vantage point on the mountain of Muqb'al Sib'. Once exposed, the enemy forces were then devastated by the supernatural power of the K'iche' lords.

[411] According to Carmack, this is the area around present-day Cubulco. The nearby ruins of Pueblo Viejo, just north of Cubulco, are still called Cawinal (Carmack 1973, 312). Cawinal is situated along the Río Blanco just north of its confluence with the Río Negro (Fox 1978, 243).

[412] *xkik'ul wi kib' ruk' aq'a'ab'*. The phrase can be interpreted to mean that they joined with the Aq'a'ab' as allies or that they intermarried with them.

[413] *ral tolob'* ("its child deer snake"). According to Ximénez and Coto, *tolob'a'om* is a great snake that in Mexico is called Matzacuat. This would be *maçacoatl* ("deer snake" or boa constrictor). The Basseta dictionary lists *tolob'on* as a "great snake that eats deer."

Figure 39. "They arrived here at Chi Ismachi'." View of the plateau of Chi Ismachi'.

22. The twenty-second citadel was this—They arrived here at Chi Ismachi'.[414] Here, then, they ground fine lime plaster.[415] They grew in number, they the descendants, the sons of the lord and the grandsons of the lord; the older brothers and the younger brothers that came after Lord B'alam K'itze'. For now they had become numerous, they the children and the sons of the Kaweqib'.

[414] Chi Ismachi' ("At Whiskers"). The ruins of this settlement are located on a hill just across a small canyon southwest of the later K'iche' capital of Chi Q'umarkaj, the principal settlement at the time of the Spanish Invasion. According to the *Título Tamub'* (*Historia Quiché de Don Juan de Torres*), the founding of this citadel marked the beginning of the true *ajawarem* ("lordship") of the K'iche' (Recinos 1957, 43–45), reinforced by the presence there of the tokens of authority brought from Tulan by K'oka'ib'. All three major lineages of the K'iche' (Nima K'iche', Tamub', and Ilokab') resided at Chi Ismachi'. The authors of the *Popol Vuh* record that Chi Ismachi' was founded by K'onache, although it was fortified and expanded by K'otuja: "It was there at Chi Ismachi' that Lord Co Tuha and Iztayul ruled as Ah Pop and Ah Pop of the Reception House. Under them it came to be a very fine citadel . . . Their hearts were united. There were no bad feelings or anger, only steadfast lordship. There was no contention or disturbance. There was only purity and a tranquil sense of community in their hearts. There was no envy or jealousy . . . They attempted to strengthen their defenses there at Chi Ismachi'. This act was surely a sign of their sovereignty. It was surely a sign of their glory, as well as their greatness" (Christenson 2007, 263–264).

[415] The lime used to make plaster for building construction was ground to a powdery consistency. In highland Maya literature, citadels built with lime plaster represent prestige and administrative authority. Chi Ismachi' is the first K'iche' settlement described as having plastered buildings as opposed to smaller communities built from adobe and wood (Christenson 2007, 262).

And of B'alam Aq'ab', numerous had become the children and the sons of the Nijayib'. And of Majukotaj, numerous had become the sons of the Ajaw K'iche'. Here, then, would sprout, in small measure, their lordship.

THE TITLES OF AUTHORITY ESTABLISHED AT CHI ISMACHI'[416]

Then was the establishment of the offices of authority there at Chi Ismachi'. The first office was held by Lord K'otuja.[417] Within the hierarchy of lordship, he came to be the Ajpop, he, the son of B'alam K'iq'ab'.

The Ajpo K'amja was Stayul, another lord, who was the son of K'onache; he entered into the office of Ajpo K'amja. We shall describe the order of authority within the lineage of Kaq Imox[418] Stayul.

This, then, is the order of lordship for the K'iche' at Chi Ismachi'. This is the order of lordship, the order of the burden of responsibility—the Ajpop was held by the K'iq'ab'il people[419] and the Ajpop K'amja was held by Stayul K'onache.

The Great Ajpop of the Valiant Men and the Lesser Ajpop of the Valiant Men[420] go before us, we, the Kaweqib'. The Lord Utza'm Pop and the Lord Laq' Pop,[421] the Lord Uchuch K'amja and the Lord Nima Lolmet,[422] they are of the Lord K'iq'ab''s people, the Kaweqib'.

These complete the Ajpop K'amja lords, they who give birth to the benches.[423] These, then, are their titles: the Ajpop Alomab' and the Alay Tem Kaweqib'.[424]

The givers of birth for the benches behind the lord Uq'alel Alomab'[425] of the Nijayib'.

---

[416] lines 2554–2610.

[417] K'otuja ("Sir Sweatbath").

[418] Kaq Imox ("Red Imox"). This may be scribal error for Kaj Imox ("Four Imox"), a day on the 260-day highland Maya calendar. It was common for individuals to adopt the day on which they were born as their personal name.

[419] As seen in the next paragraph, the K'iq'ab'il Winaq are defined as leaders of the Kaweqib' lineage. The title of Ajpop was held exclusively by the leaders of the Kaweqib'.

[420] Nima Raj[p]op Achij, Ch'uti Raj[p]op Achij ("Great Ajpop of Valiant Men, Lesser Ajpop of Valiant Men"). In this context, *achij* refers to warriors; thus these are military leaders.

[421] Ajaw Utza'm Pop ("Lord Its Edge/Leader Mat") Ajaw Laq' Pop ("Lord Companion Mat"). The implication is that these lords serve at the royal court close to the the ruling Ajpop ("He of the Mat").

[422] Ajaw Uchuch K'amja ("Lord Mother/Founder of the Reception House") Ajaw Nima Lolmet ("Lord Great Emissary").

[423] *tem* ("bench"). Benches represent positions of authority and are arranged according to the hierarchal order of the K'iche' lords.

[424] Ajpop Alomab' ("Ajpop They Who Have Borne Children") and Alay Tem Kaweqib' ("Givers of Birth Benches of the Kaweqs"). In this case, the "children" are the benches of authority.

[425] Alomab' ("They Who Have Borne Children").

Figure 40. "The crook-necked gourd and the gourd cup." The Maize God holding a crook-necked gourd. San Bartolo, ca. 100 BCE. Drawing by Heather Hurst.

The Nim Ch'okoj Alomab'[426] are of the Ajaw K'iche'.

This was their manner. There came to be only three Great Houses.

Then entered the Lord Q'alel[427] of the Nijayib' and the Ajaw Atzij Winaq, the Ajaw Q'ale K'amja and the Nima K'amja, the Uchuch K'amja and the Julajuj Tem,[428] the Ajawilix,[429] the Metasanik, and the Saqlatol. They were the Nijayib'.

Of the Ajaw K'iche' there were these—the Atzij Winaq Ajaw and the Nim Ch'okoj Ajaw, the Ajaw Lolmet and the Lord Jaqawitz.[430]

---

[426] Nim Ch'okoj Alomab' ("Great Stewards They Who Have Borne Children").

[427] Q'alel Nijayib'. *Q'alel* is the highest office among the Nijayib', the second-ranked of the ruling K'iche' lineages (see p. 142, n. 325).

[428] Julajuj Tem ("Eleven Benches").

[429] Ajawilix ("She/He/They of Awilix"). Awilix was the god of the Nijayib'.

[430] Jaqawitz. Jaqawitz was the god of the Ajaw K'iche'.

THE TOKENS OF AUTHORITY BROUGHT FROM
THE PLACE WHERE THE SUN EMERGES[431]

These, then, are the tokens of authority that came from the place where the sun emerges; that came as well from the other side of the lake, from the other side of the sea—the crook-necked gourd[432] and the gourd cup;[433] the claws of the eagle and the claws of the jaguar; the head and the hooves of the deer; the bone flute, the drum, and the great flute; the talon of the eagle and the paw of the jaguar; the shell and the net of tobacco; the tail of the deer and the bracelet of precious stones; the feathers of the beautiful bird and the feathers of the snowy egret; the braid; the *titil* stone and the yellow stone.

These are the signs of lordship, the piercings and the perforations[434] that came from the place where the sun emerges—the stone ear ornaments (nine[435] there were belonging to the Ajpop and the Ajpo K'amja); the four canopies, the three canopies, the two canopies, and the one canopy of quetzal feathers and cotinga feathers;[436] the crown[437] and the turquoise;[438] the pendant jaw[439] and the bound fire[440] of the

---

[431] lines 2611–2842.

[432] *b'us* ("crook-necked gourd"). Gourds are used as vessels for liquids. On the west wall of the San Bartolo murals (ca. 100 BCE), the Maize God bears a crook-necked gourd as a vessel for sacred water taken from the first mountain of creation (see figure 40). A similar gourd on the same wall gives birth to five human-like infants (Saturno et al. 2005). Basseta defines *b'us* as a kind of double trumpet, perhaps also made from the dried shells of gourds.

[433] *q'axeon*. This is most likely a variant of *q'o'x*, a small gourd cup. Ximénez also glosses *q'o'x* as *casca de la cabeza* ("shell of the skull").

[434] *worik k'aqik* ("piercing perforating"). In the *Título K'oyoy*, the same paired terms are also linked with the *titil* stone and the yellow stone. These are stones that are tokens of lordship placed within the pierced/perforated noses of rulers: "These lords were pierced (*xeworik*) and perforated (*xek'aqik*) with *titil* stones (*titil*) and with yellow stones (*q'ana ab'aj*) . . . They are those who have been pierced (*e worom*); they are those who have been perforated (*e k'aqom*)" (Carmack 1973, 277, author translation).

[435] *b'elejeb'* ("nine"). The text does not specify what nine things there were, but perhaps it refers to the number of ear ornaments belonging to the Ajpop and Ajpo K'amja. There were nine Great Houses or lineages of the ruling Kaweqib' who held the offices of Ajpop and Ajpo K'amja, suggesting that the number of ear ornaments matched the number of Great Houses and were perhaps distributed among them (Christenson 2007, 204, 267–268, 299).

[436] These refer to the feathered canopies placed over the thrones of high officials—four canopies for the Ajpop, three for the Ajpop K'amja, two for the Great Ajpop of the Valiant Men, and one for the Lesser Ajpop of the Valiant Men (see p. 120).

[437] *k'ub'ul* ("crown, wreath, garland").

[438] *chaltit*, derived from the Nahuatl *chalchiuitl* ("turquoise"). Among the Postclassic Maya, rulers wore headdresses or crowns adorned with jade or turquoise.

[439] *kamachal*, derived from the Nahuatl *camachalli* ("jaw, mandible, chin").

[440] *tub' q'aq'* ("bound up/tied fire"). In the Brasseur de Bourbourg (1961, 238) dictionary, *tub'q'aq'* is glossed as "exhalation" or "steam/vapor" in the context of a sweatbath heated by fire.

Figure 41. "The *titil* stone and the yellow stone. These are the signs of lordship, the piercings and the perforations." Terracotta figurine of a lord with a nose ornament. National Museum of Archaeology and Ethnology, Guatemala City.

sweatbath;[441] the three hundred sixty and the five hundred forty[442] penetrating darts[443] and thrown darts.[444]

Thus there were four progenitors.[445] The images of clefted armadillos adorned their staffs when they took their offices of authority.[446] This, then, was done at Chi Ismachi'. Thus they took their offices of authority. They achieved a small degree of glory, sovereignty, and authority.

---

[441] *tawiskal,* derived from the Nahuatl *temazcalli* ("sweatbath").

[442] *kamul b'elej kal* ("twice nine score"). In K'iche' numeration, this is the way to write the number 360 (2 × 9 × 20); *oxmul b'elej kal* ("thrice nine score"), or 540 (3 × 9 × 20).

[443] *chi q'ech'a* ("of penetrating arrows/darts"), perhaps referring to arrows shot from bows.

[444] *chi tz'ununche'* ("of thrown arrows/darts"). *Tz'unun* is derived from *tz'ununah* ("to spear or to cast a spear"). These weapons are cast or thrown, perhaps spears or atlatl darts.

[445] *alomab'* ("they who have borne children"). From the context, this refers to the first four male progenitors of the K'iche' people, although the phraseology utilizes a verb form generally used to refer to mothers who bear children. Among modern K'iche', the principal male lineage heads or respected shamans are called *chuchqajaw* ("mother father").

[446] In modern highland Maya communities, indigenous officials often hold staffs topped with a symbol that represents the nature of their authority.

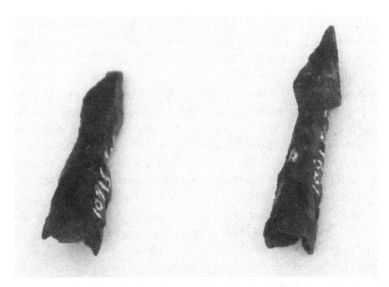

Figure 42. "The three hundred sixty and the five hundred forty penetrating darts." Highland Maya dart points. National Museum of Archaeology and Ethnology, Guatemala City.

Figure 43. "The images of clefted armadillos adorned their staffs when they took their offices of authority." Highland Maya leaders holding staffs of authority topped with their symbols of office, Santiago Atitlán, 2010.

There came to be only three Great Houses. They took their offices of authority; they exulted as well. Yet they were still humble there at Chi Ismachi'. The symbol of lordship was opened that K'oka'ib' had gone to receive when the lineages were perhaps still at Jaqawitz, the first citadel.

Surely it was not at Chi K'ix and Chi Ch'at that the first war was waged. The first true war was waged earlier at Jaqawitz. It was the second war that took place at Chi K'ix and Chi Ch'at. But it was on the mountain that wondrous power and spirit essence were manifested. For the third time did this occur here at Chi Ismachi'.

Here, then, they gave thanks at Chi Ismachi': "You, the sky and the earth; and you, Tz'aqol and B'itol, may you give to us our daughters and our sons. May you give a bit of food and drink to us, you who are on the other side of the lake, the other side of the sea. You, the Womb of the Sky, and you, the Place Where the Sun Emerges, and you, the Place Where the Sun Rises, may you give to us our sun and our light," they said; "you, the Great Star, Venus,"[447] they said.

They offered their incense and young turkeys. These the people offered before the face of Tojil here at Chi Ismachi'. Here they danced the Junajpu K'oy[448] and the Wuqub' Kaqix.[449]

Then began their drinking. They brought their honey drink[450] and they became drunk. Their daughters were borne on their backs.[451] They exchanged their daughters between themselves. They bore their daughters to the drinkers of sweet drink.

---

[447] *ek'o q'ij* ("passes before sun"). This is the planet Venus, which rises before the sun in its appearance as the morning star.

[448] Junajpu K'oy ("Junajpu Spider Monkey"). This dance recalls an episode in the *Popol Vuh* in which the twin gods Junajpu and Xb'alanke play their flutes in an effort to attract their brothers who had been transformed into spider monkeys: "Then they began to sing, to play the flute, and to play the drum. And when they had taken up their flute and their drum, the Grandmother sat down with them as well. Thus they played the flute, calling them with the music. In song they called out their names, with the music whose name is 'Junajpu Spider Monkey'" (Christenson 2007, 145).

[449] Wuqub' Kaqix ("Seven Macaw"). Wuqub' Kaqix was a prideful deity who lived before the first dawn of the sun: "While the face of the earth was only a little brightened, before there was a sun, there was one who puffed himself up named Seven Macaw. There was a sky and an earth, but the faces of the sun and moon were dim. He therefore declared himself to be the bright sign for those who were drowned in the flood. He was like an enchanted person in his essence" (Christenson 2007, 91). He was ultimately defeated by Junajpu and Xb'alanke, who shot him with their blowguns (97). This passage indicates that the story of Seven Macaw was reenacted in a dance.

[450] *kikab' ki'* ("their honey sweet drink"). The drink is specifically identified as made from honey, perhaps similar to balche.

[451] *xe'eqa'xik* ("they were borne on the back"). The verb refers to carrying something on the back by use of a tump line secured by a strap across the forehead. It is possible that the daughters were carried this way, although the verb is often used metaphorically.

Figure 44. "They offered their incense and young turkeys." Sacrifice to an ancient stone deity at the K'iche' site of Paxkwal Ab'aj, Chichicastenango.

They were given to the poor and the widowers.[452] They went to their homes to give them: "We give her to you without cost, we offer her to you,"[453] they said.

Merely one large jar of cacao[454] and one gourd cup of guacamole;[455] merely one vessel of food of some kind[456] and one platter with the thigh of a wild pig; merely

---

[452] *ajk'aqowal*. According to the Sáenz dictionary, this term refers to "orphans, widowers, and the abandoned." The passage suggests that brides were provided for all single men despite their circumstances.

[453] This passage echoes the *Popol Vuh*'s description of the lords at Chi Ismachi' who did not demand dowries during marriage negotiations: "And yet again they began to feast and to drink to their daughters. They who were called the Three Great Houses gathered together to celebrate. They would drink their drinks and eat their food, and this alone was the bride price for their sisters and their daughters. There was only joy in their hearts when they feasted within their Great Houses: 'We give only our thanks and our gratitude as a sign of our agreement; as a sign of our word regarding the boys and girls born of their mothers,' they said" (Christenson 2007, 265).

[454] *saqa'* ("cacao drink"). According to Coto, *saqya'* is "cacao" in drinkable form. Cacao was an essential part of marriage negotiations among traditionalist highland Maya well into the twentieth century (Bunzel 1952, 46, 113–117, 272; Christenson 2010, 593–597).

[455] *matul oj*. These are two types of avocado. This is either an avocado sauce (an early form of guacamole) or an avocado drink, paralleling the jar of cacao that was drunk as a liquid.

[456] *uwe* ("some kind/any kind/whatsoever").

Figure 45. "Merely one large jar of cacao." Drinking cacao at a ceremonial meal, Santiago Atitlán, 2010.

one gourd vessel of maize tamales wrapped in *q'anaq'* leaves and *kub'* leaves.[457] This was the price for their daughters that they set. It was done there at Chi Ismachi'.

Thus they came together, these three nations of the K'iche'—the Tamub', the Ilokab', and the Saqajib'. They remained with each other when they came as one from the place where the sun emerges, from Tulan Sewan.

---

[457] These are two types of large leaves that are still used to wrap steamed corn tamales, although today the K'iche' generally prefer to use plantain, banana, or *maxan* (*Calathea lutea*) leaves.

This, then, was done at Chi Ismachi'. There was no incense[458]—no *kik' alaxi* or *pom alaxi*,[459] no blood or croton sap,[460] no blue-green body paint[461] or sacrifices.[462] There were no female captives or male captives. There were no mother birds—the parrot or the macaw. There was no Great Sacrifice. There was no Pokob' Chanal dance.[463] They were still humble in their existence.

They were still deceived into calling upon wood and stone. They were the first people. There were twenty-two citadels and mountains that they passed through on their way here.

These, then, were the offices received by the noblemen,[464] the glorious grandfathers and the glorious fathers.[465] These were the burdens of authority distributed

---

[458] *pom* ("copal incense") is made from the sap of the *palo jiote* tree (*Bursera verrucosa*). It is still burned by the K'iche' as a part of both Christian and traditional Maya ceremonies.

[459] *kik' alaxi* ("blood born") *pom alaxi* ("incense born"). Tree sap and blood are analogous in K'iche' belief, and both carry the same name, *kik'*.

[460] *jolomax* ("croton/croton sap"). This is the red sap of the croton tree (*Croton draco*; Spanish: *Sangre de Dragón*—"Dragon's Blood"). Vázquez de Espinosa (1969, 1st.I.iv.590, 147, author translation) wrote that "there is a tree in this province of Chiapa and of Guatemala that is called 'dragon.' It is tall like the almond tree; the leaves are white and the stems are of the same color, and if it is struck with a knife it weeps blood, as natural as if it were human." In the *Popol Vuh*, croton sap was offered to the lords in the otherworld realm of Xib'alb'a as a substitute for the blood of the goddess Xkik' ("Lady Blood"): "Then the red secretions of the tree were collected in the bowl. There it congealed and became round. The red tree, therefore, oozed forth the substitute for her heart. The sap of the red tree was thus like blood when it came out. It was the substitute for her blood. Thus she collected the sap, the secretion of the red tree. Its surface became like bright red blood in the bowl when the maiden cut open the tree called the Sacrifice Red Tree. She named this 'blood,' and blood croton it is still called" (Christenson 2007, 133).

[461] *raxtunim* (blue-green body paint). In highland Maya languages, blue and green are shades of the same color, *rax*. Ximénez glosses the verb *raxtunij* as "to paint blue/green." Among the Postclassic lowland Maya, humans destined for sacrifice were often painted blue (Landa 1941, 117–118, n. 537; Sharer 1994, 543–544). It is possible that this was also a practice among the highland Maya, as this word is paired with *k'atoj* ("sacrifice").

[462] *k'atoj* ("sacrifice"). It is derived from the verb "to cut, tear, or perform surgery."

[463] According to the dictionaries of both Basseta and Ximénez, Pokob' Chanal was an ancient dance as well as a festival. *Pokob'* is a "shield or buckler"; therefore the dance no doubt had military overtones. *Chanal* is a "flute or whistle," suggesting that the dance had musical accompaniment.

[464] *ajtz'alam* ("they of authority"). The term denotes those holding offices of authority as well as anyone of elevated status, such as noblemen.

[465] *q'ana mama q'ana tata* ("glorious grandfathers glorious fathers"). *Q'ana* is literally "yellow"; however, it is also used as a superlative meaning "great, glorious, or abundant." Coto glosses the phrase *q'ana winaq* ("yellow person") as "patron or witness." Ximénez defines the same phrase as "to glorify, a man who passes through everything."

to them that had been brought by K'oka'ib'. First were the floral vessel of precious metal and the rattle[466] of precious metal, along with the staff bearing the image of the clefted armadillo. These were the tokens of authority for the Ajpop, the Ajpop K'amja, and the Q'alel Atzij Winaq.

Soon the token of his authority was distributed to the Ajpop of the noblemen—the floral vessel of precious metal. This belonged to the Ajpop of the noblemen, the head of his lineage. He was the first to take authority, the first to come with lordship there at Jaqawitz.

We have said before[467] that they paid heed to the misery of their people, to their sons and to their younger brothers. They were victors in war and conquerors of the land—they of the Great House, the Place of Sacrifice. They were punishers, captors, and chasteners. They were the sons and younger brothers of the white flint blade[468] and the white deer hooves.

Truly this was the means of reviving[469] the young men and the maidens—four reclinings[470] in sweatbaths, in [steam] ovens; the crushed and the ground meat; the very cold water[471] and the mirrors;[472] the mint[473] and the pennyroyal;[474] the bathing bowl and the bathing cup.[475] These were the means of reviving the generations.

---

[466] *sochi* ("rattle, rattlesnake"). It is unclear whether this is a rattle made of precious metal or the image of a rattlesnake made of precious metal.

[467] This description of the rulers at Jaqawitz is a repetition of a similar passage on p. 115.

[468] *saqi toq'* ("white flint blade"). This is no doubt the instrument by which bloodletting and sacrifice were carried out. The *Popol Vuh* mentions the *saqi toq'* three times as a sacrificial blade linked to the otherworld realm of Xib'alb'a (Christenson 2007, 124, 132, 164).

[469] *k'astab'al* ("instrument to awaken, revive, resurrect, give birth").

[470] *kaj q'alaj chi tuj chi xik'a'y* ("four reclinings in sweatbath in [steam] ovens"). *Q'alaj* is to rest, recline, or lean against something like a wall. This passage refers to the ceremonial sweatbath, which is still practiced in the Guatemalan highlands.

[471] *joronalaj ja'* ("very cold water"). Cold water is poured over hot stones in the sweatbath to produce steam and is also splashed on the body after the bath. Here it is paired with mirrors, which may suggest that another use of the water is to provide a reflective surface.

[472] *lemo* ("mirrors, crystals"). Mirrors and quartz crystals are often used among modern highland Maya *ajq'ijab'* (traditionalist K'iche' shamans) as instruments of sight into alternate worlds, divination, or scrying. They are an important part of ritual bundles used in divination ceremonies.

[473] *q'ebun* ("yerba buena," Spanish for "good herb"). This is a generic term for a number of medicinal plants belonging to the mint family. It is commonly used by K'iche' as a tea for treating stomach problems.

[474] *muchuchen* ("pennyroyal"). This is also a medicinal mint plant, considered to be particularly effective for respiratory problems when drunk as a tea or boiled to create a vapor to be breathed. In this context, the yerba buena and pennyroyal are used as aromatic herbs in the sweatbath.

[475] This is a common couplet used to refer to the vessels of water used for pouring water onto heated stones in a sweatbath.

Figure 46.
"Truly this was
the means
of reviving
the young
men and the
maidens—four
reclinings in
sweatbaths."
Traditional
K'iche' sweatbath,
Momostenango.

This, then, was the word of Nakxik to Lord K'oka'ib'. And so he carried out his word regarding the Q'alel Ajpop, the Uq'alechij, and the Rajpop Achi. "It shall not be long before you shall give lordship to them," he said to K'oka'ib'.

THE MARRIAGE OF K'OTUJA TO A DAUGHTER OF THE MALAJ TZ'UTUJIL[476]

He, then, Lord [Q'ukumatz] K'otuja,[477] reigned at Chi Ismachi'. He sent two envoys to the mountain place of the people of Malaj.[478] "Go there to Malaj. Carry[479] with

---

[476] lines 2843–2958.

[477] [Q'ukumatz] K'otuja ("Quetzal Serpent Sir Sweatbath"). This lord is most likely the Ajpop of the sixth generation of lords and the grandfather of K'iq'ab' (see p. 155, n. 543). He is referred to as Q'ukumatz K'otuja throughout most of this section.

[478] Malaj. The Tz'utujil-speaking lineages occupied the lands south and west of Lake Atitlán, extending to the southern coast of the Pacific Ocean. Carmack (1979, 111) places the territory of Malaj south of the volcano now known as San Lucas Tolimán. The *Título de Santa Clara* describes Malaj as "under the pataxte and cacao trees" (Recinos 1957, 173), an indication that Malaj must have been located somewhere on the coastal plain, as these trees do not grow in the highlands. The Malaj were of the Tz'utujil lineage, subsidiary to the Ajtz'ikinaja who ruled at Chiya' on the southwest shore of Lake Atitlán (see n. 504). Shortly before the Spanish Invasion, the Tz'utujil rebelled against their Ajtz'ikinaja overlords and briefly expelled them, although the rebellion was soon quelled (Recinos and Goetz 1953, 117–118; Maxwell and Hill 2006, 252–254). The Nima K'iche', the Kaqchikel, and the Ajtz'ikinaja were the three principal highland Maya realms at the time of the Spanish Conquest.

[479] *chiwuk'aj* ("carry"). This verb is used specifically to refer to carrying something as a message (Sáenz de Santa María 1940, 405).

Figure 47. "He sent two envoys to the mountain place of the people of Malaj." The mountainous area of Malaj looking toward the coastal plain.

you a rabbit and a quail and place them there atop the hill Mulb'a[480] where the furious valiant men of Malaj gather," said Lord K'otuja. "Hide yourselves. Do not show yourselves," the envoys were commanded by K'otuja. The rabbit and bird were the proxy petition[481] that they received.

Then they arrived. The resplendent quetzal[482] remained behind. The rabbit and the bird were his substitutes. On the fourth attempt[483] they accomplished their

[480] Mulb'a ("anthill"). This is specifically an anthill, although the term can also refer to any small hill or mound.

[481] uk'exwach tz'onoj ("its exchange petition"). This section describes an elaborate negotiation for a bride. K'exwach is an "exchange, substitution, or proxy." Tz'onoj is "to offer a petition or plead for something." The Basseta dictionary glosses the word as used specifically when asking for a bride. Rabbits are linked with females, specifically the young moon goddess. Las Casas (1967 [ca. 1550]:2, book III, ch. 238, 516) records that quail were offered to a bride when she arrived at the home of her new parents-in-law. According to the *Xajil Chronicle*, quail were also the *jaleb'al* ("transformation or animal substitute") for the ruling Kaweq lineage (Maxwell and Hill 2006, 78), of whom K'otuja was the lineage head as Ajpop. Perhaps the implication was that the rabbit represents the bride and the quail acted as the "substitute" for Lord K'otuja as the petitioner for a bride.

[482] q'uq' ("resplendent quetzal"—*Pharomachrus mocinno*). The quetzal bird was linked to royalty throughout the Maya world. In this passage, the resplendent quetzal likely refers metaphorically to Lord K'otuja, who remained behind at his capital while the rabbit and bird were borne by his envoys as symbolic representatives. In the following section, K'otuja is specifically linked with the quetzal bird through his title, Q'u[q']kumatz ("Quetzal Serpent") (pp. 147–149).

[483] Marriage negotiations among the ancient highland Maya involved a complex interchange between representatives of the young man and the family of the intended bride that required

work. On this, the fourth attempt then, the faces of the envoys were seen. Thus the envoy of Malaj spoke:

"Who are you? Are you not the envoy of Q'ukumatz K'otuja?"[484] he asked.

"I am thy messenger, the envoy of Q'ukumatz K'otuja," he said.

And so, the K'iche' envoy was escorted under guard. They arrived before Malaj. Then came the drink[485] for the envoy—one red vessel and one white vessel of beaten cacao.[486]

Lord Malaj then asked: "What is the desire of Q'ukumatz that you have heard?" "It is merely marriage[487] that he desires," said the envoy.

multiple visits: "If he was a person of quality who wanted to marry, he sent his messengers to obtain an agreement, along with presents to beg for the girl, saying that it was good for the boy to marry his daughter. If the father did not wish to give consent, then he replied that this was not a reflection on them, but excused himself by some means; but if the messenger suspected that there was hope that permission be granted, he returned a second time, on bended knee; and the third time someone older was sent, begging for whatever was necessary to conclude the marriage; and from there, if accepted, they were treated as relatives and the day was determined for the marriage" (Las Casas 1967: vol. 2, book III, chapter ccxxxviii, 516). Among modern K'iche', even if the petition is favorable, the bride's family never accepts the first approach of the intended bridegroom's representatives. The following is an account from the K'iche' community of Chichicastenango recorded between 1930 and 1932: "The father of the girl always refuses the first time. Then right away he finds out about the boy, who he is and if he will make a good husband for his daughter. And he asks the girl what she thinks. Then he goes to a diviner to make the divination to see whether it is her destiny to marry this man ... The *chinimtal* ['bride negotiator,' often the head of the boy's lineage]: 'Pardon our intrusion in entering this house. As for me, I am a *chinimtal*. It is my profession to bespeak the seven favors ... Give us the girl child of this house. Pardon our faults! Take us and hold us in your hearts.' The father of the girl: 'Pardon our faults, mother, father! I'll not give her to you. Our child is too small; she is not strong enough to hold up a man. No, go to some other house. As for me, I'll not give her to you, even if you go down on your knees, mother, father. There is no need to discuss or argue this further.' The *chinimtal*: 'Pardon our faults! We will win her yet, even if we have to come four, five times, and endure whips and lashes'" (Bunzel 1952, 113–114).

[484] This is the first time K'otuja is referred to with the additional name Q'ukumatz ("Quetzal Serpent"). Q'ukumatz is one of the principal creator deities who participated in the creation of the world (Christenson 2007, 68–69). In this context, Q'ukumatz appears to be an honorific title. It was a fairly widespread practice in Postclassic Mesoamerica to adopt "Quetzal Serpent" as a name or a title—Quetzalcoatl in Mexico or K'uk'ulkan in the Maya lowlands.

[485] *uk'iya'* ("drink"). This is a general term for "beverage," although it implies cacao in ritual circumstances.

[486] *q'utum* ("beaten cacao"). Cacao was prepared as a beverage by beating it to create a foamy head. Cacao is the standard drink offered during bride negotiations (Bunzel 1952, 115–122; Christenson 2010, 595–596).

[487] According to Fr. Bartolomé de las Casas (1967 [ca. 1550]: 2, book III, chapter ccxxxviii, 516, author translation), the ancient lords of Guatemala married women outside their own lineage as a means of establishing marriage alliances: "Under no circumstances did they

"Well, then, I have heard the word of Q'ukumatz K'otuja," said Lord Malaj. "It is given, then, the white beaten cacao and the fresh cacao cakes as a sign of my word. May they come to take the girl. You shall come as her bearers," said Malaj.

Then four emissaries[488] were sent to receive the daughter of the Malaj people. They drank therefore to her name, as well as to the yellow hammock and the red mat, the string of gold beads, the feathered fan, and the sandals. They drank to her.

Then they departed. The daughter of the Malaj people came. She arrived there at Pa K'iche', at Chi Ismachi'. Xle'm[489] was the name of the woman.

Then she arrived. [Lord Q'ukumatz K'otuja] named her Moqani.[490] He also named her Pos.[491] She had two cloaks of palm leaves as protection from the rain, and she was accompanied by tribute bearers behind her.

Thus was her arrival. The daughter of the Malaj people arrived. For thus were they invaded,[492] although not in war. It was merely to be married to Lord Q'ukumatz K'otuja that she arrived there. And also there arrived then the branches from the *pataxte* tree and the branches from the cacao tree;[493] the white *pacaya* palm leaves[494]

---

marry those of their own tribe, family, or kinship . . . If he was a lord or the son of a lord who married, he usually looked for a woman from another town, and thus he established kinship among those people. And this was the means by which they lived peacefully."

[488] *pop k'amja* ("emissaries"). According to Sáenz de Santa María (1940, 314), the *popak'amajai* are "those charged with presenting petitions from communities to their lords." They are no doubt trusted members of the K'iche' court commissioned to conclude bride negotiations.

[489] Xle'm ("Lady Bug"). *X-* is a feminine indicator, often translated as "Lady." *Le'm* is Tz'utujil for "lady bug or flower beetle."

[490] *moqani[l]* is an object of worked silver. It may have been customary to rename a royal bride, or she may have been given a new name because Xle'm has no meaning in K'iche', being a Tz'utujil name.

[491] *pos* is a pebble or smooth stone. It specifically refers to small stones in riverbeds that are polished smooth by the current.

[492] *rokib'exik* ("their being invaded"). The authors of the text contrast the arrival of the Tz'utujils from Malaj, in this case peacefully, with the invasion by another Tz'utujil-speaking lineage, the Ajtz'ikinaja, described in the following chapter. It is possible that this marriage was a political one, intended to drive a wedge between the people of Malaj and their overlords, the Ajtz'ikinaja. The Ajtz'ikinaja were centered at Chiya' on the southern coast of Lake Atitlán, and they controlled the rich coastal lands that bordered the K'iche'.

[493] *xamal ton peq' xamal ton kako* ("tree branches pataxte tree branches cacao"). Both *xamal* and *ton* refer to branches or wood cut from a tree, particularly for firewood. *Pataxte* (*Theobroma bicolor*) is an inferior grade of cacao used to sweeten food and drinks, such as the maize-based drink *chorote*. Its name is derived from the Nahuatl *pataxtli*. In this context, the branches and aromatic leaves mentioned in the following line are probably intended for the ceremonial sweatbath, an essential part of highland Maya marriage rituals.

[494] *saqi pakay* ("white pacaya palm"). The pacaya palm (*Chamaedorea tepejilote*) has a whitish-yellow sheathed flower with long tendrils of edible kernels that resemble baby maize. Both its flower and its leaves are aromatic and are often used in sweatbaths.

and the white *b'oxom* leaves;[495] the red chili[496] and the white chili; the netted shrimp and the entrapped birds.[497]

On 2 Ib'ote[498] she married Q'ukumatz K'otuja. Thus was the marriage of Q'ukumatz K'otuja with the daughter of the Malaj people of the Tz'utujil.

And thus arrived the Ajxetulul[499] along with the Ajyatza,[500] the Ajk'uke and the Laqam Kuk, the Mama Kot and the Mama Sakipat, the Wanakoj, the Yab'akoj,[501] and the Ajk'aqolkej.[502]

---

[495] *saqi b'oxom* ("white *b'oxom*"). In the Ajpacaja Tum dictionary (2001, 92–93), *b'oxom* is glossed as a plant that grows in maize fields and is related to the pacaya palm.

[496] *rixk'aq b'a*. Literally, "its claw gopher." The Coto dictionary glosses this phrase as a type of chili.

[497] The firewood and aromatic leaves for the sweatbath, the chili, and the entrapped animals all allude to items that represent the conclusion of traditional marriage negotiations among the highland Maya when the bridegroom receives his intended bride: "And now after a month they come for the girl. This time the boy himself comes with them for the first time. He carries a load of firewood for the sweatbath, and bunches of various aromatic leaves to be used in the sweatbath for the parents of the girl. His father carries a basket of food and his mother carries a jar of *puliq*, and other relatives and friends carry jars of *atole*. There are the usual greetings, and then the father of the boy speaks: 'Pardon me, mother, father, that I have intruded in your house, together with my companion and my child. This is the day, this is the hour which we have appointed. Today we come bringing food, only this poor bit of food and drink, this bit of spiced sauce for the carrying away of our daughter who is in this house and sacred place of the ancestors. And also our son has come bringing these branches of trees and these potent leaves. Thus we have come, mother, father'" (Bunzel 1952, 114). It is perhaps important to note that the shrimp and birds are specifically referred to as "netted" and "entrapped." In K'iche' tradition, the potential bride is described as a "trap" by which the family of the potential bridegroom is ensnared: "We have fallen into the trap which they [the girl and her clothing] have set for us. For thus indeed we have come to see her, the watcher and listener, the woman's skirt, the woman's blouse within this house" (Bunzel 1952. 114, n. 23).

[498] Ib'ote is a month on the highland Maya solar (365-day) calendar. It appears as Ibota in the 1685 Kaqchikel calendar, the fifteenth of eighteen named months (each consisting of twenty days). It is described as the "season of various red colors or of rolling up mats." 2 Ib'ota corresponds to November 9 on the Gregorian calendar (Weeks et al. 2009, 4, 54–55). This period is marked by the end of the rainy season and the time of the principal maize harvest.

[499] Ajxetulul ("They of Xetulul"). Xetulul ("beneath the zapote tree") is the community of San Martín Zapotitlán (Zapotitlán means "Land of the Zapote" in Nahuatl) as attested in this text (see p. 151). This is the first in a list of representatives from Tz'utujil communities and their allies who attend the marriage ceremony. The marriage apparently succeeded in bringing new allies and tributaries from lands previously aligned with the powerful Ajtz'ikinaja lineage.

[500] Ajyatza ("They of Yatza"). This settlement appears as Pa Yatza ("At Yatza") in the *Testament Ajpopolajay* (Carmack 1973, 374). Carmack and Mondloch (1983, 246, n. 271) identify this settlement as San Bartolomé Chicacao.

[501] Yab'akoj ("Sick Eagle"), or Yab'a Koj ("Sick Puma"), is the town of Cuyotenango on the Pacific Coast (Recinos 1957, 102–103).

[502] Ajk'aqolkej ("They of K'aqolkej"). K'aqol Kej ("Deer Hunter") is the town of Mazatenango (Recinos 1957, 102), which means "Land of the Deer" in Nahuatl.

THE WAR WITH THE AJTZ'IKINAJA OF LAKE ATITLÁN[503]

It was then that five people, principal people [of the Aztz'ikinaja], invaded the mountains and valleys of Malaj Tz'utujil.[504] Then were defeated the Malaj, the Tz'utujil people. Each of [the five] increased their demands for vassals among the children of women and the sons of men behind them. And thus they waged war against five territories[505] of the vassal children and sons of the K'iche' and of Q'ukumatz K'otuja.[506]

And so the K'iche' fought the Yaki people[507] and the Ajtz'ikinaja.[508] It was the tail of the squirrel that they carried as their banner. They defeated the Yakis and the Ajtz'ikinaja. Two men of the Yakis were captured and bound—Welpan[509] was the name of one, and Xukutzin[510] was the name of the other. These were brought by the furious valiant men before the face of Lord Q'ukumatz K'otuja at Chi Ismachi'. "We crossed over there. We threw down their day and their birth—they who

---

[503] lines 2959–3081.

[504] As seen below, this invasion of Malaj lands was carried out by the Ajtz'ikinaja ("They of the Bird House") and their Yaki allies. The Ajtz'ikinaja were the ruling lineage of the Tz'utujil-speaking highland Maya who occupied the southern shores of Lake Atitlán as well as the coastal lands to the south and west. The capital of the Ajtz'ikinaja was Chiya' ("At the Water"), located across a small bay from the present-day town of Santiago Atitlán. The Malaj were of a rival lineage, the Tz'utujil. According to the *Relación de los caciques y principales del pueblo de Atitlán*, written in 1571, the Tz'utujil paid tribute to the Ajtz'ikinijay: "The head and lord of all of them was called Atz'ikinijay; the other lords, together with the lord called Amaq'-Tz'utujile, knew no other lord" (Anonymous 1952 [1571], 435). Apparently, this invasion of the Malaj Tz'utujil lands was in retaliation for their recent alliance with the K'iche', described in the last chapter, which would have freed them from tribute to the Ajtz'ikinaja.

[505] *li'aj* ("territories"). *Li'aj* refers to a group of maize fields or flat lands suitable for cultivation (Sáenz de Santa María 1940, 249).

[506] This passage makes clear that the Malaj were considered vassals to the K'iche', not equal partners in an alliance.

[507] Yaki winaq ("Yaki people"). *Yaki* is the name the K'iche' used to refer to Nahuatl-speaking people of Mexican descent. The southern coastal lands of Guatemala were occupied by a number of Nahuatl-speaking groups, including the Pipil, who had occupied the land for centuries. The Tz'utujil and Pipil occupied adjacent territories until the end of the fifteenth century and were often allies during conflicts (Orellana 1984, 55–56).

[508] There is no indication that Chiya' itself was attacked by the K'iche'. More likely, the war was directed against their vassals and allied Nahuatl-speaking communities along the southern coastal plain. After the fall of Chiya' during the Spanish Invasion in 1524, the Ajtz'ikinaja rulers complimented the invaders on their military prowess and declared that until that day, "their land had never been broken into nor entered by force of arms" (Alvarado 1924, 72).

[509] Welpan ("Principal Conqueror"). A Nahuatl name derived from the adverb *wel* ("first, principally") and *panawia* ("to conquer, to be the greatest among a group, to walk ahead of others").

[510] Xukutzin ("Great Invader"). Also a Nahuatl name, derived from *xocoa* ("to take another's lands") and *tzin* (an honorific meaning "revered, great").

dwell on the shores of the lake and they who dwell on the shores of the sea.[511] We have brought these men here. Perhaps they may be of service to thee, thou Lord Q'ukumatz K'otuja," they, the furious valiant men, said when they arrived.

"It is good what you have done, you, our furious ones, you, our valiant men. Soon will be given to you your glory and your sovereignty," said Lord Q'ukumatz K'otuja to them.

Then was the deliberation of their plans by Lord Q'ukumatz K'otuja and Lord Stayul. They carried out their word.

"Establish our lordship there in Malaj in the semblance of our image and our visage.[512] Go as our envoys. Go to take captives. Go bearing a bundle of jaguar skins and a bundle of arrowheads. Go as well with their woven bundle and their standard. May they be killed—they who occupy the shores of the lake and the shores of the sea. May they be vanquished and humiliated, they of the Ajtz'ikinaja."

And thus they entered into their offices as Q'alel and Ajpop. From here went forth the burden of office belonging to the people of Xetulul, of San Martín[513] as it is called today. And again, these also received their offices of authority—they of Wanakoj and of Yab'akoj; of Q'inom, Tunati, and Is;[514] of the five territories and the five provinces; they who live below the slopes of the pataxte and the cacao. [They were given] five bundles of arrowheads and their standard; five bundles were given to them by Lord Q'ukumatz K'otuja, along with their slings and their lances, their arrows and their shields.

And thus they received their offices. They began to go forth from Pa K'iche', from Chi Ismachi', because of Lord K'otuja Q'ukumatz as well as Lord Stayul,[515] the Ajpop and Ajpo K'amja. Thus went forth the offices of Q'alel and Ajpop. There were five Q'alels and five Ajpops, five Q'alels of the Valiant Men and five Ajpops of the Valiant Men.

---

[511] The Ajtz'ikinaja occupied the lands from the southern shore of Lake Atitlán to the Pacific Coast.

[512] *qachib'al qawachib'al* ("our image/form, our visage/likeness"). The phrase implies that the envoys are to act as the representatives of the lords at Chi Ismachi' as if they themselves were present. The Ximénez dictionary glosses the phrase as "the semblance of one's visage and face."

[513] The ancient site of Xetulul was renamed San Martín Zapotitlán following the Spanish Invasion. It is located at the far western edge of Ajtz'ikinaja territory, bordering on the lands occupied by the K'iche'. The battle described here appears to be a border skirmish rather than a major invasion of Ajtz'ikinaja lands.

[514] These appear to be the five territories the K'iche' established in lands formerly occupied by the Ajtz'ikinaja near Xetulul—Wanakoj ("Striking Puma"), Yab'a Koj ("Sick Puma"), Q'inom ("Jocote," a tropical fruit), Tunati (a Nahuatl name, meaning "Sun"), and Is ("Camote," a type of sweet potato).

[515] This would be the seventh generation of K'iche' rulers, Lord K'otuja [Q'ukumatz] as Ajpop and Lord Stayul as Ajpop K'amja (see p. 155, n. 543).

"Thus are established your offices of authority, you our grandsons and sons."

Then went forth the Ajpop Alomab', they who held the offices of Alay Tem along with Mama Ajtz'alam. This, then, was done at Chi Ismachi'. Many scores of years did they pass there at Chi Ismachi'. Three great lime-plastered and whitewashed structures did they build there at Chi Ismachi'.

THE REBELLION OF THE ILOKAB' AT CHI ISMACHI'[516]

Contention was nearly instigated among the lords there at Pa K'iche', at Chi Ismachi', by two emissaries [of the Ilokab']. They spread gossip.[517] They lied to the lords:

"He [Stayul] disparages thy drink, thou Q'ukumatz—'It is merely the foam of rotten cacao[518] that he drinks,' said Stayul about thee," said Ta'om and Tumakajnej.[519]

"Not in mine," he said to them.

And then they said to Stayul: "'What use is he? It is merely atole of maize and stale water[520] mixed with maggot-infested cacao[521] that he drinks like an animal,'[522] says Lord Q'ukumatz about thee, thou lord," they said to Stayul. "'Not like me, for only fresh fish and fresh shrimp do I eat,' so says Q'ukumatz about thee," they said.

Thus they spoke the same words, these lords, behind their backs.

But then they were punished.[523] Their denials[524] were transformed by the lords. A

---

[516] lines 3082–3169.

[517] *xulisaj tzij* ("they spread gossip"). The phrase means to spread gossip, but with the implication of slander.

[518] *upulu tzoy* ("rotten grains"). *Pulu* is foam or sweat, although the Basseta dictionary also glosses *pulu* as "rotten or overripe." *Tzoy* are "ill-formed seeds or grains." The Coto dictionary defines these seeds specifically as cacao.

[519] Ta'om Tumakajnej. The names of the two Ilokab' lords given here are most likely disparaging terms rather than proper names. *Ta'om* is "to have been heard or understood," perhaps related to his role as a gossip spreader. *Tumakajnej* is derived from *tuma* ("to twist or speak ill of another") and *kajanisaj* ("to make noise") or *kajcanasoj* ("to speak insulting words") in the Ximénez dictionary.

[520] *upe'n* ("lime water"). This is water mixed with lime that is used to soak maize kernels before grinding them into dough. The implication is that Stayul's maize drink is made not of freshwater but of stale water that is usually thrown out.

[521] *rachaq' joch'a amolo* ("maggot-infested cacao"). There are two equally possible interpretations of this phrase, neither of which is complimentary to Stayul's cacao-drinking habits. *Rachaq' amolo* literally means "fly droppings," although it is also used to refer to fly larvae or maggots.

[522] *karecha'j* ("he drinks"). This is not the usual verb for "to drink." In the Coto dictionary, this is to consume something rapidly, like an animal from a trough.

[523] *xk'ajisax kiwach*. Literally, "their faces were slapped," though the phrase is used metaphorically as any kind of punishment.

[524] *kimetab'al* ("their denials"). The term is derived from the verb *metaj* ("to deny"). In other words, the K'iche' lords exposed the Ilokab' attempts to deny their lies as akin to the craftiness or trickery of foxes and weasels.

fox and a weasel[525] became the face of their denials, because they were lying words.[526] Then was the conception of malice of heart by Roqche' and Four Aj.[527] They plotted the murder of Lord K'otuja Q'ukumatz along with Lord Stayul. They quickly went to gather their Ilokab' killers.

But two furious valiant men lay in wait for them. There in an open ravine the two [K'iche'] furious valiant men bathed. Ta'om and Tumakaj encountered them at the river. Ta'om and Tumakaj led the way[528] for the Ilok'ab and their warriors. Then the furious valiant men untied their belts.[529] Ta'om and Tumakaj were struck with slings, with sling stones, by the furious valiant men of K'iche'. This was done at Chi Ismachi'.

It, then, the mountain of Chi Ismachi', had four centipides as its *nawal*.[530] For this reason, it was not true that they felt content there.[531] And thus Chi Ismachi' was abandoned by the lords.

---

[525] Weasels are linked to spies and deception among the ancient highland Maya. In the *Annals of the Kaqchikels*, a weasel is the animal transformation of the K'iche' spies: "Then the animal, weasel, was sent out; it went to see them . . . They arrived there; they were camouflaged. They did not show themselves, they did not feel that they were seen. A sign came from Weasel" (Maxwell and Hill 2006, 70–71).

[526] *tzij talom*. Literally, spun or scattered words. Carmack's K'iche' informants recognized the phrase as implying "lies" (Carmack and Mondloch 1983, 248, n. 286).

[527] Roqche' Kajib' Aj. *Roq'oche'* is "two thousand (many) trees," but in this context the term probably refers to Roqche', the principal lineage of the Ilokab'. Kajib' Aj (4 Aj) is a day on the 260-day sacred calendar, commonly used as proper names among the highland Maya. These are most likely the actual names of the Ilokab' conspirators.

[528] *k'amol kib'e ilokab'* ("takers/receivers of their road Ilokab'"). The phrase means that they were the leaders or guides for the Ilokab'. At the beginning of the section, they were described as *pop k'amja*, or emissaries.

[529] *xkikir k'ut kipam* ("they untied their waists"). In the context of the next line, it appears that this was a trick on the part of the two K'iche' "valiant men." They went to bathe in the river as a ruse to make them appear defenseless. When the two Ilokab' emissaries appeared, they untied their belts as if to disrobe for bathing, only to reveal that their belts were actually slings that they used to kill the Ilokab'.

[530] *nawal* is an animal counterpart or alter-ego. In K'iche' belief, powerful people and things have the ability to transform into their *nawal*. This may be for benevolent or malicious reasons. In this case, the implication is that the place itself became hostile. *La Historia Quiché de Don Juan de Torres* records a similar account of the dangerous *nawals* linked to the mountain of Chi Ismachi', ultimately causing the ruling K'iche' to move their capital to the nearby hilltop of Chi Q'umarkaj: "Surely they worshiped the image of the rattlesnake, the image of the viper, for surely these were the *nawals* of the mountain of Chi Ismachi', where the sons of the people lived in great numbers" (Recinos 1957, 44–45, author translation).

[531] *k'am wach* ("receive face"). This is a common phrase in K'iche' discourse, meaning "to feel established, settled, or content."

Then were engendered seventeen valiant men by Lord Q'ukumatz, the son of K'otuja. These were the K'iq'ab'il people and the Tekum Stayul people, the Tepepul[532] K'iq'ab'il people and the Tepepul Kawisimaj.[533]

THE SUCCESSORS OF B'ALAM K'ITZE'[534]

These, then, are the descendants of B'alam K'itze', the first person.

The second generation was K'ok'oja.

The third generation was Tz'ikin.[535]

The fourth generation were Aj and Kan.

The fifth generation were K'oka'ib' and K'okawib'. K'oka'ib' engendered five sons— 1. Kejnay, 2. K'oyoy, 3. Xmaykej, 4. Laqamal, and 5. Rochok'oy. Five sons, as well, were engendered by Xmaykej.[536]

Now this lord, K'otuja [Q'ukumatz],[537] was the sixth generation of lordship. K'otuja Q'ukumatz was the Ajpop. The Ajpop K'amja was the son of K'okawib', K'onache, the illegitimate child of Tzipitawar, the wife [of K'oka'ib'].[538]

And so the seventh generation was K'otuja.[539]

And now the eighth generation was this: Q'ukumatz had engendered K'otuja.[540]

---

[532] Tepepul. This name is derived from the Nahuatl *tepeuh* ("sovereignty, conqueror, majesty") and *pul/pol* ("great"), giving the reading "Great Sovereign" or "Great Conqueror."

[533] This list of people includes the names of prominent rulers from the Nima K'iche' lineage. The seventeen valiant men may have been actual sons of Lord Q'ukumatz, although it is also possible that they were military cohorts created by Q'ukumatz who served under the direction of the K'iche' rulers.

[534] lines 3170–3213.

[535] Earlier in this text, the third generation included another son of K'ok'oja named E' (see p. 122).

[536] Although not explicitly written, the implication is that one of these five unnamed sons was K'otuja Q'ukumatz, the Ajpop of the sixth generation listed in the next line. If so, then K'otuja Q'ukumatz would have been the grandson of K'oka'ib'.

[537] The full name of this lord is K'otuja Q'ukumatz, as can be seen in the same passage (see also pp. 145, n. 477). This lord is the first of two ruling Ajpops to bear this name, as his son was also named K'otuja [Q'ukumatz].

[538] Pages 116–117, 154 of this text also asserts that K'onache held the lesser title of Ajpop K'amja. This directly contradicts the *Popol Vuh*, which claims that K'onache was the first Ajpop and makes no mention of his illegitimate parentage (Christenson 2007, 262, 293). This is a major point of difference and perhaps reflects an intra-lineage struggle for legitimacy in the mid-sixteenth century when both texts were composed.

[539] Although not listed here, earlier in the text the Ajpop K'amja who served in the seventh generation was Stayul, the son of K'onache (see p. 151).

[540] Only eight generations are mentioned in this dynastic list, and later in the text it is asserted that it was the eighth generation of rulers, led by the Ajpop K'iq'ab', who organized the military sentinels that were sent out to guard the K'iche' kingdom (see p. 168). My understanding

Q'ukumatz engendered seventeen sons. Here it shall be shown that many were the names of those who were engendered [by K'otuja], including K'iq'ab' and Kawisimaj. There were seven sons[541] in all: Tekum, Tepepul, Tepepul, Kawisimaj, K'iq'ab', and Tepepul[542] were engendered at Chi Ismachi'. And K'otuja was the son of Q'ukumatz.[543]

THE ESTABLISHMENT OF CHI Q'UMARKAJ[544]

This day we shall begin the account, the declaration as well, of this esteemed citadel, the admirable citadel of Pa K'iche', Chi Q'umarkaj.[545] Chi Ismachi', the royal

of this paragraph is that the eighth generation was represented by K'iq'ab' (the Ajpop) and Kawisimaj (the Ajpop K'amja). Their names are preceded by a brief review of their lineage, beginning with their grandfather, [K'otuja] Q'ukumatz I (who had seventeen sons), and their father, K'otuja [Q'ukumatz] II (who had seven sons).

[541] The text indicates that K'otuja [Q'ukumatz] II engendered seven sons, including K'iq'ab' and Kawisimaj. But only six are listed.

[542] The name Tepepul is repeated three times in this list. Because the first two times Tepepul is listed occur before and after a line break, it may be an erroneous repetition. This type of repetition commonly occurs in the text at line breaks. Nevertheless, it is apparent that siblings, or at least half-siblings, could share the same name.

[543] This is a repetition of the statement regarding the ancestry of K'iq'ab', in which [K'otuja] Q'ukumatz I of the sixth generation engendered K'otuja [Q'ukumatz] II of the seventh generation. The following is my understanding of the genealogy of the eight generations of Kaweq lords as outlined in this section:

1st generation: B'alam K'itze'
2nd generation: K'ok'oja
3rd generation: Tz'ikin
4th generation: Aj and Kan
5th generation: K'oka'ib' (Ajpop, who had five children) and K'okawib' (Ajpop K'amja)
6th generation: K'otuja Q'ukumatz I (Ajpop, who had seventeen children including K'otuja Q'ukumatz II) and K'onache (Ajpop K'amja)
7th generation: K'otuja Q'ukumatz II (Ajpop, who had seven children, including K'iq'ab' and Kawisimaj) and Stayul (Ajpop K'amja)
8th generation: K'iq'ab' (Ajpop) and Kawisimaj (Ajpop K'amja)

[544] lines 3214–3239.

[545] Chi Q'umarkaj ("At Place of Ancient Reeds"). Following the Spanish Invasion, Chi Q'umarkaj was renamed Utatlán by the Tlaxcalan allies of the invaders. In the Tlaxcalan dialect of Nahuatl, Utatlán means "Among the Reeds," a close translation of the K'iche' name (Carmack 1981, 143). Chi Q'umarkaj was still the capital of the Nima K'iche' at the time of the Spanish Invasion. The ruins of the citadel are located approximately 2.5 kilometers west of the modern city of Santa Cruz del Quiché. Little remains of its buildings, in part because it was burned by Pedro de Alvarado during his invasion of the Maya highlands in 1524 and in part because of extensive looting of its stones for buildings elsewhere since that time. Chi

Figure 48. "This esteemed citadel, the admirable citadel of Pa K'iche', Chi Q'umarkaj."
View of the central area of Chi Q'umarkaj.

house[546] of the K'iche', was abandoned it is said. Chi Ismachi' is today called Ojer
Tinamit.[547] Thus, yet again they would be established here.

This is our word.[548] Do not lose heart, you who are our grandsons and our sons.
There, then, you shall receive knowledge. May it be so. For this is merely the manifestation and the memorial of the works of our grandfathers and our fathers.

Q'umarkaj was constructed atop a small plateau with nearly vertical cliffs on all of its sides.
Anciently, the citadel was accessible only by a narrow causeway and bridge from the southeast and by a steep stairway on the west side (Fox 1978, 22–24), making it easily defended
from attack. The move to Chi Q'umarkaj was apparently necessitated by conflict among
the major K'iche' lineages (Christenson 2007, 267). As a result, the Nima K'iche' founded
Chi Q'umarkaj as their capital ca. 1400, while the Tamub' remained at nearby Chi Ismachi',
and the Ilokab' founded a new settlement at Muqwitz Chilokab' ("Burial Mountain of the
Ilokab'"), now called Chisalin, also located in the vicinity (Recinos 1957, 43–44; Fox 1978,
36). Archaeologically, Muqwitz was by far the smallest of the three, indicating the decline in
power suffered by the Ilokab' following their rebellion (Carmack 1981, 167). See map 4.

[546] *tlekpan* or *tekpan* is Nahuatl for "royal house or the house of a great lord" (Molina 2001
[1571], 93).

[547] Ojer Tinamit ("Ancient Citadel").

[548] The text is clear that this section of the Totonicapán document was composed by multiple
authors.

THE DEFEAT OF THOSE WHO KILLED THE LORD K'OTUJA Q'UKUMATZ[549]

Two years after the death of K'otuja[550] there was a great war waged by K'iq'ab'[551] and Kawisimaj.[552] They [the enemies of the K'iche'] were captured and they were bound—all the lords of those nations. They were killed on behalf of K'otuja, they of the nations of K'oja and Uxaja, as they are called. K'iq'ab' and Kawisimaj, Tekum and Tepepul[553] went out to bind those belonging to the nations of K'oja and Uxaja. Thirteen lords were defeated.[554] They were brought here along with their vassal

---

[549] lines 3240–3281.

[550] This K'otuja, who often carried the title Q'ukumatz, represents the seventh generation of K'iche' rulers and was the father of K'iq'ab' (see p. 155, n. 543). The circumstances of how K'otuja Q'ukumatz died are not described in this text. A Kaqchikel-Maya document called *Guerras Comunes de Quiches y Cakchiqueles* includes a brief description of K'otuja Q'ukumatz's death at the hands of the K'oja, a Poqomam lineage that occupied an area near Rabinal (Carmack and Mondloch 2007, 203, n. 297). K'oja had previously been defeated by an alliance of K'iche' and Sotz'il (Kaqchikel) forces, and a great number of jewels and precious metals had been taken as spoils. Afterward, K'otuja Q'ukumatz sent his daughter to the ruler of the K'oja, Tecum Ziqom Puvak, to form a marriage alliance. But instead, the ruler of K'oja sacrificed the daughter of K'otuja Q'ukumatz, precipitating a resumption of hostilities: "And again, lord Gucumatz [Q'ukumatz] spoke: 'Tecum Ziqom Puvak has killed my daughter. Go there, you lords. My heart is enraged because of Tecum Ziqom Puvak,' he told them. 'The Zotziles and Tukuches destroyed them before. Since they are not many we will only take four hundred or we will take eight hundred,' he said to his soldiers. 'It is well,' they replied. They fasted and then went to roast meat. 'You shall eat the entrails of my dead son-in-law,' Lord Gucumatz told them. Then Lord Gucumatz died as his daughter had" (Recinos 1957, 138–139, author translation). The last sentence implies that he was captured and sacrificed in the same way his daughter had died.

[551] K'iq'ab' ("Many Hands") was one of the most powerful Kaweq K'iche' lords. K'otuja Q'ukumatz II, the ruler of the seventh generation, was his father (see pp. 155, n. 543). K'iq'ab' reigned as the Ajpop from ca. 1425 to 1475 (Carmack 1981, 122). The name of this lord suggests his power to accomplish what would be impossible for someone with only two hands (parallel- ing the name of his brother Kawisimaj ["Two Heads"]), or his name may refer to the number of vassals and servants he possessed. According to the *Popol Vuh*, K'iq'ab' and Kawisimaj "accom- plished a great many deeds. They made the K'iche' great, for their essence was truly enchanted. They broke apart and shattered the canyons and the citadels of the small nations and the great nations … These all paid homage to K'iq'ab'" (Christenson 2007, 277–278).

[552] Kawisimaj ("Two Heads/Tips Sharp"). Kawisimaj held the position of Ajpop K'amja (see p. 155, n. 543; see also Christenson 2007, 282–283). This lord's name may have a double meaning. The "sharpness" may refer to the points of the weapons under his command, but it may also refer to the "sharpness" of his mind, a common expression among the K'iche' just as it is in English. The latter is all the more impressive because he has "two heads" with which to be clever. Together, these two rulers combine the benefits of "many deeds" and "many thoughts."

[553] Tekum and Tepepul were also sons of K'otuja (see p. 155).

[554] This campaign resulted in the conquest of the northern border regions of the K'iche' terri- tory. This included the lands of the Kumatz and Tujal around Sacapulas as well as that of the Mam of Saqulew. K'iq'ab' subsequently expanded his empire by subduing the rival Sajcabaja,

children and sons. They were enslaved and subjugated. They arrived at Pa K'iche' where they were sacrificed[555] and pierced with arrows.[556] They were destroyed[557] here. It was not merely sickness that came upon them, but rather their bones and skulls were shattered.[558] This was done by K'iq'ab' and Kawisimaj as recompense for the suffering of Lord K'otuja.

Thus was the birth of K'iq'ab': "His fate[559] shall be as one who burns[560] the interior of the sky, one who burns the interior of the earth," said K'otuja.

Caukeb, and Cubulco in the east, extending his influence as far as the upper Usumacinta and Motagua River valleys. In the west, his forces reached the Ocós River near the Isthmus of Tehuantepec in Chiapas, Mexico. Further conquests extended his lands from the Alta Verapaz in the north to the Pacific Ocean near Escuintla in the south, an area of approximately 26,000 square miles (Fox 1978, 3–4).

[555] *xelotz* ("they were sacrificed or bled"). The verb refers to bloodletting or cutting with blades but may also refer to sacrifice in general, which is the likely interpretation here.

[556] *xek'aq* ("they were pierced with arrows"). Ritual sacrifice by arrows was practiced by the ancient highland Maya. The *Annals of the Kaqchikels* describe the arrow sacrifice of a captured lord named Tolgom: "Then began the execution of Tolgom. He dressed and covered himself with his ornaments. Then they tied him with his arms extended to a poplar tree to shoot him with arrows. Afterwards all the warriors began to dance. The music to which they danced is called the Song of Tolgom. Following this they began to shoot the arrows, but no one of them hit the cords [with which he was tied], but instead they fell beyond the gourd tree, in the place of Qakbatzulu where all the arrows fell. At last our ancestor Gagavitz shot the arrow which flew directly to the spot called Cheetzulu and pierced Tolgom. After which all of the warriors killed him. Some of the arrows entered [his body] and others fell farther away. And when that man died, his blood was shed in abundance behind the poplar. Then they came and completed the division [of pieces of him] among all the warriors of the seven tribes that took part in the offering and the sacrifice, and his death was commemorated thereafter in the month of Uchum. Every year they gathered for their festivals and orgies and shot at the children, but instead [of arrows] they shot at them with alder branches as though they were Tolgom" (Recinos and Goetz 1953, 74–75).

[557] *xk'isik kiwach*. Literally, "their faces were ended."

[558] *upaq'urisaxik b'aq jolom* ("their being shattered bones skulls"). According to Basseta, the verb is used to describe breaking something hard, like a ceramic plate.

[559] *chalaxik* ("his birth shall be"). *Alaxik* is literally "birth" but is also used metaphorically to refer to "fate, destiny, or tradition."

[560] *poroy* ("burner"). Although the root verb, *poroj*, simply means "to burn," it is also commonly used in a ritual sense to refer to the burning of incense and other offerings. In modern K'iche' prayers, such offerings are given to the sky and the earth, a couplet that encompasses the world in general. In the context of this section, however, it may refer to the destruction that K'iq'ab' wrought on his enemies. The *Guerras Comunes de Quiches y Cakchiqueles* interrupts the description of K'iq'ab's conquest of K'oja by saying that when he was born, the highland Maya region was "on fire" with war: "Then Quicab [K'iq'ab'] was born. When he was born all the villages were burning, at midnight, the towns of Cumatz and Tuhal. They were burned by the lords of Iyu and Cakix. They burned [also] the towns called Halic and Tabahal, Bahay and Tzitzol, all

Figure 49. "Divination was made to determine the month of Tz'ikin Q'ij." Calendric divination ceremony, Chiya', 2006.

THE GREAT DANCE OF TOJIL AT CHI Q'UMARKAJ[561]

Then was the performance of the great dance, the Dance of Tojil. Divination was made[562] to determine the month of Tz'ikin Q'ij.[563] There arrived thirteen representatives of the Seven Nations [to be sacrificed] here at Pa K'iche'. The gods of the Tamub' and the Ilokab' arrived here at Pa K'iche'.[564]

big towns, big cities" (Recinos 1957, 141). The implication is that the destruction of K'oja by fire was foreshadowed by the conflagration of the region at the time of K'iq'ab''s birth. This may have been a widespread tradition concerning K'iq'ab''s destiny. K'otuja's prophecy at the time of his son's birth thus declares him to be a destroyer of worlds.

[561] lines 3282–3385.

[562] *xb'an choloj* ("was made divination"). It is common among the highland Maya to consult an *ajq'ij*, a traditional Maya shaman, to carry out a divination ceremony to determine the best day for scheduling an important event.

[563] Tz'ikin Q'ij ("Bird Season"). According to both a Kaqchikel-Maya calendar composed in 1685 and a K'iche' calendar dated 1722, Tz'ikin Q'ij is the thirteenth of eighteen months, each composed of twenty days, that comprise the highland Maya solar calendar. The remaining five days are called Tz'api Q'ij ("Closing Days") and are observed ceremonially to renew the year. In 1685, Tz'ikin Q'ij included the days 7 Ik' to 13 Imox on the 260-day *cholq'ij*, or sacred calendar. This correlates with the days September 28 to October 17 on the Gregorian calendar of the late seventeenth century (Weeks et al. 2009, 50–51).

[564] This indicates that not only did representatives from the various lineages come to Chi Q'umarkaj for the ceremony, but they brought their gods as well.

Tojil was the god of the Q'ale Tam and the Ajpo Tam,[565] the Q'ale K'aqoj and the Atzij Winaq K'aqoj,[566] the Ye'ol and the Ajtunala. These were they who came from the Tamub'.

He, Tojil of the Ilokab', also came with the Q'ale Roqche' and the Atzij Winaq Roqche',[567] the Q'alel Kajib' Ajtzij Winaq and the Sik'a, the Lolmet and the Juwanija, they of the Ilokab'.[568]

He arrived, then, the Lord K'aqaj.[569]

Then arrived the Rab'inaleb' and the Talmalin, the Ajpop Ajb'om and the Atzij Winaq, the Jab'jalawej and the Nim Ch'okoj.

They arrived to carry out blood sacrifice; they arrived to pierce with arrows.

They arrived as well the Lord Ajpo Sotz'il and the Ajpo Xajil, the B'ak'ajolab' and the Q'eqak'uch.[570]

They arrived, then, the Uch'ab'aja and the Lord Ch'umilaja.[571]

They arrived, then, the Aq'a'ab' and the B'alamija,[572] the K'ub'ul Ka'al[573] and the Kumatz.[574]

There arrived as well the Najtija and the Ajk'ib'aja, the Ajq'uja and the K'isija, the Ajk'ab'awil and the Ajpo Tzolola, the Ajpo Wa'is and the Ajpo B'uluxa, the Ajpo Runam and the Ajpo Saqi Achaq', the B'alam and the Utiw, the Ajja'eq'oche' and

---

[565] Q'ale Tam and Ajpo Tam. These are the principal lords of the Tamub' lineage of the K'iche'.

[566] Q'ale K'aqoj and Atzij Winaq K'aqoj. *K'aqoj* ("archer") is named as one of the representatives of the Tamub' who witnessed the compilation of the Totonicapán manuscript on p. 95. It is unclear in this context whether K'aqoj is a lineage within the greater Tamub' polity or if these offices represent leadership among the division of Tamub' archers.

[567] Roqche' was the name of the Ilokab' lineage that conspired against Q'ukumatz and Stayul when the Nima K'iche' and Ilokab' occupied Chi Ismachi' (see p. 153).

[568] The *Title of the Ilokab'* gives a similar list of Ilokab' lineages, although only five are named rather than six: "the Wuqmil, Sika, Xuwanija, Roqche', Qalel Kajib' Aj, the five houses, the five places, they came from where there is the departure of the sun, Siwan Tulan" (Sparks 2017, 280).

[569] K'aqaj ("arrow shooter"). It is unclear whether this is the name of a lord or if it is a title. A major aspect of the Great Dance of Tojil is an arrow sacrifice.

[570] These are four lineages belonging to the Kaqchikel language group.

[571] Uch'ab'aja ("Arrow House") and Ch'umilaja ("Star House") are lineages that settled in the valley of Sacapulas (Recinos and Goetz 1950, 171, n. 6; Fox 1978, 84–87; Carmack and Mondloch 1983, 253, n. 304).

[572] Aq'a'ab' ("Night") and B'alamija ("Jaguar House"). Settled the Aguacatán area of the Río Negro. B'alamija is specifically identified as Aguacatec in a 1739 land dispute document (Carmack 1973, 207; Fox 1978, 106; Carmack and Mondloch 1983, 253, n. 304). The Aq'a'ab' settled the site of Cawinal (Fox 1978, 249–250).

[573] K'ub'ul Ka'al. Lineage from the area of Cubulco (Fox 1978, 249–250).

[574] Kumatz ("Serpent"). This lineage settled the west end of the Sacapulas valley near Chutixtiox (Fox 1978, 76; 1987, 113–114).

the Ajpo B'alaja, the Ajpo Ko'on and the Ajpo Tuktum, the Ajpo Jun and the Ajpo Wal, the Ajpo Sanay and the Lolmet Kawinay.

They, the Ajtz'ikinaja,[575] came—all of them.

They, then, the representatives of the Seven Nations, arrived for blood sacrifice; they arrived to be pierced with arrows; they arrived to have their breasts bled;[576] they arrived to have their breasts seized—the breasts of the thirteen lords of the nations who had killed K'otuja.[577]

Thirteen great lords donned their apparel.[578] Then they rent [the sacrificial victims].

---

[575] Ajtz'ikinaja ("They of the Bird House"). This is the principal lineage of the Tz'utujil-speaking inhabitants of the area of Lake Atitlán. The text notes that during the reign of K'otuja Q'ukumatz, the Ajtz'ikinaja were at war with the Nima K'iche' (see pp. 150–152). Either friendly relations had been reestablished by this time or hostile lineages were welcomed to the ceremony as well.

[576] *kik'uwuj tz'um chomam tz'um* ("bleed chest/breast/skin seize chest/breast/skin"). The word *tz'um* can be interpreted in this context as either "chest," in which case the phrase would indicate bloodletting or heart extraction, or "skin," suggesting flaying the victim (see n. 578). Both forms of sacrifice were practiced anciently.

[577] According to the *Popol Vuh*, Tojil received the blood of victims sacrificed in his name: "Then was given the breast [*tz'um*—the same word used here] at the place called Pa Zilizib. And behind it came blood, a rain of their blood as an offering for Tojil" (Christenson 2007, 237). This blood was rubbed inside the mouths of Tojil and other patron deities (236). Las Casas (1958 [ca. 1550], clxxvii, 152, author translation) affirms that heart extraction was a principal means of sacrifice during major festivals among the ancient highland Maya: "Upon reaching the altar of sacrifice the lord placed the victim in the hands of the butcher priest, who was there ready for them. He with his ministers removed his heart with a knife and offered it to the idol, and the priest, with three fingers, took some of the blood and sprinkled it on the idol and then toward the Sun, carrying out many ceremonies that we will leave out so as not to dwell upon it further."

[578] *xeq'unik* ("they clothed/donned apparel"). This is the intransitive form of the verb; thus no object is indicated to clarify what they clothed themselves with. It is possible that the K'iche' lords simply donned the apparel of the men who were sacrificed. Chonay, however, interpreted this passage to mean that the lords clothed themselves in the "remains" of the sacrificed captives (Recinos 1950, 235). Carmack and Mondloch (2007, 205, n. 305) agree, suggesting that the thirteen "great lords" of the K'iche's carried out the sacrifice and then clothed themselves in the skins of the thirteen sacrificial victims. In Postclassic Mexico, sacrificial victims taken in war were often flayed and their skins worn in honor of the god Xipe Totec ("Our Lord the Flayed One") (Miller and Taube 1993, 188; Sahagún 1950–1963, I.73). Once arrayed in the skin of the sacrificial victim, the deity impersonator then performed a ritual dance: "And at that time a man arrayed himself to be the likeness of Totec; he put on the skin of a captive when they had flayed him. Hence was it called the Feast of the Flaying of Men. And in this manner was [the man] arrayed" (Sahagún 1950–1963, IX.69–70). Captives sacrificed to Xipe Totec were often killed with arrows before being skinned so that their blood dripped onto the ground (Smith 2003, 218), a practice also described in this text. Skinning sacrificial victims is hinted at on p. 132, n. 400.

Figure 50. "They carried all the gods; they were borne in procession by the lords." Procession of Rilaj Mam, a traditional Maya deity, Santiago Atitlán, 2010.

They made a circumambulation. They carried all the gods; they were borne in procession by the lords.[579]

One young lord[580] led those who supported the hand of Tojil. All of them were adorned with jade and precious metal in every part of their form, in every part

---

[579] Las Casas (1958 [ca. 1550], clxxvii, 152, author translation) wrote that prior to the Spanish Invasion, great feasts were held by the K'iche' in which their gods were given a share of their drink and carried through the streets of their capitals: "They danced and leaped before the altars and gave the gods to drink of the most precious wines, soaking their mouths and faces . . . Each afternoon they walked in procession with great songs and music bearing this principal idol, or as many as there were, placing them in eminent places. And there the lords played ball before him and the rest."

[580] *ajpo k'ajol.* Ajpop is the title of a principal lord in K'iche' hierarchy. *K'ajol* may be "son, young man, or vassal" depending on the context. The parentage of the young lord is not identified. Before the Spanish Invasion, young lords led the procession of the gods at major festivals: "On the night immediately preceding the fiesta and sacrifice, the sons of the supreme lord and other lords went to retrieve the idols. They carried these idols with great reverence, stopping periodically to offer birds—macaws, doves, and other birds of various species and colors; and they periodically sent young men to tell the high lord and the other lords with him that the gods had arrived at such and such a place, and this was done many times" (Las Casas 1958 [ca. 1550], clxxvii, 151, author translation).

Figure 51. "All of them were adorned with jade and precious metal in every part of their form." Ancient copper necklace from the Guatemalan highlands. National Museum of Archaeology and Ethnology, Guatemala City.

of their raiment.[581] They were wrapped and girded in penitential clothing[582] and mantles of fasting.[583]

---

[581] Las Casas (1958 [ca. 1550], clxxvii, 151–152, author translation) describes the procession of the gods: "They wore crowns of gold or silver or another metal, the most precious that they could have, adorned with precious stones and other things by which they made them very beautiful. They had some litters, richly prepared with many jewels of gold, silver, and stones, arranged with roses and flowers upon which they placed the idols, dressed in a careful and curious manner. With these they walked in procession around the patio of the temple with great songs, music, diversions, dances, and eminent persons, all arranged in order without a hint of confusion. In some parts they walked in procession with those that were to be sacrificed; in others they did not, but rather they were in place at the end of the procession. After they had been processed in their litters, the gods were seated in an eminent place that must have been like an altar, and there the sacrifice was carried out before them. Close by were the flautists and musicians and singers and dancers, who never ceased their performances."

[582] *lamaxintzi* ("penitential clothing"). Derived from Nahuatl, *tlamaceualiztica* ("penitence or clothing of penitence" in Molina). Sacrifice is linked to the concept of penitence in highland Maya texts (Christenson 2007, 203, 225). Ximénez translates *k'ajb'* as "punishment." The related word in Classic Maya texts, *ch'ahb'*, has two related meanings with regard to war contexts. In one sense, it refers to the punishment of captives and at the same time to the notion that captives destined for sacrificial death represent a kind of penitence by proxy. Classic Maya lords saw in the person of the war captive their own penance and self-denial (Stephen D. Houston, personal communication, 2002). Sacrificial victims were thus seen by the ancient Maya as substitutes for the sacrificer in payment for penitential blood debt (Taube 1994, 669–674).

[583] *mayat* ("mantles of fasting"). Derived from the Nahuatl *mayan* or *may* ("hunger, fasting") and perhaps *tilmatli* ("clothing") (see p. 109, n. 275).

[The sky] was thick with fiery comets and phantom globes of fire; there was light-ning and Heart of Sky;[584] the four bearers, they who measure the days.[585]

They were danced—the precious metals and the precious stones,[586] the tur-quoise[587] of the dance, the quetzal feathers and the cotinga feathers.

THE TOKENS OF AUTHORITY OF THE K'ICHE' LORDS[588]

All things, whatsoever there are, we shall tell. We shall declare the manifestation of the essence[589] of all the lords. They were pierced[590] here—K'iq'ab' and Kawisimaj, Tekum and Tepepul, they who were at the court of K'iq'ab'.

The Ajpop had four canopies above his throne. There was his orator[591] and his bone flute player.

The Ajpop K'amja had three canopies above his head.

---

[584] *kaqulja' uk'u'x kaj* ("lightning its heart sky"). In the *Popol Vuh*, Uk'u'x Kaj is described as a trinity of three lightning deities who oversaw the creation of the world: "Then they gave birth, heartening one another. Beneath the light, they gave birth to humanity. Then they arranged for the germination and creation of the trees and the bushes, the germination of all life and creation, in the darkness and in the night, by Heart of Sky who is called Huracan. First is Thunderbolt Huracan, second is Youngest Thunderbolt, and third is Sudden Thun-derbolt. These three together are Heart of Sky" (Christenson 2007, 69).

[585] *kaj eqa'm ajetaq'* ("four are borne on their backs they who measure [days?]"). Carmack and Mondloch (1983, 253, n. 309) propose that the "four that are borne" are the four "Year Bear-ers," the days Kej, Ik', No'j, and E' of the 260-day highland Maya sacred calendar, or *cholq'ij*, that "bear" the progression of the solar years. This appears to be the most likely interpreta-tion. *Ajetaq'* is meaningless by itself, but in conjunction with the previous phrase it could be read as a contracted form of *ajeta'm q'ij* ("they who measure days"), which would fit the context of the couplet.

[586] *q'oq'ol*. This is "precious stones" in Colonial dictionaries, but the type of stone is left undefined.

[587] *xtekok* ("turquoise"). Ximénez defines this as *chalchigüites*, the Nahuatl term for turquoise. Turquoise is not found anywhere in the Maya region and would have had to have been obtained through trade from Mexico.

[588] lines 3386–3437.

[589] *uk'ulun kiwach*. Literally, "its appearance/manifestation their faces." The phrase implies "to reveal or make manifest the essence of a person" rather than just show his or her outward appearance.

[590] *xwor* ("was perforated or pierced"). As will be seen later in this section, this refers to the piercing of the nose to insert a precious stone ornament as a token of high office, a common practice in Pre-Columbian Mesoamerica (see p. 165).

[591] *uRajon* ("his orator"). Derived from the root verb *raj* ("to speak") according to the Ximénez dictionary. It is possible that this is a scribal error for *uraxon* ("its cotinga feathers"), suggest-ing that the canopies were composed of feathers, although this does not fit the grammatic construction of the sentence or complement the second half of the couplet, *ajsu'b'aq* ("bone flute player").

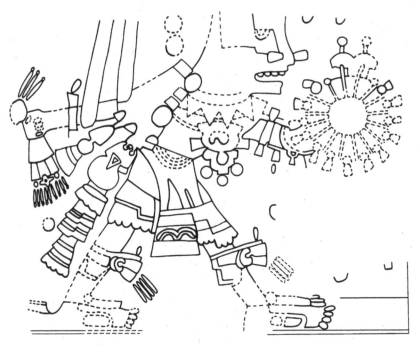

Figure 52. "The jewels to plug the noses of the Ajpop and the Ajpop K'amja. They were perforated." Mural from Chi Q'umarkaj showing a lord with a nose ornament. Drawing by Robert M. Carmack.

The Great Ajpop of the Valiant Men had two canopies above his head. The Lesser Ajpop of the Valiant Men had one canopy above his head. They took office at Plume House.[592] Thus the lords whose heads were shaded with canopies were pierced; they were perforated with the *titil* stone and the yellow stone. They had the bloodletter[593] and the red tree,[594] the tail of the deer and the bracelet of precious stones, the talon of the eagle and the paw of the jaguar, the shell and the tobacco net, the feathers of the beautiful bird and the feathers of the snowy egret, the precious stone and the turquoise—the jewels to adorn the noses of the Ajpop and the Ajpop K'amja. They were perforated. They were pierced here at Pa K'iche', at Chi Q'umarkaj, the royal house of the K'iche'.

---

[592] Pa Xik'aja ("At Plume/Wing House"). This house was mentioned earlier in the text as a place linked to military rulers (see p. 120, n. 344).

[593] *lotz kik'* ("piercer blood").

[594] *kaq che'* ("red tree"). In the *Popol Vuh*, the "red tree" refers to the croton tree (*Croton draco*; Spanish *Sangre de Dragón*—"Dragon's Blood Tree"), whose bright red sap was used as a substitute for human blood (Christenson 2007, 132–134).

THE TWENTY-FOUR GREAT HOUSES OF THE K'ICHE' AT CHI Q'UMARKAJ[595]

These, then, the nine Great Houses, were divided there.[596]

They of the lineage of Lord K'oka'ib' had nine Great Houses belonging to the Kaweqib', the people of K'iq'ab'.

There were nine Great Houses belonging to the Nijayib' lords.

There were four Great Houses belonging to the Ajaw K'iche'.

Two, then, were the Great Houses that belong to the Ajaw Saqik Tz'utuja.

Thus was the completion of twenty-four lords of the K'iche'. They ruled at the royal city of the K'iche', at Chi Q'umarkaj.[597]

THE NAMES AND TITLES OF THE NINE GREAT HOUSES OF THE KAWEQIB'[598]

These, then, are the names of the nine Great Houses [of the Kaweqib']. There are four lordly offices within the inheritance—the Ajpop of the people of K'iq'ab', the Ajpop K'amja, the Great Ajpop of the Valiant Men, and the Lesser Ajpop of the Valiant Men. They were the people of K'iq'ab'. They also were his grandsons and his sons: Leq' B'aq[599] and Lajuj No'j.[600] They took their burden of office along with K'iq'ab' and Kawisimaj. Roqche' Aj[601] was the name of the woman who gave them birth. She was an esteemed lady.[602] It was not merely a false lordship that each of them possessed.

Ajtojil, Ajq'ukumatz,[603] Chituy, Kejnay,[604] and Nim Ch'okoj Kaweq were on the left.[605]

---

[595] lines 3438–3453.

[596] There had only been nine Great Houses when the K'iche' resided at Chi Ismachi' (see p. 137)

[597] The *Popol Vuh* describes the same division of the lineages at Q'umarkaj but adds a fuller description: "They were advanced in rank, differentiated by their benches and their cushions. They were set apart, each according to their glory . . . Thus they came to be numerous. Many there were behind each of the lords. From the beginning they were the heads of numerous vassals and servants. Each of the lineages of lords became crowded" (Christenson 2007, 268).

[598] lines 3454–3481.

[599] Leq' B'aq ("Wide/Big Bones").

[600] Lajuj No'j ("Ten No'j"). This is a day on the 260-day sacred calendar, or *cholq'ij*.

[601] Roqche' is a ruling lineage among the Ilokab'. Aj is a day on the 260-day calendar.

[602] *xoqojaw* ("female ruler, princess, esteemed lady").

[603] Ajtojil Ajq'ukumatz ("She/He/They of Tojil She/He/They of Q'ukumatz"). Tojil and Q'ukumatz were the principal patron deities of the K'iche'.

[604] Chituy and Kejnay. These are abbreviated titles. In the *Popol Vuh*, these offices are listed as Popol Winaq Chi T'uy ("Counsel Person of Stacks") and Lolmet Kej Nay ("Emissary Deer House") (Christenson 2007, 269, n. 744; 270, n. 745).

[605] *xokotzil* ("left"). These five officials complete the nine Great Houses of the Kaweqib' after the four preeminent lords. In K'iche' society those seated to the right are the dominant officials in the hierarchy. Those on the left hold lesser positions of authority.

Figure 53. "These, then, the nine Great Houses, were divided there." Ruins of the Great Houses of the Kaweqib' at Chi Q'umarkaj.

REPRESENTATIVES OF THE NINE GREAT HOUSES ARE SENT FORTH[606]

And thus went forth the titles of their representatives,[607] their benches and their seats, to each of the mountains. Nine warriors and lords were the first to be given their burdens of authority by the lords. Ajtz'alam, Rajpop Ajtz'alam, and Utza'm Chinamital were their titles. There were nine Ajtz'alam, nine Rajpop Ajtz'alam, and nine Utza'm Chinamital. These were the first to take offices of authority within the Great Houses.

Merely as one they went forth; merely as one they built council houses.[608] And so they took their offices, they our grandfathers. They divided themselves on each of the mountains.[609]

---

[606] lines 3482–3501.

[607] *kiwachib'al*. Literally, "their image." In this context, it refers to representatives who act as proxies for the principal lords.

[608] *cabilto* ("council house"). Derived from the Spanish *cabildo*, a term used in Early Colonial Guatemala for a "town hall" or a building used by a council of local noblemen who administered the affairs of a community. The text emphasizes that the construction of these buildings was coordinated so that they might act in concert to defend the K'iche' capital.

[609] The *Popol Vuh* clarifies that these representatives of K'iq'ab' were sent out to garrison the mountains surrounding the capital city of Chi Q'umarkaj as sentinels in the event of an attack: "Thus the grandfathers and fathers came to be separated. All the K'iche' people were placed, each of them, on a mountain as guardians. They were guardians of arrows and bowstrings. They went as guardians against war" (Christenson 2007, 281).

MILITARY SENTINELS ARE COMMISSIONED[610]

[611]This, then, is the setting forth of the Q'alels and the Ajpops.[612] There were thirteen of Q'ulaja[613] and twelve of Tzijb'achaj,[614] along with eight timber towers of Sija Rax K'im.[615] There were three groups that were established.[616] As one they went forth. Then they left; then they were commissioned. It was the eighth generation that truly organized the work of the lords. It was then that the lords were sent forth—their older brothers and their younger brothers, the sons of the lord and the grandsons of the lord. These were sought out.[617]

And so they were commanded.[618] And this was the counsel that they gave:

"Ye, our older brothers, and ye, our younger brothers—honored and preeminent ones—our hearts cry out for you.[619] We send you forth, you our furious men, our

---

[610] lines 3502–3577.

[611] At this point in the manuscript, the text is written in a new hand with a much smaller script. Prior to this section, the subject matter is applicable to the Nima K'iche' lineage as a whole. From here on, the emphasis is on the establishment of military colonies in the area of Totonicapán where the manuscript ultimately came to reside.

[612] These are ranks within the military hierarchy of the K'iche'. They are commissioned to defeat the enemies of the Nima K'iche' and construct fortified citadels to defend their centers of power.

[613] Q'ulaja ("Beautiful/Chosen House"). This lineage settled the area of Xelaju No'j, just west of present-day Quetzaltenango (Carmack 1973, 327, n. 119). Thirteen refers to the number of military colonies established by this group in the Quetzaltenango valley.

[614] Tzijb'achaj ("Finely Ground"). The Tzijb'achaj lineage conquered the valley of Totonicapán, centered near the area known as Pueblo Viejo or Chuwi' Miq'ina' ("Above Hot Water"). It is located above a series of hot springs (Fox 1978, 161).

[615] Sija Rax K'im ("Flower Green Grass"). Both the Sija and the Q'ulaja lineages had previously attended the Great Dance of Tojil (see p. 160). The Sija settled in the area between Totonicapán and Nahuala'. An important hilltop site nearby is still known as Sija, situated on an eroded volcanic neck jutting 150 meters above the Pan-American Highway, about 11 kilometers by road west of Nahuala'. This is also the summit of the Continental Divide Range, separating the Nahuala' valley from the Quetzaltenango basin (Fox 1978, 153–155). Today, the site is located near the town of Santa Catarina Ixtahuacán (Recinos and Goetz 1953, 188, n. 33).

[616] The same three cohorts of warlords are mentioned in the *Título K'oyoy*: "The sons went to battle . . . The sons of the lords; their older brothers went . . . This testimony is not false, the thirteen K'ulaja from Xelajuj went . . . The Twelve Tzijbachaj, with . . . (the eight Tz'alam) C'oxtun Xija" (Carmack 1973, 296).

[617] *xetzukuxik* ("they were sought out"). The verb generally means "to be sought out/looked for." However, it is also used to refer to a specified term of service, which is the most likely implication here. For example, in Sáenz de Santa María (1940, 393), the transitive form of the verb, *tzukuj*, is glossed as "a time of service that the Indians had in the convents."

[618] *xepixab'ax* ("they were counseled/commanded"). The verb refers to "counsel," but it is stronger than mere "suggestions."

[619] *koq' qak'u'x chech alaq* ("cry out/weep our hearts to you"). The phrase means "to have compassion, to be preoccupied, to be worried, or to mourn."

valiant men. Go to wage war against the Seven Nations. Go to terrorize all of the mountains and valleys. Go, then, to threaten their sides and armpits,"[620] they were told. Thus they were counseled.

Their countenances were troubled; they consoled their hearts;[621] they stroked their heads[622]—they who fight with the sling and they who fight with the spear; they who came to be the guardians[623] of the plastered and whitewashed citadel. It was not their desire merely to hold the offices of Q'alel and Ajpop. They were the furious men and the valiant men of the royal house of the K'iche'. Their benches and their seats went forth.[624]

"Go, you, my older brother, and you, my younger brother.[625] Do not mourn or weep. Do not let your heart suffer. Merely find and take your female captives and your male captives. You shall go as an adversary to the royal houses of the Seven Nations—the Ajpo Sotz'il and the Ajpo Xajil,[626] the B'ak'ajolab' and the Q'eqak'uch,

---

[620] *tolok' maske'l* ("sides [below shoulder] armpits"). In K'iche' the phrase refers not only to the armpit but to the space between the upper chest and arm. This is an allusion to the method of sacrifice by heart extraction practiced by the highland Maya, cutting into the side of the victim to avoid the sternum. The same pairing of *tolok'* and *maske'l* appears in the *Popol Vuh* as an explicit reference to human sacrifice (Christenson 2007, 216–218). The *Título K'oyoy* contains an account of the same campaign into the valley of Xelaju, now called Quetzaltenango, including the counsel given by Lord K'iq'ab': " 'Go with your sons, you, our valiant warriors our watchmen, be fighters of the subject peoples of the fortified center; with bow and arrow and shield, go and trample them, grab them by the armpits and sacrifice them,' it was said to them, our grandfathers and fathers, and our sons; then indeed we left the Quiché mountains and plains and arrived here in the mountains of Xelaju" (Carmack 1973, 298).

[621] *xkikub'a' kik'u'x* ("they consoled their hearts"). It is unclear who is meant by "they" in this context. The passage may be interpreted that the lords of Chi Q'umarkaj consoled their warriors or that the warriors consoled each other or that the warriors consoled their own hearts. Any of these interpretations are valid.

[622] *xkimes kiwi'* ("they swept/stroked their heads"). According to Colonial dictionaries, the phrase refers to passing a hand over the head or face of a person as a sign of affection; when done over the head of a dead person, it is a sign of farewell.

[623] *ri'j* ("its back"). The term literally means that they are "at the back, or behind" the citadel of the K'iche' but with the implication that they are guardians, similar to the expression "they have their backs."

[624] In other words, their symbols of authority were transferred from the capital city of Chi Q'umarkaj to their new fortified centers in what would become the newly conquered territories in the valleys of Quetzaltenango and Totonicapán to the southwest.

[625] *at watz at nuchaq'* ("you my older brother you my younger brother"). This quotation is given in first-person singular, presumably by K'iq'ab' himself, and is addressed to a single individual (second-person singular), making it an unusually personal statement from the ruler to his vassal. It also utilizes the familiar *at*, a form that implies intimacy, rather than the more formal *la*, used in the earlier speech by the lords.

[626] Ajpo Sotz'il and Ajpo Xajil. The Sotz'il and the Xajil were the two principal ruling lineages of the Kaqchikel. At this point, the text identifies the principal enemies of the K'iche' who

Figure 54. "You shall go as an adversary to the royal houses of the Seven Nations—the Ajpo Sotz'il and the Ajpo Xajil." Ruins of Iximche', capital of the ancient Ajpo Sotz'il and Ajpo Xajil.

along with the Ajpo Ko'on and the B'uluxa, the Ajpo Runam and the Junajpwale. Show your furor[627] and your valor,"[628] they were told.

---

occupied the Totonicapán and Quetzaltenango valleys as the Kaqchikel. Previously, they had been allies of the K'iche', but this alliance broke down toward the end of the reign of K'iq'ab' as the result of an internal revolt by factions opposed to him (Recinos and Goetz 1953, 96–100; Maxwell and Hill 2006, 166–180). Although K'iq'ab' survived the revolt, his power and authority were severely diminished. He was forced to "humble himself" before the rebel warriors, who "seized the government and the power" (Recinos and Goetz 1953, 96–100). One by one the former vassal states in K'iq'ab's empire broke away. His old allies, the Kaqchikel, had remained loyal during the revolt but were soon beset by attacks and insults from the new lords of Q'umarkaj. Contrary to this passage, the *Annals of the Kaqchikels* assert that it was K'iq'ab' himself who counseled them to leave the city, as well as their old settlement at Chiawar, to establish their own capital independent of the K'iche': "The die is cast. Tomorrow you will cease to exercise here the command and power which we have shared with you. Abandon the city to these *k'unum* (penises) and *k'achaq* (dung). Let them not hear your words again, my sons" (Recinos and Goetz 1953, 97). Soon thereafter, in ca. 1470, the Kaqchikels under their lords Jun Toj and Wuqu[b'] B'atz' (who had fought alongside K'iq'ab' as his allies) founded the citadel of Iximche', an act that initiated a series of disastrous wars between the K'iche' and the Kaqchikel that persisted until the coming of the Spaniards in 1524. The *Title of Totonicapán* is silent regarding the revolt and the unsuccessful wars to subjugate the Kaqchikel.

[627] *iwoyewal.* Literally, "your furor/anger," although the term also implies "courage" in battle.
[628] *iwachijilal.* Literally, "your manliness," although the term implies "valor, strength."

THE ESTABLISHMENT OF MILITARY OUTPOSTS[629]

Thus they went forth from Pa K'iche' and Chi Ismachi'. They arrived at Ikiyak;[630] they arrived at Tza'm Chinq'aj; they climbed Jokol[631] and Q'ana Pek;[632] they climbed up Chi Patz'an and Chi Kaqk'ix; they climbed up Ch'ay B'amet[633] and Kaqikil.

And so it was there that they separated themselves from the Q'ulaja to inhabit the mountains and valleys. For there they constructed their buildings and their towers[634] at Kaqikil and Joyam Q'anaq'.[635] There they were established.

Then they received their ranks of lordship as Q'alel and as Ajpop. There were thirteen with the rank of Q'alel and thirteen with the rank of Ajpop among the people of Q'ulaja.[636]

And there were as well twelve Tzijb'achaj, twelve Q'alel and twelve Ajpop, twelve Q'alel of the Valiant Men and [twelve of] the Ajpop of the Valiant Men that took their ranks of office there before Joyam Q'anaq'.[637]

Surely they multiplied, they came to be many there. They began to propagate many children and sons.

---

[629] lines 3578–3744.

[630] Ikiyak. A hill between Chichicastenango and Totonicapán (Carmack and Mondloch 1983, 257, n. 330). The list of toponyms that follows describes a route leading toward the valleys of Totonicapán and Quetzaltenango to the southwest of Chi Q'umarkaj.

[631] Jokol. A river whose origin lies near the present town of San Antonio Ilotenango and flows toward Totonicapán.

[632] Q'ana Pek ("Yellow/Orange Cave"). The *Título K'oyoy* also describes this expedition and lists a number of the same toponyms. It mentions a site called Cakapek (Kaqa Pek, "Red Cave") that may be a variant name for this site. If so, then it is located south of Quetzaltenango near the Volcano of Santa María on the route leading toward the Pacific Coast (Carmack 1973, 333, n. 154).

[633] Ch'ay B'amet. An *aldea* ("dependent community") of Totonicapán (Carmack and Mondloch 1983, 257, n. 330).

[634] *k'oxtum* ("towers, fortifications"). The term includes both fortresses and fortified walls. These are often distinguished in the text as constructed of *tz'alam* ("timber"), as opposed to the paired term *tz'aq* ("buildings"), which were constructed of stone and mortar.

[635] Carmack identifies this first military outpost in the Totonicapán valley as having been established in the present-day *aldea* of Chimente (Carmack and Mondloch 1983, 258, n. 331).

[636] The implication is that the warriors sent by K'iq'ab' from Chi Q'umarkaj now divide the territory conquered by the Q'ulaja lineage (comprising the area of present-day Quetzaltenango) into thirteen districts administered by regional lords who assume the ranks of Q'alel and Ajpop by right of conquest.

[637] Carmack and Mondloch (1983, 258, n. 331) identify these military outposts with the region of Totonicapán called Chimente. According to the *Título K'oyoy*, it was the Tzijb'achaj lineage that inhabited Joyam Q'anaq', while the Q'ulaja lineage occupied the area of Xelaju No'j (Quetzaltenango).

Then they began to terrorize the land there. The mountains and valleys were given names by them.[638]

Then they gathered together their standards[639] there above K'uch Ulaq'am.[640] They proclaimed three standards. One belonged to the K'iq'ab'il people—K'iq'ab' Nima Yax[641] along with Tepepul. These were the K'iq'ab'il people. Another belonged to the Q'ale Nijayib' and the Atzij Winaq Nijayib'. The other belonged to the Ajaw K'iche'. Thus three standards were placed together.[642]

And also there were eight belonging to the Sija, eight citadels for the people of Xeyojowt and Rax K'im.[643]

Sab'ache'[644] was raised up. They climbed to Raxtum Pek to establish Chi Sub'it. Soon they constructed their buildings. There they resided. There was their foundation.[645] There it was that they divided Sab'ache'—Little Sab'ache' and Great Sab'ache' they are called.

And then it was that Xeyojowt was enlarged—thus they were named the people of Raised-Up Xeyojowt.

---

[638] Although these areas were inhabited and no doubt already had names, the K'iche' warlords renamed the newly conquered territories as a means of claiming sovereignty over them.

[639] *kilaq'am* ("their standards"). *Laq'am* can be a standard or a flag.

[640] K'uch Ulaq'am ("Vulture Their Standard"). Carmack and Mondloch (1983, 258, n. 334) identify this site as a hill south of present-day San Antonio Ilotenango, along the ancient road leading from Chichicastenango to Totonicapán.

[641] *ima Yax* ("Great Crab"). *Yax* is glossed as "crab" in the Basseta dictionary. The authors of the *Título Yax*, composed ca. 1560, claim to be descendants of this lord, who conquered the area of Totonicapán on behalf of K'iq'ab': "He only used his staff to divide the town. Suddenly the earth was rent like when a stone is struck by lightning and breaks, causing fear" (Carmack 1989, 84–85). According to the same text, he then ruled Totonicapán on behalf of K'iq'ab' and paid tribute. His full name is given as Nima Yax K'iq'ab' Topon Xink'ar Itzcot (84–85).

[642] The three standards represent the three ruling lineages of the K'iche' at Chi Q'umarkaj—the Kaweq (here referred to as the K'iq'ab'il people, named after Lord K'iq'ab', the current Ajpop and thus head of the Kaweq lineage), the Nijayib', and the Ajaw K'iche'.

[643] According to Colonial documents, Yojowt refers to a mountainous area northeast of the present-day city of Nahuala' (Carmack and Mondloch 1983, 259, n. 336). Rax K'im is the string of mountains that surrounds the valleys of Totonicapán, Nahuala', and Santa Catarina Ixtahuacán (259, n. 336)

[644] Perhaps the same as Tzib'ache', a site near Santa Catarina Ixtahuacán (Carmack and Mondloch 1983, 259, n. 336).

[645] *çemiento* ("foundation"). This is a rare appearance of a Spanish word in the narrative portion of the text. It is a K'iche' spelling of *cimiento* ("building foundation, origin, base, root"). The same Spanish term appears in an analogous section of the *Título K'oyoy* that describes the conquest of the Quetzaltenango valley (Carmack 1979, 280), an indication that perhaps the authors of the *K'oyoy* text based their account on this section from the Totonicapán document.

And so they went. They led the way of the people of Kaqsay and the people of Samayak[646] as they are called today. They accompanied the Tamub' and the Ilokab'—the Wuqmil, Sik'a, and Juwanija.[647] It was there, then, that they took their offices as Q'alel and Ajpop.

Now it was the Ch'ajkar people who departed for B'alax Ab'aj Lemoja. And they, the twelve of Tzijb'achaj, were left divided at Joyam Q'anaq' by the Q'ulaja along with the people of Sija Rax K'im. The enlargement of the mountan places was carried out by them.

Thus they guided [the people] here on their roads and on their pathways. These, then, were their roads and their pathways. These twelve of the Tzijb'achaj, they were the guides for the roads of the K'iq'ab'il people. First was the Lord Ajpop K'iq'ab' Nima Yax, second was the Lord Q'alel Nijayib', and third was the Lord Atzjij Ajaw K'iche'. They guided their vassal children and sons on their roads and on their pathways.

Then they climbed Rax Chuj.[648] They arrived at Much'ulik B'aq,[649] O'much' K'ajolab'[650] and Yiq' Ch'opi Siwan,[651] Q'axion[652] and K'ak'amab'al.[653]

---

[646] These are allies from the Pacific Coastal region that the K'iche' had recently taken from the Ajtz'ikinaja. Samayak is still known today as Samayac, a small town located southwest of Lake Atitlán.

[647] The Sik'a and Juwanija are lineages of the Ilokab' people. They participated in this campaign as allies of K'iq'ab'.

[648] Rax Chuj ("Green/Fresh Seeds"). There is still a small settlement by this name southeast of Totonicapán near the border with lands belonging to Chichicastenango (Carmack and Mondloch 1983, 260, n. 342). This section of the *Title of Totonicapán* lists the places conquered by the Tzijb'achaj in the area of Totonicapán. Robert Carmack wrote that the Yax family, as well as other indigenous informants in Totonicapán, recognized nearly all the landmarks listed in this section and could identify them as communities that still exist within the boundaries of present-day San Miguel Totonicapán (260, nn. 341–342).

[649] Much'ulik B'aq ("Decayed/Crumbled Bones"). This is a small hilltop settlement belonging to the present-day *cantón* of Pank'ix (Carmack and Mondloch 1983, 260, n. 342).

[650] O'much' K'ajolab' ("Four Hundred [five eighties] Boys"). According to the *Popol Vuh*, "four hundred boys" were killed by the demigod Zipacna, after which they rose into the sky as the Pleiades (Christenson 2007, 104). It is identified with a small hill called Pamuch in *cantón* Pank'ix.

[651] Yiq' Ch'opi Siwan ("Conquest Broken-up Canyon"). This is a canyon located near Popab'aj in the Totonicapán *aldea* of Argueta (Carmack and Mondloch 1983, 260, n. 342).

[652] Q'axion ("River Crossing").

[653] K'ak'amab'al ("Guarded Place"). Perhaps identified with Q'uq'umab'al ("Place of the Quetzals"), now known as Rancho de Teja, a community at the southeastern edge of the territory of Totonicapán (Carmack and Mondloch 1983, 260, n. 342).

Figure 55. "Then they descended to Nawala'." K'iche' men in traditional clothing, Nahuala', 1979.

They entered Xe'juyub'[654] where there were many *nawals*.[655] Then they descended to Nawala'.[656]

They climbed Chutanab'al Juyub'[657] and they climbed Pa Uwa'l Xukuq'ab'.[658]

[654] Xe'juyub' ("Below Mountain"). The Yax family of Totonicapán identifies this site as a hill near Nahuala' (Carmack and Mondloch 1983, 260, n. 342).

[655] *nawal* (derived from the Nahuatl, *naualli*). In K'iche' belief, all things both living and inanimate have a spirit essence that they call *nawal*. This spirit essence is believed to give them power to act or communicate on a supernatural plane, for example, to transform their usual form into that of a powerful animal or force of nature. When used as a verb it means "to work miracles, to enchant." Father Coto (1983 [ca. 1656], 328, 369, author translation), with his Christian bias, defines the word *naual* as "the magical means whereby the devil spoke to the K'iche' through their idols. Thus they would say that the life of the tree, the life of the stone, of the hill, is its *naual*, because they believed there was life in these objects. If a man asks his wife for something to eat or drink when there is nothing in the house, the wife would reply, '*xa pe ri tin naualih*? (Do you expect me to perform miracles?).'" *Nawal* may also refer to an animal spirit companion. Ximénez (1985 [1701], 409, author translation) defines *naual* as "witch, sacrifice, miracle, animal, or demon that accompanies the Indian; and it has been seen many times that to kill the animal is to kill the Indian."

[656] Nawala' ("Nawal/Enchanted Water"). This is the modern town of Nahuala'.

[657] Chutanab'al Juyub' ("At Steps Mountain"). A hill with a cave just west of the hill of Sija in the valley of Totonicapán. It is currently located south of Totonicapán near the Pan-American Highway (Carmack and Mondloch 1983, 260, n. 342).

[658] Pa Uwa'l Xukuq'ab' ("At Its Fluid Secretions Arch of the Sky"). *Wa'l* is the liquid secretions of a living thing—juice from fruit, tears from eyes, sweat from the brow, honey from bees,

Then they passed through Pan K'ix[659] and Xol Takar Ab'aj.[660] They passed through Tz'ultz'ul Pek,[661] Chi Jul,[662] and Chaqi'j Cho.[663]

They arrived atop the mountain of the Tzijb'achaj,[664] to the fortified citadel.

These, then, are the names of the first conquerors[665]—K'iq'ab' Nima Yax and Yaxom B'alam. They were the established sages of the Kaweq K'iq'ab'il people, along with the Q'alel Nijayib' and the Atzij Winaq Ajaw K'iche'. They were the first people to come from Pa K'iche'[666] and Chi Ismachi'.

Then they arrived at Miq'ina'[667] and Tz'ikiche',[668] at Pa Uwa'l and Sajoq'. Then was their admirable greatness[669] atop Saqmal Ajaw.[670] They climbed Q'uxlikel and Chuja Tz'ikin.

---

and the like. According to Basseta, *xucucab* is the *arco del cielo* ("arch of the sky"). This is most likely a poetic reference to "rain." Xukuq'ab' is a community in Cantón Vásquez, north of the hill of Sija (Carmack and Mondloch 1983, 260, n. 343).

[659] Pan K'ix ("At Spine"). This is a common toponym for a place dedicated to the ritual practice of bloodletting, which was carried out using spines to prick the body. There is a *cantón* bearing the same name southeast of Totonicapán near Chi Jul (Carmack and Mondloch 1983, 260, n. 344).

[660] Xol Takar Ab'aj ("Center Plain Stone"). Takarab'aj, Chaqi'j Cho, and Chi Jul are located southeast of Totonicapán near a dry lake bed (Carmack and Mondloch 1983, 260, n. 344).

[661] Tz'ultz'ul Pek ("Adorned Cave").

[662] Chi Jul ("At the Well/Hole").

[663] Chaqi'j Cho ("Dry Lake").

[664] This is the first fortified citadel, built atop a flat mesa dominating the eastern approach to the Totonicapán valley. Carmack's informants identify it as the settlement of Ojer Tinamit ("Ancient Citadel"), also known as Chutinamit ("At the Citadel") (Carmack and Mondloch 1983, 260, n. 345).

[665] *ajyiq'* ("flame kindler/conqueror"). *Yiq'* is "to kindle a flame or set fire to something." As seen in the latter portion of this section, the term implies conquest. In this context, Matsumoto (2017, 166n53) points out that *yiq'* may be a variant of *yaq'* ("to conquer"), *a* to *i* being a relatively common substitution.

[666] Pa K'iche' ("At K'iche' ") refers to the central area of the K'iche' region, which would include both Chi Q'umarkaj and Chi Ismachi'.

[667] Miq'ina' ("Hot Water"). These are the hot springs that were the focus of the settlement of ancient Totonicapán. The ruins of this citadel are known today as Pueblo Viejo (Spanish for "Old Town"). The K'iche' name for modern city of Totonicapán is Chuwi' Miq'ina' ("Above the Hot Water").

[668] Tz'iki[n]che' ("Bird Tree"). Along with Chuja Tz'ikin ("At the House of Birds"), these sites represent the communities that were established furthest to the southwest within the Totonicapán district. Today, they are located just west of the Pan-American Highway.

[669] *kimayjanik* ("their admiration/greatness"). It is difficult to accurately translate this noun, as *mayjanik* can mean "admiration, authority, miracle, marvel, illustriousness, greatness, offering, or reverence," all of which could potentially fit the context of the sentence.

[670] Saqmal Ajaw ("Egg Lord"). It is the most prominent hill in the Totonicapán valley, located

Figure 56. "Then they arrived at Miq'ina." View of the hot springs of Miq'ina' below the plateau of Totonicapán. Photograph by John Fox, 1971.

These were the sons of K'iq'ab'.[671] Five were the sons that he engendered and they are these—his first son was Xitapul, the second was Sun, the third was Isk'wat, the fourth was Yamu, and the name of the fifth was Q'anil. He then, Xitapul, separated himself from his younger brothers. Thus there were five sons who were engendered by K'iq'ab' and there were five buildings there at Chwi' Xtoka[672] and Chi K'wa.[673]

<hr />

southwest of the city. The modern-day *aldea* of Xesaqmalja ("Beneath Egg House") is at the foot of the hill. There are widespread rumors in the area that the hill contains buried treasure, hence the Spanish name for the hill, Cerro de Oro (Spanish, "Hill of Gold").

[671] These are the sons of K'iq'ab' Nima Yax, the lord of Totonicapán, and not K'iq'ab', the Ajpop at Chi Q'umarkaj.

[672] Chwi' Xtoka ("Atop Xtoka"). This settlement, as well as Chik'wa, are sites located just north and west of Chuja Tz'ikin. According to the *Título Paxtoka*, there was a fort atop the hill of Xtoka occupied by a lord named Excamparitz and his court at the time of the Spanish Conquest (Carmack 1973, 359–361). He appears in the *Título K'oyoy* as Lord Xkamparij of Xtoka.

[673] Chi K'wa ("At the Springs/Well"). According to the *Título K'oyoy*, the ruler of Chi K'wa was Lord Quemaxitapul, the same name as the eldest son of K'iq'ab' Nima Yax who held the rank of Q'alel Ajaw (Carmack 1973, 300). He survived the Spanish Conquest and adopted a Spanish name. He may be the same lord who was a signatory of the *Títulos de la Casa Ixquin-Nehaib', Señora del Territorio de Otzoya* (also known as the *Título de Quetzaltenango and Momostenango*) under the name Don Diego Pérez Quemaxidapul (Recinos 1957, 93). He also appears as a signatory for the *Título Real de Don Francisco Izquin Nehaib'* as Don Diego Pérez Kemaxitapul (Recinos 1957, 103; Matsumoto 2017, 238–239, 386–387).

It was there that the message arrived regarding Don Pedro de Alvarado, Donatii.[674] There is only one that would conquer, that would set aflame the houses. It was at Pa Xkaqtunum that K'iq'ab' carried out his conquest by fire.[675]

THE CAMPAIGN AGAINST LAKE ATITLÁN AND THE SOUTH COAST[676]

These, then, went forth—K'iq'ab' and Kawisimaj—from Pa K'iche', from Chi Q'umarkaj. He was accompanied by the thirteen Q'ulaja and the twelve Tzijb'achaj.[677] Thus was the creation of great glory and sovereignty by K'iq'ab' and Kawisimaj,

---

[674] Don Pedro de Alvarado was the Spanish conqueror who defeated the K'iche' in 1524. Donatio or Donadi is the K'iche' spelling of the Mexica god of the sun, Tonatiuh. The anonymous author of the *Isagoge* wrote that this was a title the Maya of Guatemala used to refer to Alvarado: "During Lent arrived Donadí, who is Don Pedro de Alvarado, who the Mexicans called *Tonatio*, the Indians of these provinces corrupting the word in various ways, some calling him Donatio, others Donativo, and here Donadi" (Anonymous 1935 [ca. 1700]:2, iv, 191). Pedro de Alvarado was widely known by this name among the highland Maya, as seen in the numerous references to him as Donadiu in indigenous texts composed in the sixteenth century, including the *Popol Vuh* (Christenson 2007, 295), the *Títulos de la Casa Ixquin-Nehaib, Señora del Territorio de Otzoya* (Recinos 1957, 84; Matsumoto 2017, 358), and the *Título Real de Don Francisco Izquin Nehaib* (Recinos 1957, 97; Matsumoto 2017, 160–161). The Tlaxcalan chronicler Diego Muñoz Camargo wrote: "They called Don Pedro de Alvarado 'the sun,' because they said he was the son of the sun for being blond and ruddy, of very beautiful face, charming, and of good appearance" (in Acuña 1984, 238, author translation). Alvarado's hair was more red than blond, but it was considered to be fair in color compared to the dark hair of the K'iche'. Light-colored hair was a physical trait unknown in the Pre-Columbian New World, other than albinos, who are often called *ralk'walab' q'ij* ("children of the sun").

[675] *uyiq' K'iq'ab'* ("his kindling K'iq'ab'"). *Yiq'* is to illuminate or to kindle fire. The authors of the text compare the destruction by fire caused by K'iq'ab' Nima Yax, the conqueror of the Totonicapán valley, at the unknown site of Pa Xkaqtunum to the conquests of Don Pedro de Alvarado. Alvarado burned the K'iche' capital city of Chi Q'umarkaj as well as its kings: "And I saw that by occupying their land and burning it, I could bring them into the service of His Majesty. Thus I decided to burn the lords who, at the time I desired to burn them, would appear in their confessions, admitted that they were the ones who had ordered and carried on the war ... Therefore, since I knew them to have such ill will toward the service of His Majesty and for the good and tranquility of the land, I burned them, and I commanded to be burned the town of Utatlán [the Nahuatl language version of Q'umarkaj as named by Alvarado's Tlaxcalan mercenaries] to its foundations, for it was dangerous and strong ... All they that were taken prisoners of war were branded and made slaves" (Alvarado 1946, 457-459, author translation).

[676] lines 3745–3855.

[677] The Tzijb'achaj lineage conquered the Totonicapán area. The *Title of Totonicapán* concludes with this campaign, perhaps to emphasize their conquests as allies of Lord K'iq'ab' of Q'umarkaj.

Figure 57. "They passed by the shores of the lake called 'Mirror Water.'" Laguna Lemo'a' ("Mirror Water"), Guatemala.

our grandfathers, we, the Kaweq people.

Then he made a circuit around the borders of the lands of the K'iche', the K'iche' mountains and valleys. They left Pa K'iche'. They passed by the shores of the lake called "Mirror Water."[678] There he was reflected in the waters as an eagle, as a quetzal.

Then they passed by Kaqixkan. They climbed Pab'al Ab'aj, Chajaxaq'[679] and Chi Q'apoj, Tza'm Tzolola Pek[680] and B'alam Ab'aj. From the center of the lake, he divided the lake in half. Half belonged to the Ajpo Sotz'il[681] and half belonged to K'iq'ab'.[682]

---

[678] Cho Lemo'a' ("Lake Mirror Water"). A small lake located south of Chi Q'umarkaj, which still bears the name Lemoa.

[679] Chajaxaq' is a *cantón* just north of present-day Solola (Carmack and Mondloch 1983, 262, n. 355).

[680] Tza'm Tzolola Pek ("Border Tzolola Cave"). This is present-day Solola, northeast of Lake Atitlán. There is a large cave, often used as a ceremonial site, located just below Solola to the south, near the present-day town of San Jorge.

[681] Ajpo[p] Sotz'il ("Ajpop of the Sotz'il"). This is the Ajpop, or leader, of the Sotz'il lineage (also written as Tzotz'il in the text), one of the two major branches of the Kaqchikel who occupied the northern shore of Lake Atitlán.

[682] *nik'aj re ajpotzotz'il nik'aj rech k'iq'ab'* ("half belonged to Ajpotzotz'il half belonged to K'iq'ab'"). According to the Early Colonial text *Guerras Comunes de Quiches y Cakchiqueles*,

Figure 58. "He divided the lake in half. Half belonged to the Ajpo Sotz'il and half belonged to K'iq'ab." View of Lake Atitlán looking south toward the Tz'utujil-speaking people who occupy the lands on the south shore. The K'iche' lands are to the east, and the Kaqchikel (led by the Ajpo Sotz'il) hold the lands on the northern and western shores, 1979.

Then he entered Choy Juyub',[683] He entered Chi Jukb'a'ikaj and Pa Meseb'al. They passed Chi Ruk'ab'ala' Q'uq'[684] and Chi Q'ojom, Tza'm Q'ana Ulew, and before the face of the Naranjos River.[685]

all of these conquered lands belonged to the Tz'utujil-speaking people of the Ajtz'ikinaja lineage prior to this campaign by K'iq'ab' (Recinos 1957, 146–147). The Ajpo Tzotz'il is the head of the principal ruling lineage of the Kaqchikel. Even today, the Kaqchikel inhabit most of the northern and northeastern shores of Lake Atitlán. The K'iche' occupy lands in the hills above the northwestern shores. The text does not mention that the southern shores of the lake continued to be ruled by the Ajtz'ikinaja with their capital, Chiya', situated on the lower slope of Volcano San Pedro, where it meets the waters of a large inlet of the lake.

[683] Choy Juyub' ("Lake Mountain" in the Kaqchikel and Tz'utujil languages). Lake Atitlán is surrounded by mountains, as it is a caldera lake. These include three great volcanoes on its southern shore, one of which may be this mountain. Carmack and Mondloch (1983, 263, n. 356) suggest that it may be Volcano San Pedro, as it is the furthest west of the three and the campaign is directed toward the western territories held by the Ajtz'ikinaja on the south coast (see figure 58). If so, the K'iche' would have passed the mountain below its western slopes, as the well-defended stronghold of the Ajtz'ikinaja, Chiya', dominates the east side.

[684] Ruk'ab'ala' Q'uq' ("Their Drinking Place Quetzals"). This must be at a high elevation, the habitat for quetzals.

[685] Chwa Naranjos ("Before Naranjos"). Carmack and Mondloch suggest that this is the river that still bears the name Naranjos (Spanish for "Oranges"), with headwaters in the

Figure 59. "Then he entered Choy Juyub." Bay of Lake Atitlán with Volcano San Pedro and the Ajtz'ikinaja capital of Chiya' atop the hill at its base.

Then he descended to Muqulik and Xikat. He went to establish his borders at the mountain,[686] [he went with those called Yakis[687] to the Ceiba Inup;[688] from here to Makol Ab'aj-Tab'alamin, where K'iq'ab' Kawisimaj left those of K'ulaja and

present-day Department of San Marcos and that empties into the Pacific halfway between Tapachula and Retalhuleu. The sites listed here, near the Naranjos River, are apparently located in the southern coastal lowlands, but they are difficult to identify.

[686] The upper portion of folio 31r of the manuscript is missing at this point. Fortunately, Father Dionisio Chonay based his partial translation of the document either on this same manuscript before it was damaged, which appears likely, or on an intact copy. I have inserted the missing portion from Chonay's translation in brackets (Recinos and Goetz 1953, 194). The only alterations I have made are to the orthography of names and toponyms for consistency.

[687] The Yakis are Nahua speakers. The text affirms that the Yakis, at least in part, were allies of the K'iche' during this campaign and subsequently established military outposts guarding the southwestern borders of K'iche' territory. The *Título de Santa Clara* describes the same area and mentions the River Zaki Oca (Ocós River) as the K'iche' territorial boundary near the present-day border between Guatemala and Mexico. The same text also mentions the ceiba tree nearby, perhaps functioning as a boundary marker (Recinos 1957, 176–177).

[688] *Inup* ("ceiba"). The original text, now missing, perhaps only read *inup* here. Chonay appears to have included the original word and then translated it for the benefit of Spanish speakers. In the *Título de Santa Clara*, the marker is simply called Inup (Recinos 1957, 176–177). Large trees such as the ceiba were used as landmarks or boundary markers in the Guatemalan highlands.

Figure 60. "Then were planted two ceiba trees by K'iq'ab' and Kawisimaj." Ceiba tree, Guatemala.

Figure 61. "This other formed the border of the mountain of the people of Saqulew and Yok." The ruins of Saqulew, capital of the Mam

Tzijb'achaj.[689]

He went to Kajakalkat Nawal[690] beside the mouth or passage of the Samala';[691] from here to Siwan and, accompanied by all the valiant warriors, he arrived at the mouth of Rewe, an arm of the sea. There ended the measuring of the lands] before the faces of the Yakis.

---

[689] The implication here is that K'iq'ab' and Kawisimaj left garrisons made up of the K'ulaja (conquerors of the Quetzaltenango valley) and the Tzijb'achaj (conquerors of the Totonicapán valley) to guard the approaches to the coast.

[690] The Nahua-speaking Yaki who had participated as allies of the K'iche' in this campaign occupied the area around the mouth of the Samala' River, centered at a place called Kajakalkat Nawal. Carmack and Mondloch (1983, 263, n. 357) identify this as the modern community of Nahuatán, between Tapachula and Ayutla in the coastal region of Chiapas near the Guatemalan border. This would represent the extreme southwestern extent of the lands ruled by the K'iche'. The *Testament Catalina Nijay*, composed in Nahuatl and dated 1587, asserts that the Yakis in this area of the Pacific Coast continued to have close relations with the K'iche' in the late sixteenth century (Carmack 1973, 372).

[691] The Samala' River still bears the same name. Its headwaters form near Totonicapán and empty into the Pacific Ocean.

Then were planted two ceiba trees[692] by K'iq'ab' and Kawisimaj. "Clefted Ceiba" and "Clefted Altar"[693] they were called. One belonged to the Yaki people—they of Ayutlekat[694] and they of Masatlekat.[695] The other formed the border of the mountain of the people of Saqulew and Yok, Q'anchib'ix and Q'aq'alix.[696]

---

[692] These two ceiba trees are also described in the *Título de Quetzaltenango and Momostenango*, where they appear as boundary markers near the Pacific Coast. Although that text ascribes the campaign in the Soconusco to an earlier ruler, Q'ukumatz K'otuja, it follows the same route and mentions the same battles as those of K'iq'ab'. Q'ukumatz K'otuja in this case is most likely used as a title for K'iq'ab', as suggested by Recinos (1957, 15–16): "And then they went and entered through two very large ceibas, there they came to a halt. They put the cacique and [the] leaders in these two ceibas, they put their eagle weapons [there], because a cacique called Q'ukumatz K'otuja ordered it, that they put those weapons in those two ceibas as a sign of their boundary marker where they had reached their conquest. Then from there he went to the sea to conquer and to win the land and to rest by the sea. And then the aforementioned cacique, in order to please his soldiers, turned into an eagle, he submerged himself in the sea, demonstrating that he was also conquering the sea. And after having left the sea, they were very glad of [the] great outcome that they had had" (Matsumoto 2017, 393).

[693] Laq'alik Mumus ("Clefted Altar"). *Mumus* is derived from the Nahuatl *mumuztli*, meaning "altar" (Molina 2001 [1571], 61).

[694] Ayotecatl is the ancient name for the southwestern coast of Guatemala and the district of Soconusco (the extension of the south coast westward into Chiapas, Mexico) (Recinos and Goetz 1953, 194, n. 44). The *Títulos de la Casa Ixquin-Nehaib, Señora del Territorio de Otzoya* describes the same campaign: "Then he entered through another village called Ayutecat, also fighting, he killed 200 Ayutec Indians, and he took from them many pearls, gold, emeralds, and many riches. Through Mazatán, another village of many Indians, he entered to fight [at] midday. Those of Mazatecat, seeing the destruction that he had made in the rest of the villages, they did not want war, but rather then they gave him peace" (Matsumoto 2017, 391). Recinos (1957, 79, n. 69) notes that this area of the Soconusco was conquered soon afterward by the Mexica ruler Ahuitzotl (reigned 1486–1502), according to various Mexica chronicles.

[695] Masatlekat. Today, this is the area of Mazatán, the region of the Soconusco coast just west of Tapachula, Chiapas, near the border with Guatemala.

[696] These four toponyms all refer to regions occupied by the Mam to the north and west of K'iche' territory. Saqulew is a large Mam citadel built on a mesa top approximately 3 kilometers north of the modern city of Huehuetenango. The *Popol Vuh* (Christenson 2007, 278), the *Título K'oyoy* (Carmack 1973, 300), and the *Título de Santa Clara la Laguna* (Recinos 1957, 178–179) use Saqulew to refer to the Mam people in general, which is the meaning here. The Mam region was conquered soon after the campaigns of K'iq'ab' against the Sacapulas valley sites. The Mam remained subject to the K'iche' and fought with them against the Spaniards (Fox 1978, 147). According to the *Títulos de la Casa Ixquin-Nehaib'*, Yok is the term for the head of a community among the Mam people (Recinos 1957, 75); Q'anchib'ix is mentioned several times in Early Colonial titles as a Mam community (75, n. 48), often listed next to Bamac, a Mam site in the region of San Miguel Ixtahuacán, Department of San Marcos; Q'aq'alix is located in a region of Mam speakers west of Quetzaltenango near a hill known as Siete Orejas (Recinos 1957, 76; Carmack and Mondloch 1983, 264, n. 360).

Thirteen score [days]⁶⁹⁷ passed Lord K'iq'ab' there. He was truly our grandfather and our father, of we the Kaweqib'. Thirteen score [days] he demonstrated his wondrous power and his spirit essence with fiery comets and phantom globes of fire, clouds and mist, Sudden Thunderbolt and Youngest Thunderbolt.⁶⁹⁸ It was then that he devastated⁶⁹⁹ all of the nations.

These, then, are the borders of the lands of the K'iche' people with Aq'a'ab' and K'oxom Xaq, before Usiatik and before Ab'al Tza'm. There were many K'iche' before Laq'am Ab'aj, Tza'm Yaki, Aq'a Yoqa, and B'alam Kolob'.⁷⁰⁰

⁷⁰¹[Now on the twenty-eighth of September 1554, we sign this attestation in which we have written that which by tradition our ancestors told us, who came from the other part of the sea, from Siwan-Tulan, bordering on Babylonia. We the firstborn of the Kaweqib' sign, we the descendants of B'alam K'itze'.]

---

⁶⁹⁷ *oxlaj winaq* ("thirteen twenties/score"). *Winaq* in this context refers to a period of twenty days. Thirteen times twenty days is 260, the length of the sacred Maya calendar, or *cholq'ij*, which is still used in the Maya highlands. The implication is that the campaign of K'iq'ab' was timed to complete an entire sacred cycle of 260 days. The list of wonders he performed during this time attests to the ceremonial nature of the campaign.

⁶⁹⁸ Raxa Kaqulja' Ch'ipa Kaqulja' ("Sudden Thunderbolt Youngest Thunderbolt"). These are two of the three lightning deities who collectively are known as "Heart of Sky" and who presided over the creation of the world according to the *Popol Vuh* (Christenson 2007, 69–73).

⁶⁹⁹ *xe'upaxij* ("he devastated them"). The term also implies "breaking apart" or "scattering."

⁷⁰⁰ The Aq'a'ab' people settled the area of Cawinal on the Río Blanco approximately 14 kilometers north of Cubulco in the Baja Verapaz (Fox 1978, 243–250). This would represent the northeastern border of the K'iche' territory. Alternatively, Recinos (1957, 109, n. 26) links a major branch of the Aq'a'ab' to the area of present-day Sacapulas along the Río Chixoy, which is the more likely interpretation in this context. Usyatik, Laq'ama B'aj, and possibly Ab'al Tza'm K'iche' are located in the area to the west of Quetzaltenango (Recinos 1957, 76–77; Carmack and Mondloch 1983, 264, n. 362). The Tza'm Yaki ("borders/edge/ leader of the Yaki") refers to the southern Pacific coastal areas where Nahuatl speakers were concentrated. The Aq'a Yoka and B'alam Kolob' are located in the Mam region west of Quetzaltenango according to the *Título K'oyoy* (Carmack 1973, 279, 330).

⁷⁰¹ The final folio page of the manuscript is missing its upper section and is heavily damaged along its right edge. A fragmentary phrase at the beginning of the page can be read "this day . . . in the year 155 . . ." The missing date can be restored as September 28, 1554, from Father Dionisio Chonay's translation of the intact document (Recinos and Goetz 1953, 194).

[Don José Kokoa K'iq'ab']⁷⁰²

---

[702] Because of the damaged page, some of the names are missing in whole or in part. I have placed the missing portions of the signatories in brackets as recorded by Chonay (Recinos and Goetz 1953, 195). Recinos suggested that Kokoa is scribal error for Kortes (Cortés). The first two signatories are thus the same principal lords who appear at the end of the page (195, n. 45). At some point following the Spanish Conquest, the surviving lords of the highland Maya lineages were baptized as Christians and adopted Spanish names. Ximénez (1929–1931, I.xli.128) doubted that this took place when Alvarado invaded highland Maya territory and suggested that the baptisms began several years later when the first missionaries arrived in Guatemala. Early evangelization efforts focused on survivors of the old highland Maya nobility in the hope that they would set an example for the rest of the people. Baptism was also a necessary step for any Maya of noble birth who aspired to a place in the new political order, since without it the Spanish authorities would not recognize their legitimacy or territorial claims. The fact that this is the case here is evident by the title "Don." This title was given to Maya noblemen who professed faith in Christ as well as those who could prove their legitimacy in court. Many of the documents composed by the Maya in the sixteenth century were "titles" written for the purpose of establishing the legitimacy of former ruling lords and their descendants in an effort to recover hereditary honors. As noblemen recognized by the Spanish Crown, they were allowed to receive some tribute from their subjects, to be exempt from compulsory labor, and to ride horses. In addition, baptism afforded a measure of protection from the excesses of Spanish rule. Without it, unconverted Maya were subject to enslavement until the reforms of Governor Alonso López de Cerrato abolished the practice after 1548. Don José/Joseph Cortés does not appear in any other known Early Colonial document, although Don Juan Cortés held the position of Ajpop K'amja when the *Popol Vuh* was composed (ca. 1554–1558), shortly after the Totonicapán manuscript was signed. It is possible that Don José Cortés was a predecessor to Don Juan Cortés, although I think it is more likely that they are the same person. Juan Cortés, son of Tepepul, was recognized by the Spaniards as the Ajpop K'amja and, along with Don Juan de Rojas, who is the next signatory, represented the fourteenth generation of ruling lords after the founder B'alam K'itze' (Christenson 2007, 297). Don Juan Cortés petitioned the Spanish Crown to restore the rights and privileges of lordship the ancient K'iche' lords had enjoyed prior to the Conquest. Accompanied by a Dominican priest, he sailed to Spain in 1557 to press his claim before King Philip II (Carrasco 1967). He would certainly have taken with him copies of indigenous texts to prove his claims, possibly including a version of the *Title of Totonicapán*. Unfortunately, his ship was attacked by French pirates who seized his documents and any tribute he may have carried with him. He was nevertheless granted audiences before high officials in Spain. Franciscans, who opposed the efforts of Dominican missionaries to support petitions by K'iche' lords, succeeded in opposing these claims on the grounds that they would foster further revolts by the Indians. Spanish authorities in Guatemala also urged caution in granting too much authority to the old K'iche' nobility. In a letter to the Spanish Crown written in 1552, Alonso López Cerrato, governor of Guatemala, wrote that the ancient K'iche' lords wielded tremendous religious as well as political power over their subjects and could prove dangerous if they were to rebel "because anciently they were revered as gods, and if this persists, the lords could raise the land easily" (Carmack 1973, 379).

[Don Juan de Rosa] K'iq'ab'[703]   [Don José Pérez] [?] Ajaw K'iche'

Don Diego García Chituy   [Christóbal Fer]nánd[ez Nija]yib'

Don Jorge Nijayib'   Don Cristóbal de Velasco Nim Ch'okoj Kaweq

Don Diego Pérez Ajq'ukumatz   Juan Lucas Ajtojil

Don Cristobal,[704] scribe of the town hall   Don Pedro Xikitzal Tepe

These are our signatures,[705] we the first K'iche'—the Kaweqib', the Nijayib', and the Ajaw K'iche'; the Ajtojil and the Ajq'ukumatz; the Chituy and the Kejnay.[706] I, Don Joseph Cortés K'iq'ab', I give my signature at the end of this Act of K'iq'ab' Nima Yax.

I, Don Juan de Ro[sa] K'iq'ab', we give this ... Act of the Ajpop of Chuwi' Miq'ina'.[707]

---

[703] This is the K'iche' spelling for the Spanish name Don Juan de Rojas. He was the son of Tekum and the fourteenth successor to the founding ancestor, B'alam K'itze', of the Kaweq lineage (Christenson 2007, 297; Matsumoto 2017, 387, n. 305). Don Juan de Rojas was probably named after the Spanish captain Diego de Rojas who came to Guatemala at the orders of Hernán Cortés in the second half of 1524 with fifty Spanish soldiers (Akkeren 2003). Juan de Rojas must have been born sometime between this year and ca. 1530 when Diego de Rojas departed for Peru. When his father was hanged in ca. 1535, Juan de Rojas would have been too young to rule, leaving the K'iche' without effective leadership for some time. He had begun to exercise some measure of power by at least 1550 when he became involved in a land dispute and demanded that certain merchants from the Chi Q'umarkaj area pay tribute to him (Lutz 1994, 25–26, n. 28). In his mature years as a native *cacique*, Juan de Rojas collected tribute, carried out censuses, provided labor, enforced church attendance and instruction, and acted as the principal judge in local disputes (Carmack 1981, 313). According to Ximénez (1929–1931, I.xxviii.79), Juan de Rojas was eventually given a special hall at the Royal Palace of Guatemala next to the king's representative. Here, he administered the affairs of the Maya as a vassal lord of the Spaniards.

[704] Carmack and Mondloch (1983, 266, n. 366) suggest that this is the same Don Cristobal who acted as scribe for the *Título de Caciques de Totonicapán*, dated 1544.

[705] *qafirma* ("our signatures"). This combines the K'iche' first-person plural possessive pronoun *qa* ("our") with the Spanish word *firma* ("signature"). No signatures appear on the document, as this is a later copy of the original, which is now lost. The concept of signatures on documents is no doubt a Spanish introduction, and it is interesting that the practice is now adopted for indigenous texts. No such signatures appear at the conclusion of the *Popol Vuh*, although in the case of the latter the lack of signatures may have been for the purpose of anonymity to protect the authors from persecution (Christenson 2007, 36, 64–65, n. 36).

[706] Chituy Kejnay. These are abbreviated titles. In the *Popol Vuh*, these offices are listed as Popol Winaq chi T'uy ("Counsel Person of Stacks") and Lolmet Kej Nay ("Emissary Deer House") (Christenson 2007, 269–270, nn. 744–745).

[707] Chuwi' Miq'ina' ("Above Hot Water"). This is the K'iche' name for the town now known as Totonicapán. The text makes clear that this is the *Auto* ("Act") of K'iq'ab' Nima Yax, the Ajpop of Chuwi' Miq'ina', and not of the signatories. K'iq'ab' Nima Yax was the lord who conquered the Totonicapán region on behalf of the Ajpop K'iq'ab' of the Kaweq lineage (see pp. 173–175). He would have long since died, but the document serves as a legal land title based on right of conquest and was duly signed by the ruling K'iche' lords who held office in 1554.

Literal English Translation with Parallel K'iche' Text in Modern Orthography

Folio i

tz'aq re aj[a]w k'iche'	building of ajaw k'iche'
wa'e sokib'al	this place of sacrifice
tz'aq re nima raj[p]op achij	building of great their ajpop valiant men
wa'e tzumpan	this skull rack
wa'e tz'aq re q'alel nijayib'	this building of q'alel nijayib'
wa'e tz'aq rech k'iq'ab' ajpop kaweq	this building of k'iq'ab' ajpop kaweq
[wa']e k'ut chun saqkab'[708] pa nima k'iche'	[these] thus plaster whitewash in nima k'iche'
chi q'u[m]arkaj, Santa Cruz kuchax kamik	chi q'umarkaj, Santa Cruz it is called this day

---

[708] *q'aq'kab'* in the original manuscript. I agree with Carmack and Mondloch (1983, 204, n. 4) who suggest that this is an example of scribal error and should read *saqkab'*.

Folio ii

AUTo del Señor D[on] Ju[an]   Coat of Arms of Señor Don Juan
De Aguilar conquistador   de Aguilar conqueror

Folio 1r

WA'E UKAJ[709] tzij
nima b'ixel

THIS FOURTH word
great song

wa'e ub'i'
Parayiso Terrenal[710]

this its name
Paradise Earthly

Rulewal Q'anal
Raxal chuchaxik

Its Land Yellowness
Greenness it is called

chita' wakamik
xchinb'ij chiwech

hear you all this day
I shall speak to you all

uk'oje'ik
parayiso terrenal

its nature
paradise earthly   10

xa ju paj tzij
xchinb'ij chiwech

merely one division word
I shall speak to you all

k'o wi[711] ucholotajik
uq'ijil:

there is its ordering
its time periods:

xb'an wi jujun
chi b'anoj

was done each one
of works

rumal *Dios*
nima ajaw:

by him God
great lord:

unab'e wa'e *do[mi]ngo*
xuwinaqirisaj nima saq

first this sunday
he conceived great light   20

ri *dios*
nima ajaw:

the god
great lord:

---

[709] Garry Sparks suggests that the original manuscript, which reads *ukab'* ("second"), is scribal error for *ukaj* ("fourth"). This section corresponds to chapter 30 of the *Theologia Indorum*, which is the *ukaj nima b'i'* ("fourth great name") (Sparks 2017, 219, n. 17).

[710] In this modern orthographic version of the text, Spanish words are italicized to distinguish them from indigenous languages. Non-indigenous proper names retain the original spelling, although variants have been standardized according to the most common spelling of the name as written in the original manuscript.

[711] *wi* is a locative particle or a marker of emphasis. It has no equivalent in the English language and is not translated.

lunes ukab' q'ij	monday second day
b'elej tas chi kaj xk'ase'	nine divisions of sky were raised
rumal *dios*	by him god
n[ima a]j[a]w[712]	great lord
ub'elejichal kesolow chirij ulew	each of the nine encircles around earth
kesutuw puch	they rotate as well
chi ronojel[713] q'ij ula ju tas chi silab'ik:	on all days each division of moving:
junelik kub'ul	forever adorning 30
rochoch	their homes
utinamit chi ronojel q'ij:	their towns on all days:
Rox q'ij	Third day
xuwinaqirisaj	he[714] conceived
ronojel juyub'	all mountains
taq'aj	valleys
che'	wood
ab'aj	stone
xk'oje' ronojel	came to be all of them
pa *mardes* =	on tuesday = 40
Miergoles	Wednesday
ukaj q'ij	fourth day
q'ij	sun
ch'umil xya' kisaqil	stars were given their light

---

[712] *nhu* in the original manuscript (*njw* in modern orthography), a contracted form of *nima ajaw* ("great lord"), the most common title for God in the *Theologia Indorum*. The Totonicapán text periodically uses the contracted form from here on.

[713] *rononojel* in the original manuscript, scribal error for *ronojel*.

[714] This is a third-person singular pronoun. Pronouns are not gendered in K'iche', so this could be translated as "she," "he," or "it." It is probable that Vico, the author of the *Theologia Indorum* on which this section of the Totonicapán document is based, had in mind "he" to refer to the Judaeo-Christian God. At times, both Vico and the K'iche' authors of this text adopted the K'iche' deities Tz'aqol B'itol as the equivalent of God (see p. 63). In traditional Maya literature, Tz'aqol and B'itol are gendered as paired female and male deities in highland Maya documents, but here the pronoun is singular; therefore, the reference is likely based on Vico's understanding of the nature of God as a monotheistic male deity.

ru[mal] *Dios*	by him God	
nima ajaw	great lord	
unimaqil	its greatness	
ch'umil	stars	
ruk' q'ij	with sun	
ik'	moon	50
retal saq[715]	its sign light	
retal aq'ab' =	its sign night =	
Juebes	Thursday	
Ro' q'ij	Fifth day	
xwinaqir wi kar pa ja'	were conceived fish in water	
kuk' tz'ikin	with them birds	
[x]winaqir wi ch'uti kar =	were conceived small fish =	
nima kar	large fish	
biernes	friday	
uwaq[716] q'ij xwinaqir	sixth day were conceived	60
ch'uti kumatz	small serpents	
nima kumatz	great serpents	
ronojel chikop pa ulew	all animals on earth	
xwinaqir	were conceived	
rumal *dios*	by him god	
nima ajaw	great lord	
xare k'ut xwinaqir	moreover thus were conceived	
pa *viernes*	on friday	
keje' k'ut uk'asb'axik	then thus were given life	
ronojel ub'anoj *dios* chupam jujun chi	all his works god within each of days	70
q'ij		

---

[715] The text reads *cak* ("red") in the original orthography, possibly referring to the reddening of the sky at dawn. More likely it is a scribal error for *çak* ("white, light, brightness, clarity"), which is the parallel word used in the *Theologia Indorum* for the creation of the sun and moon on the fourth day (folio 44v, lines 10–11).

[716] *uwaqaq* in the original manuscript, scribal error for *uwaq*.

chiwalaj iwib'	propagate yourselves
chik'iyarisaj iwib'	increase yourselves
chitz'ab'ej iwib'[717]	multiply yourselves
xcha' *dios*	said god
nima ajaw	great lord
chikech ub'anoj	to them his works
keje' k'ut kipixab'axik ronojel ub'anoj	then thus their being commanded all his works
rumal tz'aqol	by framer
b'itol	shaper
¶ Wakamik k'ut xchiqatikib'a' ub'ixik	¶ This Day thus we shall begin its telling 80
ucholik puch	its account as well
Parayiso Terrenal	Paradise Earthly
xawi jere rachb'anik ulew	similarly its care earth
ta xutzin	then was completed
ri *parayiso*	the paradise
kojcha' chirech	we speak to it
keje' k'ut xchintikib'a' ucholik ——	then thus I shall begin its account ——
Ukaj paj tzij	Fourth division word
wa'e ub'ixik	this its telling
b'elej ch'ob' chi	nine groups of
b'elej tas puch chi *angeles*	nine divisions as well of angels 90
qitzij chi utz	true that good
chi jeb'elik	that beautiful
ub'anoj	their making
[u]winaqirik puch *angeles*	their conception as well angels
rumal *dios*	by him god
nima ajaw	great lord
chub'elej tananaj	in their nine levels
chub'elej le'	in their nine orders
chub'elej tas puch xuxik	in their nine divisions as well came to be 100

---

[717] The manuscript reads *chitzeb'ej*, scribal error or variant for *chitz'ab'ej* ("multiply").

qitzij chi utz	true that good
jeb'elik	beautiful
ucholotajik	their arrangement
ucholik xuxik chujutaq tas	their order came to be in each division
xa nab'e jun ub'inatisaxik chi *angeles*	merely first one their being named of angels
ronojel unima[l] k'ut ub'inatisaxik	all their greatness thus their being named
chi kijujunal	to each of them
chi j[u]taq le'	to each order
chi jutaq tanaj	to each level

k'o chi nay puc[h] kib'i'	there are now as well their names	110
jutaq ch'ob' chi *angeles*	to each assembly of angels	

Wa'e nab'e tas	This first division
nab'e le' *arcangeles* =	first order archangels =

uka le': *principados*	second order: principalities	
rox le' *podestades*	third order powers	
ukaj le' *virtudes* kib'i'	fourth order virtues their names	
ro' le' *dominaçiones*	fifth order dominions	
uwaq le' *dronos*	sixth order thrones	
[u]wuq tanaj *herubines* =	seventh level cherubim =	
uwa[j]xaq le' *serafines*	eighth order seraphim	120
ub'elej tanaj *angelicos espiritus* ———	ninth level angelic spirits ———	

are' k'ut kib'i' ri' chi kijutaq ch'ob'	these thus their names these of their each assembly
chi tinamit	of citadel
e k'o chwi' jutaq tanaj	they are above each level
jutaq tas	each division
ri k'o wi ub'elej uch'akat	it is ninth his throne
nima ajaw *dios* chila' chi kaj	great lord god there in sky
are' kib'i' chi kijujunal *angeles*	these their names for each of them angels
xare q'alaj ri jun ka'ib' kinimaqil	but clear the one two their greatness

ri san Miguel *arcangel*	the saint Michael archangel	130
reqale'n	his burden of authority	

san cabriel ub'i' jun chik:	saint gabriel his name one other:

San Rafael ub'i' jun chik rox[718]	Saint Raphael his name one other third
San Uriel ukaj:	Saint Uriel fourth:
Jeremia ro'	Jeremiah fifth
Numiel	Numiel
Pamiel	Pamiel
romiel	romiel
samiel:	samiel:
açael	asael
Sehutiel	Sejutiel
horchiel	jorchiel
escaltiel =	escaltiel =
xere k'u q'alaj	so thus clear
kib'i' ri'	their names these
keje' k'ut kik'oje'ik *angeles*	then thus their places angels
ri mi xqab'ij[719]	that we just now said
e ajloq'	they esteemed
e ajmayin chirij	they honored behind
dios	god
nima ajaw	great lord
ARe' chi k'ut xchiqab'ij	THese now thus we shall say
kib'i'	their names
adan	adam
eva	eve
Ro' paj tzij k'o wi	Fifth division word there are
ub'i'	their names
adan	adam
eva	eve
nab'e achi	first man
nab'e ixoq	first woman
qachuch	our mother
qaqajaw	our father

140

150

160

---

[718] The text reads *ros*, a variant spelling in the text for *rox*.
[719] The text reads *skab'ij*, a variant spelling for *xkab'ij*.

ARe' uk'u'xlaxik winaq[720]	THey their being ensouled people
ub'anik puch winaq	their making as well people
tz'aq	framed
b'it[721]	shaped
chuk'u'x *dios*	in his heart god
nima ajaw	great lord
rumal tolon kanoq chi kaj	because desolate left behind in sky 170
xtolob'a' kanoq rumal luçifer	he was desolated left behind by him lucifer
ta xunimarisaj rib'	when he aggrandized himself
kuk' e rach ajmak	with them they his companions malevolent ones
xcha' k'ut *dios*	said thus god
nima ajaw	great lord
ma wi chutzinik chi tole'ik	not will be improved of desolation
ri chi kajil ja	the at sky house
xa chinb'an kik'exel chi laq'ab'en ri'	merely I will make their replacement as dwellers these
chi kajil ja	in sky house
xcha' nima ajaw	said great lord 180
dios	god
k'ate k'ut utz'aqik winaq	then thus its framing person
rumal *dios* nima ajaw	by him god great lord
ulew xrokesaj	earth he inserted
dios nima ajaw	god great lord
chirij ulew xel wi uq'oral winaq	from its surface earth came out his soft flesh person
uti'ojil puch	his firm flesh as well
juq'ataj xb'ititajik uq'ab'	one moment were given shape his arms
raqan	his legs

---

[720] The original manuscript reads *winaq,* scribal error for *winaq*. When used as a verb, *winaq-irik*, the text more consistently uses the correct spelling. The scribe often substitutes q' for q throughout the text, although the Parra alphabet is followed more closely in the first seven folios of the manuscript that are based on the *Theologia Indorum*. Subsequent pages that are based on indigenous traditions are far less consistent in their use of the Parra alphabet.

[721] The text reads *b'ik*, scribal error for *b'it*.

xutzin uk'oje'ik uchi'	were completed their placement his mouth 190
uwach	his face
uxikin	his ears
utza'm	his nose
xok ub'aqil	entered his bones
rib'och'il	his tendons
xwiqaje' taq raqan	were added his legs
uq'ab'	his arms
k'o k'ut uwi'	there are thus their ends
xuxik	they came to be
xok unima ti'ojil	entered his great flesh 200
xok utz'umal	entered his skin
xok re'	entered his teeth
rixk'aq	his nails
xwiqitaj k'ut chi winaqil	was adorned thus of humanity
ti'ojil xuxik =	flesh it came to be =
4 chuyujik	4 to its combining
xok uti'ojil	entered his flesh
ulew	earth
q'aq'	fire
ja'	water 210
kaq'iq'	wind
ulew xok wi unima ti'ojil[722]	earth entered his great flesh
ja' k'ut uq'anal	water thus his yellowness
ukik'el puch	his blood as well
q'aq' k'ut xel wi umiq'inal	fire thus came out his warmth
uk'atanal ——	his heat ——
kaq'iq' k'ut xokesax ruxlab'	wind thus was inserted his breath

---

[722] There is no paired concept linked with the "earth" component of human flesh and no paired concept linked with "wind (line 17)." This is anomalous for this text and perhaps reflects the non-Maya nature of the four elements, which is a wholly European theory; therefore, there is no tradition of indigenous literary forms to describe it.

keje' k'ut chi kaj molaj wi	then thus that four types
xokisax uwinaqil ti'ojil	were inserted his humanity flesh
jeb'elik xuxik	beautiful he came to be 220
rumal *dios*	by him god
❡ k'ate k'ut ta xk'amowan chirech	❡ then thus that he gave thanks to
tz'aqol	tz'aqol
b'itol	b'itol
k'amo chech la	thanks to thee
lal nuchuch	thou my mother
lal nuqajaw	thou my father
mi xitz'aq la	just now thou framed me
mi xib'it la xcha' chirech *dios*	just now thou shaped me he said to god
❡ k'ate k'ut ub'anik	❡ then thus their making 230
ka'ib' chi nima'q tulul	two of great zapote trees
xub'an *dios*	he did it god
nima ajaw chunik'ajal *parayiso terrenal*	great lord in its center paradise earthly
jun tulul	one zapote tree
k'aslem tulul	life zapote tree
achinaq chilo'w uwach	whoever will eat its fruit
junelik chik'ase'ik rumal	forever will live because of it
xcha' *dios*	said god
nima ajaw	great lord
❡ jun chi tulul	❡ one other zapote tree 240
eta'mab'al tulul	knowledge zapote tree
ub'i'	its name
are' ub'i'nam wi eta'mab'al tulul	this its having been named knowledge zapote tree
achinaq chilowik	whoever will eat it
chireta'j utz	will know good
chireta'maj utz	will come to know good
chireta'maj ma wi utz	will come to know not good
keje' k'ut uk'oje'ik	then thus their placement

ka'ib' tulul ri' ——	two zapote trees these ——
Ukaj paj tzij	Fourth division word 250
uwab'axik adan chupam *Parayiso terrenal*	his placement adam within Paradise earthly
rumal *dios*	by him god
nima ajaw	great lord
waral katochin uwi'	here you make your home above
xcha' *dios* nima ajaw	said god great lord
waral puch katamaq'elab' wi	here as well you remain
xuchaxik rumal *dios* nima ajaw	he was told by him god great lord
keje' k'ut ta xmolob'ax ch'uti chikop	then thus then were gathered small animals
nima chikop chwach	great animals before his face
rumal *D[ios]*	by him God 260
nima ajaw	great lord
ke'ab'i'natisaj	name them
chawokesaj kib'i' chi kijujunal	put within them their names to each one
xuchaxik rumal *dios*	he was told by him god
nima ajaw	great lord
xa utukel	merely alone
adan	adam
xtz'aqik	he was framed
xb'it puch rumal *dios*	he was shaped as well by him god
nima ki'kotem	great joy 270
nima saq amaq' xk'oje' wi	great light nation there was
nima ki'kotem	great joy
li'anik	peace
su	purity
saqil amaq'	light nation
xuya' *dios* chirech	he gave god to him
k'is rech ronojel	completed its all
uki'il	its sweetness
uqusil	its deliciousness
uk'ok'al	its sweet fragrance 280

upam	its womb
parayiso terrenal	paradise earthly
e k'o ka'ib' tz'ikin	there are two birds
paloma ruk'	doves with him
kakitz'ub'aj ki' chi kiwach	they suck sweet liquid before their faces
e kub'ay uk'u'x	they consolers his heart
ta xuk'u'xlaj k'ut	then he considered in his heart thus
adan	adam
ta xub'ij chirech *dios*	then he said to god
nima ajaw	great lord 290
lal *dios*	thou god
nima ajaw	great lord
chiya' ta la wach ajki'kotel	give then thou fellow giver of joy
wach ch'awel	fellow speaker
wach tzijonel	fellow converser
in tz'aq la	I framed one thine
in b'it la	I shaped one thine
xcha' chirech *D[ios]*	said to God
nima ajaw	great lord
ta xuta' k'ut *dios* roq'ej	then he heard thus god its plea 300
uk'u'x adan	his heart adam
ta uya'ik	then its giving
rachkoj	his companion
keje' k'ut ta xwartisax adan	then thus then was put to sleep adam
rumal *D[ios]*	by him God
nima ajaw	great lord
kawar k'ut adan	he sleeps thus adam
ta xelesax jun uk'alk'ax chumox	then was taken out one his rib from his left
xel wi jun ub'aqil uk'alk'ax ixoq	came out one his bone his rib woman
k'ut xuxik juq'ataj	thus she came to be in a moment 310
xutzin rumal	she was completed by him

nima ajaw	great lord
dios	god
xawi jutzu xok *ranima'*	merely an instant entered her soul
utzininaq chik	her completion now
ta xk'astaj uwach adan	then was revived his face adam
ta xk'asux rumal *rangel dios*	then he was awakened by him his angel god
adan adan katk'astajoq	adam adam wake up
chach'ab'ej ak'ulil	speak to your bride
aloq'	your beloved one
ak'anij	your cherished one
xcha' *rangel dios*	said his angel god
chirech adan	to adam
ta xuk'amowaj chirech *dios*	then he gave thanks to god
k'amo chi[r]ech la	thanks to thee
lal tz'aqol	thou tz'aqol
b'itol	b'itol
wech	mine
mi xya' la wachb'il	just gave thou my companion
xcha' chirech *dios*	he said to god
nima ajaw	great lord
jutzu k'ut xch'a'ow adan chirech ixoq	immediately thus spoke adam to woman
xcha' adan chirech ixoq	said adam to woman
at nub'aqil	you my bone
at nuti'ojil	you my flesh
at elenaq chupam nuti'ojil	you came out from within my flesh
xcha' chirech ixoq	he said to woman
ta xek'ulub'ax k'ut	then they were joined thus
rumal *dios* nima ajaw	by him god great lord
ri awachijil[723]	the your husband
ri awixoqil le	the your wife her

320

330

340

---

[723] There is an extraneous *e* here that has no apparent meaning in this context.

chiloq'oj iwib'	love each other
chik'axk'omaj iwib'	cherish each other
chik'anijaj iwib'	take care of each other
kixmi'alanik	give birth to daughters
kixk'ajolanik xe'uchaxik	give birth to sons they were told
keje' k'ut upixab'axik adan ruk' eva	then thus their being commanded adam with eve
rixoqil adan xuxik	his wife adam she came to be
rumal *dios*	by him god
nima ajaw	great lord 350
ta kipixab'axik k'ut	then their being commanded thus
chirech ri awas tulul	about the forbidden zapote
kanukanaj wawas tzij	I leave my inviolable word
wawas pixab' chiwech	my inviolable commandment to you
milo' uwach awas tulul	do not eat its fruit forbidden zapote tree
eta'mab'al tulul	knowledge zapote tree
mixkam Rumal are'	do not die Because Of it
chilo' ri k'aslem tulul	eat the life zapote
junelik kixk'ase' rumal	forever you live because of it
xe'uchaxik adan	they were told adam 360
eva	eve
rumal *D[ios]*	by him God
nima ajaw	great lord
ta utikerik k'ut	then its beginning thus
kikawachixik	their being deceived
rumal *diablo*	by him devil
k'axtok'	demon
rumal are' k'ax	because of him pain
chi kik'u'x	in their hearts
uya'ik	its giving 370
usipaxik chi kajil ja chikech	its being gifted in the sky house to them
adan	adam
eva	eve

ta xul kik'axtok'oj ri eva	then he arrived to their deception the eve
chulo'ik awas tulul	to its eating forbidden zapote
xujalk'atij uwach ri *diablo* chi *angel*	he transformed his face the devil to angel
kumatz k'u uje'	serpent thus his tail
lo' la wa'e uwach eta'mab'al tulul	eat thou this its fruit knowledge zapote tree
lal eva xcha' chire	thou eve he said to her
ma wi kinwaj[724] taj rumal kanajinaq	not I want to because of it left behind 380
rawas *dios* chiqech xcha' eva	his inviolable [word] god to us said eve
majay	do not reject
mapa'in usamajel	do not mock his messenger
machutzin pa la keje' taj	not will be completed in thee thus
xa rumal rewab'al *dios*	merely because of it his hiding god
are' karaj	he desires
ma wi katz'aqat eta'mab'al alaq[725]	not is perfected knowledge thine
lo' la xcha'	eat thou he said
keje' k'ut ulo'ik awas tulul rumal eva	then thus its eating forbidden zapote by her eve
keje' k'ut uwinaqirik mak	then thus its conception malevolence 390
lab'al kumal	enmity by them
ta xe'oq'otax k'u uloq	then they were removed thus hither
chupam *parayiso terrenal*	within paradise earthly
ta xewul waral	then they fell here
chwach ulew	before its face earth
pa ra	in suffering
pa k'ax	in pain
pa wa'ijal	in hunger
pa chaqi'j[726] chi'	in dryness mouth
chi oq'ib'al	in place of weeping 400

---

[724] The manuscript reads *kawaj* ("you want"), most likely scribal error for *kinwaj* ("I want").

[725] The original text consistently reads *allaq'*. I have modified the orthography according to the modern spelling, which does not utilize a double *ll* or terminal glottalization.

[726] The text reads *chajij*, probable scribal error for *chaqi'j*.

chi sik'ib'al	in place of wailing
keje' k'ut ta xkitz'onoj chik kalk'wal	then thus then they pleaded for now their
chirech *dios* nima ajaw	children to god great lord
xoq' kik'u'x	wept their hearts
xe'oq'ik	they wept
xesik'inik	they wailed
ta xkitz'onoj kalk'wal	then they pleaded for their children
chiya' ta la qami'al	give then thou our daughter
qak'ajol xecha'	our son they said
ala taj	boy perhaps
ali taj xecha' chirech	girl perhaps they said to him 410
dios	god
nima ajaw	great lord
ta uya'ik kalk'wal	then his giving their children
xuta' *dios*	he heard god
roq'ej kik'u'x	its lament their hearts
roq'ej kipam	its lament their bowels
¶ ju paj chik tzij	¶ one division more word
k'o wi ub'ixik	there is its telling
oxib' chi b'i':	three more names:
cayin abel: xeth	cain abel: seth 420
maja' jayoq uk'ajol adan	not yet engendered his sons adam
ta xel uloq	when he left hither
pa *parayiso terrenal*	from paradise earthly
anim k'ut xuya' *dios*	quickly thus he gave [them] god
xalax[727] cayin	was born cain
xalax chi k'ut abel	was born next thus abel
e ka'ib' chi alab'om	they two of boys
kichaq' kib'	their brothers themselves
uk'ajol adan	his sons adam
are' k'u ri ralk'wal ——	they thus the his children —— 430

---

[727] *xalas* in the original manuscript, variant or scribal error for *xalax*.

jutzu xemakun	soon they committed offense
chik	later
nab'e are' ri cayin	first him the cain
nab'e al qitzij meb'a':	first child truly poor:
are' k'u ri':	he thus him:
abel	abel
xuya' *dios* chirech uq'inomal	he gave god to him his abundance
utikilem	his riches
itzel k'ut xril cayin	evil thus he saw it cain
ta xukamisaj uchaq' chi ewajkil	then he killed his younger brother in secret 440
qitzij k'ut uloq' *dios* ri abel	true thus his love god the abel
rumal xuya' unimaqil wach	because he gave its best harvest
utiko'n chi	his planted field then
are' k'u ri cayin	he thus the cain
xa upich'olil xuya' chirech *dio[s]*	only its rejects he gave to god
are' k'u ri abel	he thus the abel
kasik'in ri ukik'el chwach *dios*	calls out the his blood before his face god
keje' k'ut uya'ik uk'axel	then thus its giving its punishment
umak cayin	his offense cain
xawi ma wi utzilaj kamik xok chirech	merely not very good death entered to him 450
xa xk'aq ru[mal] jun *casador*	merely shot by a hunter
k'o pa rab'ix[728]	he is in his maize field
ta xilitaj rumal	when he was seen by him
ri wub'anel	the blowgunner
turnio	turnio
sqaqi'n chi moymot uwach	a little now blinded his face
ta xwub'ax k'ut	when he was blowgunned thus
masat xrilo	deer he saw
xa tojorisaxik umak rumal *dios*	merely forgiven his offense by him god
ma wi umak ta	not his offense 460
ri [w]ub'anel	the blowgunner

---

[728] *rab'is* in the original manuscript, variant or scribal error for *rab'ix*.

chita' k'ut usuk'ulikil	hear you all thus its straightening out
nab'e mak	first offense
xkib'an	they did
ralk'wal	their children
adan	adam
eva	eve
wa'e //k'ut uk'ajol adan	these //thus his sons adam
cayin abel:	cain abel:
are' chi k'ut uk'ajol cayin abel	they then thus their sons cain abel 470
wa'e: e[noch?]729 nowe matuxalem	these: e[noch?] noah methuselah
wa'e nowe.	these [his sons] noah.
wa'e. xen. chan. .Jabet. .	these. shem. ham. .Japheth. .
¶ wa'e chi k'ute ju paj tzij	¶ this now thus a division word
ub'ixik ujalk'atijik ch'ab'al rumal *dios*	its telling its change language by him god
chikech e ralk'wal nowe xb'ano	to them his children noah it was done
ma ri nab'e b'ut'ik chwach nowe:	after the first flood before his face noah:
kaminaqa chik nowe	dead now noah
ta xkik'u'xlaj ralk'wal nowe	when they planned his children noah
ub'anik jun nima tz'aq	its making a great building 480
nima k'oxtun	great tower
chupam	in its womb
chwach kaj xecha'	in its face sky they said
we chib'an chi ri b'ut'ik jumul chik	if should make again the flood one time again
chiri' k'ut kojkolotaj wi' xecha'	there thus we are saved they said
ta xeq'il rumal *dios* nima ajaw	then they were stopped by him god great lord
ta xuq'at tzij *dios* pa kiwi'	then he made judgment god on their heads
ta xuljalk'atij *dios* nima ajaw kich'ab'al	then he arrived to change god great lord their language
oxlaju ch'ob' chi chi' ch'ab'al	thirteen kinds in mouths languages
kich'ab'al xuxik	their languages came to be 490

---

729 The initial *e* of this line doesn't fit grammatically. The passage is based on chapter 49 of the *Theologia Indorum*, which bears a title that lists the descendants of Abel as Enoch, Matusalem (Mathuselah), and Noe (Noah). It is possible that the initial *e* represents an aborted attempt to write the name Enoch.

ma chi chi' xkita' kich'ab'al chi kib'il kib'	not at mouths they understood their language among themselves
keje' k'ut kipaxik ri'	then thus their division this
rumal *dios*	by him god
nima ajaw	great lord
are' chi k'ut uk'ajol xen chan Jabet	these then thus their sons shem ham Japheth
wa'e abrahan yssac. esau Jacob	these abraham isaac. esau Jacob
wa'e chi k'ut uk'ajol Jacob	these then thus his sons Jacob
Ruben:	Reuben:
Simon:	Simeon:
Lewi.	Levi.
Jutas.	Judah.
Ysacab:	Issachar:
çabulen.	zebulun.
Samin	Samin
Dan.	Dan.
Cat.	Gad.
Betalen	Benjamin
aset	asher
Joseph	Joseph

500

Ri' k'ute umam ADan:	These thus his grandsons ADam:
uk'ajol puch nowe.	his sons as well noah.
Ri Abrahan: Jacob puch	The Abraham: Jacob as well
¶ wa'e k'ut ub'i' juyub' canaan:	¶ this thus its name mountain canaan:
xek'oje' wi Jacob	they abode Jacob
kuk' e ralk'wal: puch	with them they his children: as well
chi k'u chiri' xe'opon chi k'u chila' egipto	now thus there they arrived then thus there egypt
o' much' chi k'u junab'	five eighties then thus years
xkib'an chila' ri umam Jacob	they did there the his grandsons Jacob
ta xalax chi k'u kanoq moyses	then was born then thus left moses
chuxol ebreos xalax wi moyses =	among hebrews was born moses =
katajin k'ut moy[s]es yuq'ul chij	he is thus moses tender sheep
ta xsik'ix	when he was called
rumal *dios* nima ajaw	by him god great lord

510

520

k'o pa	he is in
tukan:	blackberry bush:
ma wi kak'at taj	not it burns up
kaporotaj ta puch	it is burned then as well
uxaq tukan	its leaves blackberry bush 530
k'o wi	he is
dios nima ajaw	god great lord
ta xusik'ij	when he called
moyses	moses

moyses moyses	moses moses
katpe ta wuk'	come then with me

kinulta'awila'	come to see me
chulata' nutzij	come to hear my word

xcha' *dios* nima ajaw chirech	said god great lord to him
ta xopon k'ut moyses	then he arrived thus Moyses 540

k'o wi tukan kajuluwik chi q'aq'	there is blackberry bush burning with fire
xrilo	he saw it

chawelesaj kanoq axajab'	remove behind your sandals
k'ate katul waral wuk'	then arrive here with me

xcha' *dios* chirech moyses	said god to moses
ta ub'ixik chire moyses	then its being said to moses

jat egipto	go to egypt
ruk' paraon	with pharaoh

keb'e'awelesaj uloq nuloq'	bring out hither my beloved
e nuk'anij ajysrael	they my cherished israelites 550

xuchax moyses	was told moses
xuk'ulub'a' moyses	he responded moses

ma wi in rokik uch'ab'exik ri ajaw paraon	not I worthy his speech the lord pharaoh
xaqi in uk'i'al meb'a':	merely I their relation poor ones:

we ta jun chikech	perhaps then one of them
nima'q *propetas* chib'ek	great prophets should go

lal ajaw xcha' moyses —	thou lord said moses —
chirech nima ajaw *dios*:	to great lord god:

xax katb'e wi	merely you go
chab'ij nutzij chirech paraon	speak my word to pharaoh 560
maxib'ij awib'	do not frighten yourself
in k'o awuk'	I am with you
xcha' *dios*	said god
nima ajaw chirech moyses	great lord to moses
ta ub'[e]'ik k'ut moyses	then his going thus moses
ruk' paraon	with pharaoh
rachb'il uchaq'	his companion his younger brother
aron	aaron
ma wi k'o taj lab'alib'al xruk'aj	not there was weapon he carried
xawi xare uch'ami'y [yu]q'ub'al chij	but only his staff for tending sheep 570
ta ub'[e]'ik k'ut moyses	then his going thus moses
xopon k'ut ruk' pa[ra]on	he arrived thus with pharaoh
xub'ij k'ut utzij n[ima] [a]j[a]w *dios* chire	he said thus his word great lord god to him
xcha' moyses lal ajaw paraon	said moses thou lord pharoah
in achb'ilay ke ri e uloq'	I companion of theirs the they his beloved
uk'anij *dios* ajysrael	his cherished god israelites
rumal keje' nutaqikil	because of him thus my task
rumal nima ajaw *dios*	because of him great lord god
xcha' moyses	said moses
chirech paraon	to pharaoh 580
paraon chi k'ut	pharaoh then thus
ma wi xunimaj utzij moyses	not he obeyed his word moses
¶ Ta ub'anik k'ut	Then its doing thus
7 chi nima'q pus nawal	7 of great wondrous power spirit essences
unimal	his greatness
chi nima'q pus nawal	of great wondrous power spirit essences
xub'an *dios*	he did it god
milagro chuchaxik chi kiwach ajegipto	miracle it is called before their faces egyptians
chwach puch paraon	before his face as well pharaoh
ta utzolq'omitajik	then its being transformed 590
uch'ami'y aron chi kumatz	his staff aaron into serpent

¶ ukab' q'ij chik ta xtzolq'omitaj chik
ja' chi kik'

¶ second day next when transformed next
water into blood

¶ rox[730] q'ij chi k'ut ta xewinaqir
  xpeq
  xtutz'
  ruk' kalatz[731]

¶ third day next thus when they were conceived
  toads
  frogs
  with other frogs

¶ ukaj mul k'ut xewinaqir.
  Us.
  xkatz.
  xpeper
  amolo
  ronojel ti'onel chikop

¶ fourth time thus they were conceived.
  Mosquitoes.
  horseflies.   600
  moths
  flies
  all biting insects

¶ ro' mul ta xwinaqir
  lem
  amolo

¶ fifth time then were conceived
  biting flies
  flies

¶ uw[aq] mul ta[732] xewinaqir
  nima saqb'och
  nima kaqulja'
  ruk' nima kumatz xim chwach che'

¶ sixth time then they were conceived
  great hail
  great lightning
  with great serpent wound before its face tree   610

xwi[na]qirik ta
  xok nima q'equ'm rumal *dios* nim ajaw
  xkam jun kinab'e'al ajegipto

was conceived then
  entered great darkness by him god great lord
  died one their firstborn egyptians

k'ate k'ut kitzoqopitajik uloq
ajysrael rumal paraon

then thus their being freed hither
israelites by him pharaoh

xa ta keb'ek mojkam
kumal lal [moy]ses aron xcha' paraon =

merely then they go may we not die
because of thee moses aaron said pharaoh =

keje' k'ut kipetik ralk'wal ysrael
e ajutinamit *dios*

then thus their coming their children israel
they of the citadel of god

nim k'axk'ol xepe wi ral
uk'ajol ysrael

great affliction they came their children   620
their sons israel

ajcanaan

canaanites

---

[730] The text reads *ros*, variant for *rox*.

[731] The text reads *kalat*, derived from *kalatz* (Nahuatl for "toad").

[732] *tax* in the original manuscript, most likely scribal error for *ta* ("then").

oj puch ebreos	we as well hebrews
ta kik'amik ub'ik rumal moyses	then their being brought out by him moses
ta xe'opan chi palo	then they arrived at sea
ta xub'ij *dios*	then said god
chirech moyses	to moses
chatzaqa' kab'lajuj ab'aj[733] pa palo	throw twelve stones in sea
kab'lajuj k'ut chawesewaj	twelve thus cast forth
ta xtzaj k'ut palo rumal *dios* nima ajaw	then dried thus sea by him god great lord 630
kab'lajuj nima'q b'e xk'oje' chupam palo	twelve great pathways there were within sea
ta xojik'ow uloq	then we passed through hither
xax sqaqi'n chik	only a little more
ma wi tz'aqatinaq	not completed
kaj kalab' chi winaq	four multitudes of people
oj ral	we their children
uk'ajol	their sons
ajysrael	israelites
ajcanaan	canaanites
oj puch ebreos	we as well hebrews 640
Ri' k'ute qapetik relib'al q'ij	This thus our coming its coming out place sun
wa'e ta xchinchol chik kik'owib'al uloq	this then I shall give account now their passage hither
pa k'im	in grasslands
pa k'echelaj	in forests
ukab'	second
xelimkutz	xelimkutz
chi marakow	at marakow
k'aylaj ja'	very bitter water
xe'el chi k'u chiri'	they left again thus there
xe'opon chi k'u chila' xim ub'i'	they arrived again thus there xim its name 650
xe'el chi k'u chiri'	they left again thus there
xe'[o]pon chi k'u chila' Papitin	they arrived again thus there Papitin

---

[733] *asab'* in the manuscript, most likely scribal error for *ab'aj* ("stone").

xawi xere xk'oqon chi wi kik'u'x chiri'	but only suffered then their hearts there
ajebreos	hebrews
chiri' k'ut xkich'ak wi	there thus they defeated
amalech	amalek
k'ate k'ut ropanik ralk'wal Jacob	then thus their arrival his children Jacob
chila' chi k'ates	there chi k'ates
chiri' k'ut xkam wi maria	there thus she died maria
ranab' santo moyses	his sister saint moses 660
k'ate k'ut ta xe'opan chik ralk'wal Jacob:	then thus then they arrived again his children Jacob:
chila' hor	there hor
ukamik moyses are k'o chiri' moab	his death moses when he is there moab
naqaj chik canaan	near now canaan
ta xeq'ax chi k'ut Jortan	then they crossed next thus Jordan
ta xech'akataj herico ——	then was defeated jericho——
¶ Are' k'ut kajawar ri Joseph pa ki[wi']	¶ He thus he reigned Joseph over them
¶ ukamik Josue	¶ his death Joshua
ujachik ulew	its division land
ulew cana[a]n ——	land canaan —— 670
ujuwinaq 5[734] nima b'i'	twenty-[fifth] great name
ub'i' saniwel	his name samuel
¶ ukab' tzij[735] uwab'axik:	¶ second word his being raised up:
Saul chi ajawarem	Saul in lordship
¶ ujuwinaq 6 nima b'i'	¶ twenty-sixth great name
ub'i' ala Davit	his name young boy David

---

[734] In the original manuscript, Saniwel (Samuel) appears as the twentieth in the list of great prophets recognized by the authors, although Sparks (2019, 253) suggests that this is a scribal error. Based on the order of prophets listed in the *Theologia Indorum*, Samuel should be the twenty-fifth great name. The subsequent list of prophets are in the correct order.

[735] The story of Saul is found in chapter 88 of the *Theologia Indorum*, which begins with the phrase *vca pah tçih* (*uka paj tzij* in modern orthography). The first word could be interpreted as either *uka[b']* ("second") or *uka[j]* ("fourth"). The previous chapter 86 is clearly identified as the first division of the theme; therefore, this should be *ukab'* ("second-division word"). The authors of the Totonicapán document chose the second alternative *ukaj* in error.

¶ ujuwinaq 7 nima b'i'   ¶ twenty-seventh great name
ub'i' Salamon ruk' k'iya b'i' chik   his name Solomon with many names more

¶ ujuwinaq [8] nima b'i'   ¶ twenty-eighth great name
ub'i' *propetas* ruk' nay puch: *patriargas*[736]   their names prophets with also: patriarchs   680

elias *propeta*[737] ub'i'   elijah prophet his name
eliseo *propeta* ub'i'   elisha prophet his name
taniel[738] *p[ro]peta* ub'i'   daniel prophet his name

esayas *P[ro]peta*   isaiah Prophet
ruk' Jowanes *propeta* ——   with Jonah prophet ——

¶ ulaju paj tzij   ¶ tenth division word
kitzalijik uloq Jubias   their return hither Jews

chi kijuyub'al   to their mountain place
ub'i' Jerusalem   its name Jerusalem

kipetik chila' babilonia //   their coming from there babylonia //   690
axiria// —————   assyria// —————

¶ ujulaju paj tzij   ¶ eleventh division word
k'o wi chi ma wi kopanik chik   there is now not arrives again

lajuj chi chinamital ajysrael   ten other lineages israelites
chi kijuyub'al chila'   to their mountain place there

chi kijuyub'al   to their mountain place
xepe wi babilonia   they came from babylonia

xul kilaq'ab'ej[739] chik   they arrived at their habitations again
kamaq'   their homeland

xa jun chi'al   only one tribe   700
jun puch chinamital   one also lineage

---

[736] *Pa patriargas. Pa* appears at the end of one page and appears to be an erroneous repetition of the initial *pa* in *patriargas* at the top of the next page.

[737] *Propetas* in the manuscript. From the context, this should be singular.

[738] Spelled Daniel in the *Theologia Indorum*, but the authors of the *Title of Totonicapán* altered it here as there is no *d* sound in K'iche'.

[739] The manuscript reads *kailaq'ab'ej*, scribal error for *kilaq'ab'ej*.

xa e ju ch'ob' chik	only they one group now
chinamital	lineage
e uk'ajol Jacob	they his sons Jacob
uk'ajol	his sons
chuk'oje'ik xa kitukel chik	to its settlement only they alone now
xkilaq'ab'ej chik Jerusalem +++ — —	they occupied again Jerusalem — —
¶ Are' k'u ri e lajuj chi chinamital	¶ They thus the ten other lineages
xeb'e chila' asiria rumal salmanasar	they went there assyria because of him shalmaneser
xma lo chi wi xetzalij chi wi uloq	not perhaps again they returned again hither 710
chila' xsach wi kitzijoxik	there was lost their being spoken of
xma k'o wi	not there are
xek'utun uwi'	they manifested its head
qitzij chi e k'i chi kopanik	true that many that their arrival
ma chi k'ut xetzalij uloq	not then thus they returned hither
xa che'	only wood
xa ab'aj	only stone
xkisik'ij chila'	they called upon there
xepe wi	they came
¶ xa kimak	¶ only their offense 720
xa pu kitzelal	only as well their wrongdoing
xe'oq'otax	they were banished
uwi'	their heads
rumal *dios*	by him god
nima aja[w]	great lord
wa'e ub'i' juyub' mi xcholotajik	this its name mountain that was just declared
xe'ik'ow wi mi xcholotajik:	they passed through it that was just declared:
mara ub'i' nab'e juyub'	mara its name first mountain
ta xujq'ax uloq ch'aqa palo:	when we crossed hither other side sea:
ukab' xelimkutz:	second xelimkutz: 730
rox sin:	third sin:

ukaj rabitin:	fourth rabitin:
ro' xiney:	fifth xiney:
uwaq[740] kaxerot:	sixth kaxerot:
uwuq chi k'ates	seventh chi k'ates
uwajxaq: eton:	eighth: eton:
ub'elej: hor:	ninth: jor:
ulajuj chi boch	tenth chi boch
ujulaj chi abatin.	eleventh chi abatin.

ukab'laj: saret:	twelfth: saret:	740
roxlaj: arnon	thirteenth: arnon	
ukajlaj matan	fourteenth matan	
ro' laj xchamel:	fifteenth xchamel:	
uwaqlaj: bemot	sixteenth: bemot	
uwuqlaj chi moab ——————	seventeenth chi moab ——————	

Ri' k'ute kik'oje'ik	These thus their residences
kik'owib'al	their abodes

Rumal *dios*	By Him god
nima ajaw	great lord

kiyiq' puch ajcanaan:	their conquests as well canaanites:	750
ajebreos puch	hebrews as well	
ajysrael	israelites	

oxib' chi b'i' chi konojel ajysrael	three then names for all of them israelites
ajcanaan	canaanites
ajebreos ke'uchaxik	hebrews they are called

e qamam	they our grandfathers
qaqajaw ri oj	our fathers the us

ri' k'ute qaxe'	this thus our root
qak'oje'ik puch	our existence as well

qelik pu uloq	our coming out as well hither	760
relib'al q'ij	its coming out place sun	

xchita' k'u alaq	you shall hear thus you all
xchiwachin puwach wumal	you shall give heed to its face by me
xchinb'ij k'ut usuk'ulikil chech alaq	I shall tell thus its straightness to you all

xa pa lab'al	merely in war

---

[740] The manuscript reads *uwaq'aq'*. From the context, this is most likely scribal error for *uwaq* ("sixth").

xesach wi	they were lost
qamam	our grandfathers
qaqajaw	our fathers
oj umam	we their grandsons
uk'ajol	their sons · 770
adan	adam
eva:	eve:
enoc	enoch
abrahan	abraham
yssac	isaac
Jacob	Jacob
xa k'u rumal xkisach *kidios*	merely thus because they forgot their god
XA k'u cha' xe'ixowax	MERELY thus said they were abandoned
rumal *dios*	by him god
nima ajaw	great lord · 780
ri' k'ute	this thus
usuk'ulikil ———	its straightness ———
//xa xkipo'o	//merely they corrupted
xa xkijalk'atij kitzij	merely they changed their words
wuqub' pek	seven caves
wuqub' siwan	seven ravines
sewan tulan xecha' chirech	ravine tulan they said to it
pan parar	pan parar
pan[741] paxil	pan paxil
pan k'ayela' xecha' =	pan k'ayela' they said = · 790
are' k'[ut] ri pan paxil	these thus the pan paxil
pan k'ayela' xkib'ij are' ri'	pan k'aela' they said they these
chupam *parayiso terrenal* xojtz'aq wi	within paradise earthly we were framed
xojb'it wi	we were shaped
rumal *dios*	by him god
nima ajaw	great lord

———

[741] The manuscript reads *pam*, variant or scribal error for *pan*.

ma wi xutzin chi ub'i' kumal	not honored then his name by them
rumal k'ut kimak	because of it thus their offense
are' k'u ri sewan tulan xkib'ij	this thus the ravine tulan they said
cha' k'ut usuk'ulikil sineyeton	called thus its straightness sineyeton 800
are' k'ut ri wuqub' pek	these thus the seven caves
w[u]qub' siwan	seven ravines
qitzij wi are' ri' pa pek	truly they these in caves
pa siwan	in ravines
xewar wi chila'	they slept there
chi Relib'al q'ij	at Its Coming Out Place sun
xa kejunelik uloq	merely they are united hither
xa pu e ju sachik	merely as well they as one lost
ta xesach chila' asiria	then they were lost there assyria
rumal salmanasar————————	because of him shalmaneser —————— 810
¶Wa'e ju paj tzij	¶This one division word
xchinb'ij	I shall say
wa'e uk'oje'ik ajawarem	this its establishment lordship
uxe' puch tzij	its root as well authority
ri ub'ixik ri q'analaj juyub'	the its telling the very yellow mountain
raxalaj ujuyub' ri'	very green their mountain these
pa sewan	at ravines
pa tulan xkib'ij	at tulan they said
utz'ib'al pek	its writings caves
utz'ib'al sewan. Tulan xecha'	its writings ravines. Tulan they said 820
ta xenimataj	then they festered
chupam ri tz'aqb'al tzij	within the lies
ta xecha'[742]	then they said
chirech ri q'ij	to the sun
ik'	moon
jun q'apoj	one maiden

---

[742] This is a common type of chiasm in highland Maya literature in which a gendered pair is listed with the titles or associated symbols given in reverse order (ex. Christenson 2007, 62, n. 25).

jun k'ajol	one young boy	
xecha':	they said:	
junajpu xecha'	junajpu they said	
chirech ri q'ij	to the sun	830
xb'alankej chuchax	xb'alankej it is called	
ri ik' kumal	the moon by them	
usik' k'iq'ab' chuchax	his cigar kiq'ab' it is called	
ri ch'umil kumal	the stars by them	
oj umam	we their grandsons	
oj uk'ajol	we their sons	
ajysRael	israelites	
santo moyses	saint moses	
chupam kichinamital	within their lineages	
ajysRael	israelites	840
xel wi e qamam	they came out they our grandfathers	
e qaqajaw	they our fathers	
ta xepe chi relib'al q'ij	then they came from its coming out place sun	
chila' pabelonia	there babylonia	
kowisanoq ajaw	powerful lord	
nakxik[743]	nakxik	
ri uxe' qamamaxik	the its root our being grandfathered	
qak'ajolaxik	our being fathered	
ta xkik'u'xlaj kipetik e nawal winaq	then they planned their coming they enchanted people	
naj xe'opam wi	far they arrived	850
kimuqub'al chi kaj	their obscurity in sky	
chi ulew	on land	
ma wi k'o ta kujunamaj ruk'	not there is then equals with them	
xkimuq'uj ronojel xe' kaj	they saw everything beneath sky	
e nima'q eta'manel	they great sages	

---

[743] There are two variant spellings for the name of this lord in the text, Naq'xik (appearing four times) and Nakxik (appearing five times). I have standardized the spelling as Nakxik for consistency.

e k'amol ub'e	they guides their road
ronojel wuq amaq'	all seven nations
tlekpan	tribes
keje' k'ut kipetik wa'e ch'aqa cho	then thus their coming these other side lake
ch'aqa palo	other side sea 860
pa tulan	from tulan
pa sewan	from sewan
wa'e k'ute kib'i' nab'e winaq	these thus their names first people
wa'e nab'e k'iche' e 4 chi winaq =	these first k'iche' they 4 of people =
are' nab'e ajaw wa'e	he first lord this
B'alam k'itze'	B'alam k'itze'
ri qamam	the our grandfather
qaqajaw oj kaweqib'[744] =	our father we kaweqib' =
are' k'ut ukab' ajaw	he thus second lord
ri B'alam aq'ab'.	the B'alam aq'ab'. 870
umam	their grandfather
uqajaw ajaw nijayib' =	their father lord nijayib' =
rox k'ut ajaw	third thus lord
ri majukotaj	the majukotaj
ri kimam	the their grandfather
kiqajaw e ajaw k'iche' =	their father they ajaw k'iche' =
ukaj k'ut ajaw	fourth thus lord
ri ik'i b'alam	the ik'i b'alam
are' k'ut	they thus
wa'e nab'e k'iche'	these first k'iche' 880
B'alam k'itze' nab'e ajaw.	B'alam k'itze' first lord.
Kaqapaluma ub'i' rixoqil	Kaqapaluma her name his wife
B'alam aq'ab' ukab' ajaw:	B'alam aq'ab' second lord:
Sunija ub'i' rixoqil	Sunija her name his wife
Majukotaj rox ajaw	Majukotaj third lord
kaqixaja ub'i' rixoqil	kaqixaja her name his wife
ik'i b'alam	ik'i b'alam

---

[744] *muchib'* in the original manuscript. Carmack and Mondloch (1983, 71) read this as *kaweqib'*, which fits the context here. This is most likely the result of scribal error.

xa kik'ajol xpe chi relib'al q'ij	merely their son he came from its coming out place sun

¶wa'e k'ut ukab' k'iche'	¶these thus second k'iche'
ub'i' tamub':	their name tamub': 890

wa'e nab'e ajaw k'opichoch	these first lords k'opichoch
k'ochojlan.	k'ochojlan.

majk'inalom.	majk'inalom.
k'oq'anawil.	k'oq'anawil.

xawi xa kajib' chi winaq	only four of people
qi' uxe' wa'e ajawab' tamub'	truly their roots these lords tamub'

wa'e k'aqoj eq'omaq'	these k'aqoj eq'omaq'
xa uq'ana winaq rib' chupam wa'e wuj	merely their witnesses themselves within this book

xa e junelik uloq ch'aqa cho	merely they unified hither other side lake
ch'aqa palo relib'al q'ij	other side sea its coming out place sun 900

pa tulan	at tulan
pa sewan ————————	at sewan ————————

¶ xawi keje' kech ri' - ilokab'	¶ merely then theirs these - ilokab'
Rox k'iche'	Third k'iche'

xawi 4 chi winaq.	merely 4 of people.
wa'e ub'i' nab'e ajaw	these their name first lords

chiya' toj	chiya' toj
chiya' tz'ikin	chiya' tz'ikin

yol chitum.	yol chitum.
yol chiramaq'.	yol chiramaq'. 910

ch'ipel kan	ch'ipel kan
muq'el [kan]:	muq'el [kan]:

wa'e kimam	these their grandfathers
kiqajaw	their fathers

e ajawab':	they lords:
q'ale	q'ale
sik'a	sik'a

Juwanija
e ilokab'

Juwanija
they ilokab'

e oxib'[745] amaq' chi k'iche'
xa jun kitzij
xa pu jun kiwach
chi oxib' amaq' chi k'iche'

they three nations of k'iche'   920
only one their word
only as well one their face
of three nations of k'iche'

e ral
uk'a[jol][746] YsRael

they their children
their sons Israel

oj
k'iche' winaq

we
k'iche' people

ta xujpe Babilonia
relib'al q'ij —————————————

when we came Babylonia
its coming out place sun —————————————

¶ Wa'e k'ut kipetik
chi relib'al q'ij

¶ This thus their coming   930
from its coming out place sun

ta xeyakataj k'u uloq
are' k'amol b'e

then they were raised up thus hither
they guides road

ri B'alam k'itze'.
ruk' b'alam aq'ab'.
Majukotaj.
Ik'i b'al[am][747] =

the B'alam k'itze'.
with b'alam aq'ab'.
Majukotaj.
Ik'i b'alam =

wa'e k'ut kipetik
ta xya' uloq pison q'aq'al chikech
rumal ajaw nakxik
ta kipetik waral

this thus their coming ·
then was given hither bundled glory to them
by him lord nakxik   940
then their coming here

e sonolik

they uncovered

---

[745] *oxixib'* in the original manuscript, scribal error for *oxib'* ("three"). The error most likely arose because the word is split at the end of a line and continues at the beginning of the next line.

[746] This is a common couplet in K'iche' literature. *Ral* refers to the child (of any sex) of a woman. The paired term should be *uk'ajol* (son of a male). *Uk'a* appears at the end of the line, but the scribe apparently neglected to complete the word on the next line.

[747] The original manuscript spells this progenitor's name three different ways: *yqui balam* (Iki B'alam in modern orthography), *yꝥui balam* (Ik'i B'alam), and *yꜫui balam* (Iq'i B'alam). For consistency, I have chosen Ik'i B'alam in this translation, as it is the spelling used in other Colonial-era documents, including the *Popol Vuh*.

e ch'analik xepetik	they naked they came
xa kito[q']	only their spears
xa kixaq po't k'olik	only their leafy tunics there are
ta kulik k'ut	then he arrived thus
chuchi' palo	at its mouth sea
¶ Ta xuk'am k'ut uch'ami'y	¶ Then he took thus his staff
ajaw B'alam k'itze'	lord B'alam k'itze'
ta xuq'osij k'ut palo	then he struck thus sea 950
jutzu k'ut xtzaj ri palo	immediately thus was dried the sea
xaqi b'olob'ik sanayeb'	merely bare sand
xux chik	it came to be now
keje' k'ut kik'owik uloq	then thus their passing hither
chi konojel	of all of them
ox ch'ob' nab'e k'iche'	three groups first k'iche'
kuk' k'ut oxlaju ch'ob'	with them thus thirteen clans
chi wuq amaq'	of seven nations
tlekpan	tribes
e teren chikij	they followers behind their backs 960
xa k'i kik'owik[748] uloq	merely many their passage hither
ta xutzapaj rib'	then it closed itself
palo	sea
xax uloq'ob'al wi *dios* chikech	merely his love god to them
rumal xa juna	because only one
tz'aqol	framer
b'itol	shaper
xkisi[k'i]j unik'ajal kaj	they called upon its center sky
ulew xecha'	earth they said
rumal xa xewi uk'ajol	because merely their sons 970
umam	their grandsons

---

[748] *k'ik'owik* in the original manuscript, scribal error for *kik'owik*.

abrahan	abraham
Jacob	Jacob
ta kiq'axik k'u uloq	then their passage thus hither
waral uloq ch'aqa palo	here hither other side sea
Ta xkik'am uloq uxe' che'	Then they brought hither their roots trees
uxe' k'a'm	their roots bushes
chi ma wi wa	now no food
chi ma wi ja'	now no water
xaqi uwi' kich'ami'y chikisiqo	only its head their staffs they would sniff 980
chi kub'e' k'u kik'u'x	now they console thus their hearts
xepetik	they came
ta xe'ul k'ut	they arrived thus
chuchi' jun ch'uti cho chiri'	at its shore a small lake there
nimsoy karchAj	nimsoy karchAj
xkib'an	they built
kitz'aq chiri'	their buildings there
e k'o wi q'uq'	there are quetzals
raxon	cotingas
punpun[749]	ducks 990
q'ana xko	yellow parrots
raxa xko	green parrots
q'an b'ulul	yellow gatherer birds
q'an tz'ikin	yellow birds
xawi ma wi xuk'an ta kiwach	merely not they find then their faces
ta xkoq'otaj chi k'u kanoq	then they abandoned again thus behind
ta xkik'am chi uloq uxe' che'	then they brought again hither their roots trees
uxe' k'a'm	their roots bushes
ta xe'ul chi k'u chiri' chi xpa'ch	then they arrived again thus there chi xpa'ch
xkiya'	they gave 1000

---

[749] It is unusual that ducks are not paired with another similar bird, consistent with the other paired birds in this passage.

retal	its sign
pa ja ayin ab'aj	pa ja ayin ab'aj
retal	its sign
xkiya'o	they gave it
ta kipetik chi k'ut chila'	then their coming again thus there
ta kulik chwi'	then their arrival atop
jun nima juyub'	a great mountain
ub'i'	its name
chi k'iche' xecha' chirech	chi k'iche' they said to it
xawi xeyaluj chiri'	merely they delayed there
ta xkikanaj chi k'ut	then they left it again thus
ri juyub'	the mountain
chi k'iche'	chi k'iche'
ta xepe chik	then they came again
ta kulik k'ut chiri' chwi'	then they arrive thus there atop
juyub'	mountain
Jaqawitz ch'ipaq ub'i'	Jaqawitz ch'ipaq its name
chi k'ut xejeqe' wi chi nima[750] [juyub']	again thus they settled at great [mountain]
konojel chiri' puch xjeqe' wi	everyone there as well settled
e ajk'ix	they bloodletters
e ajkaj	they sacrificers
ri B'alam k'itze'	the B'alam k'itze'
b'alam aq'ab'.	b'alam aq'ab'.
Majukotaj:	Majukotaj:
ik'i b'alam ———————	ik'i b'alam ———————
xa k'u kuk'am kib' chi	merely thus they gathered themselves again
konojel	all of them
kuk' tamub'	with them tamub'
ilokab'	ilokab'
kuk' puch e	with them as well they
oxlajuj [ch'ob'][751] chi	thirteen [clans] now

750 *chi nima* ("at great"). "At great [mountain]" is implied.

751 From the context, *oxlajuj* ("thirteen") refers to the *oxlajuj ch'ob'* ("thirteen clans").

wuq amaq'	seven nations
tlekpan	tribes
xe k'ut xepetajinaq chik	merely thus grown in number now
xu k'iyala chik junab'	merely many now years
e k'o chiri' ta xkik'u'xlaj k'ut	they are there when they planned thus
relik kiq'aq'	its coming forth their fire
ta xcha' b'alam k'itze'	then said b'alam k'itze'
mi b'a xqana' tew	recently then we felt cold
xa ta chiqelesaj qaq'aq'	merely then we will bring forth our fire 1040
xcha' b'alam k'itze'	said b'alam k'itze'
chikech wuq amaq'	to them seven nations
tlekpan	tribes
utz b'a la'	good then that
naqipa chiqach'ako'	what shall we reward you
xecha' wuq amaq'	they said seven nations
tlekpan	tribes
apachinaq nab'e chel uq'aq'	whoever first will bring forth their fire
chiqaya'	we shall give
jun qal	one our child of mother 1050
qak'ajol chirech xecha' wuq amaq'	our son of father to them they said seven nations
utz b'a la'	good then that
keje' chuxik xcha' B'alam k'itze'	then may it be so said B'alam k'itze'
ta xkich'ak kitzij	then they achieved their lighting fire
ta xkitikib'a' k'ut ub'aqik kiq'aq'	then they began thus its igniting their fire
nab'e k'ut xel kiq'aq'	first thus it came forth their fire
ri B'alam k'itze'	the B'alam k'itze'
b'alam aq'ab':	b'alam aq'ab':
Majukotaj	Majukotaj
ik'i b'alam	ik'i b'alam 1060
are' k'u ri wuq amaq'	they thus the seven nations
tlekpan	tribes
xa xma xel wi kiq'aq'	merely in no way came forth their fire
¶ k'ate k'ut utz'onoxik q'aq' kumal	¶ then thus its being pleaded for fire by them

chikech: b'alam k'itze'	to them: b'alam k'itze'
b'alam aq'ab'	b'alam aq'ab'
Majukotaj	Majukotaj
jun ik'i b'alam =	one ik'i b'alam =
xa ta b'a chiya' alaq	merely then give thou
s[qa]qi'n qaq'aq'	a little our fire 1070
xecha' k'ut ri wuq amaq'	they said thus the seven nations
tlekpan	tribes
chiya' b'a ri qach'akon	give then the our reward
xe'uchax k'ut	they were told thus
naqi ta la' k'ut ri ch'akom chiqaya'o	what then it thus the reward we will give
xecha' =	they said =
we b'a chiwaj	perhaps then you will want
chiqatz'umaj wach ik'u'x	we will suck face your hearts
xe'uchax k'ut rumal b'alam k'itze'	they were told thus by him b'alam k'itze'
utz b'a la' xecha' k'ut	good then that they said thus 1080
ta utz'ub'axik k'ut uwa[ch] kik'u'x	then its being sucked thus its face their hearts
kimaske'l	their armpits
keje' k'ut kich'akatajik ri e wuq amaq'	then thus their being defeated the seven nations
ajlab'a[l]	warriors
are' k'ut xRetaj ri kal	they thus gave its sign the their children
kik'ajol	their sons
xkiya'	they gave it
chi ch'akik	in defeat
[Capitulo 2°][752]	[Chapter Second]
¶ wakamik chi k'ut	¶ this day now thus
xchiqatikib'a' chik	we shall begin now 1090

---

[752] *Capitulo 2°* (Spanish for "Chapter Second") is written in a different hand and in Spanish. Carmack suggests that the phrase was inserted by Father Dionisio Chonay to mark the place where he believed the K'iche' had begun a new story (Carmack and Mondloch 1983, 10, 219, n. 105). Chonay's translation does include numbered chapters and headings of his own invention, and this is where his second chapter begins (Recinos and Goetz 1953, 172). There is no indication that the K'iche' authors conceived of dividing the text into chapters in this way.

ucholik wa'e   its account this
kijachowik kib'   their division themselves

ta xecha' ri b'alam k'itze':   then they said the b'alam k'itze':
b'alam aq'ab'.   b'alam aq'ab'.
Majukotaj   Majukotaj
ik'i b'alam =   ik'i b'alam =

xa ta b'a chiqajach qib'   merely then we shall divide ourselves
alaq ajawab'   thou lords

k'opichoch.   k'opichoch.
k'ochojlan   k'ochojlan   1100

k'oq'anawil.   k'oq'anawil.
majk'inalom: majk'inalom:

alaq puch: chiya' toj   thou as well: chiya' toj
chiya' tz'ikin   chiya' tz'ikin

jal chitum   jal chitum
jal chiramaq'   jal chiramaq'

ch'ipel kan   ch'ipel kan
muq'el kan = xcha' b'alam k'itze'   muq'el kan = said b'alam k'itze'

ma b'a qasachik taj   not then our loss
et chiqak'ulu' wi qib'   little later we will meet together   1110

maja' chiqariq qajuyub'al   not yet we have found our mountain place
qataq'ajal   our valley place

xa umaytzij xchiqab'ano waral   merely its tarrying for a time we shall do here
Jaqawitz ch'ipaq   Jaqawitz ch'ipaq

are' xchib'i'naj wi chi pixab'   they would give names chi pixab'
chi mamaj   chi mamaj

keje' chikib'i'j chi q'iyaj   then they will give its name chi q'iyaj
chi qamamaj xe'uchan k'u kib'   chi qamamaj they spoke thus themselves

ta kiq'axik k'ut   then their passage thus
tamub'   tamub'   1120

chwi' juyub'   atop mountain
amaq' tan =   amaq' tan =

xawi keje' ke[ch] Ilokab'	likewise then theirs Ilokab'
xeq'ax	they journeyed

chwi' juyub'	atop mountain
uk'in =	uk'in =

xawi k'u xetere	merely thus they followed	
ri wuq amaq'	the seven nations	
tlekpan	tribes	
chikij	behind their backs	1130

xa k'u kitukel ri ajk'ix	only thus they alone the bloodletters
ajkaj	sacrificers

ri b'alam aq'ab'	the b'alam aq'ab'
b'alam k'itze'	b'alam k'itze'
Majukotaj	Majukotaj
ik'i b'alam	ik'i b'alam

xekanaj chiri'	they remained there
chwi' juyub' Jaqawitz ch'ipaq	atop mountain Jaqawitz ch'ipaq

chiri' k'ut xemi'alan wi	there thus they engendered daughters	
xek'ajolan wi	they engendered sons	1140

chiri' xk'ajolax wi	there were engendered
k'oka'ib'	k'oka'ib'
k'okawib'⁷⁵³	k'okawib'
rumal ajaw B'alam k'itze' —	by him lord B'alam k'itze' —

ta kipoq'otajik k'ut kal	then their being multiplied thus their children
kik'ajol	their sons

wuq amaq'	seven nations
ajlab'al =	warriors =

wiqil achi k'ut	armed men thus	
kitz'aq	their buildings	1150

ri ajk'ix	the bloodletters
e ajkaj	they sacrificers

---

⁷⁵³ K'oq'awib' in the original manuscript. The *Popol Vuh* spells this lord's name as K'okawib' (Christenson 2007, 253). The scribe for the Totonicapán document often substitutes ɛ (q' in the modern orthography) for c (k in the modern orthography), and this appears to be another example of this substitution.

ri e qamam	the they our grandfathers
qaqajaw	our fathers
oj kaweqib':	we kaweqib':
nijayib'.	nijayib'.
Ajaw k'iche'	Ajaw k'iche'
are' k'u ik'i b'alam	he thus ik'i b'alam
· xaqi xkam chupam uk'ajolal	merely he died within his youth

¶ B'alam k'itze' Tojil uk'ab'awil	¶ B'alam k'itze' Tojil his god	1160
B'alam aq'ab' awilix uk'ab'awil.	B'alam aq'ab' awilix his god.	
Majukotaj: Jaqawitz uk'ab'awil.	Majukotaj: Jaqawitz his god.	

chi k'wal ab'aj	at precious stone
ri pison k'ak'al	the bundled glory
xpe relib'al q'ij	came from its coming out place sun
chiri' k'ut xkikir wi Jaqawitz	there thus they unwrapped [on] Jaqawitz
are' e q'aq' wi	they glory
e tepew wi xe'uxik chikiwi'	they sovereignty they came to be on their heads

wuq amaq'	seven nations	
tlekpan	tribes	1170

k'iya may xkib'an chiri'	many cycles of twenty years they did there
kijachamachik kib' =	their division themselves =
ta xtiker k'ut	then began thus
usachik	their disappearance
kimi'al	their daughters
kik'ajol	their sons
wuq amaq'	seven nations
tlekpan	tribes

xa ma wi q'alaj	only not clear	
kisachik	their disappearance	1180

ta kesachik	then they disappear
kumal chalamakat	because of them enchanters
xa rixkolob' chik k'o kanoq	only their entrails now there are left behind
ta chikiriq wuq amaq'	then they would find it seven nations

naqipa kojb'anowik	what do we do
we xa juyub' lo xecha'	perhaps merely mountain maybe they said
xkitaq'ej raqan	they looked for its footprints
ri b'anol re	the doer of it
xa raqan b'alam	only its pawprints jaguar
xa raqan utiw k'o kanoq—	only its pawprints coyote there are left behind— 1190
xa k'ut ukik'el kab'e chwach k'ab'awil	only thus their blood goes before their faces gods
chwach tojil awilix Jaqawitz:	before their faces tojil awilix Jaqawitz:
keje' k'ut uk'u'xlaxik	then thus its planning
kikamisaxik	their being killed
e qamam	they our grandfathers
qaqajaw	our fathers
B'alam k'itze'	B'alam k'itze'
b'alam aq'ab'	b'alam aq'ab'
majukotaj	majukotaj
ik'i b'alam	ik'i b'alam 1200
kumal wuq amaq'	by them seven nations
ajlab'al:	warriors:
chi juq'ataj k'ut	soon thereafter thus
xnataj chikech b'alam k'itze'	came to know to them b'alam k'itze'
jutzu xe chu[wa]ch tojil awilix	immediately he went before their faces tojil awilix
xkib'ij kikamisaxik kumal wuq amaq'	they said their being killed by them seven nations
ta xuk'ulab'a' tojil	then he responded tojil
mixib'ij iwib'	don't frighten yourselves
q'alaj chich'ikitaj uq'ijil lab'al	clear it will be set its day war
chulib'ij chwe	you will arrive to say it to me 1210
xcha' tojil	said tojil
awilix	awilix
Jaqawitz——	Jaqawitz——
ta uch'ikitajik	then its being set
k'u q'ij	thus day

kumal wuq amaq'	by them seven nations
tlekpan	tribes

kikamisaxik B'alam k'itze'	their being killed B'alam k'itze'	
b'alam aq'ab'	b'alam aq'ab'	
majukotaj	majukotaj	1220
ik'i b'alam	ik'i b'alam	

ta xkiwiq k'u ulo kib'	then they armed thus hither themselves
ajlab'al	warriors

chi tzol	with slings
chi tz'ununche'	with lances

chi yach'wach wach[754] pwaq	with crowns precious metal
chi tesakaw pwaq	with lip plugs precious metal

ta xkib'an nab'e lab'al	then they did first war
chila' Jaqawitz	there Jaqawitz

¶ e k'ut xa: b'a ma chik oyew achi	¶ they thus only: then not now furious men	1230
e kamasotz'	they death bats	

xa k'ut xewar	only thus they slept
xesayab' ri ajlab'al	they were sleepy the warriors
are' k'ut kewarik	they thus they sleep

ta xmaj kitzol	then were taken their slings
kitz'ununche'	their lances

kiyach'wach	their crowns
kiq'alq'ab'[755]	their bracelets

ruk' jujun kich'ipa q'ab'	with each their little fingers hands	
kich'ip aqan	their little toes feet	1240

xaqi e sonosoj chik	merely they naked now
ta xk'astaj kiwach	when were revived their faces

xax ma k'o wi lab'al xkib'ano	but not there is war they did
xetzalij chi kijuyub'al	they returned to their mountain place

---

[754] *wach* is written twice in the manuscript, scribal error because of a line break.

[755] *chiq'alq'aj* in the original manuscript, probable scribal error for *kiq'alq'ab'*.

ukamul chi k'ut	second time again thus
xkimol chi na kib'	they gathered again surely themselves
rumal tzatz ri kal	because multitude the their children
kik'ajol kesachik	their sons they disappear
keje' k'ut k'o wi lab'al chi kik'u'x	then thus there is war in their hearts
ma k'u kakuchaj	not thus they can do it 1250
k'a chiri' xk'ulun wi	even there they came together
ri kitu' xtz'umaxik	the their breasts were sucked
ta xkitz'onoj q'aq'	then they pleaded for fire
xa ma wi xkina'o	merely not they understood
wa'e chi k'ute	this again thus
ukamul lab'al	second time war
ta xch'ikitaj	then was set
chi q'ij	again day
kumal wuq amaq'	by them seven nations
ajlab'al	warriors 1260
chi kikamisaxik e qamam	to their being killed they our grandfathers
qaqajaw	our fathers
B'alam k'itze'	B'alam k'itze'
b'alam aq'ab'	b'alam aq'ab'
majukotaj	majukotaj
ik'i b'alam	ik'i b'alam
ta reta'maxik chik rumal tojil	then their being instructed again by him tojil
awilix	awilix
Jaqawitz	Jaqawitz
ta xkib'ij k'ut	then they said thus 1270
b'alam k'itze'	b'alam k'itze'
chirech tojil	to him tojil
awilix	awilix
mi xch'ikitaj q'ij	recently was set day
qakamisaxik chik	our being killed again

kumal wuq amaq'	by them seven nations
ajlab'al	warriors
at tojil	you tojil
awilix	awilix
Jaqawitz xecha' chirech	Jaqawitz they said to them 1280
cha' k'u ri tojil	said thus the tojil
chire b'alam k'itze'	to him b'alam k'itze'
chib'ana' kab'lajuj kech	make twelve theirs
ri poy	the effigies
are' ri kitzol	these the their slings
kitz'ununche'	their lances
ximaj kanoq nab'e	you took left behind first
are' chikikoj	these you will place on them
ri poy ajam che'	the effigies carved wood
keya' chwi' taq k'ej	they are placed on top palisades 1290
ruk' chiya' chik 4 sokob'	with them you will give now 4 great pots
chukaj tz'uk taq tz'aq	at its four corners buildings
jun sokob' q'awonon:	one great pot bumblebees:
jun sokob' sital	one great pot wasps
jun sokob' q'atz'itij:[756]	one great pot hornets:
jun sokob' wonon——	one great pot bees——
rumal ma na e ta k'i R[i] b'alam k'itze':	because not surely they many The b'alam k'itze':
b'alam aq'ab'	b'alam aq'ab'
Majukotaj	Majukotaj
jun ik'i b'alam	one ik'i b'alam 1300
xa k'u charaj	merely thus they would desire
xetza'ix	they were persecuted
kumal wuq amaq'	by them seven nations
ajlab'al	warriors
ka'oq q'ij	ka'oq day

---

[756] *q'atz'utuj* ("poisonous snake") in the original manuscript. From the context, this is most likely scribal error for *q'atz'itij* ("hornet").

ta raj xekamik'axik	then its desire they were to be killed	
ri qamam	the our grandfathers	
qaqajaw	our fathers	
ta ub'anik k'ut nima mayjab'al	then its doing thus great wonders	
kwonal chi	strength again	1310
chiri' k'ut xkik'ut wi	there thus they showed	
kib'inib'al	their stride	
kipus	their wondrous power	
kinawal	their spirit essence	
ta xetzalow	then they fought	
poy ajamche'	effigies carved wood	
uchuk[757]	hot coals	
saqlaq'	braziers	
wonon	bees	
sital	wasps	1320
ch'ab'i q'aq'	shooting fire	
kaq tijax	red flint knife	
q'eteb'	strangulation	
pub'a'ix:	being blowgunned:	
sutz'	clouds	
mayul	mist	
nima saqb'och:	great hail:	
kab'raqan:	earthquake:	
kaqulja'	thunderbolt	
ri kib'inib'al	the their stride	1330
kichakab'al:	their gait:	
ta rokik k'ut	then its entrance thus	
lab'al	war	
kumal wuq amaq'	by them seven nations	

---

[757] *uchuch* ("her/his/its mother") in the original manuscript. Mallory Matsumoto (personal communication, 2020) suggests that this is scribal error for *uchuk* ("hot coals").

tlekpan	tribes
xa k'ut poy ajamche'	merely thus effigies carved wood
ri'	them
xkilab'alij	they waged war
xk'is na kichuq'ab'	ended surely their strength
k'ate k'ut xjaqataj sokob'	then thus were opened great pots
kumal xoq'ojawab' rixoqil	by them beloved their wives
b'alam k'itze'	b'alam k'itze'
b'alam aq'ab'	b'alam aq'ab'
majukotaj	majukotaj
ik'i b'alam	ik'i b'alam
are' k'ut ta xjaqataj sokob'	they thus then were opened great pots
ta xjaqataj	then were opened
wonon	bees
sital	wasps
q'awonon:	bumblebees:
Are' k'ut xqasan kech wuq amaq'	They thus conquered theirs seven nations
ajlab'al	warriors
chwach ulew	on its face earth
are' k'ut e k'o chwach ulew	they thus they are on its face earth
ta xq'ol kanoq kitzol	then were thrown down left behind their slings
kitz'ununche'	their lances
xaqi kich'ab'	even their arrows
kipokob'	their shields
k'o xkam kanoq	there were they who died left behind
k'o xanumaj chi	there were they who fled now
chik[e]ch wuq ama[q']	to them seven nations
tlekpan	tribes
chi ma wi k'o ta lab'al xkib'ano	now not there is then war they made
xaloq' xkib'ana' lab'al =	in vain they would make war
keje' k'ut unimarik	then thus its aggrandizement
k'iche'	k'iche'

1340

1350

1360

wa'e e q'aq'	these they glorious	
e tepew xe'ux chi	they sovereign came to be now	
kib'i' wa'e wuq amaq' =	their names these seven nations	
wa'e k'ute kib'i' wuq amaq'	these thus their names seven nations	1370
raj xelab'alinik	their desire they waged war	
chila' Jaqawitz	there Jaqawitz	
¶ rot[z]jayib':	¶ rotzjayib':	
k'ib'aja:	k'ib'aja:	
uxab':	uxab':	
b'akaj:	b'akaj:	
keb'atzunja ri'	keb'atzunja these	
ta xeb'anow lab'al	then they caused to be made war	
utikerik lab'alin rib'	its beginning war against themselves	
utikerik puch ch'ab'	its beginning as well arrows	1380
pokob'	shields	
qi' uxe' keje' k'ut	truly its roots then thus	
uk'utunik	its manifestation	
q'aq'al	glory	
tepek'wal[758]	sovereignty	
rumal k'iche' winaq	by k'iche' people	
chwach ronojel rajlab'al	before their faces all of them their warriors	
xel wi k'u apanoq	came forth thus outward	
kinimal =	their greatness =	
Roxmul[759] chi k'ut lab'al Raj	Third Time again thus war Their Desire	1390
xkik'u'xlaj chik	they plotted again	
wuq amaq'	seven nations	
tlekpan	tribes	
ta xkikamisaj chi kitzij	then they killed with their words	
chirech kich'akik chik	to them their defeat now	

---

[758] Variant of *tepewal*, meaning "sovereignty" in Nahuatl.

[759] *Roxmal* in the original manuscript, scribal error for *Roxmul*.

e qamam	they our grandfathers
e qaqajaw	they our fathers
b'alam k'itze'	b'alam k'itze'
b'alam aq'ab'	b'alam aq'ab'
Majukotaj	Majukotaj 1400
ik'i b'alam =	ik'i b'alam =
rumal [w]uqu taq q'ij	because seven days
ke'atin wi	they bathe
ri ajkaj	the sacrificers
ajkix	bloodletters
e qamam	they our grandfathers
qaqajaw =	our fathers =
ta xecha' chi k'ut wuq amaq'	then they said now thus seven nations
xa ta keb'e qach'aka'	merely then they go to our victory
chi miq'ina'	at hot water 1410
chi katinab'al	at their bathing place
ma pa xa rumal ma wi kakil	not merely because not they see
uwach ixoq	her face woman
are' k'u rumal qitzij e q'aq'	they thus because truly they glorious
e tepe[w]	they sovereign
xa ta k'ut keqawik	merely then thus we adorn them
keqakaw[a]j ub'ik	we ornament them with jewels thither
oxib' josq'ilaj	three beautiful
alitom	girls
we ta pu chib'e kik'u'x chikech	perhaps then as well will go their hearts to them 1420
chet k'elax ta k'ut uk'u'x	soon deadened then thus their hearts
tojil.	tojil.
Awilix	Awilix
Jaqawitz. Chikech	Jaqawitz. To Them
xa k'u cha'utz kikamisaxik	merely thus will be accomplished their being killed
chux qumal xecha' k'ut	it will be so by us they said thus

ta xb'anataj kitzij	then was accomplished their word	
xch'ikitaj k'ut: uq'ijil kich'akik	it was set thus: its day their defeat	
qamam	our grandfathers	
qaqajaw	our fathers	1430
kumal wuq amaq'	by them seven nations	
ajlab'al =	warriors =	
jutzu k'ut	immediatly thus	
chi anim	now quickly	
xketa'maj	they learned it	
b'alam k'itze':	b'alam k'itze':	
ta kib'ek⁷⁶⁰ e·atinel	then they go they bathers	
pa miq'ina':	at hot water springs:	
e chi k'u k'o chik oxib'	they now thus there are now three	
josq'ilaj⁷⁶¹ alitom pa miq'ina'	beautiful girls at hot water springs	1440
ta xe'opanik =	then they arrived =	
jutzu k'ut xepe ri alitom	immediately thus they came the girls	
kaniman alaq	honor to thee	
alaq ajawab'	ye lords	
mi xujpe uk' alaq	we just now came with thee	
uj kitaqon qaqajaw	we their envoys our fathers	
ojix kuk'	go with them	
ajawab'	lords	
B'alam k'itze'	B'alam k'itze'	
b'alam aq'ab'	b'alam aq'ab'	1450
majukotaj	majukotaj	
ik'i b'alam:	ik'i b'alam:	
je'ich'ab'ej	go to speak	
wa'e	this	
naqi chikaj chiya' chiqech	what will you want to give to us	

---

⁷⁶⁰ *kib'ik* in the original manuscript, a common variant in this text for *kib'ek* ("their going").

⁷⁶¹ *q'ilaj* is repeated twice due to scribal error at the line break.

we pu chikaj kixk'ule' quk'[762]	perhaps also you will want to join with us
kecha'	they say
e qaqajaw	they our fathers
Rotzjayib':	Rotzjayib':
uxab':	uxab': 1460
k'ib'aja:	k'ib'aja:
b'akaj	b'akaj
keb'atzunja:	keb'atzunja:
xecha' k'ut q'apojib'	they said thus maidens
chikej b'alam k'itze':	to them b'alam k'itze':
ta xechoq'ob'ex k'ut	then they were in accord thus
utz b'a la'	good then that
ix	you
qami'al	our daughters
mi b'a xeqach'ab'ej ri ajawab'	recently then we spoke to them the lords 1470
mi puch qil kiwach	recently as well we saw their faces
kixcha' b'a apanoq	you say then out there
chikech iqajaw	to them your fathers
ix	you
qami'al	our daughters
xecha'	they said
b'alam k'itze'	b'alam k'itze'
Are' b'a	It then
ri qataqikil	the our task
Alaq	Ye 1480
ajawab'	lords
chik'ama' uloq retal	bring hither its sign
chi qitzij xe'ich'ab'ej	that truly you spoke with them

---

[762] These two lines are grammatically problematic. From the context, these should be the words the lords of the Seven Nations want the young ladies to say to the progenitors. But the manuscript reads *chikech* ("to them") in line 1455, whereas it should be *chiqech* ("to us"), and the manuscript reads *kuk'* ("with them") in this line, which should be *quk'* ("with us"). If my interpretation is correct, this must be scribal error.

we ma wi k'o retal	if not there is its sign	
chul iwumal	will arrive by you	
kixqakamisaj	we kill you	
kixchoy	you are cut in pieces	
chwach ja'	before its face river	
chwach siwan	before its face ravine	
kecha'	they say	1490
qaqajaw chiqech	our fathers to us	
alaq	ye	
ajawab'	lords	
toq'ob' k'u qawach	favor thus our faces	
chiya' ta alaq retal chiqe	give then thee its sign to us	
xecha' k'ut	they said thus	
q'apojib' =	maidens =	
ta xkik'ulu b'a k'ut	then they responded in accord then thus	
b'alam k'itze'	b'alam k'itze'	
chiweyeb'ej	wait	1500
na chiqaya' retal chiwech	surely we will give its sign to you	
xe'uchax k'ut	they were told thus	
q'apojib'	maidens	
ta kib'[e]ik k'ut	then their going thus	
b'alam k'itze'	b'alam k'itze'	
chwach tojil:	before their faces tojil:	
awilix:[763]	awilix:	
Jaqawitz.	Jaqawitz.	
at tojil	you tojil	
awilix	awilix	1510
naqipa retal wa'e tzij	what its sign this word	
chiqaya'	we will give	

---

[763] *ajilis* in the original manuscript, scribal error for *awilix*.

chikech	to them
wa'e q'apojib'	these maidens
kimi'al	their daughters
wuq amaq'	seven nations
xecha' k'ut tojil	they said thus tojil
awilix	awilix
chitzib'aj oxib' k'ul[764]	paint three robes
chiya' chikech:	give to them: 1520
jun sital upam	one wasps its interior
jun k'ut b'alam upam:	one thus jaguar its interior:
jun k'ut kot upam	one thus eagle its interior
chikiq'uwuj apanoq	they will drape about
kiqajaw loq'ob'al ke	their fathers gift theirs
xcha' k'ut tojil:	said thus tojil:
awilix.	awilix.
Jaqawitz	Jaqawitz
chike	to them
b'alam k'itze'	b'alam k'itze' 1530
keje' k'ut utz'ib'axik	then thus their being painted
oxb'usaj[765] chi k'ul	three of robes
kumal	by them
b'alam k'itze'	b'alam k'itze'
xkiya' ub'ik chikech	they gave thither to them
oxib' q'apojib'	three maidens
kimi'al	their daughters
wuq amaq'	seven nations
wa'e kib'i'	these their names
q'apojib':	maidens: 1540
jun puch	jun puch

---

[764] *k'al* in the original manuscript, scribal error for *k'ul* ("robe, tunic").

[765] According to Sáenz de Santa María (1940, 69), *b'usaj* indicates enumeration (*jub'usaj wuj* is "one book," *kab'usaj wuj* is "two books," and *oxb'usaj wuj* is "three books").

jun tax.	jun tax.
Jun k'ib'atzunja:	Jun k'ib'atzunja:
ta xkuk'aj oxib' tzib'am k'u loq'ob'al	then they bore three painted thus gifts
rech kiqajaw	of their fathers
keki'kot chik xeb'ek —	they rejoice now they went —
ta kopanik ruk' kiqajaw	then they arrive with their fathers
nim xeki'kot ajawab'	greatly they rejoiced lords
chirech kiloq'[e]xik	to their being gifted
rajawal	their lords 1550
wuq amaq' —	seven nations —
are' b'a wa'e k'ul jujun kech	they then these robes each theirs
jujun kech iqajaw	each theirs your fathers
kecha' ajawab'	say lords
b'alam k'itze'	b'alam k'itze'
xecha' chikech	they said to them
kiqajaw =	their fathers =
jutzu k'ut	immediately thus
xuk'am uk'u[l]	he took his robe
ri jun chikech	the one to them 1560
are' ri sital upam	it the wasps its interior
xukoj chirij	he put it on his back
jutzu k'ut	immediately thus
xk'astaj kiwach chi sital	came to life their faces of wasps
xuti' uti'ojil ajaw	they stung his flesh lord
xawi keje' ri kot upam	likewise then the eagle inside
xk'astaj kiwach kot b'alam	came to life their faces eagle jaguar
xeti' k'ut ajawab'	they bit thus lords
rajawal amaq'	their lords nations
maqipa chi k'axk'ol wa'e	was it not to torment these 1570
xb'e'ik'ama' uloq[766]	you went to bring hither

---

[766] *uloq* is repeated twice at this point, most likely scribal error.

ix	you
k'axtok'anel	demons
xecha' chikech.	they said to them
kimi'al	their daughters
keje' k'ut uq'ilitajik	then thus its being stopped
lab'al ri'	war that
kumal	by them
amaq'	nations
chila' Jaqawitz	there Jaqawitz 1580
ch'ipaq	ch'ipaq
unimal	their greatness
uq'aq'al k'iche'	their glory k'iche'
keje' k'ut uk'utunik uq'aq'al	then thus its manifestation their glory
utepewal k'iche' winaq	their sovereignty k'iche' people
chwach ronojel	before their faces all of them
Rajlab'al	Their Warriors
xel wi k'u apanoq	went forth thus outward
kinimal	their greatness
e qamam	they our grandfathers 1590
qaqajaw	our fathers
B'alam k'itze':	B'alam k'itze':
b'alam aq'ab'.	b'alam aq'ab'.
Majukotaj.	Majukotaj.
ik'i b'alam	ik'i b'alam
waral k'ut cheta'max wi q'aq'al	here thus they would come to know glory
tepewal	sovereignty
xb'an Jaqawitz	it was done Jaqawitz
ch'ipaq	ch'ipaq
chi uk'iyal may	again its multitude twenty year cycles 1600
xkib'an chiri' Jaqawitz ————	they did there Jaqawitz ————
❡wa'e k'ut una'ojixik ajawarem	❡this thus its being considered lordship
kumal b'alam k'itze'	by them b'alam k'itze'

| chwi' kich'akatajik | upon their being defeated |
| wuq amaq' | seven nations |

| Ta xecha' xa ta b'a chib'e | Then they said merely then go |
| qasamajel | our envoys |

| chila' chwach ajaw nakxik | there before his face lord nakxik |
| chi relib'al q'ij | at its coming out place sun |

| ma ta kojkich'ak | not then they defeat us   1610 |
| ri wuq amaq' ajlab'al | the seven nations warriors |

| ma ta pu kojkisacho | not then also they disappear us |
| kojkimayj | they destroy us |

| ma ta pu chiqaj qaq'ij | not then as well will be thrown down our day |
| qalaxik | our birth |

| qab'i' | our names |
| qawach | our faces |

| ta wi chux apanoq | then may it be henceforward |
| xecha' | they said |

| keje' k'ut kitaqik ub'ik | then thus their being sent thither   1620 |
| e ka'ib' uk'ajol B'alam k'itze' | they two his sons B'alam k'itze' |

| wa'e k'ut kib'i' | these thus their names |
| e ka'ib' uk'ajol b'alam k'itze' | they two his sons b'alam k'itze' |

| ta xya' kitaqikil | then was given their authority |
| wa'e | these |

| k'oka'ib'. | k'oka'ib'. |
| k'okawib' | k'okawib' |

| ta xeb'e chi relib'al q'ij | then they went to its coming out place sun |
| e[767] k'ama' ajawarem chi relib'al q'ij | [to] obtain lordship at its coming out place sun |

| jun xb'e chikej chi relib'al q'ij | one went by order to its coming out place sun   1630 |
| jun k'ut xb'e chuqajib'al q'ij | one thus went to its setting place sun |

| k'oka'ib' xb'e chi relib'al q'ij = | k'oka'ib' went to its coming out place sun = |

---

[767] It is unclear how the *e* functions here grammatically. This may be the result of scribal error. The element *chi* would make better sense in this context.

k'okawib' xb'e chuq[a]jib'al q'ij	k'okawib' went to its setting place sun
are' k'u ri k'oka'ib'	he thus the k'oka'ib'
jusu suk'ulik xb'e chi relib'al q'ij	quickly straightaway went to its coming out place sun
are' k'u ri k'okawib'	he thus the k'okawib'
xa xtzalij ulo[q]	merely he returned hither
chi palo	from sea
ma wi xq'ax[768] palo	not he crossed sea
ta xtzalij uloq	then he returned hither 1640
[me]xiko	mexico
ta xuch'utinaj uk'u'x	then he diminished his heart
ta xjoxow kanoq	then plowed behind
ruk' rixnam	with his sister-in-law
rixoqil k'oka'ib'	his wife k'oka'ib'
ta xk'ajolan k'u	then he engendered a son thus
na ri b'alam k'okawib' =	surely the b'alam k'okawib' =
k'o la' chi k'u ak'al	there is he now thus child
chi kusul	in cradle
ta xk'ulun utzijoxik	then it happened his being informed 1650
k'oka'ib'	k'oka'ib'
ta xb'e uk'ama' muj	then he went to receive canopy
q'alib'al:	throne:
tzikwil koj	paw puma
tzikwil b'alam	paw jaguar
ta xul puch: titil	then arrived as well: titil
q'an ab'aj	yellow stone
xb'anataj	it was accomplished
xb'e ub'ana' k'oka'ib'	he went to its doing k'oka'ib'
ta xul puch kotz'i'jab'al pwaq	then arrived as well flower vessel precious metal 1660

---

[768] This word is nearly illegible in the manuscript and is possibly written by another hand than the rest of the page. *Xq'ax* ("crossed") is reconstructed from the context of the sentence.

sochi pwaq[769]

rech mama ajtz'alam
rajpop ajtz'alam
utza'm chinamital

k'ate ta xcha' chi k'ut k'okawib'
qitzij b'a chiyan

mi xinb'an kanoq
xa ta ki[n]b'e jitz'axoq

chupam ri' b'a
xi[n]tzalij wi uloq rumal

mi xpe ri aja[w]
k'oka'ib'

naqipa xchijachaj
ri ak'al xcha'

ta xumalij uk'u'x
are' k'u xkib'an ri'

are' pu ujech'b'al rib'
kajawarem

ri' ri k'ute retal
rajawarem k'oka'ib'

qitzij wi muj
q'alib'al

koj
b'alam

waqachib'al
kotz'i'jab'al pwaq k'ut

rech rajpop ajtz'alam
utza'm chinamital

nab'e chapel
ta'ol upe uwinaq

rattle precious metal

theirs mama ajtz'alam
rajpop ajtz'alam
utza'm chinamital

then he said now thus k'okawib'
truly then right away

I just then did it left behind
merely then I go to be hanged

within this then
I returned hither because of it   1670

recently he came the lord
k'oka'ib'

who shall separate
the child he said

then he lost his heart
they thus did it

it also his division himself
their lordship

this the thus its sign
his lordship k'oka'ib'   1680

truly canopy
throne

puma
jaguar

shiny image
flower vessel precious metal thus

theirs rajpop ajtz'alam
utza'm chinamital

first chosen ones
listeners their misery their people   1690

---

[769] *pwach* in the original manuscript, scribal error for *pwaq*.

chi uk'ajol	to their sons
uchaq'	their younger brothers
qasam	victors in war
ajch'atam ulew[770]	conquerors earth
nim ja	great house
sokb'a[l] kiwi'	place of sacrifice their heads
are' ximonel	they punishers
are' Rapanel	they Captors
tijoy	chasteners
uk'ajol	their sons 1700
uchaq' ri mama ajtz'alam	their younger brothers the mama ajtz'alam
nab'e xpe ri keqale'n	first came the their burden of authority
rumal k'oka'ib'	by him k'oka'ib'
wa'e k'ut xb'an chi[771] Jaqawitz	this thus was done at Jaqawitz
xawi b'a chiq'alajin apanoq	merely then will be manifested outward
oxmul oxlaju winaq	three times thirteen score
xk'ulun wi k'oka'ib'	he journeyed k'oka'ib'
ta xpe	then he came
chi relib'al q'ij	from its coming out place sun
k'o la' chi k'ut	there is he now thus 1710
ak'al chi kusul ta xulik	child in cradle when he arrived
Apachina	Who Is He
ri ak'al	the child
xcha' k'ut ajaw k'oka'ib'	said thus lord k'oka'ib'
chirech xoqojaw	to her lady lord
je xawi b'a ti'ojil la	like merely then flesh thine
tz'umal la	skin thine

---

[770] The original manuscript reads *ulee*, scribal error for *ulew*. An identical parallel passage occurs on p. 23v, line 15, where the word is clearly *ulew*.

[771] The second *chi* is written below the line and is probably scribal error. Although some toponyms carry a *chi* prefix, Jaqawitz does not in this text; therefore, the second *chi* is unlikely to be part of the name of this mountain.

xawi pu atz la	merely as well older brother thine	
chaq' la	younger brother thine	
ajchoq'e xcha' k'ut	responsible one said thus	1720
ixoq	woman	
no'j b'a[772] la ma b'a xchiwixowaj taj	so be it then not then he shall be rejected	
ma pu xchiwitzelb'ij taj	not as well he shall be cursed	
xawi b'a chinya' rajawarem	merely then I will give his lordship	
xawi pu chinya' uq'aq'al	merely as well I will give his glory	
utepewal	his sovereignty	
xcha' k'ut	he said thus	
k'oka'ib'	k'oka'ib'	
ta xuk'onok'a' uwach	then he uncovered its face	
kusul	cradle	1730
are' b'a wa'e ala	he then this little boy	
b'alam k'onache chuchaxik	b'alam k'onache he will be called	
chib'e q'ij	it will go sun	
chib'e saq	it will go light	
xcha' k'ut	he said thus	
k'oka'ib'	k'oka'ib'	
keje' k'ut rulik	this thus its arrival	
nab'e ajawarem	first lordship	
ri' rumal	it because of him	
k'oka'ib'	k'oka'ib'	1740
ta xk'ajolan kanoq k'okawib'	then he engendered left behind k'okawib'	
chirij rixnam	behind his sister-in-law	
keje' k'ut uwinaqirik b'i' ri chi	then thus its conception name it now	
k'onache ristayul ajaw kuchax wakamik	k'onache ristayul lord he is called this day	
keje' puch uwinaqirik	then also its conception	
ajpo[p] k'amjayil[773]	ajpop k'amjayil	

---

[772] *b'a* is repeated erroneously at the line break.

[773] *ajpo k'amjayil*. The fuller spelling is *ajpop k'amjayil*, but the text frequently abbreviates the title.

ri ukab' ajawarem	the second lordship
ajaw stayul chuchaxik	lord stayul he is called
are' k'u ri nab'e ajaw	he thus the first lord
k'oka'ib'	k'oka'ib' 1750
uk'ajol	his son
b'alam k'itze'	b'alam k'itze'
ri ajaw	the lord
ajpop kaweq ——	ajpop kaweq ——
xchita' chi k'u alaq	hear now thus ye
usuk'ulikil	its straightness
xchicholotajik	it shall be recounted
xchinloq'b'ij k'ut kik'oje'ik	I shall speak with honor thus their nature
xchintz'ib'aj k'ut	I shall write thus
in Diego reynoso	I Diego reynoso 1760
popol winaq	popol winaq
¶ uk'ajol laju no'j	¶ his son laju no'j
Are' chi k'ut xchiqatikib'a' chik	It now thus we shall begin now
ub'ixik	its being said
wa'e kib'ik chik	this their going again
e oxib' nawal winaq chukamul chik	they three enchanted people for second time again
ta xeb'e chik	then they went again
chi relib'al q'ij	to its coming out place sun
wa'e	these
kib'i':	their names: 1770
k'oka'ib'.	k'oka'ib'.
k'okawib'.	k'okawib'.
k'o'akul akutaq' ——	k'o'akul akutaq' ——
Ri' xeb'ek	These they went
chi relib'al q'ij	to its coming out place sun
chwach ajaw	before his face lord

nakxik	nakxik
e k'amol rech	they receivers theirs
ajawarem	lordship
q'alib'al koj	throne puma 1780
q'alib'al b'alam:	throne jaguar:
su'b'aq[774]	bone flute
chamcham	drum
rajawarem	their lordship
ajaw	lords
ajpop	ajpop
ajpo k'amja:	ajpo k'amja:
q'alel atzij winaq	q'alel atzij winaq
ta xb'e ri nim ch'okoj kaweq	then went the great ch'okoj kaweq
xa ch'okojil tem xuxik	merely sitter bench he came to be 1790
ma wi xub'ij	not he said
tzok'otz	leaders
nima'q ajmewa	great fasters
k'axko'ol	sufferers
ma wi kajawarem taj	not their lordship
xb'ekik'ama' kitaqikil	they went to receive their authority
rumal ajaw	because of him lord
b'alam[775] k'itze'	b'alam k'itze'
ta xe'[o]pan[776] chwach ajaw nakxik	then they arrived before his face lord nakxik
xkitz'onoj k'ut	they pleaded for it thus 1800
kitaqikil	their authority
chirech ajaw nakxik	to him lord nakxik
ta xmolob'ax k'u uloq	then was delivered thus hither
ajawarem chikech	lordship to them

---

[774] *sukb'aq* in the original, most likely scribal error for *su'b'aq* as it is spelled elsewhere in the text.

[775] *b'alan* in the original, variant or scribal error for *b'alam*

[776] *xepam* in the original, variant or scribal error for *xe'opan.*

rumal ajaw	by him lord
nakxik	nakxik
ta xetzalij uloq ri k'oka'ib'	then returned hither the k'oka'ib'
k'okawib'.	k'okawib'.
ruk' nim ch'okoj kaweq	with them nim ch'okoj kaweq
ta kulik k'ut	then they arrived thus 1810
xkimolob'a' k'ut	they delivered it thus
kitaqikil	their authority
xb'anataj	it was done
xqab'ano	we did it
xpe	it has come
wa'e ajawarem	this lordship
retal	its sign
xpetik xecha'	it has come they said
ta xkimolob'a'	then they distributed it
kitaqikil	their authority 1820
ma wi xkib'ij	not they said
tzok'otz nima'q	leaders great
ajtz'isomcha.	ajtz'isomcha.
ajkuk'umam	ajkuk'umam
k'a'm	k'a'm
b'elej winaq	nine periods of twenty days
oxlaju winaq	thirteen periods of twenty days
chi mewa	of fasting
chi k'axk'ol	of suffering
uk'axk'ol	its suffering 1830
ajawarem	lordship
ta xkimolob'a'	then they distributed
chirech b'alam k'onache	to him b'alam k'onache
wa'e muji q'uq'	these canopy quetzal
muji raxon	canopy cotinga

q'alib'al koj	throne puma	
q'alib'al b'alam	throne jaguar	
su'b'aq	bone flute	
chamcham	drum	
tatil	stone	1840
q'an ab'aj	yellow stone	
jolom	head	
pich kej	hooves deer	
tzikil wil kot	talon eagle	
tzikil b'alam	paw jaguar	
t'ot'	shell	
matak'us	net tobacco	
ch'ayom[777]	beautiful bird feathers	
astapulul[778]	snowy egret feathers	
je' k'uch	tail vulture	1850
makutax:	bracelet of precious stones:	
malili	braid	
nakat ab'aj	ear ornament of stone	
retal ajawarem chila'	its sign lordship there	
xnuk' wi uloq	was arranged hither	
chi relib'al q'ij	at its coming out place sun	
chikech samajel are'	to them envoys them	
ta kechapoq' ajawab'	then may they take them lords	
keje' retal	as their signs	
wa' xe'uchax	this they were told	1860

---

[777] *Chiyom* in the original manuscript. This is most likely a variant or scribal error for *ch'ayom*, glossed as a "beautiful bird" in Colonial dictionaries but otherwise unidentified. Alternatively, it could be a Mayanized form of *chiltotl*, a Nahuatl name for an unidentified "bird with colored feathers" (Molina 2001 [1571]). The same pairing of this bird and the snowy egret appears elsewhere in the text as symbols of authority brought from Tulan (see lines 2630–2631, 3424–3425).

[778] *ajtjtapulul* in the original manuscript, variant or scribal error for *astapulul* as it is written elsewhere in the text.

samajel	envoys
Are'	He
ri ajaw ajpop	the lord ajpop
kajib' muj pa uwi'	four canopies at its head
jun uq'alib'al:	one his throne:
k'o	there is
uraxon	its cotinga feathers
ri ajsu'b'aq	the player bone flute
ajchamcham	player drum
Are' k'u	He thus
ri ajpo k'amja	the ajpo k'amja
oxib' umuj	three his canopies
pa uwi'	at his head
Are' k'u	He thus
ri nima Raj[p]op achij:	the great Their Ajpop valiant men:
ka'ib' umuj	two his canopies
pa uwi'	at his head
Are' k'u	He thus
ri ch'uti Rajpop achij	the small Their Ajpop valiant men
jun umuj	one his canopy
pa uwi'	at his head
pa xik'aja	in plume house
chichap wi	he will take it
ma na k'o ta usu'b'aq	not surely there is their bone flute
uchamcham	their drum
rumal k'al	because child
k'ajolaxel	son
ri' k'ute kajawarem ajawab'	these thus their lordship lords
ta xulik	when they arrived
xpe chi relib'al q'ij	they came from its coming out place sun
xa junulik ajawarem	merely eternal lordship

Line numbers in right margin:
1870 (aligned with "He thus / the ajpo k'amja")
1880 (aligned with "one his canopy / at his head")
1890 (aligned with "they came from its coming out place sun")

ta xulik q'alelay tem	then arrived q'alelay bench
atzij winaqil tem	atzij winaqil bench
nim ch'okojil tem	nim ch'okojil bench
q'ale k'amja'il tem	q'ale k'amja'il bench
nima k'amja'il tem	nima k'amja'il bench
kajib' ajtojil	four ajtojil
oxib' ch'okojib'	three ch'okojib'
oxib' utza'm pop	three utza'm pop
oxib' yakol ja	three yakol ja 1900
k'i k'ut pop k'amja	many thus pop k'amja
chirij k'iche'	behind k'iche'
// keje' k'ut rech ajaw k'iche'	// then thus theirs ajaw k'iche'
ta rulik atzij winaqil tem	then its arrival atzij winaqil bench
e lolmet ajaw	they lolmet ajaw
// nim ch'okoj ajaw	// nim ch'okoj ajaw
// ajaw Jaqawitz	// lord Jaqawitz
Rech ajaw k'iche'	Of Him ajaw k'iche'
xa oxib' chi nima'q ch'okojib'	merely three then great ch'okojib'
alay tem	givers of birth benches 1910
xawi rach	merely their companions
chapik	take as office
upop	their pop
uk'amja ajawab'	their k'amja lords
xawi chi relib'al q'ij	merely at its coming out place sun
xpe wi ub'i'natisaxik	came their being named
k'iche' ajawarem	k'iche' lordship
k'iche' pop	k'iche' pop
k'iche' k'amja	k'iche' k'amja
ajawal winaq————	lordly people———— 1920
mi k'ut xkub'e'	just then thus were consoled
uk'u'x	their hearts
b'alam k'itze'	b'alam k'itze'
B'alam aq'ab'	B'alam aq'ab'
Majukotaj	Majukotaj

ik'i b'alam	ik'i b'alam
mi xwiqitaj	just then were invested
ajawarem	lordship
kumal	by them
e kik'ajol	they their sons 1930
chwi' juyub'	atop mountain
Jaqawitz ch'ipaq—	Jaqawitz ch'ipaq—
wakamik k'ut xchita' chi alaq	this day thus hear then ye
wa'e kik'axk'ol	this their suffering
qamam	our grandfathers
qaqajaw	our fathers
chi mewa	in fasting
chi k'axk'ol	in affliction
xek'oje' chwi' juyu[b']	they were atop mountain
Jaqawitz	Jaqawitz 1940
B'alam k'itze'	B'alam k'itze'
wa'e qamam	this our grandfather
oj	we
kaweqib'	kaweqib'
waral k'ut mi xtikel wi	here thus just then was begun
uk'ajolanik	their engendering sons
b'alam k'itze' =	b'alam k'itze' =
b'alam aq'ab'	b'alam aq'ab'
Majukotaj:	Majukotaj:
are' k'u ik'i b'alam[779]	he thus ik'i b'alam 1950
xkam chupam uk'ajolal	he died within his youth
wa'e k'ute uk'ajol b'alam k'itze'	these thus his sons b'alam k'itze'
wa'e unab'e k'ajol =	these his first sons =
k'ok'oja:	k'ok'oja:
k'oraxonamaq'	k'oraxonamaq'

---

[779] The manuscript reads *b'allam*.

kib'i' e ka'ib'	their names they two	
uk'ajol b'alam k'itze' =	his sons b'alam k'itze' =	
xek'ajolan chi k'u ri k'ok'oja:	they engendered sons then thus the k'ok'oja:	
k'oraxonamaq' =/	k'oraxonamaq' =	
e'	e'	1960
tz'i[ki]n[780]	tz'ikin	
chi k'ut	then thus	
xkik'ajolaj =	they engendered sons =	
xek'ajolan	they engendered sons	
chi k'u ri tz'ikin	then thus the tz'ikin	
aj	aj	
kan	kan	
chi k'ut kib'i'	then thus their names	
xkik'ajolaj =	they engendered sons =	
ukaj le' uwinaq =	fourth generation their people =	1970
5 Ro' le' winaq k'ut wa'e	5 Fifth generation people thus these	
k'oka'ib'	k'oka'ib'	
k'okawib' //	k'okawib' //	
xkik'ajolaj	they engendered	
aj	aj	
kan	kan	
Ro' le' winaq =	Fifth generation people =	
¶ job' k'ut[781] xuk'ajola[j]	¶ five thus he engendered sons	
k'oka'ib'	k'oka'ib'	
kejnay.	kejnay.	1980
k'oyoy //	k'oyoy //	
xmaykej //	xmaykej //	
chokoy—	chokoy—	
r[i] laq'amal	the laq'amal	
ri' xuk'ajolaj	these he engendered sons	
k'oka'ib' ——	k'oka'ib' ——	

---

[780] The manuscript reads *tzin*, a contraction of *tz'ikin*.

[781] The original reads *k'utt*, variant or scribal error for k'ut.

// are' k'ut	// he thus
k'okawib'	k'okawib'
k'onache xuk'ajolaj	k'onache he engendered son
joxb'al[782] al	illegitimate child 1990
tzipitawar ub'i'	tzipitawar her name
rixoqil	his wife
xwaq le'oq k'ajolax.	six generations engendered.
Taxik	Ordered
ta xb'ek'amoq ajawarem	then they went to receive lordship
chi relib'al q'ij	at its coming out place sun
wa'e k'ut	this thus
kipixab'axik	their being counseled
B'alam k'itze'	B'alam k'itze'
b'alam aq'ab'	b'alam aq'ab' 2000
kumal tojil	by them tojil
awilix	awilix
Jaqawitz	Jaqawitz
ix	you all
ajawakob'	lords
xa sqaqi'n chik	merely a little more
ma wi chisaqirik	not it will dawn
china' k'u iwib'	prepare thus yourselves
kujiwelesaj ta waral	take us out then here
rumal toq'ob' iwach	because favor your faces 2010
chux apanoq	it will come to be henceforward
kojiya' ta	place us then
chupam ewam k'echelaj	within hidden forest
chiri' k'ut	there thus
kojich'ab'ej wi	you speak with us

---

[782] From the context, this should be *joxb'al* ("illegitimate/result of fornication") rather than *josb'al* ("scraper"), as it appears in the original manuscript.

rumal kape nima saq	because it comes great light	
kape pu q'ij	it comes as well sun	
ik'	moon	
ch'umil	stars	
uj ta k'utewachim chik	we then have been manifested again	2020
iwumal	by you	
xcha' ri tojil	said the tojil	
chikech	to them	
B'alam[783] k'itze'	B'alam k'itze'	
b'alam aq'ab'	b'alam aq'ab'	
majukotaj	majukotaj	
ik'i b'alam	ik'i b'alam	
ta xunimaj k'ut	then he obeyed thus	
b'alam k'itze'	b'alam k'itze'	
xb'e ri tojil	he went the tojil	2030
chupam jun nima k'echelaj	within a great forest	
jutzu xub'i'naj ri k'echelaj	immediately he named it the forest	
pa tojil	pa tojil	
e k'o wi b'[784] k'ula wi kot	they are among eagle	
k'ula wi b'alam	among jaguar	
k'ula wi sochoj	among rattlesnake	
k'ula wi k'anti'	among viper	
xk'oje' wi uk'ab'awil	there he was his god	
B'alam k'itze' =	B'alam k'itze' =	
Are' k'ut rech	He thus his	2040
b'alam aq'ab'	b'alam aq'ab'	
xb'e pa awilix	he went pa awilix	
pa ewam k'echelaj =	in hidden forest =	
are' k'u rech	he thus his	

---

[783] B'alalam in the original manuscript, scribal error for B'alam.

[784] It is unclear why the letter *b* (or possibly the number 6) appears here, but it does not appear to have any known meaning in this context.

Majukotaj	Majukotaj
xawi chiri' xk'oje' wi	merely there he was
chwi' juyub'	atop mountain
Jaqawitz	Jaqawitz
xawi k'o chiri' ta xsaqirik ---	merely they are there when it dawned ---
keje' k'ut xeki'kot wi	then thus they rejoiced 2050
xaqi xkeyeb'ej chi usaqirik	merely they awaited now its dawn
chila' chwi' juyub'	there atop mountain
Jaqawitz	Jaqawitz
junelik xk'ixe'[785] chwach	always they bloodlet before its face
chi relib'al q'ij	to its coming out place sun
chireyeb'exik usaqirik———	to its being awaited its dawn———
ta usaqirik k'u——	then its dawn thus——
nab'e xel uloq ri nima ch'umil	first it came out hither the great star
k'amol ub'e q'ij	guide its path sun
k'ate k'ut relik ula q'ij	then thus its coming out hither sun 2060
xsaqir k'ut	it dawned thus
ta xe'oq' k'ut tz'ikin	then they cried out thus birds
are' nab'e ri ajpop k'eletza	it first the lordly parrot
k'a chiri' k'ut xkil wi q'ij	even there thus they saw sun
saq	light
chwi' juyub'	atop mountain
Jaqawitz =	Jaqawitz =
k'ate k'u ri' ta xeki'kotik	then thus this then they rejoiced
xek'amowanik	they gave thanks
xeb'ixanik	they sang 2070
k'ate pu ri' ta xkikir kipom[786]	then as well this they unwrapped their incense
xare wi xkixim uloq kipom chi relib'al	for they bound hither their incense at its coming
q'ij	out place sun

---

[785] *xxk'ixe'*. An extraneous *x* appears at the beginning of the word due to a line break.

[786] *kipam* ("their bellies/waists") in the original manuscript, scribal error for *kipom* ("their incense").

ta xepetik ral	then they came their vassals
maylo kipetik	delayed their coming
ta xek'amowan k'ut	then they gave thanks thus
ta xkijaq k'ut	then they opened thus
kipom	their incense
kik'amowab'al	their means of giving thanks
B'alam k'itze':	B'alam k'itze':
kasiwastan upom //	kasiwastan his incense // 2080
B'alam aq'ab':	B'alam aq'ab':
mixtan[787] pom re	mixtan incense his
majukotaj	majukotaj
k'ab'awil pom rech —	k'ab'awil incense his —
ta xkiporoj	then they burned it
kamul k'amo	twice thanks
oxmul k'amo	thrice thanks
at tz'aqol	you framer
at b'ito[l]	you shaper
at k'u unik'ajal kaj	you thus its center sky 2090
ulew	earth
at kaj tz'uk	you four corners
kaj xuk'ut k'amo	four sides thanks
mi xqil[788] ri usaqirik	just now we saw the its dawn
upakatajik	its brightening of the sky
mi xqil q'ij	just now we saw sun
mi xqil ch'umil =	just now we saw stars =
at k'ut	you thus
at qajuyub'al	you our mountain place
tulan	tulan 2100

---

[787] *mistan* in the text, a variant of *mixtan*, as this incense is called in the *Popol Vuh* (Christenson 2007, 228). The *x* is commonly substituted for *s* in this text.

[788] *xq'ij* in the original manuscript, scribal error for *xqil* ("we saw"), paralleling the subsequent couplet.

sewan	sewan
q'analaj juyub'	very yellow mountain
raxalaj juyub' xecha'	very green mountain they said
ta xkiporoj	then they burned it
ri kipom	the their incense
are' k'u ri usib'el	it thus the its smoke
kipom	their incense
suk'ulik xb'e chi kaj	straight it went to sky
nab'e ta xsuk'ma'ij[789] k'u uwach	first then it straightened thus its face
xb'e chi relib'al q'ij	it went to its coming out place sun
rumal	because of it
aretal xopan chupam kijuyub'al	when it arrived within their mountain place
xopan puch roq'ej kik'u'x	it arrived as well its crying out their hearts
chwach ajaw	before his face lord
nakxik rumal xecha'	nakxik by them they said
xa ta jun mi xqil wi q'ij	merely then one just now we saw sun
saq	light
iwuk' ix	with you
q'uk' qatzab'	with us our older brothers
qatz	our older brothers
qachaq'	our younger brothers
tlekpan	tribes
ix k'o kana	you are left behind
chi qajuyub'al	at our mountain place
chi qataq'ajal xecha'	at our valley place they said
roq'ej kik'u'x e qamam	its crying out their hearts they our grandfathers
qaq[a]jaw	our fathers
ta xkil usaqirik	then they saw its dawn
ta xek'amowan	then they gave thanks

[789] *xk'uk'ma'ij* in the original manuscript, which has no known meaning. I agree with Carmack and Mondloch (1983, 233, n. 190) who suggest that this should be *xsuk'ma'ij* ("to straighten").

k'ot saq k'ut	sculpted stone radiant thus	2130
xkisa' kib'	they dried themselves	
chwi' taq che'	atop trees	
juyub'	mountains	
wa'e k'ut usaqirik	this thus its dawn	
kik'axkol	their affliction	
e qamam	they our grandfathers	
qaqajaw———	our fathers———	
wa'e k'ute kipixab' chikech kik'ajol	this thus their counsel to them their sons	
chwi' usaqirik	above its dawn	
ix qak'ajol mi xixtz'aqatik	you our sons just now you were completed	2140
mi pu xixpoq'otajik	just now also you were multiplied	
chik'ama' k'u wa'e	take thus this	
pison k'ak'al	bundled glory	
k'olo wi na	take care of it surely	
chichokonik	keep it	
maja' kaqariq	not yet we find it	
qajuyub'al	our mountain place	
chib'an wi q'aq'al	you will achieve glory	
tepewal	sovereignty	
k'a chiri' k'ut chijaqataj wi	even there thus you will open it	2150
ri retal ajawarem xpe chi relib'al q'ij	the its sign lordship came from its coming out place sun	
chik'ajolaj chi na ri ajpop	you will engender surely the ajpop	
ajpo k'amja	ajpo k'amja	
q'alel atzij winaq	q'alel atzij winaq	
chib'anow	you will attain	
q'aq'al	glory	
tepek'wal	sovereignty	
chux apanoq	it will come to be henceforward	
rumal kojkamik	because we die	
kojsachik	we vanish	2160

kojb'ek	we go
kojtzalilik	we go back
mi xixqaya' kanoq pa utzil	just now we left you in peace
maji chik lab'al	there is not now war
kumal wuq amaq'	by them seven nations
ajlab'al	warriors
mixb'ison k'ut	do not mourn thus
chiwila' ichuch xecha'	look after your mothers they said
ma wi e yawab' taj ta xepixab'ik	not they ill when they counseled them
utz kiwach	good their faces 2170
ta xok aq'ab' =	when it entered night =
are' chi k'ut ta xsaqirik	they now thus when it dawned
e chi k'ut maji chik	they now thus were not now
xa k'a et xesachik =	merely until a little later they vanished =
ma ta k'u chisach ik'u'x[790]	not then thus lose your hearts
chita'ow wa'e tzij	hear this word
xawi qi' are' b'alam[791] k'itze'	merely true he b'alam k'itze'
xkib'i'naj kik'ajol:	they named their sons:
b'alam aq'ab'	b'alam aq'ab'
majukotaj	majukotaj 2180
ik'i b'alam	ik'i b'alam
xe'uchax chik	they were called now
chupam usaqirik	within its dawn
e k'u k'i chik kimam	they thus many now their grandsons
kik'ajol	their sons
chi kaweq	of kaweq
chi nijayi[b']	of nijayib'
chi ajaw k'iche'	of ajaw k'iche'
ta xb'i'naj ri juyub'	then they named the mountain
saqirib'al tojil rech kaweq	saqirib'al tojil theirs kaweq 2190

---

[790] *uk'u'x* ("her/his heart") in the original manuscript, scribal error for *ik'u'x* ("your hearts").

[791] *b'alan* in the original manuscript, variant or scribal error for *b'alam*.

saqirib'al awilix
rech nijayib':

saqirib'al Jaqawitz
rech ajaw k'iche'———

kech tamub'
saqirib'al [a]maq' tan

kech k'aqoj
eq'omaq'———

saqirib'al ajuk'in
kech ilokab'

sik'a'ab'
Juwanija———

// xa k'u jun xek'oje' chiwi' pa tojil
kuk' nijayib'

qi' xub'i'naj ch'aqa ja kaweq
ch'aqa ja nijayib' xecha'

retwach
kitzij junam

xkib'an kitz'aq———
nab'e saqiri[k]

ta roq'otaxik nab'e tinamit q'aq'awi[tz]
2[792] xkoq'otaj chi k'u ri tojil

ukab' tinamit ta xe'opan chi k'u
sib'aqija naj kib'an chiri'

xawi keqa'm ri pison k'ak'al

retal ajawarem xpe chi relib'al q'ij

saqirib'al awilix
theirs nijayib':

saqirib'al Jaqawitz
theirs ajaw k'iche'———

theirs tamub'
saqirib'al amaq' tan

theirs k'aqoj
eq'omaq'———

saqirib'al ajuk'in
theirs ilokab'

sik'a'ab'
Juwanija———

// merely thus one they were atop pa tojil
with them nijayib'

truly they named it other side house kaweq
other side house nijayib' they said

they distributed equally
truly united

they built their buildings———
first dawn

then was abandoned first citadel q'aq'awitz
2 was abandoned now thus the tojil

second citadel then they arrived now thus
sib'aqija long time they do there

merely they had borne on backs the bundled glory

its sign lordship it came its coming out place sun

792 This line appears at the end of folio 18v in error, where it interrupts the narrative of the naming of the three mountains of the Nima K'iche'. It appears to belong here, where the abandonment of the first K'iche' settlement is described. The line begins with the number 2, which does not appear to be part of the narrative. The number should have preceded the next line, which begins with *ukab'* ("second"), consistent with the pattern in the remainder of this section that ennumerates the stops along the K'iche' route of migration.

chi ma wi wa	now not food
chi ma wi ja'	now not water
ta xe'opan chi kak	then they arrived in thirst
chi wa'ij	in hunger 2220
3 = rox tinamit	3 = third citadel
chiwa'ij	chiwa'ij
nima kab'al xkib'an chiri'	great dwelling they built there
xkikotoj ukoq	they sculpted their images
uwach taq che'	its face wood
ab'aj	stone
chi wa'iya	in hunger
chi chaqi'j[793] chi ————————	in thirst now ————————
4 ukaj tinamit	4 fourth citadel
pakaja xejoyan	pakaja xejoyan 2230
xaq'an chi wi	they raised up again
kitz'aq chiri'	their buildings there
naj xkib'an chiri'——	long time they did there——
5. Ro' tinamit	5. Fifth citadel
————————————[794]	————————
6: uwaqaq tinamit	6: sixth citadel
b'arab'ik chun	b'arab'ik chun
b'oqotajinaq sanaylo —	b'oqotajinaq sanaylo —
naj chi wi xkib'an chiri'	long time again they did there
7 wuq tinamit	7 seventh citadel 2240
pan jilil pan tz'okon naj xkib'an chiri'	pan jilil pan tz'okon long time they did there
xa ral wonon	only its child bees
sital xkechaj	wasps they ate [meat]
xkilo'o	they ate [plants]
xa uk'atib'al che'	merely its charred remains wood

---

[793] The text in its original orthography reads *chi cakih*, probable variant or scribal error for *chi chakih*.

[794] The name of the fifth citadel is left blank here.

xk[i]wajwij wi kaqix	they made loud eating noises macaws
alRaj	parrots

8 uwajxaq tinamit wa'e	8 eighth citadel this	
tikaj ch'alib'	tikaj ch'alib'	

xaq'an chi wi	raised up again	2250
kitz'aq chiri'	their buildings there	

xa wi kuk'am ri retal ajawarem	merely were brought the its signs lordship
xpe chi relib'al q'ij	come from its coming out place sun

chi mewa	in fasting
chi k'axkol	in affliction

9. ub'elej tinamit	9. ninth citadel
tib'atzi rajawiche'	tib'atzi rajawiche'

xaq'an chi wi	raised up again
kitz'aq chir[i']	their buildings there

chiri' xtiker wi	there began	2260
kaq'iq'	wind	

ta xkikayij uwi' soq'oj	then they rent their tops soq'oj
uk'in	uk'in

la'e	la'e
la'e xecha'	la'e they said

10 ulajuj tinamit	10 tenth citadel
job'alam q'ana ulew	job'alam q'ana ulew

ub'i' juyub' xe'ik'ow wi	its name mountain they passed by
xawi xemayin chiri'	merely they paused there

11 ujulaj tinamit	11 eleventh citadel	2270
chi wa'an chi q'aq'	chi wa'an chi q'aq'	

k'i ub'i'	many their names
juyub'	mountains

xek'oje' chi wi	they were now
xawi xemayin chiri'	merely they paused there

1 2 ukab'laj tinamit wa'e xech'ayab' ximb'axuk	1 2 twelfth citadel this xech'ayab' ximb'axuk
xawi keqa'm ri retal ajawarem xpe chi relib'al q'ij	merely they had borne on backs the its sign lordship it came from its coming out place sun
chi wa'ij chi chaqi'j chi xek'oje'	in hunger 2280 in thirst again they were
1 3 roxlaj tinamit wa'e ta xopan tz'utuja	1 3 thirteenth citadel this then they arrived at tz'utuja
k'a chiri' k'ute xkikanab'eq wi jun ajaw tz'utuja	even there thus they captured one lord tz'utuja
ta xriqitaj payo pab'aq'oj	then he was discovered at payo pab'aq'oj
kub'an roq'ib'al saqkorowach	it makes crying out quail
ta xkita' b'alam aq'ab' b'alam k'i[tze'] majukotaj	then they heard it b'alam aq'ab' 2290 b'alam k'itze' majukotaj
ta xok k'u pa xuq' ta xkanab'exik	then he entered thus in net then he was captured

ta xch'aw k'ut
  ma ta kiniwuchaj
  ix
    ajawab'
  ma ta kinikamisaj
xcha'
	then he spoke thus
	    not then you take me by force
	    you
	    lords
	    not then you kill me
	he said 2300

xuchax k'ut apa katuxik	he was told thus who you come to be
in b'a tz'utuja kinuchaxik xcha' k'ut	I then tz'utuja I am called he said thus
xa ta b'a in iwajil itz'aqat chuxik xcha' k'ut	merely then I your recompense your completion will come to be he said thus

qitzij pa la' kab'ij	true that you say	
utz b'a la'	good then that	
keje' chuxik at ta	as will come to be you then	
ulaq'el n[u]wach	its pair my face	2310
nutzij puch	my word as well	
chuxik	will come to be	
xecha' b'alam k'itze'	they said b'alam k'itze'	
chirech tz'utuja	to him tz'utuja	
at uk'axel	you his substitute	
qajaw	father	
ik'i b'alam	ik'i b'alam	
chuxik xuchax k'ut	will come to be he was told thus	
keje' k'ut riqitajik	then thus his being discovered	
ajaw tz'utuja	lord tz'utuja	2320
ri saqik utz'aqat[795] k'ut	the saqik its completion thus	
majukotaj xuxik	majukotaj he came to be	
uk'axel	his replacement	
ik'i b'alam xuxik	ik'i b'alam came to be	
ri xkam	who died	
chupam uk'ajolal	within his youth	
keje' k'ut utz'aqatik	then thus its completion	
kajib' nab'e wi u[796]	four first	
ri xpe	that came	
chi relib'al q'ij	from its coming out place sun	2330
keje' k'ut ub'i'natisaxik	then thus his being named	
chi saqik ajaw k'iche'	as saqik lord k'iche'	
k'a chiri' xkam wi	even there he died	
pa tz'utuja	in tz'utuja	

---

[795] The manuscript reads *uk'aaut*, which has no known meaning. I agree with Carmack and Mondloch (1983, 114–115) that this should be *utz'aqat* and that it is a scribal error.

[796] This is an extraneous letter with no apparent meaning. It is most likely the result of scribal error.

ma ta chisach	not you lose
ik'u'xlal[797] kumal	your hearts because of them
qak'ajol	our sons
qaman	our grandsons
xawi chiri' xkisik'ij [j]un ab'aj	merely there they called on a stone
xkik'ab'awilaj k'wal ab'aj	they venerated precious stone 2340
ukab' k'u ri xpe chi relib'al q'ij	second thus that came from its coming out place sun
xtz'aqat k'ut ka'ib' k'wal chiri'	it was completed thus two precious stones there
tz'utuja	tz'utuja
naj xkib'an chir[i']	long time they did there
14 ukajlaj tinamit wa'e k'ut	14 fourteenth citadel this thus
ub'e chi uk'ab'al	ub'e chi uk'ab'al
xawi xaq'an kochoch chiri'	merely they raised up their homes there
xemay[i]n chi wi chiri'	they paused again there
xawi kuk'a'm ri retal ajawarem	merely they had brought the its sign lordship
xpe relib'al q'ij	it came from its coming out place sun 2350
15 Ro'laj tinamit wa'e	15 Fifteenth citadel this
yamukutu raxaj	yamukutu raxaj
naj[798]	long time
xkib'an chiri'	they did there
xa tum	merely straw
xa ral wonon	merely its larvae bees
xa ral sital kakecha'j	merely its larvae wasps they ate
e qamam	they our grandfathers
qaqajaw	our fathers
16 uwaqlaj tinamit wa'e	16 sixteenth citadel this 2360
chi tzaq'eb' chi yaki	chi tzaq'eb' chi yaki
xeyaluj chi k'u chiri'	they paused again thus there

---

[797] *uk'u'xlal* ("her/his heart"), probable scribal error for *ik'u'xlal* ("your hearts").

[798] *maj* ("none") in the original manuscript, scribal error for *naj* ("a long time") from the context of the sentence.

xkib'an chi chiri'	they built again there
kitz'aq	their buildings
kik'oxtun	their towers
chi nima k'axk'ol	in great affliction
xek'oje' wi	they were
juwuq q'ij chikiq'umej ixim	every seven days they would eat mouthful maize
chikub'e k'u kik'u'x chiri'	to comfort thus their hearts there
xaqi jun kiwach kaweq	merely one their faces kaweq 2370
nijayib'	nijayib'
17 wuqlaj tinamit wa'e	17 seventeenth citadel this
q'ale mi'al kukur ab'aj	q'ale mi'al kukur ab'aj
xawi xeyaluj chi	merely they paused again
chiri'	there
xemolomanik	they gathered together
xech'ijomanik	they endured hardship
pa siwan	in ravines
pa k'echelaj	in forests
chi wa'ij	in hunger 2380
chi chaqi'j chi' ——	in thirst ——
18 uwajxaqlaj tinamit wa'e	18 eighteenth citadel this
pa che' chi q'ojom ub'i' juyub'⁷⁹⁹	pa che' chi q'ojom its name mountain
xek'oje' wi naj chi k'u	they were long time again thus
xkib'an chiri'	they did there
e qamam	they our grandfathers
e qaqajaw	they our fathers
b'alam aq'ab'	b'alam aq'ab'
b'alam k'itze'	b'alam k'itze'
maju[ko]taj	majukotaj 2390
Ri e ajkix	The they bloodletters
e ajkaj ————	they sacrificers ———

⁷⁹⁹ *juyab'* in the manuscript, scribal error for *juyub'* ("mountain"), matching the rest of the section.

19 ub'elelaj tinamit wa'e chi k'ab'awilanik	19 nineteenth citadel this chi k'ab'awilanik
k'a chiri' k'ut xkik'ab'awilaj wi ri ab'aj k'wal xpe chi relib'al q'ij	even there thus they venerated the stone precious came from its coming out place sun
ta xejeqe' chi k'u chiri' xkib'an chi wi kitz'aq chiri'	then they laid foundations again thus there they built again their buildings there

xawi kuk'am kib' chi kaweq
   chi nijayib'
      chi ajaw k'iche'
ri B'alam k'itze'
   b'alam aq'ab'
   majukotaj
	merely they united themselves the kaweq
	   and nijayib'
	      and ajaw k'iche'
	the B'alam k'itze'
	   b'alam aq'ab'
	   majukotaj

xawi k'u kachb'ilam chi ri tz'utuja	merely thus they had joined to the tz'utuja
uk'exewach chi ik'i b'alam =	his replacement for ik'i b'alam =
chiri' k'ut xkitikib'a' wi tzukun masat	there thus they began to hunt deer
are' k'u ri ukik'el xkiya' chwach k'ab'awil tojil	it thus the its blood they gave before his face god tojil
k'a chiri' k'ut xkitikib'a' wi k'ab'awilanik	even there thus they began veneration
chi k'ix chi ch'at	chi k'ix chi ch'at
ketajin k'ut e pilol rech ri masat chwa ja	they are engaged thus as skinners of the deer before its face house
ta xe'ik'ow ka'ib' k'echelajil winaq xawi are' kuk' wuq amaq'	then passed by two forest people merely they with them seven nations

jutzu k'ut xecha'
   naqipa ri kipilo
   we xa quk' qatzab' ke'ipilo
	immediately thus they said
	   what is it that you skin
	   perhaps merely with us our brothers you skin
	   them

2400

2410

2420

xecha' k'u kanoq wuq amaq'

they said thus behind seven nations

keje' chi k'ut unuk'ik chiri' lab'al kumal amaq'
k'u waral chik xkik'ut wi kib'

then again thus its fomenting there war by them nations
thus here again they embarrassed themselves

xare wi xkitijtob'ej lab'al chila' Jaqawitz
jutzu k'ut xkik'u'xlaj lab'al

for they attempted war there Jaqawitz
immediately thus they plotted war

wa'e ajk'alaqam
ajtib'ilkat

these they of k'alaqam
they of tib'ilkat   2430

xul chi k'u
jun chik

arrived now thus
one now

uq'u'um uxikin k'a[x]tok'ol[800]
uxikin chuq'ul raqan nik'wachinel

he was cloaked his ears deceiver
his ears would be cloaked his legs spy

k'u ri' chirech kikamisaxik e qamam

e qaqajaw

thus this to their being killed they our grandfathers
they our fathers

jutzu k'u xna'taj chikech qamam

qaqajaw

immediately thus it became known to them our grandfathers
our fathers

are' e k'o chiri' chi k'ix
chi ch'at

they are there chi k'ix
chi ch'at   2440

k'a chiri' k'ut xril wi lab'al
  ri ajaw
  tz'utuja saqik
maji xril lab'al Jaqawitz

even there thus he saw war
  the lord
  tz'utuja saqik
not he saw war Jaqawitz

jutzu k'ut xeterenib'ex ub'ik
ri samajel

immediately thus they were followed thither
the envoy

utz b'a la'
kojkamoq

good then that
we shall die

xecha' qamam
qaqajaw

they said our grandfathers
our fathers   2450

---

[800] *k'a tok'ol* in the original, scribal error for *k'axtok'ol* ("deceiver"), complementing *nik'wachinel* ("spy") in the next line.

ta kib'ik k'ut oyew·achij	then they go thus furious valiant men
e ilol kech ri ajlab'al	they watchers theirs the warriors
apa k'o wi kochoch	away there are their homes
ta xil k'ut chwi' juyub'	then they saw thus atop mountain
are' xub'i'naj wi	he named it
muq'b'a[l] sib'	muq'b'al sib'
ta tob'ob' kisib'	then arose their smoke
tajkil apanoq	message outward
oyew achij e sonolik	furious valiant men they naked
e ch'analik	they nude 2460
ajmewa	fasters
ajk'axk'ol	sufferers
xa k'ut xkik'ut kipus[801]	merely thus they demonstrated their wondrous power
kinawal	their spirit essence
chwi' ri juyub'	atop the mountain
muq'b'al sib'	muq'b'al sib'
xkisik'ij kaq'iq'	they called upon wind
kaq' sut	whirlwind
kumkab'och	hailstorm
kaqulja'	thunder 2470
q'eteb'	sudden lightning
pub'a'ix chir[i']	blowgunned there
pa kiwi' wuq amaq'	on their heads seven nations
ajlab'al	warriors
xax ma k'o wi lab'al xkib'ano	merely not there was war they made
xa loq' xkik'u'xlaj lab'al	merely undone they plotted war
ri: ajk'alaqam[802]	the: they of k'alaqam
ajtib'ilkat	they of tib'ilkat

---

[801] *kipus* is repeated twice in error.

[802] *ajk'alaqan* in the original manuscript, variant or scribal error for *ajk'alaqam* as seen elsewhere in the text.

xa keje' xux e wuq amaq'	merely then came to be they seven nations
ajlab'al ————————	warriors ——————— 2480
20 ujwinaq tinamit wa'e	20 twentieth citadel this
ta xe'opan chik jume'taja	then they arrived now jume'taja
utukel jume't kochoch	alone bark their homes
xkib'ano	they built
xawi k'ab'awilanik	merely veneration
xkib'ano	they did
xa q'ul	merely mushrooms
xa yajom oqox[803]	merely misshapen mushrooms
xa ral tz'ikin	merely their children birds
xkiya' chwach	they gave before their faces 2490
k'ab'awil	gods
xawi nima k'axk'ol	merely great suffering
xek'oje' wi	they were
xemolomanik	they gathered together
xech'ijomanik	they endured hardship
pa taq k'echelaj	in forests
xawi k'u k'a'm	merely thus bushes
ri tojil	the tojil
awilix	awilix
Jaqawitz	Jaqawitz 2500
ruk' ri pison k'ak'al	with the bundled glory
ri Retal ajawarem	the Its Sign lordship
xpe chi	it came from
relib'al q'ij ——	its coming out place sun ——
21 uj[u]winaq jun tinamit wa'e	21 twenty-first citadel this
k'ulb'a kawinal	k'ulb'a kawinal
xaq'an chi wi	they raised up again
kitz'aq	their buildings

---

[803] *k'ox* in the original manuscript, probable variant or scribal error for *oqox* ("mushroom").

chiri'	there
k'ulb'a kawinal	k'ulb'a kawinal 2510
chiri' k'ute xkik'ul wi kib'	there thus they joined themselves
ruk' aq'a'ab'	with them aq'a'ab'
lal qamam	ye our grandfathers
lal qaqajaw	ye our fathers
lal qawi'	ye our leaders
lal qajolom xcha' ajaq'a'ab'	ye our heads they said they of the aq'a'ab'
chikech e qamam	to them they our grandfathers
e qaqajaw	they our fathers
b'alam k'itze'	b'alam k'itze'
b'alam aq'ab'	b'alam aq'ab' 2520
majukotaj	majukotaj
ruk' ajaw saqik tz'utuja	with him lord saqik tz'utuja
uk'exewach ik'i b'alam	his substitute ik'i b'alam
xkiya' kisib'	they gave their smoke
kimayij chwach kik'ab'awil	their offerings before their faces their gods
xa ral tolob'	only their children deer snakes
xa ral kuyuch'	only their children parakeets
xkiya' chwach kik'ab'awil	they gave before their faces their gods
chiri' kulb'a kawinal ———————	there kulb'a kawinal ———————
22 uj[u]winaq ka'ib' tinamit wa'e	22 twenty-second citadel this 2530
ta kulik waral chi ismachi'	then they arrive here chi ismachi'
k'a waral k'ut xq'aj wi	even here thus they ground
jule' chun	fine lime plaster
chiri' chi ismachi'	there chi ismachi'
k'iyarinaq chi k'ut k'ajolaxel	grown in number now thus sons
uk'ajol ajaw	his sons lord
umam ajaw	his grandsons lord
atz	older brothers
chaq'	younger brothers

chirij ajaw	behind lord	2540
B'alam k'itze'	B'alam k'itze'	
k'iyarinaq chik ral	grown in number now their children	
uk'ajol kaweqib' =	their sons kaweqib' =	
xawi keje' b'alam aq'ab'	merely then b'alam aq'ab'	
xawi k'iyarinaqa	merely grown in number	
ri ral	the their children mothers	
uk'ajol nijayib' =	their sons fathers nijayib' =	
xawi ma[ju]kotaj	merely majukotaj	
xawi e k'iyarinaq chi	merely they grown in number now	
uk'ajol	their sons	2550
ri ajaw k'iche'	the ajaw k'iche'	
k'a waral k'ut xchiwachin wi	even here thus would sprout	
sqaqi'n ajawarem ————————	a little lordship ————————	
¶ k'ate k'ut ub'anik chaponik	¶ then thus its doing taking offices	
chiri' chi ismachi'	there chi ismachi'	
nab'e chaponik	first taking office	
ta xchap ajaw k'otuja	then he took office lord k'otuja	
chi ajawarem ajpop xuxik	in lordship ajpop he came to be	
uk'ajol b'alam k'iq'ab' —	his son b'alam k'iq'ab' —	
xawi keje' chik ajpo k'amja:	merely then now ajpo k'amja:	2560
stayul jun chi ajaw	stayul one other lord	
uk'ajol k'onache	his son k'onache	
ri xok chi ajpo k'amjayil	that entered now ajpo k'amjayil	
wa'e k'ute xchiqacholo	this thus we shall give order	
kik'ajolaxik kaq imos stayul	their being engendered kaq imos stayul	
¶ wa'e chi k'ute ucholik	¶ this now thus its order	
ajawarem pa k'iche' chi i[s]machi':	lordship in k'iche' chi ismachi':	
wa'e ucholik ajawarem	this its order lordship	
eqale'n puch	burden of authority as well	

¶ ajpop
k'iq'ab'i[l] winaq

¶ ajpop
k'iq'ab'il people   2570

¶ ajpop k'amja
stayul k'onache =

¶ ajpop k'amja
stayul k'onache =

¶ Nima Raj[p]op achij
¶ ch'uti Raj[p]op achij

¶ Great Their Ajpop valiant men
¶ small Their Ajpop valiant men

¶ chiqawach
oj kaweqib'

¶ before our faces
we kaweqib'

¶ ajaw utza'm pop
¶ ajaw laq' pop

¶ ajaw utza'm pop
¶ ajaw laq' pop

¶ ajaw[804] uchuch k'amja
¶ ajaw nima lolmet =

¶ ajaw uchuch k'amja   2580
¶ ajaw nima lolmet =

Rajawal k'iq'ab'il winaq
kaweqib'ab'

Their Lords k'iq'ab'il people
kaweqib's

j[u]wi wa'e ¶ ajaw ajpop k'amja:
e alay tem k'ut

unified these ¶ lord ajpop k'amja:
they alay tem thus

wa'e k'ute kib'i' ajpop alomab'
alay tem kaweqib'

these thus their names ajpop alomab'
alay tem kaweqib'

alay tem chikij
ajawab'

givers of birth benches behind their backs
lords

---

uq'alel alomab'
nijayib' =

their q'alel alomab'
nijayib' =   2590

nim ch'okoj alomab'
ajaw k'iche' =

nim ch'okoj alomab'
ajaw k'iche' =

uwachib'alal =
xa oxib' nim ja xuxik

their manner =
merely three great houses came to be

¶ Ta xok k'ut ajaw q'alel nijayib'
¶ ajaw atzij winaq

¶ Then entered thus ajaw q'alel nijayib'
¶ ajaw atzij winaq

---

[804] *ajaw* is repeated at the line break in error.

¶ ajaw q'ale k'amja
¶ nima k'amja

¶ ajaw q'ale k'amja
¶ nima k'amja

¶ uchuch k'amja
¶ julajuj tem

¶ uchuch k'amja   2600
¶ julajuj tem

¶ ajawilix
¶ metasanik
¶ saq'latol

¶ ajawilix
¶ metasanik
¶ saq'latol

e nijayib'ab' =
¶ ajaw k'iche' k'u wa'e

they nijayib's =
¶ ajaw k'iche' thus these

¶ atzij winaq ajaw
¶ nim ch'okoj ajaw

¶ atzij winaq ajaw
¶ nim ch'okoj ajaw

¶ ajaw lolmet
¶ ajaw Jaqawitz

¶ ajaw lolmet
¶ ajaw Jaqawitz   2610

Ri' k'ute kichapob'al
xpe relib'al q'ij

These thus their tokens of authority
came from its coming out place sun

xpe puch ch'aqa cho
ch'aqa palo #

came as well other side lake
other side sea #

b'us
q'axe'on

crook-necked gourd
gourd cup

rixk'aq kot
rixk'aq b'alam #

its claws eagle
its claws jaguar #

jolom[805]
pix kej[806] #

head
hooves deer #   2620

su'b'aq
chamcham #
nima su'[807]

bone flute
drum #
great flute

tzikil kot

talon eagle

---

[805] *jolop* in the original text, scribal error for *jolom*.

[806] *pix kej* in the original manuscript, scribal error for *pich kej*. Both *pich kej* and its paired term, *jolom*, appear correctly earlier in the text as tokens of authority brought from Tulan (see p. 251, lines 1842-1843).

[807] *tzu* in the original manuscript, variant for *su'* ("flute").

tzikil b'alam #	paw jaguar #
t'ot'	shell
mata kus #	net tobacco
je' kej:	tail deer:
makutax #	bracelet of precious stones #
ch'ayom	beautiful bird feathers
astapulul #	snowy egret feathers #
malili	braid
titil[808]	titil
q'an ab'aj	yellow stone
retal	its sign
ajawarem	lordship
worik	piercing
k'aqik	perforating
xpe	it came from
relib'al q'ij:	its coming out place sun:
nakat[809] ab'aj:	ear ornament stone:
b'elejeb' chuk'oje'ik	nine would there be
rech ajpop	of ajpop
ajpo k'amja'il	ajpo k'amja'il
kajib' muj	four canopies
oxib' muj:	three canopies:
ka'ib' muj:	two canopies:
jun muj	one canopy
chi q'uq'	of quetzal feathers
chi raxon:	of cotinga feathers:
chi k'ub'ul:	of crown:
chi chaltit:	of turquoise:

(line numbers in right margin: 2630, 2640, 2650)

---

[808] *tatil* in the original manuscript, variant or scribal error for *titil*.

[809] *nanakat* in the original manuscript, most likely scribal error for *nakat* as this token is spelled in line 1853.

jeke kamachal:	pendant jaw:
tub' q'aq' tawiskal:	bound fire sweatbath:
kamul b'elej k'al:	twice nine twenties:
oxmul b'elej k'al:	thrice nine twenties:
chi q'ech'a	of penetrating darts
chi tz'ununche'[810] ———	of thrown darts ———
¶ Are' k'u ri kajib'	¶ They thus the four
alomab':	they who have borne children: 2660
ib'oy ch'arab'	armadillo clefted
uwachib'al kich'ami'y	its image their staffs
ta kechaponik:	then they take offices of authority:
¶ Ri' k'ute xb'an chi ismachi'	¶ This thus they did chi ismachi'
ta xb'an chaponik	then they did taking office of authority
ta xb'an ch'ute q'aq'al	then they did small glory
tepewal	sovereignty
taq[i]ki[l]	authority
chuxe'	would come to be
xa oxib'	merely three 2670
nim ja	great houses
xuxik	came to be
xare k'u[811] xchap	for thus they took office of authority
ri' xq'ob' puch	this they exalted as well
xa k'a ch'utinoq	merely till they would be humble
k'a waral chi ismachi'	still here chi ismachi'
jaqataj wi wa'e retal	opened this its sign
ajawarem ri'	lordship this
xb'e' uk'ama'	he went to receive it
k'oka'ib'	k'oka'ib' 2680
k'a e k'o la' chila' Jaqawitz	until they are perhaps there Jaqawitz
nab'e tinamit	first citadel

---

[810] *tununch'a* in the original manuscript, most likely scribal error for *tz'ununche'*.

[811] *ik'u* in the original manuscript, most likely scribal error for *k'u*.

xawi pu ma na keje' xb'an	merely as well not surely then was done
chi k'ix	chi k'ix
chi ch'at	chi ch'at
xa qi' lab'al	merely true war
xb'an ojer	was done earlier
Jaqawitz	Jaqawitz
nab'e lab'al	first war
ukamul lab'al	second time war 2690
chi k'ix	chi k'ix
chi ch'at	chi ch'at
xare wi juyub'	for mountain
ri' xb'an wi	it was done
pus	wondrous power
nawal	spirit essence
chi rox k'ut wa'e	at third thus this
chi ismachi' —	chi ismachi' —
waral k'ut xek'amowan wi	here thus they gave thanks
chi ismachi'	chi ismachi' 2700
at kaj	you sky
ulew	earth
at pu tz'aqol	you as well framer
b'itol	shaper
chaya' ta qami'al	give then our daughters
qak'ajol	our sons
chaya' uxer wab'al[812]	give its bit eating place
uk'ab'al chiqe	drinking place to us
at pa ch'aqa cho	you on other side lake
ch'aqa palo	other side sea 2710
at upam	you its womb
kaj	sky

---

[812] The manuscript reads *web'al*, probable scribal error for *wab'al* ("eating place"), paralleling the complementary phrase in the next line, *uk'ab'al* ("drinking place").

at relib'al q'ij	you its coming out place sun
at raq'anib'al q'ij	you its rising up place sun
chaya' ta qaq'ij	give then our sun
qasaq[813] xecha'	our light they said
at nima ch'umil	you great star
ek'o q'ij xecha' #	passer sun they said #
xkiya' kipom	they gave their incense
tz'ikin ral ak'	bird its child turkey 2720
xkiya' ri winaq chwach tojil	they gave the people before his face tojil
waral chi ismachi'	here chi ismachi'
waral xkixaj wi junajpu k'oy	here they danced junajpu k'oy
wuqub' kaqix	wuqub' kaqix
ta xkitikib'a' ruk'axik che kikab' ki'	then they began its being drunk of their honey drink
xeq'ab'arik	they became drunken
xe'eqa'xik	they were borne on their backs
xkisipaj kimi'al chikib'il kib'	they gifted their daughters between themselves
kimi'al	their daughters
eqa'b'al kech e uk'al ki'	borne to them they drinkers sweet drink 2730
xkisipaj chirech meb'a'	they gifted to them poor ones
ajk'aqowal	widowers
xa xb'e ya'oq	merely they went to give
chi rochoch	at their homes
mi xujloq'onik	just now we gave her to you without cost
mi xujmayjanik xecha'	just now we offered her to you they said
xa jun q'eb'al chi saqa'	merely one large jar of cacao drink
xa jun tol chi matu'l[814] oj	merely one gourd cup of guacamole avocado
xa pu ju[n] tik'ab' chi tzukurum uwe	merely as well one vessel of food any kind
puch jun peral chi ra juyub'al aq	as well one platter of its leg mountain pig 2740

---

[813] *qasakq* in the original, scribal error for *qasaq*.

[814] *matuj* in the original manuscript, scribal error for *matu'l*, a small avocado according to the Basseta dictionary, paralleling the following word, *oj* ("avocado").

jun tol k'u chi wa	one gourd cup thus of maize tamales
sub'an pa xaq q'anaq pa xaq kub'	wrapped in leaf q'anaq in leaf kub'
rajil kimi'al xkib'ano chiri' xb'an wi chi ismachi' ————	their price their daughters they did there they did it chi ismachi' ————
¶ xawi k'ut kachb'ilam kib' oxib' amaq' chi k'iche'	¶ merely thus they had accompanied themselves three nations of k'iche'
tamub' ilokab' saqajib'[815]	tamub' ilokab' saqajib'
xa sk'ataq kixo'l xawi junam xepe	merely they remained with each other merely as one they came
chi relib'al q'ij tulan sewan	from its coming out place sun tulan sewan
ri' k'ute xb'an chi ismachi'	this thus was done chi ismachi'
maja' b'i'oq[816] pom	there was no incense
kik' alaxi pom alaxi	blood born incense born
kik' jolomax	blood croton sap
raxtunim k'atoj	blue-green body paint sacrifices
maja' b'i'oq kanab' teleche	there were no female captives male captives

815 The original orthography reads *cakahib*, scribal error for *çakahib* (Saqajib' in modern orthography). The Saqajib' are mentioned in the *Popol Vuh* as one of the thirteen allied nations that were united with the Tamub' and Ilokab' when they migrated from Tulan (Christenson 2003, 163, line 5216; 2007, 204).

816 *maja b'i'oq* ("not yet named"). This is a common phrase that means "there isn't any." In K'iche' phraseology, a thing unnamed is a thing that does not exist.

maja' b'i'oq uchuch	there were no their mothers
tz'ikin	birds

xko	parrots	2770
kaqix	macaws	

majaja' b'i'oq ¶ nima k'atoj	there was not ¶ great sacrifice
majaja' b'i'oq pokob' chanal	there was not pokob' chanal

xa k'a uch'utinaloq	merely still their being humbled
k'olik[817] —	existence —

xa k'al xam xek'axtok'axik chusik'ixik che'	merely still they were deceived to being called on wood
ab'aj	stone

e nab'e	they first
winaq	people

ju[w]inaq ka'ib' chi tinamit	twenty-two of citadels	2780
chi juyub' xe'ik'o wi uloq ———	of mountains they passed through hither ———	

wa'e k'ut kichapik	this thus their taking offices
ajtz'alamib'	noblemen

we puch q'ana mama	perhaps as well yellow grandfathers
q'ana tata	yellow fathers

keqale'n ri ta xmolob'ax chikech[818]	their burdens that then were distributed to them
ri keqale'n ri xb'e' uk'ama' k'oka'ib'	the their burdens that he went to receive k'oka'ib'

nab'e ri kotz'i'jab'al pwaq[819]	first the flower vessel precious metal
sochi pwaq	rattle precious metal

ruk' ri wachib'al ch'ami'y	with it the image staff	2790
ri ib'oy ch'arab'	the armadillo clefted	

kichapab'al chi chirech ajpop	their taking office of authority now to them ajpop
ajpo k'amja	ajpop k'amja

---

[817] *k'olik* is repeated twice at the line break in error.

[818] *chi kej* ("at deer") in the original. This may be a toponym, although it does not appear elsewhere in the text. The K'iche' resided at Jaqawitz when K'oka'ib' returned with the tokens of authority granted by Nakxik, as affirmed later in this section. Alternatively, this is scribal error for *chikech* ("to them"), which better fits the context and syntax of the phrase.

[819] *pwach* in the original, scribal error for *pwaq*, as it appears in the parallel section on folio 14v, lines 18–19.

q'alel atzij winaq	q'alel atzij winaq
xa sqaqi' na chik xawi xmob'ax rech rajpop ajtz'alam	merely a little surely now was distributed his rajpop ajtz'alam
reqale'n wachib'al[820] kotz'i'jab'al pwaq k'ut	his burden of authority image flower vessel precious metal thus
rech rajpop ajtz'alam utza'm chinamital	his rajpop ajtz'alam utza'm chinamital 2800
nab'e chapel nab'e ulel rajawarem chila' Jaqawitz	first takers of offices of authority first arrivers their lordship there Jaqawitz
xqab'ij kanoq ta'ol upe uwinaq	we spoke before listeners their misery their people
chi uk'ajol uchaq'	of their sons their younger brothers
qasam ch'atam ulew	victors in war conquerors land
nim ja sokb'a[l]ki	great house place of sacrifice 2810
are' Rapanel ximonel tijoy	they Punishers captors chasteners
uk'ajol uchaq'	their sons their younger brothers
saqi toq' saq uk'a kej	white flint blade white hooves deer
k'astab'al uwach k'ajol q'apoj	instrument of revival their faces young men maidens
kaj q'alaj chi tuj chi xik'a'y	four reclinings in sweatbaths 2820 in ovens
kajim muchum ti'j	crushed ground meat
xawi k'ut joronalaj ja' lemo	merely thus very cold water mirror

---

[820] *iwachib'al* ("your image/token") in the original. This is most likely scribal error for *wachib'al* ("image/token"), paralleling the phrase *wachib'al ch'ami'y* just previous to this in line 2790.

q'eb'un	mint	
muchuchen	pennyroyal	
atinib'a[l] sel	bathing bowl	
atinib'al kukub'	bathing cup	
k'astab'al uwach	means of reviving their faces	2830
q'ajol tzij	generations	
keje' utzij	then his word	
ajaw nakxik	lord nakxik	
chire	to him	
ajaw k'oka'ib'	lord k'oka'ib'	
xawi k'ut are'	merely thus them	
keb'anow tzij	they carry out word	
chirij q'alel ajpop	behind q'alel ajpop	
uq'alechij	uq'alechij	
rajpop achi[j]	rajpop achij	2840
ma wi xa et chiya' ajawarem	not merely long time you will give lordship	
chikech are' xcha' chirech k'oka'ib'[821]	to them said k'oka'ib'	
¶ Are' k'ut kajawar	¶ He thus reigned	
ajaw k'otuja chi ismachi'[822]	lord k'otuja chi ismachi'	
xa xe'utaq ka'ib' samajel chila'	merely he sent two envoys there	
chupam kijuyub'al malaj winaq	within their mountain place malaj people	
jix[823] chila'	go there	
pa malaj	to malaj	
chiwuk'a'j umul	carry rabbit	
saqkorowach	quail	2850
chiya' chiri'	give them there	
chwi' mulb'a	atop mulb'a	
kul wi oyew achij	they arrive furious valiant men	
rech malaj xcha' ajaw k'otuja =	of malaj said lord k'otuja =	

---

[821] The manuscript reads *xcha' k'oka'ib'* ("said k'oka'ib'"). From the context, it is more likely that the passage should be *xcha' chirech k'oka'ib'* ("he [referring to Nakxik] said to k'oka'ib'").

[822] *ismachi'* is repeated erroneously here at the line break.

[823] *oxjix* in the original manuscript. *Ox* ("three") appears to be the result of scribal error, as only two envoys were sent and it doesn't fit grammatically here.

chiwewaj k'u iwib'	hide thus yourselves
mik'ut iwib'	do not show yourselves
xe'uchax samajel	they were told envoys
rumal k'otuja	by him k'otuja
uk'exwach tz'onoj	their exchange petition
are' k'u	them thus 2860
ri umul	the rabbit
tz'ikin k'amom chik	bird received now
ta xe'opanik =	then they arrived =
q'uq' chi k'o kanoq	resplendent quetzal now remains behind
uk'axel	his substitute
ri umul	the rabbit
tz'ikin	bird
chi kajmul	on fourth time
xkib'an	they did
kib'ano	their doing 2870
keje' wa'e chukajmul k'ut	then this on fourth time thus
ta xe'ilow	then they saw
kiwach samajel	their faces envoys
¶ xcha' k'ut	¶ he said thus
usamajel malaj	his envoy malaj
naqipa at uxik	who are you come to be
ma at on usamajel	not you his envoy
q'ukumatz	q'ukumatz
k'otuja xcha' k'ut	k'otuja he said thus
¶ in ib'a[j] la	¶ I courier thine 2880
usamajel	his envoy
q'ukumatz	q'ukumatz
k'otuja xcha' k'ut	k'otuja he said thus
ta xachb'ilax k'u ub'ik	then he was escorted thus thither
usamajel k'iche' —	their envoy k'iche' —
ta xopan k'ut	then he arrived thus
chwach malaj winaq	before his face malaj person
¶ ta xpe k'ut	¶ then it came thus

ruk'iya'q samajel	his drink envoy	
jutik'ab' kaq uwach	one vessel red its face	2890
jutik'ab' saqi q'utum:	one vessel white beaten cacao:	
xcha' k'ut ajaw malaj	he said thus lord malaj	
naqipa karaj q'ukumatz[824] xita'o xcha' //	what desires q'ukumatz you heard he said //	
xa b'a k'ulalem	merely then marriage	
karaj xcha' k'ut samajel	he desires said thus envoy	
¶ mi b'a xinta' ri utzij	¶ just now then I heard the his word	
q'ukumatz k'otuja	q'ukumatz k'otuja	
xcha' k'u	he said thus	
ajaw malaj =	lord malaj =	
ta uya'ik uloq saqi q'utum	then its giving hither white beaten cacao	2900
rax jok'on	fresh cacao cakes	
Retal	Its Sign	
Nutzij	My Word	
chulk'ama' ri alit	may they arrive to take the girl	
chipe k'amol re xcha' malaj	may they come as takers of her said malaj	
ta ub'ik k'ut kajib' pop k'amja	then their going thus four emissaries	
k'amol re umi'al malaj winaq	receivers of her his daughter malaj person	
xkuk'aj k'u ub'i'	they drank thus her name	
wa'e q'ana ab':	these yellow hammock:	
kaqa pop:	red mat:	2910
patachi'on	string of gold beads	
wal	fan of feathers	
xajab'	sandals	
xkuk'aj	they drank	
ta xeb'ek	then they went	
ta upetik	then her coming	
kimi'al	their daughter	
malaj winaq	malaj people	
ta rulik k'ut	then her arrival thus	
chiri'	there	2920
pa k'iche'	pa k'iche'	

---

[824] *q'uq'umatz* in the original text. This is a variant spelling of *q'ukumatz*, which is the more common spelling of the name.

chi ismachi'	chi ismachi'
xle'm	xle'm
ub'i' ixoq	her name woman
ta xulik //	then she arrived //
moqani chi k'ut xub'i'naj	moqani then thus he named her
pos chi xub'i'naj:	pos then he named her:
ka'ib' utut	two her cloaks of palms
rachb'[i']el ajpata chirij	her accompaniment tribute bearers behind
keje' k'u upetik wa'e	then thus her coming this 2930
ta xpeti[k] – kimi'al malaj winaq	then she came – their daughter malaj people
keje' k'u rokib'exik ri'	then thus her invasion this
ma wi chi lab'al taj[825]	not now war
xa xji'ax apanoq	merely she was married out
ajaw q'ukumatz k'ojtuja chila'	lord q'ukumatz k'ojtuja there
ta upetik k'ut xamal ton peq	then its coming thus branches tree pataxte
xamal ton kako	branches tree cacao
saqi pakay	white pacaya palm
saqi b'oxom	white b'oxom
rixk'aq b'a	red chili 2940
saq ton ik	white tree chili
sejeb'am chom	netted shrimp
kante'el tz'ikin	entrapped birds
ka'ib'[826] ib'ote xk'ulun ruk'	two ib'ote she married with him
q'ukumatz k'otuja ————	q'ukumatz k'otuja ————
keje' k'ut uk'ule'ik	then thus his marriage
q'ukumatz k'otuja ri'	q'ukumatz k'otuja this
ruk' kimi'al malaj winak	with her their daughter malaj people
tz'utujil ————	tz'utujil ————
¶ x k'u keje' koponik ajxetulul ri'	¶ thus then their arrival ajxetulul these 2950
ruk' ajyatza	with them ajyatza

---

[825] *taj* is repeated twice in error.

[826] The text reads *kab'i*, which does not have any known meaning in this context. It is most likely scribal error for *ka'ib'* ("two").

¶ ajk'uke
¶ laqam kuk

¶ mama kot
mama sakipat

¶ wanakoj
yab'akoj ———
¶ ajk'aqolkej #

ri' k'ute job' chi winaq
nab'e winaq

xokib'en juyub'
taq'aj

malaj
tz'utuj[il]

ta xch'akataj malaj
tz'utujil winaq

ta xk'iyaj
uk'ut

al
k'ajol

chikij
chi kijujunal

¶ ta ub'anik k'ut lab'al
kumal o' li'aj chi k'iche' winaq

ral
uk'ajol q'ukumatz: k'otuja

ta xkik'ulelaj [y]aki winaq
ajtz'ikinaja

xa uje' kuk
xkilaq'amij

xkiqasab'ej kech yaki
ajtz'ikinaja

¶ ta uximitajik k'u uloq ka'ib' kachijilal

yaki =

¶ ajk'uke
¶ laqam kuk

¶ mama kot
mama sakipat

¶ wanakoj
yab'akoj ———
¶ ajk'aqolkej #

they thus five of people
first people   2960

they invaded mountain
valley

malaj
tz'utujil

then were defeated malaj
tz'utujil people

then they increased
their demands

vassal children of women
vassal sons of men   2970

behind their backs
to each of them

¶ then its making thus war
by them five territories of k'iche' people

his vassal children
his vassal sons q'ukumatz: k'otuja

then they fought yaki people
ajtz'ikinaja

merely its tail squirrel
they carried as banner   2980

they defeated theirs yaki
ajtz'ikinaja

¶ then their binding thus hither two their valiant men

yaki =

welpan ub'i'	welpan his name
xukutzin ub'i' =	xukutzin his name =
ta upetik k'ut chwach ajaw	then their coming thus before his face lord
q'ukumatz k'otuja =	q'ukumatz k'otuja =
ta kulik k'ut oyew achij	then their arrival thus furious valiant men
chi ismachi'	chi ismachi' 2990
mi xujk'ulunik	just now we fought
mi xq'aq'asaj	just now we brought low
kiq'ij	their day
kalaxik	their birth
ajuwa cho	they of its shore lake
ajuwa palo	they of its shore sea
wa'e mi xq'axim uloq	these have just crossed over hither
we k'ut k'o chupatanij chech la	perhaps thus they are to be of use to thee
lal ajaw	thou lord
q'ukumatz k'otuja	q'ukumatz k'otuja 3000
xecha' k'ut	they said thus
oyew achij ta xe'ulik:	furious valiant men when they arrived:
utz mi xib'ano ix qoyewal	good just now you did you our furious ones
ix qachijilal	you our valiant men
et b'a la' uya'ik chiwech iq'aq'al	soon then that its giving to you your glory
itepewal	your sovereignty
xcha' k'ut ajaw	said thus lord
q'ukumatz k'otuja chikech ———	q'ukumatz k'otuja to them ———
¶ ta uk'u'xlaxik k'ut kumal	¶ then its being planned thus by them
ajawab'	lords 3010
q'ukumatz k'otuja	q'ukumatz k'otuja
ruk' ajaw stayul	with him lord stayul
ta xkib'an kitzij	then they did their word
xa ta b'a chib'an qajawarem	merely then will be done our sovereignty
chila'	there
pa malaj	at malaj
kumal qachib'al	by them our image
qawachib'al	our visage

chib'e taj qasamajel	go you then our envoys	
keb'e ta chapoq'	go then to take captives	3020
chib'etaj jub'otaj chi tz'um b'alam	may there be taken one bundle of skin jaguar	
jub'otaj chi cha	one bundle of arrowheads	
chib'e pu kitzok'otz	go as well their woven bundle	
kilaqam chikamisab'ex	their standards to their being killed	
kech ri ajuwa cho[827]	theirs the they of its shore lake	
uwa palo	its shore sea	
chiqasab'ex	may they be vanquished	
pu kemerib' ajtz'ikinaja	as well humiliated ajtz'ikinaja	
keje' k'u rokik kiq'alelal	then thus their entering their office of q'alel	
kajpopol ri'	their office of ajpop these	3030
waral xel wi keqale'n ri ajxetulul	here went out their burden the they of xetulul	
ri ajxsanm[art]in kuchax wakamik	the they of san martin it is called this day	
ukamul chi k'ut	second time now thus	
ta xechap ri':	then they received their offices these:	
wanakoj	wanakoj	
yab'akoj	yab'akoj	
q'inom	q'inom	
tunati	tunati	
is	is	
o' li'aj	five territories	3040
o' rem	five provinces	
ajxe'raqan peq	they of below its slopes pataxte	
kako	cacao	
o' b'otaj cha	five bundles arrowheads	
are' [k']u kilaq'am	these thus their standards	
o' b'otaj xya' rumal	five bundles were given by him	
ajaw q'ukumatz k'otuja	lord q'ukumatz k'otuja	
* rachb'il kitzol	together with their slings	
kitz'ununche'	their lances	

---

[827] The manuscript reads *cho palo*, probably due to scribal error, as *palo* appears in the next line as the paired couplet with *cho*.

kichab'	their arrows	3050
kipokob'	their shields	

keje' k'ut ub'anik chaponik ri'	then thus its doing taking offices of authority these
utikerik waral xel wi	its beginning here they left

pa k'iche'	pa k'iche'
chi ismachi'	chi ismachi'

rumal ajaw k'otuja q'ukumatz	by him lord k'otuja q'ukumatz
rumal puch stayul	by him as well stayul

ajaw ajpop	lord ajpop
ajpo k'amja	ajpo k'amja

keje' k'u relik ub'ik q'alelal	then thus its coming out thither office q'alel	3060
ajpopol ri':	office of ajpop these:	

job' q'alel	five q'alel
job' ajpop	five ajpop

job' uq'ale[l] achij[828]	five their q'alel valiant men
job' rajpop achij =	five their ajpop valiant men =

xa k'u keje' utikerik	merely thus then its beginning
chaponik ri'	taking offices of authority these

alaq qamam	ye our grandsons
k'ajol	sons

ta xeb'[e]	then they went	3070
ajpo[p] alomab'	ajpop alomab'	

e chaponel alay tem	they takers of office alay tem
ruk' mama ajtz'alam	with him mama ajtz'alam

ri' k'ute xb'an	this thus was done
ch[i] ismachi'	chi ismachi'

k'iya may xkib'an chiri'	many twenty year periods they did there
chi ismachi'	chi ismachi'

oxib' nima'q chun	three great lime plastered
saqkab'	whitewashed

xkib'an chiri'	they did there	3080

---

[828] The manuscript reads *uq'ale chila*. From the context, this is most likely scribal error for *uq'ale achij*, which is the standard office coupled with *rajpop achij*.

chi ismachi'	chi ismachi'
raj k'ut winaqir kich'a'oj ajawab'	nearly thus was conceived their conflict lords
chiri' pa k'iche' chi ismachi'	there pa k'iche' chi ismachi'
kumal ka'ib' pop k'amja	by them two emissaries
xkulisaj xkib'anesaj tzij chikech ajawab'	they spread gossip they made up words to them lords
kayoq' ri uk'i'a la lal q'ukumatz	he disparages the drink thine 3090 thou q'ukumatz
xa upulu tzoy karuk'aj	merely its rotten foam ill-formed cacao he drinks
kuchax la rumal ajaw stayul	it is said of thee by him lord stayul
xecha' ri ta'om tumakajnej	they said the ta'om tumakajnej
ma pa wech xcha'j chike	not in mine he said to them
xawi k'ut keje' kakib'ij chirech stayul	merely thus then they say to him 3100 stayul
naqipa upatan ri'	what his use him
xa ixim xa upe'n	merely maize merely lime water
xa pu rachaq' joch'a amolo karecha'j	merely as well its larva cacao fly he drinks
kacha' ajaw q'u[ku]matz che la lal ajaw	he says lord q'ukumatz of thee thou lord
kecha' chirech stayul	they say to him 3110 stayul
ma pa keje' ta ri' wech	not in then this mine

rax kar	fresh fish
rax chom kawekaj	fresh shrimp I eat
kacha' q'ukumatz	says q'ukumatz
chech la xecha'	of thee they said
keje' k'ut ujunum kitzij	then thus its same their words
a[ja]wab' ri' chikij	lords these behind their backs
ta xk'ajisax[829] kiwach =	then was slapped their faces =
xjalk'atix uwach kimetab'al kumal ajawab'	transformed its face their denials by them lords

3120

jun yak	one fox
jun saqb'in	one weasel
chirech uwach	to its face
kimetab'al	their denials
xb'anik =	it was done
rumal e tzij talom —	because words scattered —
keje' k'u uwinaqirik	then thus its conception
uq'aq'anib'al k'u'x ri'	its malice heart these
kumal[830] roqche'	by them roqche'
kajib' aj ri'	four aj these

3130

ta uk'u'xlaxik chi	then its planning of
kikamisaxik	their being killed
ajaw k'otuja q'ukumatz	lord k'otuja q'ukumatz
ruk' ajaw stayul	with him lord stayul
ri' xb'e kik'ama'	these went to gather them
ilokab' kamisay kech taj	ilokab' killers theirs hopefully
ta xe'oyob'ex[831] k'ut	then they were awaited thus
kumal e kab' oyew achij	by them two furious valiant men
chiri' woronik siwan ke'atin	there open ravine they bathe
k'u ri e ka'ib' oyew achij	thus the two furious valiant men

3140

ta xek'ulun k'ut ri ta'om	then they encountered thus the ta'om
tumakaj	tumakaj

---

[829] *xsk'ajisax* in the original manuscript, scribal error for *xk'ajisax*.

[830] *kumaj* in the original manuscript, probable scribal error for *kumal*.

[831] *xe'ob'ex* in the original manuscript, variant or scribal error for *xe'oyob'ex*.

e k'amol kib'e ilokab'	they guides their road ilokab'
e ajlab'al =	they warriors =
ta xkikir k'ut	then they untied thus
kipam	their waists
ri oyew achij	the furious valiant men
ta xe'ikaq'ix k'u	then they were slinged thus
ri ta'om	the ta'om 3150
tumakaj	tumakaj
chi ikaq' kumal	by sling stones by them
e royewal rachijilal k'iche'	they their furious valiant men k'iche'
ri' k'ut xb'an chi ismachi'	this thus was done chi ismachi'
are' k'u ri juyub' chi ismachi'	it thus the mountain chi ismachi'
xa kajib' chi stz'ul	merely four of centipedes
unawal	its nawal
xa k'u cha ma wi qi'	merely thus for this reason not true
xuk'am k'ut wach	they received thus face
keje' chi k'u roq'otaxik chi ismachi'	then now thus its being abandoned chi ismachi' 3160
ri' kumal ajawab' =	this by them lords =
ta xek'ajolax k'ut	then they were engendered thus
wuqlajuj chi achij	seventeen of valiant men
rumal ajaw q'ukumatz[832]	by him lord q'ukumatz
uk'ajol k'otuja	his son k'otuja
k'iq'ab'il winaq	k'iq'ab'il people
Tekum[833] stayul winaq	Tekum stayul people
tepepul k'iq'ab'il winaq	tepepul k'iq'ab'il people
Tepepul kawisimaj	Tepepul kawisimaj
wa'e e umam b'alam k'itze'	these they his grandsons b'alam k'itze' 3170
nab'e winaq	first person
uka le' k'ok'oja	second generation k'ok'oja
¶ rox le' tz'ikin	¶ third generation tz'ikin
ukaj le' aj kan	fourth generation aj kan
ro' le' k'oka'ib'	fifth generation k'oka'ib'
k'okawib'	k'okawib'

---

[832] The manuscript reads *q'ukumaq'* in several places, scribal error or an alternative spelling for *q'ukumatz* ("quetzal serpent").

[833] *Dekum.* There is no D sound in highland Maya languages. Where it appears in the text, it is an alternative for the more commonly used T.

job' k'ut xuk'[aj]olaj
k'oka'ib'[834]

five thus he engendered sons
k'oka'ib'

1. kejnay
2. k'oyoy.
3 xmaykej
4 laqamal
rochok'oy. 5.

1. kejnay
2. k'oyoy.
3 xmaykej
4 laqamal
rochok'oy. 5.

3180

job' xuk'ajolaj uk'ajol
chi k'ut xmaykej

five he engendered his son
now thus xmaykej

wa'e ajaw k'otuja —
waq le' ajawarem

this lord k'otuja —
sixth generation lordship

wa'e k'otuja q'ukumatz
ri ajpop =

this k'otuja q'ukumatz
the ajpop =

are' k'u ri ajpo k'amja uk'ajol [k'o]kawib'
k'onache joxb'al al

he thus the ajpo k'amja his son k'okawib'
k'onache illegitimate child

3190

tzipitawar
ub'i' rixoqil

tzipitawar
her name his wife

chi wuq le'
k'o wi xwa'e k'otuja———

of seventh generation
there is this k'otuja———

wajxaq le' chi k'u
wa'e q'ukumatz xuk'ajolaj chi k'otuja =

eighth generation now thus
this q'ukumatz engendered now k'otuja =

q'ukumatz k'ut xchik'ajolaj 17 lajuj[835]
chi k'ajolaxel

q'ukumatz thus would engender seventeen
of engendered sons

waral k'ut xchiq'alajin wi
k'iya b'i' waral k'ut

here thus it shall be shown
many names here thus

3200

xk'ajolax wi k'iq'a[b']
kawisimaj[836] wuq al chikech

were engendered sons k'iq'ab'
kawisimaj seven children to them

---

[834] The manuscript reads k'oka'iub', scribal error for k'oka'ib'. These same five names are listed as the sons of k'oka'ib' earlier in the text (lines 1980–1984).

[835] 17 lajuj ("17 ten"). It is unclear what this phrase means. The K'iche' numbering system is vigesimal (base 20); therefore, they would not have written a number such as 17 tens (170). In the previous section, Q'ukumatz is said to have engendered seventeen sons. The number should therefore be read here as simply 17, written as an Arabic numeral. The author(s) perhaps then attempted to write out the number as *[wuq]lajuj* ("seventeen").

[836] *k'awisimaj* in the original manuscript. The scribes of the text give two variant spellings for this name, K'awisimaj and Kawisimaj. I have chosen the latter, as it is consistent with the spelling in other Colonial period highland Maya texts, including the *Popol Vuh*.

Tekum
Tepepul
Tepepul
kawisimaj
k'iq'ab'
Tepepul

mi xek'ajolax	just then they were engendered	3210
chi ismachi'	chi ismachi'	

xawi k'otuja   merely k'otuja
uk'ajol q'ukumatz   his son q'ukumatz

¶ wakamik chi k'ut   ¶ this day now thus
xchiqatikib'a' chik   we shall begin now

ub'ixik   its account
utzijoxik puch[837]   its declaration as well

wa'e loq'olaj tinamit   this esteemed citadel
mayjalaj tinamit   admirable citadel

pa k'iche'[838]	pa k'iche'	3220
chi q'umarkaj[839]	chi q'umarkaj	

chi ismachi'   chi ismachi'
tlekpan k'iche'   royal house k'iche'

mi xq'oq'otaj kanoq   just then was abandoned behind
ub'ixik ri'   its account that

chi ismachi'   chi ismachi'
ojer tinamit kuchax wakamik   ancient citadel it is called this day

xa chi wi k'ut   merely again thus
xchiraq'anib'ej uloq   they would be established hither

qatzij ma ta chisach ik'u'x	our word not then you lose your hearts	3230
chirech ix	to you	

qamam   our grandsons
qak'ajol   our sons

chiri' ta chik'am wi ina'oj   there then you will receive your knowledge

---

[837] *pach* in the original manuscript, scribal error for *puch*.

[838] *k'ichi'* in the original, scribal error for *k'iche'*.

[839] Here the manuscript spells the name of the citadel as *q'umarka'aj*, but it is spelled *q'umarkaj* more frequently in the text.

chux apanoq	may it be henceforward
xa usuk'ulikil xa pu una'taxik	merely its manifestation merely as well its memorial
kib'anoj qamam qaqajaw	their works our grandfathers our fathers
¶ ukab' k'u junab' ukamik k'otuja	¶ second thus year his death k'otuja
ta xb'an nima lab'al	then was done great war
rumal k'iq'ab' kawisimaj	by him k'iq'ab' kawisimaj
k'is xekanab'exik xetelechexik	finished they were captured they were bound
konojel kajawal amaq' ri'	all of their lords nations those
xekamisanik rech k'otuja	they killed his k'otuja
ri amaq' k'ojayil uxajayil ke'uchaxik	the nations k'ojayil uxajayil they are called
ta xeb'ek k'iq'ab' kawisimaj	then they went k'iq'ab' kawisimaj
Tekum Tepepul	Tekum Tepepul
ta xeb'etelechexoq[840] amaq' k'ojayil uxajayil	then they were bound nation k'ojayil uxajayil
oxlajuj rajawal k'is k'ut xepetik	thirteen their lords ended thus they came
ruk' kal kikajol	with them their children their sons
xemunixik xetz'i'ixik	they were enslaved they were subjugated
xe'ul pa k'iche'	they arrived pa k'iche'

[840] *xeb'atelechexoq* in the original manuscript, scribal error for *xeb'etelechexoq*.

chiri'	there
xelotz wi	they were sacrificed
xek'aq wi	they were pierced with arrows
xk'isik kiwach waral	they ended their faces here 3270
ma wi xa qi' yab'il xok chikech	not merely true sickness entered to them
xa upaq'urisaxik b'aq	merely their being shattered bones
jolom	skulls
rumal k'iq'ab'	by him k'iq'ab'
kawisimaj	kawisimaj
rumal k'exelwachix kanoq	because of recompense behind
ra ajaw k'otuja	his suffering lord k'otuja
ralaxik k'iq'ab'	his birth k'iq'ab'
chalaxik	shall his birth
poroy upa kaj	burner its interior sky 3280
poroy upa ulew xcha' k'otuja	burner its interior earth said k'otuja
¶ keje' k'ut ub'anik nima poqob'	¶ then thus its doing great dance
upokob' tojil	his dance tojil
ta xb'an choloj	then was done divination
tz'ikin q'ij	tz'ikin q'ij
xul oxlajuj chi wuq amaq'	arrived thirteen of seven nations
waral pa k'iche'	here at pa k'iche'
xul uk'ab'awil tamub'	arrived their gods tamub'
ilokab' waral k'iche'	ilokab' here k'iche'
¶ tojil uk'ab'awil q'ale tam	¶ tojil their god q'ale tam 3290
ajpo tam	ajpo tam
q'ale k'aqoj	q'ale k'aqoj
atzij winaq k'aqoj	atzij winaq k'aqoj
ye'ol	ye'ol
ajtunala	ajtunala
xpe	they came
chi tamub'	of tamub'
¶ are' k'u tojil	¶ he thus tojil
xpe chi ilokab'	came of ilokab'

q'ale roqche'   q'ale roqche'   3300
atzij winaq roqche'   atzij winaq roqche'

q'alel kajib' ajatzij winaq   q'alel kajib' ajatzij winaq
sik'a   sik'a

lolmet   lolmet
juw[anija] ilokab'   juwanija ilokab'

❡ xul k'u   ❡ he arrived thus
ajaw k'aqaj   lord k'aqaj

❡ k'ate k'u rab'inaleb'   ❡ then thus rab'inaleb'
Talmalin   Talmalin

ajpop ajb'om   ajpop ajb'om   3310
atzi[j] winaq   atzij winaq

jab'jalawej   jab'jalawej
nim ch'okoj[841]   nim ch'okoj

xe'ul lotzowoq   they arrived to blood sacrifice
xe'ul k'aqwoj   they arrived to pierce with arrows

❡ xul nay pu ajaw ajpo sotz'il   arrived surely as well lord ajpo sotz'il
ajpo xajil   ajpo xajil

b'ak'ajolab'   b'ak'ajolab'
q'eqak'uch   q'eqak'uch

❡ xul k'u uch'ab'aja[842]   ❡ arrived thus uch'ab'aja   3320
ajaw ch'umilaja   ajaw ch'umilaja

❡ aq'a'ab'   ❡ aq'a'ab'
b'alamija   b'alamija

k'ub'ul ka'al   k'ub'ul ka'al
kumatz   kumatz

❡ xul nay puch najtija   ❡ arrived also then najtija
ajk'ib'aja   ajk'ib'aja

❡ ajq'uja   ❡ ajq'uja
k'isija   k'isija

ajk'ab'awil   # ajk'ab'awil   3330
ajpo tzolola   # ajpo tzolola

---

[841] *nin ch'okoj* in the original, variant or scribal error for *nim ch'okoj*.
[842] *ch'ub'aja* in the original, scribal error for *ch'ab'aja*.

ajpo wa'is
ajpo b'uluxa

ajpo runam
ajpo saqi achaq'

b'alam
utiw

ajja'eq'oche'
ajpo b'alaja

ajpo kon
ajpo tuktum

ajpo jun
ajp[o] wale

aj[p]o sanay
lolmet kawinay

are' k'u xepe chi ajtz'ikinaja ri'
ronojel ri' ————

Ri' k'ute kiwach
wuq amaq'

xe'ul lotzowoq
xe'ul k'aqowoq

xul kiq'uwuj tzu'um
chomam tzu'um

kitzu'mal
oxlajuj rajawal amaq'

ri' xekamisan
k'otuja

xawi oxlajuj chi nima'q ajawab' xeq'unik
ta xb'an poch'oj

xb'an sutinem
xb'in ronojel k'ab'awil

xeqexaje'ik
kumal ajawab'

= jun k'u ajpo k'ajol xnab'eyejik
e q'o uq'ab' tojil

---

ajpo wa'is
ajpo b'uluxa

ajpo runam
ajpo saqi achaq'

b'alam
utiw

ajja'eq'oche'
ajpo b'alaja

ajpo kon   3340
ajpo tuktum

ajpo jun
ajpo wale

ajpo sanay
lolmet kawinay

they therefore came of ajtz'ikinaja them
all of them ————

They thus their faces
seven nations

they arrived to blood sacrificing   3350
they arrived to piercing with arrows

arrived to piercing breasts
to be seized breasts

their breasts
thirteen their lords nations

these they killed
k'otuja

merely thirteen of great lords they clothed
then they did rending

they did circumambulation   3360
they walked all gods

they were borne in procession
by them lords

= one thus lord young man led
they sustainers his hand tojil

ronojel xitam	all adorned with jade
pwaqim	adorned with precious metal
uwachib'al jumaj	his form in every part
kojb'al jumaj	raiment in every part
sutum	wrapped 3370
pamam	girded
lamaxintzi	penitential clothing
mayat	fasting clothing
tzatz chi ch'ab'i q'aq'	crowded with shooting fire
kaq tijax	phantom globes of fire
kaqulja'	lightning
uk'u'x kaj	heart of sky
kaj eqa'm	four bearers
ajetaq'	they who measure
xpokob'axik	they were danced 3380
upokob'a' pwaq	their dancing precious metal
q'oq'ol	precious stones
xtekok	turquoise
q'uq'	quetzal feathers
raxon[843]	cotinga feathers
ronojel janik' xchiqab'ij[844]	all whatsoever we shall tell
xchiqacholo'	we shall declare
uk'ulun k'u kiwach	its manifestation thus their essence
konojel ajawab' ——	all of them lords ——
wa'e k'ut waral	this thus here 3390
xwor wi	was pierced
k'iq'ab'	k'iq'ab'
kawisimaj	kawisimaj
Tekum	Tekum
tepepul	tepepul
e	they
k'iq'ab'il winaq ——	k'iq'ab'il people ——

---

[843] *raron*, scribal error for *raxon*.

[844] *xchab'ij* in the original manuscript, most likely scribal error for *xchiqab'ij*.

¶ ajpop
kajib' muj pa uwi' jun uq'alib'al

¶ ajpop
four canopies above one his throne

k'o uRajon
ajsu'b'aq

there is his Orator   3400
bone flute player

¶ ajpo k'amja
oxib' muj pa uwi'

¶ ajpo k'amja
three canopies at his head

¶ Nima raj[p]op achij
ka'ib' muj pa uwi'

¶ Great their ajpop valiant men
two canopies at his head

ch'uti raj[p]op[845] achij
jun muj pa uwi'

small their ajpop valiant men
one canopy at his head

xchap
pa xik'aja

they took offices of authority
at plume house

xare [r]i' k'u ajawab'
ri' kamuj pa kiwi'

only these thus lords   3410
these are shaded at their heads

xeworik
xek'aqik

they were pierced
they were perforated

chi titil
q'an ab'aj

with titil
yellow stone

lotz kik'
kaq che'

piercer blood
red tree

je' kej
makuTaj

tail deer
bracelet of Precious Stones

tzikil kot
tzikil b'alam

talon eagle   3420
paw jaguar

t'ot'
matakus

shell
tobacco net

ch'ayom
astapulul

beautiful bird feathers
snowy egret feathers

q'oq'ol
xtekok

precious stone
turquoise

chi k'wal
usapil tza'm

with jewels
its adornment nose

---

[845] *jajop* in the original manuscript, scribal error for *raj[p]op*.

chikech ajpop	to them ajpop	3430
ajpo k'amja	ajpo k'amja	
ri' xekaqik	these were perforated	
xeworik	were pierced	
waral	here	
pa k'iche'	pa k'iche'	
chi q'umarkaj	chi q'umarkaj	
tlekpan k'iche'	royal house k'iche'	
¶ Are' k'u	¶ They thus	
ri b'e[le]jeb' nim ja	the nine great houses	
chiri' xpaxin wi ri'	there were divided these	3440
pa rochoch ajaw k'oka'ib'	in his home lord k'oka'ib'	
b'elejeb' nim ja rech kaweqib'[846]	nine great houses of kaweqib'	
k'iq'ab'il winaq	k'iq'ab'il people	
¶ b'elejeb' k'u nim ja	¶ nine thus great houses	
rech nijayib' ajaw	of nijayib' lords	
¶ kajib' nim ja	¶ four great houses	
rech ajaw k'iche':	of ajaw k'iche':	
2 k'ut nim ja	2 thus great houses	
rech ajaw[847] saqik tz'utuja	of lord saqik tz'utuja	
k'u je k'u utz'aqatik	then thus its completion	3450
24 rajawal k'iche' ri'	24 lords k'iche' these	
ri' kajawar tlekpan k'iche'	these rule royal house k'iche'	
chi q'umarkaj	chi q'umarkaj	
wa'e k'ut kib'i'	these thus their names	
e b'elejeb' nim ja	they nine great houses	
4 ajawarem[848] k'o	4 offices of lordship there are	
chupam ri nab'e'al	within the inheritance	

---

[846] The original text reads *kawaqib'*, a variant or scribal error for *kaweqib'*.

[847] *asjk'ib'* in the original manuscript. The word is poorly written in the manuscript, with attempts to cross out the final letter. It is most likely scribal error for either *ajtzij* ("warriors") or, more probably, *ajaw* ("lord"), which appears before the title *saqik tz'utuja* elsewhere in the text (see lines 2442–2443, 2522).

[848] *ajawarerem* in the original manuscript, scribal error for *ajawarem*.

ajpop k'iq'ab'il winaq
ajpo k'amja

ajpop k'iq'ab'il people
ajpo k'amja

nima Raj[p]op[849] achij
ch'uti[850] raj[p]op[851] achij

great Their Ajpop valiant men   3460
small their ajpop valiant men

e
k'iq'ab'il winaq

they
k'iq'ab'il winaq

e chi wi uk'ajol
umam

they also his sons
his grandsons

e leq' b'aq
laju no'j

they leq' b'aq
laju no'j

e rach chapik k'iq'ab'
kawisimaj:

they together took offices of authority k'iq'ab'
kawisimaj:

roqche' aj
ub'i' ixoq

roqche' aj   3470
her name woman

xe'alanik xoqojaw
ma na xa jalum ajawarem

they were born to esteemed princess
not surely merely false lordship

k'o wi jujun chike
Ri'

there is each of them
These

ajtojil
ajq'ukumatz

ajtojil
ajq'ukumatz

chituy
kejnay

chituy
kejnay

nim ch'okoj kaweq
xokotzil———

nim ch'okoj kaweq   3480
on the left———

xel k'u ub'i'
kiwachib'al

went out thus their names
their image

kitem
kich'akat pa jujun chi juyub'

their benches
their seats at each of mountains

ri b'elejeb' chi achijab'
ajawab'

the nine of valiant men
lords

---

[849] *Rajob'* in the original manuscript, scribal error for *Raj[p]op*.

[850] *chutō* in the original, scribal error for *chutī*.

[851] *rajup* in the original, scribal error for *raj[p]op*.

wa'e k'ute nab'e xya' b'ik reqale'n
kumal ajawab'

these thus first were given their burdens
by them lords

ajtz'alam
rajpop ajtz'alam
utza'm chinamital

ajtz'alam   3490
rajpop ajtz'alam
utza'm chinamital

9. ajtz'alam.
9. rajpop ajtz'alam
9 utza'm chinamital

9. ajtz'alam.
9. rajpop ajtz'alam
9 utza'm chinamital

nab'e xkichap
pa nim ja

first they took offices of authority
in great houses

xa jun xel wi
xa pu jun xb'an wi *cabilto*

merely one they went out
merely as well one they built council houses

ta xechapik e mama'ib'
ta xkipaxij kib' pa jujun chi juyub'

then they took office they grandfathers   3500
then they divided themselves on each of
mountains

wa'e k'ute kelik ub'ik e q'alel
e ajpop

these thus go forth thither they q'alel
they ajpop

ri. 1 3. q'ulaja
kab'lajuj: tzijb'achaj #

the. 1 3. q'ulaja
twelve: tzijb'achaj #

ruk' wajxaqib' tz'alam k'oxtun
Ri sija rax k'im

with them eight timber towers
The sija rax k'im

e oxch'ob'
chi kik'oje'ik

they three groups
of their residence

junam k'ut
xe'el ub'ik

unified thus   3510
they left thither

ta xeb'ek
ta xepixab'ax ub'ik ————

then they went
then they were commissioned ————

❡ uwajxaq le' tzij k'o wi ucholik
kib'anoj ajawab':

❡ eighth generation truly there is its arrangement
their works lords:

ta xetaq k'u ub'ik
e ajawab':

then were sent thus thither
they lords:

katz
kichaq':

their older brothers
their younger brothers:

uk'ajol ajaw
umam ajaw: ri' xetzukuxik

his son lord   3520
his grandson lord: these were sought out

k'ate k'ut ta xepixab'axik	then thus then they were counseled
are' k'ut kipixab' xkib'ano	this thus their counsel they did
alaq qatz	you our older brothers
alaq qachaq':	you our younger brothers:
nim	honored
nab'eq	preeminent
koq' qak'u'x chech alaq:	weeps our hearts to ye:
are kaqataq wi alaq ub'ik:	as we send ye thither:
alaq qoyewal	ye our furious men 3530
qachijilal =	our valiant men =
kab'e k'ulelaj alaq wuq amaq' aj	go ye to wage war seven nations
chib'e yeq'uj alaq	go ye to terrorize
ronojel juyub'	all mountains
taq'aj:	valleys:
chib'e k'u yek'uj tolok'	go thus to threaten sides
maske'l alaq	armpits ye
xe'uchaxik	they were told
ta xepixab'axik	they were counseled
xkoq'ej ki . . .[852] kiwach	they wept . . . their faces 3540
xkikub'a' kik'u'x	they consoled their hearts
xkimes kiwi'	they stroked their heads
chi kiwach e ajtzol	before their faces they slingers
e ajtz'ununche'	they lancers
e rij chun	they its back plastered
saqkab' xe'uxik	whitewashed they came to be
ma wi xa kirayim kiq'alelal	not merely their desire their q'alel office
kajpopol	their ajpop office
e Royewal	they Their Furious Men
rachijilal	their valiant men 3550
tlekpan	royal house

---

[852] The manuscript is very difficult to read here. Sparks (personal communication, 2020) suggests that the distorted word may be *chi'* ("mouth"), commonly paired in K'iche' texts with *wach* ("face") as a couplet. The same pairing appears in lines 190–191 of this text and three times in the *Popol Vuh* (Christenson 2003, lines 5600–5601, 8381–8382, 8395–8396). If this is a correct reading, then lines 3540–3543 would be two couplets rather than a tercet.

k'iche' =	k'iche' =
elenaq wi kitem	left their benches
kich'akat =	their seats =
katb'ek at watz	you go you my older brother
at nuchaq'	you my younger brother
matb'isonik	do not mourn
matoq'ik	do not weep
mawuchaj ak'u'x	do not let suffer your heart
xawi katulik	merely you encounter
xawi pu katk'ulunik	merely thus you take
ruk' akanab'	with them your female captives
ateleche	your male captives
keje' xkatb'e wi	then you shall go
at k'ulelay	you adversary
rech wuq amaq'	of seven nations
tlekpan ——————	tribes ——————
¶ Ri ajpo sotz'il	¶ The ajpo sotz'il
Ajpo xajil:	Ajpo xajil:
b'ak'ajolab'	b'ak'ajolab'
q'eqak'uch	q'eqak'uch
¶ ruk' ajpo ko'on:	¶ with him ajpo ko'on:
b'uluxa #	b'uluxa #
ajpo runam	ajpo runam
junajpwale ——	junajpwale ——
chib'ana' iwoyewal	do your furor
iwachijilal xe'uchaxik ————	your valor they were told ————
wa'e k'ut kelik ub'ik pa k'iche'	this thus their going thither pa k'iche'
chi ismachi'	chi ismachi'
xe'opon ikiyak	they arrived ikiyak
xe'opon tza'm chinq'aj:	they arrived tza'm chinq'aj:
xe'aq'an jokol:	they climbed jokol:
q'ana pek:	q'ana pek:
xe'aq'an apanoq chi patz'an	they climbed up chi patz'an
chi kaqk'ix #	chi kaqk'ix #

3560

3570

3580

xe'aq'an apanoq ch'ay b'amet	they climbed up ch'ay b'amet
kaqikil ——	kaqikil ——
k'a chiri' k'ute xejachow kib'[853]	until there thus they separated themselves
kuk' q'ulaja	with them q'ulaja
ulaq'ob'exik juyub'	their being inhabited mountains 3590
taq'aj	valleys
xawi k'u chiri' xkib'a[n] wi kitz'aq	merely thus there they built their buildings
kik'oxtun	their towers
kaqikil	kaqikil
joyam q'anaq' ——	joyam q'anaq' ——
e k'u k'o la' chiri'	they thus they are there
ta xechapik chi ajawarem	then they took offices in lordship
chi q'alelaj	as q'alelaj
chi ajpopol	as ajpopol
wa'e oxlajuj q'alel	these thirteen q'alel 3600
oxlajuj ajpop ajq'ulaja ——	thirteen ajpop they of q'ulaja ——
¶ wa'e chi k'ute	¶ these also thus
kab'lajuj tzijb'achaj	twelve tzijb'achaj
kab'lajuj q'alel[854]	twelve q'alel
kab'lajuj ajpop	twelve ajpop
kab'lajuj uq'ale[l] [a]chij	twelve their q'alel valiant men
rajpop achij	their ajpop valiant men
xechapik chiri'	they took office there
chwa joyam q'anaq'	before its face joyam q'anaq'
xek'iyar na	they multiplied surely 3610
xetzatzar na chiri'	they became many surely there
ta xechapik k'iyarinaqa chik kal	then they began to mulitiply now their children
kik'ajol	their sons
ta xechapik xeyaylaj chiri'	then they began to terrorize there
are' xb'i'naj wi	they were named
juyub'	mountains

---

[853] *wib'* ("myself") in the original manuscript, most likely scribal error for *kib'* ("themselves").

[854] *q'ulel* in the original, scribal error for *q'alel*.

taq'aj kumal:

valleys by them:

Ta xkikuch kilaq'am chiri'
chwi' k'uch ulaq'am

Then they gathered their standards there
atop k'uch ulaq'am

xecha' chire
oxib' chi laq'am ———

they said to them   3620
three now standards ———

jun kech k'iq'ab'il winaq
    k'iq'ab' nima yax[855]
    ruk' tepepul
k'iq'ab'il winaq =

one theirs k'iq'ab'il people
    k'iq'ab' nima yax
    with him tepepul
k'iq'ab'il people =

xawi jun rech q'ale nijayib'
atzij winaq nijayib'

merely one their q'ale nijayib'
atzij winaq nijayib'

jun k'ut rech
ajaw k'iche'

one thus theirs
ajaw k'iche'

chi oxib'
chi laq'am yaxik

of three   3630
of standards placed together

Are' chi k'u ri wajxaqib' sija
wajxaqib' chi tz'alam k'oxtum

They now thus the eight sija
eight of timber forts

are' chi k'u ri ajuxeyojowt
rax k'im[856]

they now thus the they of uxeyojowt
rax k'im

sab'ache'[857]
yakalik

sab'ache'
raised up

xe'aq'an pa raxtum pek
utik'ilib'exik k'ut ri chi sub'it

they climbed to raxtum pek
its establishment thus chi sub'it

jusu xkib'an kitz'aq chiri'
xk'oje' k'u kanoq *kisemiento* chiri'

quickly they built their buildings there   3640
remained thus their foundation there

k'a chiri' chi k'ut xejacho wi kib'
sab'ache'

until there now thus they divided themselves
sab'ache'

ch'uti sab'ache'
nima sab'ache' chuchaxik

small sab'ache'
great sab'ache' they are called

---

[855] *yas* in the original manuscript. The authors of this text frequently substitute *s* for *x*. This lord is consistently named as Nima Yax in other Early Colonial texts.

[856] *ral k'im* in the original, scribal error for *rax k'im*.

[857] *sab'ab'ache'* in the original, scribal error for *sab'ache'* as seen later in this passage (lines 3643–3645).

| k'ate chi k'ut uq'ob'ik | then thus its enlargement |
| xeyojowt | xeyojowt |

| keje' k'u ri kib'i'k k'ut | then thus the their naming thus |
| ri ajxeyojowt yakalik | the people of xeyojowt raised up |

| xeb'ek | they went   3650 |
| ta xkik'am kib'e | then they guided their road |

| ajkaqsay | people of kaqsay |
| ajajsamayak kuchax wakamik | people of samayak is called this day |

kachb'ilam k'u kib' kuk' tamub'	they were accompanied thus themselves with
	them tamub'
ilokab'	ilokab'

wuq'mil	wuq'mil
sik'a	sik'a
Juwanijayib'	Juwanijayib'

| k'a chiri' k'ut xechap chi wi chi q'alelal | even there thus they took office now as q'alel |
| chi ajpopol | as ajpop   3660 |

| keje' chi k'u ch'ajkar ri' | then now thus ch'ajkar these |
| xe'el pa b'alax ab'aj lemoja ——— | they went to b'alax ab'aj lemoja ——— |

| Are' k'u wa'e kab'lajuj tzijb'achaj | They thus these twelve tzijb'achaj |
| xejach kanoq joyam q'anaq' | they divided behind joyam q'anaq' |

| kumal q'ulaja | by them q'ulaja |
| ruk' sija rax k'im | with sija rax k'im |

| xa k'u uq'ob'ik juyub' | merely thus their enlargement mountains |
| kumal | by them |

| ta xkik'am uloq kib'e | then they guided hither their roads |
| kijok ——— | their pathways ———   3670 |

| wa'e k'ute[858] k'ute kib'e | these thus their roads |
| kijok | their pathways |

| wa'e kab'lajuj tzijb'achaj | these twelve tzijb'achaj |
| are' k'aMol b'e wa'e k'iq'ab'il winaq | they Guides roads these k'iq'ab'il people |

| ajaw ajpop | lord ajpop |
| k'iq'ab' nima yax | k'iq'ab' nima yax |

---

[858] *k'ute* ("thus/therefore") is repeated here twice in error. From the context of the sentence, this should likely be *xkik'am* to parallel the next phrase.

ukab' k'ut	second thus
ajaw q'alel nijayib':[859]	lord q'alel nijayib':
rox k'ut	third thus
ajaw atzij winaq ajaw k'iche'	lord atzij winaq ajaw k'iche' 3680
kik'amom ub'e	they have guided their roads
ujoq'	their pathways
kal	their children
kik'ajol ————————	their sons ————————
Ta xe'aq'an raxchuj #	Then they climbed raxchuj #
xe'opan much'ulik b'aq #	they arrived at much'ulik b'aq #
o' much' k'ajolab'	o' much' k'ajolab'
yiq' ch'opi siwan #	yiq' ch'opi siwan #
q'axi'on #	q'axi'on #
k'ak'amab'al	k'ak'amab'al 3690
xe'ok	they entered
xe' juyub':	xe' juyub':
ri' k'u taq nawalaq	these thus many nawals
ta xeqaj nawala' #	then they descended to nawala' #
xe'aq'an chutanab'al juyub' #	they climbed chutanab'al juyub' #
xe'aq'an pa uwa'l xukuq'ab' #	they climbed pa uwa'l xukuq'ab' #
ta xe'ik'ow pan k'ix #	then they passed through pan k'ix #
xoltakar ab'aj #	xoltakar ab'aj #
xe'ik'ow tz'ultz'ul pek #	they passed through tz'ultz'ul pek #
chi jul #	chi jul # 3700
chaqi'j[860] cho	chaqi'j cho
ta kulik chwi' juyub' tzijb'achaj	then they arrived atop mountain tzijb'achaj
tz'aq tinamit ————————	fortified citadel ————————
Wa'e k'ut kib'i'	These thus their names
nab'e ajyiq'	first conquerors
k'iq'ab' nima yax	k'iq'ab' nima yax
yaxom b'alam	yaxom b'alam
e juk'isik eta'manel kaweq	they established sages kaweq

---

[859] *nijajayib'* in the original manuscript, scribal error for *nijayib'*.

[860] *q'ij* is repeated at the line break in error.

k'iq'ab'il winaq	k'iq'ab'il winaq	
Ruk' q'alel nijayib'	With Him q'alel nijayib'	3710
atzij winaq ajaw k'iche'	atzij winaq ajaw k'iche'	
nab'e winaq xepe pa k'iche'	first people they came pa k'iche'	
chi ismachi'	chi ismachi'	
ta kulik miq'ina'	then they arrive miq'ina'	
tz'ikiche'	tz'ikiche'	
pa uwa'l	pa uwa'l	
sajoq'	sajoq'	
ta kimayjanik	then their admirable greatness	
chwi' saqmal ajaw #	atop saqmal ajaw #	
xe'aq'an q'uxlikel #	they climbed q'uxlikel #	3720
chuja tz'ikin	chuja tz'ikin	
Wa'e k'ute uk'ajol k'iq'ab'	These thus his sons k'iq'ab'	
job' xuk'ajolaj	five he engendered	
wa'e nab'e uk'ajol xitapul.	this first his son xitapul.	
2 sun.	2 sun.	
3. isk'wat.	3. isk'wat.	
4 yamu	4 yamu	
5° ub'i' q'anil #	5th his name q'anil #	
are' k'u ri xitapul xkijach kib'	he thus the xitapul they separated themselves	
kichaq' kib'	their younger brothers themselves	3730
ri e job' chi k'u k'ajolaxik	the they five now thus engendered sons	
rumal k'iq'ab'	by him k'iq'ab'	
chiri' k'o wi job' chi	there are five now	
chi tz'aq	of buildings	
chwi' xtoka	chwi' xtoka	
chi k'wa	chi k'wa	
chiri' e k'o wi	there they are	
ta xul utzijoxik	when arrived his message	
don p[edro] alvarado	don pedro alvarado	
Donatii	Donatii	3740
xawi jun chiyiq'	merely one will conquer	
chipulput wi ja =	will set aflame houses =	

pa xkaqtunum
uyiq' k'iq'ab' ——

// wa'e k'ut xelik ub'ik k'iq'ab'
kawisimaj

pa k'iche'
chi q'umarkaj

ta xerachb'ilaj oxlajuj q'ulaja
kab'lajuj tzijb'achaj

ta xwinaqir nima q'aq'al
te[pe]wal

rumal k'iq'ab'
kawisimaj

qaman
oj kaweqib'

ta xusut uchi' ulew
k'iche' ulew

k'iche' juyub'
taq'aj

ta xe'el
pa k'iche'

xe'ik'ow chuchi' cho lemo'a'
chiri' xulemowaj wi rib'

chi kotal
chi q'uq'il

ta xe'ik'ow kaqixkan
xe'aq'an pab'al ab'aj:

chajaxaq:
chi q'apoj

tza'm tzolola pek
b'alam ab'aj

nik'aj cho
ta xujach ri cho nik'aj

nik'aj re ajpotzotz'il
nik'aj rech k'iq'ab'

pa xkaqtunum
his conquest k'iq'ab' ——

// these thus went thither k'iq'ab'
kawisimaj

pa k'iche'
chi q'umarkaj

then he was accompanied by thirteen q'ulaja
twelve tzijb'achaj   3750

then was conceived great glory
sovereignty

by him k'iq'ab'
kawisimaj

our grandfathers
we kaweqib'

then he walked the circuit its border land
k'iche' land

k'iche' mountains
valleys   3760

then they left
pa k'iche'

they passed by its shore lake mirror water
there he reflected himself

as eagle
as quetzal

then they passed by kaqixkan
they climbed pab'al ab'aj:

chajaxaq:
chi q'apoj   3770

tza'm tzolola pek
b'alam ab'aj

center lake
then he divided the lake center

half his ajpotzotz'il
half his k'iq'ab'

ta xok ch'oy juyub'	then he entered ch'oy juyub'	
ta xok chi jukb'a ikaj	then he entered jukb'a ikaj	
pa meseb'al	pa meseb'al	
xe'ik'ow chi ruk'ab'ala' q'uq'	they passed chi ruk'ab'ala' q'uq'	3780
chi q'ojom	chi q'ojom	
tza'm q'ana ulew	tza'm q'ana ulew	
chwa[ch]	before its face	
naranjos	naranjos	
ta xqaj apanoq muqulik	then he descended muqulik	
xikat	xikat	
ta xb'e' uya' kanoq	then they went to establish	
uchi' juyub'	its border mountain	
[861] ... chi kiwach	... before their faces	
yaki'ab'	yakis	3790
[t]a utikik	then its planting	
ka'ib' inup	two ceiba trees	
rumal k'iq'ab'	by him k'iq'ab'	
kawisimaj	kawisimaj	
laq'alik inup	clefted ceiba tree	
laq'alik mumus chuchaxik	clefted altar they are called	
jun rech yaki winaq ayutlekat	one theirs yaki people ayutlekat	
masatlekat xuxik	masatlekat came to be	
wa'e chi k'ut	this other thus	
uchi' juyub'	its border mountain	3800
kech saqulewab'	theirs saqulewab'	
yok	yok	
q'anchib'ix =	q'anchib'ix =	
q'aq'alix	q'aq'alix	
oxlaj winaq xub'an	thirteen score he did	
ri ajaw k'iq'ab' chiri'	the lord k'iq'ab' there	
ri' qitzij qama[m]	he truly our grandfather	
qaqajaw	our father	

---

[861] The upper portion of folio 31r is missing until this point.

oj	we
kaweqib'aq //	kaweqib'aq // 3810
oxlaj winaq xuk'ut upus	thirteen score he showed his wondrous power
unawal	his spirit essence
chi ch'ab'i q'aq'	of shooting fire
kaq tijax[862]	phantom globes of fire
sutz'	cloud
mayul	mist
raxa kaqulja'	sudden thunderbolt
ch'ipa kaqulja'	youngest thunderbolt
ta xe'upaxij	then he devastated them
ronojel amaq'———	all of nations——— 3820
wa'e[863] chi k'ute uchi' ulew	this now thus its borders land
rech k'iche' winaq	theirs k'iche' people
aq'a'ab'	aq'a'ab'
k'oxom xaq =	k'oxom xaq =
chwach usiatik	before his face usiatik
chwach ab'al tza'm	before his face ab'al tza'm
k'i k'iche' # chwa laq'am ab'aj #	many k'iche' # before laq'am ab'aj #
tza'm yaki //	tza'm yaki //
aq'a yoqa	aq'a yoqa
k'ut[864] b'alam kolob'———	thus b'alam kolob'——— 3830
[865]wakam[ik] ...	this day ...
año 1 5 5 ...	year 1 5 5 ...

---

[862] *kat tijax*. Scribal error for *kaq tijax* as seen on folio 27v, line 21.

[863] *q'a'e*. Scribal error for *wa'e* based on context.

[864] *k'ut* is repeated twice errorneously.

[865] The upper portion of folio 31v is missing until this point.

[Don José Kokoa K'iq'ab']⁸⁶⁶

[Don Juan de Rosa] k'iq'ab' ξ————   [Don José Pérez] [?] ajaw k'iche'

Do[n] diego carcia chituy ξ   [Christóbal fer]nánd[ez Nija]yib'

Do[n] Jorje nijayib' ξ   Do[n] cptoual de belasco nim ch'okoj kaweq

Do[n] diego peres ajq'ukumatz   Ju[an] Lugas ajtojil

do[n] cpual *escr[ibano] cabilto*⁸⁶⁷ ξ   Do[n] p[edro] xiqiutzal tepe ξ

wa'e *qafirma* oj	these our signatures we	
nab'e k'iche'	first k'iche'	3840

kaweqib'   kaweqib'
nijayib'   nijayib'
ajaw k'iche'   ajaw k'iche'

ajtojil   ajtojil
ajq'ukumatz   ajq'ukumatz

tituy⁸⁶⁸   chituy
kejnay ————————   kejnay ————————

in do[n] Joseph cordes k'iq'ab'   I don Joseph cordes k'iq'ab'
kanuya' *nufirma*   I give my signature

chirij wa'e *auto*	at its back this act	3850
rech k'iq'ab' nima yax	of k'iq'ab' nima yax	

in do[n] Ju[an] de Ro[sa k'iq'ab']   I don Juan de Rosa k'iq'ab'
kaqaya' wa...   we give it this...

auto rech a[j]pop   act of ajpop
chwi' miq'ina'   chwi' miq'ina'

---

⁸⁶⁶ The following list of names is given in the original arrangement, in double columns.

⁸⁶⁷ *escr[ibano] cabilto* (Spanish, "scribe of the municipal council/office").

⁸⁶⁸ *tituy*, scribal error for *chituy*.

K'iche' Text with Original Sixteenth-Century Parra Orthography

Folio i

tzaɛ	vae çoqui	caɛ re
re ahu	bal	nima
ɟiche		rahop
		achih —
	vae tzũpan	
vae		vae tzaɛ
tzaɛ ɽe		rech ɟikab
ɛalel ni		ahpop ca
hayib		veɛ

gut chũ ɛaɛcab pa nima ɟiche chi ɛu
arcaah Santa Cruz cuchax camic

https://doi.org/10.5876/9781646422647.c003

Folio ii

AUTo del Señor D Ju°
De auila conquistador

Folio 1r

1: VAE VCAb tzih nima bixel vae vbiɜ
2: parayiso Terrenal Ruleual Ɛa
3: nal Raxal ————
4: chu chaxic chita vacamic xchinbiih chi
5: uech vɜoheic [10]parayiso terenal xa hu pah
6: tzih xchinbih chiuech ɜo ui vcholotahic
7: uɛihil: xban vi hujun chi banoh rumal
8: Dios nima ahau: vnabe vae doñ ɜo
9: [20]xuvinakiriçah nima çak ri dios ni
10: ma ahau: lunes vcab ɛih belej taz chi
11: cah xɜaçe rumal dios nħu vbeh hichal
12: queçolou chirih vleu que çutuu puch
13: chi rononohel ɛih vla hutaz ɜut chi
14: çilabic: [30]hunelic cubul rochoch vtiɛ
15: mit chi ronohel ɛih: Rox ɛih xuuinaki
16: riçah ronohel huyub taɛah che abah
17: xqohe ronohel [40]pamardes = Miergoles
18: vcah ɛih ɛih ɜhumil xya quiçakil ru
19: Dios nħu vnimakil qhumil ruɜ ɛih
20: [50]yɜ retal cak retal aɛab = Juebes
21: Ro ɛih xvinakir ui car pa ha cuɜ giquin
22: vinakir ui ɜhuti car nima car =

Folio 1v

1: biernes ⁶⁰vuakak ɛih xvinakir ꝗhuti cumatz
2: nima cumatz ronohel chicop pa vleu xui
3: nakir rumal dios nima ajau xare ꝗut xui
4: nakir pa viernes quehe ꝗut vꝗazbaxic
5: ⁷⁰ronohel vbanoj dios chupam huhū
6: chi ɛih chivalaj yuib chiꝗiyariçah yuib
7: chiꝗebeh yuib xcha dios nħu chiquech
8: vbanoj quehe ꝗut quipixabaxic ro
9: nohel vbanoh rumal ꝗakol bitol
10: ¶ ⁸⁰Vacamic ꝗut xchikatiquiba vbixic v
11: cholic puch Parayso Terrenal
12: xaui jere rachbanic vleu ta xutzin ri
13: parayso cojcha chirech quehe ꝗut xchinti
14: quiba vvcholic ——————
15: Vcah pah tzih vae vbixic ⁹⁰beleh ꝗhob chi
16: beleh taz puch chi angeles kitzih chi vtz
17: chi hebelic vbanoh vuinakiric puch
18: angeles rumal dios .nħu. chubeleh
19: tananah chubelej le ¹⁰⁰chubeleh taz puch
20: xuxic kitzih chi vtz hebelic vcholotahic
21: vcholic xuxic chuhutak taz xa nabe hun
22: vbinatiçaxic chi angeles ronohel vnima
23: ꝗut vbinatiçaxic chiquihuhunal chi h . . .‑
24: tak le chi jutaɛ tanah ¹¹⁰ꝗo chi nay puc . . .

Folio 2r

1: quibi hutaɛ 4hob chi angeles vae nabe taz
2: nabe le arcangeles = vca le principados
3: Ros le podestades Vcah le virtudes quibi
4: Ro le dominaçiones: vuak le dronos vuk ta
5: nah herubines = [120]vuaxak le serafines
6: vbeleh tanah angelicos espiritus ———
7: are 4ut quibi ri chiquihutaɛ 4hob chi tinamit
8: e 4o chui hutak tanah hutak taz ri 4o ui
9: vbeleh v4hacat nima ahau dios chila chi
10: cah are quibi chiquihuhunal angeles
11: xare ɛalah ri hun cayb quinimakil
12: [130]ri san miguel arcangel rekalem san
13: cabriel vbi hun chic: San Rafael vbi
14: hun chic ros San Uriel ucah: Jeremia ro
15: numiel pamiel romiel samiel: [140]açael
16: Sehutiel horchiel escaltiel = xere 4u
17: ɛalaj quibi ri quehe 4ut qui4oheyc angeles
18: riteskabij e ahloɛ e ahmayin chirij
19: [150]dios nhu ARe chi 4ut xchikabij qui
20: bi adan eva Ro pah tzih co ui vbi adā
21: eva [160]nabe achi nabe yxoɛ kachuch kaka
22: hau ARe v4axlaxic vinaɛ vbanic puch
23: vinaɛ gak bic chu4ux dios .nhu. [170]rū tolon

Folio 2v

1: canoɛ chicah xtolobas canoɛ rū luçi
2: fɛr ta xunimariçah rib cuɜ e rach aj
3: mac xcha ɜut dios nima ahau maui
4: chutzinic chitoleyc ri chicahil ha xa
5: chinban quiɜaxel chilaɛaben ri chica
6: jil ha ¹⁸⁰xcha .nħu. dios ɜate ɜut uga
7: kic vinaɛ rumal dios .nħu. vleu xro
8: que çah dios .nħu. chirij vleu xel ui vɛo
9: ral vinaɛ vtiojil puch huɛatah xbiti
10: tahic vɛab raɛan ¹⁹⁰xutzin vɜoheyc vchi
11: vuach uxiquin vtzam xoċ vbakil ri bo
12: ɜjil xviɛahe taɛ rakan vɛab ɜo ɜut vui
13: xuxic ²⁰⁰xoc vnima tiojil xoc vtzumal
14: xoc re rixɜak xvikitaj ɜut chi uina
15: kil tiojil xuxic = 4 chuyuhic xoc vti
16: ojil vleu ɛaɛ ²¹⁰ha cakiɛ vleu xoc ui
17: vnima tiojil ha ɜut vɛanaal vqui
18: ɜel puch ɛaɛ ɜut xel ui vmiɛinal
19: vɜatanal — cakiɛ ɜut xoqueçax rux
20: lab quehe ɜut chi cajmolaj ui xoqui
21: çax vuinakil tiohil ²²⁰hebelic xuxic rū dios
22: ¶ ɜate ɜut ta xɜamovan chirech gakol bitol
23: ɜamo chech la la. nuchuch lal nukahau
24: mixigak la mixibit la xcha chirech dios
25: ¶ ²³⁰ɜate ɜut vbanic cayb chi nimak tulul
26: xuban dios .nħu. chuniɜahal parayso
27: terenal

Folio 3r

1: hun tulul Ꝫazlem tulul achinaε chi
2: loou vuach hunelic chiꝪaçeyc rumal xcha
3: dios .nhu. ꝅ [240]hũ chi tulul etamabal tulul
4: vbi are vbinaam ui etamabal tulul achi
5: naε chilouvic chiretah vtz chiretamah vtz
6: chiretamah maui vtz quehe Ꝫut vꝪoheyc
7: cayb tulul ri———————
8: [250]Vkah pah tzih vuabaxic adan chupã
9: Paraysso terrenal rũ dios .nhu. varal cat
10: ochochin vui xcha dios .nhu. varal puch cat
11: amaεelab ui xuchaxic rũ .dios nhu. quehe Ꝫut
12: ta xmolobax Ꝫhuti chicop nima chicop chuach [260]rũ
13: D .nhu. queabinatiçaj chauoqueçah quibi
14: chiquihuhunal xuchaxic rũ dios nima ahau
15: xa vtuquel adan xgakic xbit puch rũ dios
16: [270]nima quicotem nima çak amaε xꝪohe ui nima
17: quicotem lianic çu çakil amaε xuya dios chi
18: rech Ꝫiz rech ronohel vquiyl vkuçil [280]vꝪo
19: Ꝫal vpam paraysso derrenal e Ꝫo cayb tzi
20: quin paloma ruꝪ caquigubaj qui chiquivuach
21: e cubay vꝪux ta xuꝪuxlah Ꝫut adan ta xubij
22: chirech dios [290]nhu. lal dios nima ahau chiyata
23: la vach ahquicotel vach Ꝫhavel vach tziho
24: nel yn gak la yn bit la xcha chirech D .nhu

Folio 3v

1: [300]ta xuta ɜut dios roεeh vɜux adan ta vyayc
2: rach coj quehe ɜut ta xvartiçax adan rumal
3: .D nhu. cavar ɜut adan ta xeleçax hun vɜal
4: ɜax chumos xel ui jun vbakil vɜalɜax yxok
5: [310]ɜut xuxic huεatah xutzin rumal nima ahau
6: dios xaui hutzu xoc ranima vtzininaε chic ta x
7: ɜaztah vuach adan ta xɜaçux rū rangel dios
8: adan adan catɜaztahok chachabej aɜulil [320]aloε
9: aɜanij xcha rangel dios chirech adan ta xuɜa
10: movah chirech dios ɜamo chiech la lal tzakol bi
11: tol vech mi xyala vachbil [330]xcha chirech dios nima
12: ahau: hutzu ɜut xɜhaou adan chirech yxok xcha
13: adan chirech yxoε at nubakil at nutiohil at
14: elenaε chupam nutiohil xcha chirech yxoε
15: ta xeɜulubax ɜut rū dios nima ahau [340]ri avachi
16: jil e ri auixokil le chiloεoj yuib chiɜaxɜomaj yuib
17: chiɜanihah yuib quixmialanic quixɜaholanic xe
18: uchaxic quehe ɜut vpixabaxic adan ruɜ eva ri-
19: xokil adan xuxic rū dios [350].nhu. ta quipixaba
20: xic ɜut chirech ri avaz tulul canucanaj va
21: uaz tzij vauaz pixab chiuech milo vuach avaz
22: tulul etamabal tulul mixcam Rumal are
23: chilo ri ɜazlem tulul hunelic quixɜaçe rū [360]xevcha
24: xic adan eva rū D. nhu ta vtiqueric ɜut quica
25: vachixic rumal diablo ɜaxtoc rumal are ɜax chi
26: quiɜux [370]vyayc vçipaxic chicajil ja chiquech adā
27: eva ta xulquicaxtoɜoj ri eva chuloyc avaz tu
28: lul

Folio 4r

1: xuhal4atij vuach ri diablo chi angel cumatz 4u
2: vhe loo la vae vuach etamabal tulul lal
3: eva xcha chire [380]maui cauaj taj rū canahinaɛ
4: ravaz dios chiɛech xcha eva majay mapayn
5: vçamajel machutzin pa la queje taj xa rumal
6: revabal dios are caraj maui cagaɛat etamabal
7: allaɛ loo la xcha queje 4ut vloyc avaz tulul rū eva
8: [390]quehe 4ut vuinakiric mac labal cumal
9: ta xeokotax 4u vloɛ chupan paraysso terenal
10: ta xevul varal chuach vleu pa rapa4ax pa va
11: yhal pa chahij chi [400]chi oɛibal chi çi4ibal quehe
12: 4ut ta xquigonoj chic cal4ual chirech dios
13: nima ajau xoɛ qui4ux xeoɛic xeçi4inic ta xqui
14: tzonoj cal4ual chiya ta la kamial ka4ahol xecha
15: ala taj [410]ali taj xecha chirech dios nhu. ta vyayc
16: cal4ual xuta dios roɛej qui4ux roɛej quipam
17: ¶ hu pah chic tzih 4o ui vbixic oxib chi bi: [420]cayin
18: abel: xetj Mahahaiok v4ahol adan ta xel
19: vloɛ pa paraysso terenal anim 4ut xuya dios
20: xalas: cayn: xalax chi 4ut abel e cayb chi alabō
21: quichaɛ quib v4ahol adā [430]are 4u ri ral4ual—
22: hutzu xemacun chic nabe are ri cayin nabe
23: al kitzij meba: are 4u ri: abel xuya dios chirech
24: vɛinomal vtiquilem ytzel 4ut xril cayin [440]ta
25: xucamiçaj vchaɛ chi evahquil kitzij 4ut vloɛ dios
26: ri abel rumal xuya vnimakil vuach vticon chi
27: are 4u ri cayin xa vpi4holil xuya chirech dio

Folio 4v

1: are 4u ri abel caçi4in ri vqui4el chuach dios que

2: he 4ut vyayic v4axel vmac cayin [450]xaui maui

3: vtzilaj camic xoc chirech xa x4ak rū jun ca

4: sador 4o pa rabis ta xilitah rumal ri vubanel

5: turnio z4akin chimoymot vuach ta xvubax

6: 4ut maçat xrillo xa tohoriçaxic vmac rū dios

7: [460]maui vmac ta ri vbanel chita 4ut vçu4uli

8: quil nabe mac xquiban ral4ual adan eva vae

9: //4ut v4ahol adan cayin abel: [470]are chi 4ut

10: v4ahol cayin abel vae: e noe matuxalem

11: noe. vae. xen. chan. .Jabet.. ¶ vae chi 4ute hu

12: paj tzij vbixic vhal4atijic 4habal rū dios

13: chiquech e ral4ual noue xbano ma ri nabe bu

14: ttic chuach noue: caminaka chic noue ta xqui

15: 4uxlaah ral4ual noue [480]vbanic hun nima gaɛ

16: nima 4oxtun chupam chuach caj xecha vue

17: chiban chi ri buttic humul chic chi ri 4ut coj

18: colotaj ui xecha ta xeɛil rū dios .nħu. ta xu

19: cat tzih dios paquiui ta xulhal4atih dios nħu

20: qui4habal oxlahu 4hob chi chi4habal [490]qui4ha

21: bal xuxic ma chichi xquita qui4habal chiqui

22: bil quib quehe 4ut quipaxic ri rū dios .nħu.

23: are chi 4ut v4ahol xen chan Jabet vae abrajan

24: ysahac. esau Jacob vae chi 4ut v4ajol Jacob

25: Ruben: Simon: ~~Jutas.~~ [500]Leui. Jutas. Ysacab: çabu

26: len. Samin Dan. Cat. Betalen aset Joseph

Folio 5r

1: [510]Ri 4ute vmā ADan: v4aho. pachinoc. Ri

2: Abrahan: Jacob puch ¶ vae 4ut vbi huyub cana

3: an: xe4ohe ui Jacob cu4 e ral4ual: puch chi 4u

4: chiri: xeopō chi 4u chila egipto ~~xaui rala.4aheltJa~~

5: ~~cob~~ omu4h chi 4u hunab [520]xquiban chila ri

6: vmam Jacob: ta xalas chi 4u canoɛ moyses chu

7: xol ebreos xalas ui moyses = caŦahin 4ut moy

8: es yuɛul chij Ŧa xçi4ix rumal dios .nħu. 4o

9: pa tucan: maui ca4at taj caporotaj ta puch

10: [530]vxak tucan 4o ui dios .nħu. ta xuçi4ij moyses

11: moyses moyses catpe ta vu4 quinultaauila

12: chulata nutzij xcha dios .nħu. chirē [540]ta xopō 4ut

13: moyses 4o ui tucan cajuluyc chi ɛaɛ xrilo chauele

14: çah caNoɛ axahab 4ate catul varal vu4 xcha

15: dios chirech moyses Ŧa vbixic chire moyses hat e

16: gipto ru4 paraon quebeaueleçah vloɛ nuloɛ

17: [550]e nu4anih ahysrael xuchax moyses xu4u

18: luba moyses maui yn roquic v4habexic ri ahau

19: paraon xaki yn v4ial meba: vue ta hun chi

20: quech nimak propetas chibec lal ahau xcha moy

21: ses chirech nħu dios: xax catbe ui [560]chabij nu

22: tzij chirech paraon maxibij avib yn 4o avu4 xcha

23: dios nima ahau chirech moyses ta ubic 4ut moy

24: ses ruc paraon rachbil vchaɛ aron maui 4o t

25: ah labalibal xru4aah [570]xaui xare v4hamiy

26: ɛubal chij ta vbic 4ut moyses xopō

Folio 5v

1: ꝗut ruc paon xubih ꝗut vtzih .nhu. dios chirē

2: xcha moyses lal ahau paraon yn achbilay que

3: ri e vloꜫ vꝗanij dios ahysRael rū queje nu

4: takiquil rū .nhu. dios xcha moyses [580]chirech para

5: on: paraon chi ꝗut maui xunimah vtzih moyses

6: ❡ Ta vbanic ꝗut 7 chi nimaꜫ puz naval vnimal

7: chi nimaꜫ puz naval xuban dios milagro chu-

8: chaxic chiquivach ahegipto chuach puch

9: paraon [590]ta vtzolꜫomitajic vꝗhamiy aron chi cu

10: matz ❡ vcab ꜫij chic ta xtzolꜫomitaj chic ja

11: chi quiꝗ ❡ ros ꜫih chi ꝗut ta xeuinakir xpek

12: xtug ruꝗ calat ❡ vcah mul ꝗut xeuina

13: kir. Vz. [600]xcatz. xpeper amolo ronohel tionel chi

14: cop ❡ ro mul ta xvinakir lem amolo ❡ vu . . .

15: mul tax xeuinakir nima çaꜫboch nima ca

16: kulja [610]ruꝗ nima cumatz xim chuach chaxvi

17: kiric ta xoc nima ꜫekum rū dios nim a

18: jau xcam jun quinabeal ajegipto ꝗate ꝗut

19: quitzokopitahic vloꜫ ahysRael rumal pa

20: raon xa ta quebec mohcam camal lal . . .

21: ses aron xcha paraon = quehe ꝗut quipetic

22: ralꝗual yxrael e ahvtinamit dios [620]nim

23: caxꝗol xepe ui ral vꝗahol ysrael ahcana

24: an oj puch ebreos ta quiꝗamic vbic rumal

25: moyses ta xeopan chi. palo ta xubij dios

26: chirech moyses chatzaka cablajuj azab

Folio 6r

1: pa palo cablah + h 4ut chaueçeuah
2: ⁶³⁰ta xtzah cut palo rũ dios nima ahau cablahuj
3: nimaɛ be xcohe chupam palo ta xohy4ou vloɛ
4: xax zgakin chic maui tzakatinaɛ cah calab chi
5: vinaɛ oh ral v4ahol ahysRael ahcanaan
6: ⁶⁴⁰oh puch ebreos Ri 4ute kapetic relibal ɛih vae
7: ta xchinchol chic qui4euibal vloɛ pa 4im pa 4e
8: chelah vcab xelimcutz chimaracou 4aylah
9: ha: xeel chi 4u chiri ⁶⁵⁰xeopon chi 4u chila xim vbii
10: xeel chi 4u chiri xepon chi 4u chäla Papitin
11: xaui xere x4okon chi ui qui4ux chiri ahebreos
12: chiri 4ut xqui4hac ui amalech 4ate 4ut ro
13: panic ral4ual Jacob chila chi 4ates chiri 4ut
14: xcam ui maria ⁶⁶⁰ranab sanlo moyses 4ate 4ut
15: ta xeopan chic ral4ual Jacob: chila hor vcamic
16: moyses are 4o chiri moab nakah chic canaan ta
17: xeɛax chi 4ut Jortan ta xe4hacatah herico ——
18: ¶ Are 4ut cahauar ri Joseph paqui ¶ vcamic Josue
19: vhachic vleu canaanvleu ⁶⁷⁰canan ————————
20: vhuinaɛ nima bi vbii saniuel ¶ vcah tzih vua
21: baxic: Saul chi ahavarem ¶ vhuuinaɛ 6
22: nima bi vbi ala Davit ¶ vhuinaɛ. 7. nima
23: bii vbi Salamon ru4 quia bi chic ¶ vhuinaɛ
24: nima bi ⁶⁸⁰vbi propetas ruc nay puch: pa

Folio 6v

1: patriar4as elias propetas vbi eliseo pro

2: peta vbi taniel ppeta. vbi esayas Ᵽ

3: peta ruc Jouanes propeta——

4: ¶ vlahu pah tzih quitzalihic vloɛ Jubias chiqui

5: huiubal vbi Jerusalem ⁶⁹⁰quipetic chila babi

6: lonia // axiria//————

7: ¶ vhulahu pah tzih co ui chi maui copanic

8: chic lahuh chi chinamital ahysRael chi

9: quihuyubal chila chi quihuyubal

10: xepe ui babilonia xulqailaɛabeh chic

11: camaɛ ⁷⁰⁰xa hun chial hun puch chinamital

12: xa e hu 4hob chic chinamital e u4ahol Jacob

13: v4ahol chu4oheyc xa quituquel chic xquila

14: ɛabeh chic Jerusalem————

15: ¶ Are 4u ri e lahuh chi chinamital xebe chila

16: asiria rumal salmanasar ⁷¹⁰xma lo chi ui

17: xetzalih chi ui vloɛ chila xçach ui quitzihoxic

18: xma . . . ui xe4utun uvi kitzih chi e 4i chi copanic

19: ma chi 4ut xetzalih vloɛ xa che xa abah x ¶

20: quiçi4ih chila xepe ui ⁷²⁰xa quimac xa pu qui

21: tzelal xeoɛotax vui rumal dios nima aha

22: vae vbi huyub mi xcholotahic xey4ou ui——

Folio 7r

1: mi xcholotahic: mara vbi nabe huyub ta xuhꜫax
2: vloꜫ ꜭhaka palo: [730]vcab xelimcutz: rox sin: vcah
3: rabitin: ro xiney: vuaꜫaꜫ caxerot: vuuꜫ chiꜭates
4: vuahxaꜫ: eton: vbeleh: hor: vlahuj chiboch v
5: hulah chiabatin. [740]vꜭablah: çaret: roslah: arnō
6: vcahlah matan rolah xchamel: vuaꜫlah: bemot
7: vuuꜫlah chi moab————
8: Ri ꜭute quicoheyc quiꜭouibal Rumal dios nima
9: ahau [750]quiyiꜫ puch ahcanan: ahebreos puch ahyx
10: rael oxib chi bi chi conohel ahysRael ahcana
11: an ahebreos quevchaxic e kamam ꜫaka
12: hau ri oh ri ꜭute kaxe kaꜭoheyc puch [760]kelic pu
13: vloꜫ relibal ꜫih xchita ꜭu allaꜫ xchiuachin puv
14: vach vumal xchinbih ꜭut vçuꜭuliquil chi
15: ech allaꜫ xa palabal xeçach ui kamam kaka
16: jau oh vmam [770]vꜭahol adan eva: enoc abra
17: han yssac Jacob xa ꜭu rumal xquiçach quidios
18: XA ꜭu cha xeyxouax rumal dios [780]nima ahau
19: ri ꜭute vçuꜭuliquil————
20: //xa xquipoo xa xquihalꜭatih quitzij vuꜫub pec vu
21: ꜫub çiuan çeuan tulan xecha chirech pan pa
22: rar pam paxil [790]pan ꜭaela xecha = are ꜭ

Folio 7v

1: ri pan pasil pan Ɵaela xquibih are ri chu
2: pam parayso terenal xohƟzak ui xohbit ui
3: rumal dios nima ahau mavi xutzin chi
4: vbi cumal rumal Ɵut quimac are Ɵu ri
5: çeuan tulan xquibih 800cha Ɵut vçuƟuliquil
6: sineyeton are Ɵut ri vuɛub pec vɛub çiuan
7: kitzih ui are ri pa pec pa çiuan xevar ui chila chi
8: Relibal ɛih xa quehunelic vloɛ xa pu e huça
9: chic ta xeçach chila asiria 810rumal salmana
10: sar————————————————
11: ⁋Vae hu pah tzih xchinbih vae vƟoheic aha
12: varem vxe puch tzih ri vbixic ri ɛanalah
13: huyub raxalah vhuyub ri pa çeuā pa tulan
14: xquibih vgibal pec 820vtzibal çeuan.
15: tulan xecha ta xenimatah chupam ri tzaɛbal
16: tzih ta xecha 830chirech ri ɛih yc hun ɛapoh hū
17: Ɵahol xecha: hunahpu xecha chirech ri ɛih
18: xbalanqueh chuchax ri yc cumal vçiƟ Ɵiɛab
19: chuchax ri Ɵhumil cumal oh vmam oh vƟa
20: hol ahysRael santo moysen chupan quichina
21: mital 840ahysRael xel ui e kamam e kakahau
22: ta xepe chi relibal ɛih chila pabelonia couiça
23: noɛ ahau naɛxic ri vxe kamamaxic

Folio 8r

1: kaɜaholaxic ta xquiɜuxlaah quipetic e na. .

2: val vinaɛ [850]nah xopam vi quimuɛubal chicah

3: chivleu maui ɜo ta cuhunamah ruc xquimu

4: ɛuh ronohel xecah e nimaɛ etamanel e ɜamol

5: vbe ronohel vukamaɛ tlecpan quehe ɜuɛ

6: quipetic vae ɜhaka cho [860]ɜhaka palo pa tulan pa

7: çeuan ─────────────

8: vae ɜutɛ quibi nabe uinaɛ vae nabe ɜiche

9: e 4. chi uinaɛ = are nabe ahau vae Balam

10: ɜitze ri kamam kakahau oj muchib = are ɜuɛ

11: vcab ahau [870]ri Balam aɛab. vmã vɛahau ahau

12: nihayib = ros ɜuɛ ahau ri mahucotah ri

13: quimam quikahau e ahau ɜiche = vcah ɜuɛ

14: ahau ri yqui balam Are ɜuɛ [880]vae nabe ɜiche

15: Balam ɜitze nabe ahau. cakapaluma vbi rixokil

16: Balam aɛab vcab ahau: çuniha vbi rixokil

17: Mahucotah rox ahau cakixaha vbi rixokil

18: yqui balam xa kiɜahol spe chi relibal ɛih

19: ¶vae ɜuɛ vcab quiche [890]vbi tamub: vae nabe

20: ahau ɜopichoch. ɜochohlan. mahɜinalom.

21: ɜoɛanauil. xaui xa cahib chi uinaɛ ɛi vxe

22: vae ahauab tamub vae cakoh eɛomaɛ

23: xa vɛana uinaɛ rib chupã vae vuh xa

Folio 8v

1: e hunelic vloɛ ϑhaka cho [900]ϑhaka palo reli
2: bal ɛih pa tulan pa çeuan————————————
3: ¶ xaui quehe quech ri - ylocab Ros quiche xa
4: ui 4 chi uinaɛ. vae vbi nabe ahau chiya toh
5: chiya ǥiquin yolchitum. [910]yol chiramaɛ. ϑhi
6: pel can muɛel: vae quimam quikahau e
7: ahauab: ɛale çiϑa Juaniha e ylocab [920]e oxi
8: xib amaɛ chi ϑiche xa hun quitzih xa pu hū
9: quivach chi oxib amaɛ chi quiche e ral vϑa
10: ysRael oh ϑiche uinaɛ ta xuhpe Babiloni
11: a relibal ɛih————————————
12: ¶[930]Vae ϑut quipetic chi relibal ɛih ta xe
13: yacatah ϑu vloɛ are ϑamol be ri Balam ϑi
14: tze. ruϑ balam aɛab . . Mahucotah . yqui
15: bal = vae ϑut quipetic ta xya vloɛ piçon caϑal
16: chiquech [940]rumal ahau nacxic ta quipetic
17: varal e çonolic e ϑhanalic xepetic xa quito
18: xa quixaɛpot ϑolic ta culic ϑut chuchi palo
19: ¶Ta xuϑam ϑut vϑhamiy ahau Balam ϑitze
20: [950]ta xuɛoçih ϑut palo hutzu ϑut xtzah ri pa
21: lo xaki bolobic çanayeb xux chic quehe ϑut
22: quiϑouic vloɛ chi conohel ox ϑhob nabe ϑiche

Folio 9r

1: cu4 4ut oxlahu 4hob chi vuεamaε tlecpam [960]e te
2: ren chiquih xa ki 4i4ouic vloε ta xutzapāh rib pa
3: lo xax vloεobal ui dios chiquech rumal xa huna
4: ǥakol bitol xquiçih vni4ahal cāh vleu xecha
5: [970]rumal xa xeui v4ahol vmam abrahan Jacob
6: ta quiεaxic 4u vloε varal vloε 4haka palo Ta s
7: qui4am vloε vxe che vxe 4am chi maui va chi
8: maui ha [980]xaki vui qui4hamiy chiquiçiko chi
9: cube 4u qui4ux xepetic ta xevl 4ut chuchi hū
10: 4huti cho chiri nimsoy carchAh xquiban quitzaε
11: chiri e 4o ui εuε raxon [990]punpun εana xco raxa
12: xco εan bulul εan ǥiquin xaui maui xu4an ta
13: quivach ta xcoεotah chi 4u canoε ta xquicam chi
14: vloε vxe che vxe 4aam ta xeul chi 4u chiri chix
15: pach [1000]xquiya retal pahaayin abah retal xqui
16: yao ta quipetic chi 4ut chila ta culic chui hun
17: nima huyub vbi chi4iche xecha chirech [1010]xa
18: ui xeyaluh chiri ta xquicanah chi 4ut ri hu
19: yub chi4iche ta xepe chic ta culic 4ut chiri chui
20: huyub haεauitz 4hipaε vbi chi 4ut xeheke ui
21: chi nima conohel chiri puch xheke ui [1020]e ah4ix
22: e ahcaj ri Balam 4itze balam aεab. Ma
23: hucotah: y4ui balam ——————————————

Folio 9v

1: xa 4u cu4am quib chi conohel 4u4 tamub ylocab

2: [1030]cu4 puch e oxlahuj chi vuɛamaɛ tlecpan

3: xe 4ut çepetahinaɛ chic xu 4iala chic ~~ɛih~~ hu

4: nab e 4o chiri ta xqui4uxlaah 4ut relic

5: quiɛaɛ ta xcha balam 4itze mi ba xɛana teu

6: [1040]xa ta chiɛeleçah kaɛaɛ xcha balam 4itze

7: chiquech vuɛamaɛ tlecpam vtz ba la na

8: kipa chika4haco xecha vuɛamaɛ tlec

9: pam apachinaɛ nabe chel vɛaɛ chika

10: ya [1050]hun kal ka4ahol chirech xecha vuɛ

11: amaɛ vtz ba la quehe chuxic xcha Balam

12: 4itze ta xqui4hac quitzij ta xquitiquiba

13: 4ut vbakic quiɛaɛ nabe 4ut xel quiɛaɛ

14: ri Balam 4itze balam aɛab: Mahu4otah [1060]y

15: qui balam are 4u ri vuɛamaɛ tlecpam xa x

16: ma xel ui quiɛaɛ ¶ 4ate 4ut vgonoxic ɛaɛ cumal

17: chiquech: balam 4itze balam aɛab Mahucotah

18: jun yqui balam = xa ta ba chiya allaɛ [1070]z4in kaɛaɛ

19: xecha 4ut ri vukamaɛ tlecpan chiya ba ri ka4hacō

20: xevchax 4ut naki ta la 4ut ri 4hacom chikayao xe

21: cha = vuɛ ba chiuah chikatzumaj vach y4ux xe

22: vchax 4ut rumal balam 4itze [1080]vtz ba la xecha

23: 4ut ta vgubaxic 4ut vua qui4ux quimazquel

Folio 10r

10

1: quehe 4ut qui4hacatahic ri e vueamae ahlaba
2: are 4ut xRetah ri cal qui4ahol xquiya chi4haquic
3: Capitulo 2° \
4: ¶ vacamic chi 4ut [1090]xchikatiquiba chic vcholic vae
5: quihachouic quib ta xecha ri balam 4itze: balam
6: aeab. Mahucotah yqui balam = xa ta ba chi
7: kahach eib allae ahauab 4opichoch. [1100]4ochoh
8: lan 4oeanauil. mah4inalom: allae puch: chi
9: ya toj chiya giquin hal chi tum
10: hal chi ramae chipel can mueel can = xcha
11: balam 4itze ma ba kaçachic tah [1110]et chika4ul
12: vui kib maha chi karie kahuyubal kata.
13: eahal xa vmay tzih xchikabano varal ha
14: eauitz chipae are xchibinah ui chipixab
15: chimamah quehe chiquibih chieiyah chika
16: mamah xeuchan 4u quib ta quieaxic 4ut [1120]ta
17: mub chui huyub amae tan = xaui quehe que
18: ylocab xeeax chui huyub v4in = xaui 4u
19: xetere ri vueamae tlecpam [1130]chiquih
20: xa 4u quituquel ri ah4ix ahcah ri balam
21: aeab balam 4itze Mahucotah yqui balam
22: xecanah chiri chui huyub haeauitz 4hi
23: pak chiri 4ut xemialan ui [1140]xe4aholan ui
24: chiri x4aholax ui 4ocayb 4oeauib rumal
25: ahau Balam 4itze — ta quipoeotahic

Folio 10v

1: ɜut cal quiɜahol vukamaε ahlabal = vikil
2: achi ɜut [1150]quitzak ri ahɜix e ahcah ri e ka
3: mam kakahau oj caueεib: nihayib. ahau
4: ɜiche are ɜu yqui balam xa kixcam chupā
5: vɜaholal ¶ [1160]Balam ɜitze Tohil vɜabauil
6: Balam aεab auilis vɜabauil. mahuco
7: tah: haεauitz vɜabauil. Chi ɜual abah
8: ri piçon ɜaɜal xpe relibal εih chiri ɜut
9: xquiquir ui haεauitz are e εaε ui e tepeu
10: vi xevxic chiquiui vuεamaε [1170]tlecpam
11: ɜia may xquiban chiri quihachamachic qui
12: b = ta xtiquer cut vçachic quimial qui
13: ɜahol vuεamaε tlecpan xa maui εalah [1180]qui
14: sachic ta queçachic cumal chalamacat
15: xa rixcolob chic ɜo canoε ta chiquiriε vuεa
16: maε naεipa cojbanouic vue xa huyub lo
17: xεcha xquitaεeh rakan ri banol re xa
18: rakan balam [1190]xa rakan vtiu co canoε ———
19: xa ɜut vɜuiɜel cabe chuach ɜabauil chuach
20: tohil auiliz haεauitz: quehe ɜut vɜuxla
21: xic quicamiçaxic e kamā kakahau Balā ɜitze
22: balam aεab mahucotaj [1200]yɜui balam cumal
23: vuεamaε ahlabal: chi juεatah ɜut xna

Folio 11r

1: tah chiquech balam 4itze hutzu xe chuch
2: toil auilis xquibij quicamiçaxic cumal
3: vuɛamaɛ: ta xu4ulaba tohil mixibih yuib
4: ɛalaj chi4hiquitah vɛihil labal [1210]chulybij
5: chue xcha tohil auilis haɛauitz———ta v4hiqui
6: tahic 4u ɛih cumal vukamaɛ tlecpan qui
7: camiçaxic Balam 4itze balam aɛab [1220]mahu
8: cotah yqui balam] ta xquiviɛ 4u vlo quib
9: ahlabal chi tzol chi gununche chiya chuach
10: vach puaɛ chiteçacau puaɛ ta xquiban
11: nabe labal chila haɛauitz ¶ [1230]e 4ut xa:
12: ba ma chic oyeu achi e 4amaçog xa 4ut
13: xevar xe sayab ri ahlabal are 4ut que
14: varic ta xmah quitzol quigununche
15: quiya4hvach quiɛalɛah ruc huhũ
16: [1240]qui4hip aɛab qui4hip aɛan xaki e çonoçoh
17: chic ta x4aztah quivach xax ma 4o ui labal
18: xquibano xetzalih chiquihuyubal vca
19: mul chi 4ut xquimol chi na quib rumal
20: tzatz ri cal qui4ahol queçachic quehe
21: 4ut 4o ui labal chi qui4ux [1250]ma 4u cacu
22: chah 4a chiri x4ulun vi ri quitux gu

Folio 11v

1: maxic ta xquitzonoh ɛaɛ xa maui xquinao
2: vae chi ꝗute vcamul labal ta xꝗhiqui
3: tah chi ɛih cumal vuɛamaɛ ¹²⁶⁰ahlabal chi
4: quicamiçaxic e kamā kakahau Balam ꝗitze
5: balam aɛab mahucotah yqui balam ta re
6: tamaxic chic rumal tohil auilis haɛauitz
7: ¹²⁷⁰ta squibih ꝗut balam ꝗitze chirech tohil aui
8: lis mi xꝗhiquitah ɛih kacamicaxic chic
9: cumal vuɛamaɛ ahlabal at tohil aui
10: lis ¹²⁸⁰haɛauitz xecha chirech xcha ꝗu ri tohil
11: chire balam ꝗitze chibana cablahuh
12: quech ri poy are ri quitzol quitzununche
13: ximah canoɛ nabe are chiquicoh ri poy
14: ahamche ¹²⁹⁰queya chui taɛ ꝗeh ruꝗ chi
15: ya chic 4 çocob chucah guc tak gak hū
16: çocob ɛauonon: hun çocob çital hun ço
17: ꝗob ɛagutuh: hun çocob vonon——
18: rumal ma na e ta ꝗi R balam ꝗitze: balam aɛab
19: Mahucotah ¹³⁰⁰hun yqui balam xa ꝗu charah xe
20: tzayx cumal vuɛamaɛ ahlabal caoɛ ɛih
21: ta rah xecamiꝗaxic ri kamam kakahau ta
22: vbanic ꝗut nima mayhabal ¹³¹⁰cuonal chi

Folio 12r

12

1: chiri ɜut xɜuiɜut ui quibinibal quipuz quinaual

2: ta xetzalou poy ahamche vchuch çaklaɛ vonon

3: [1320]çital ɜhabiɛaɛ cak tihax ɛeteb pubayx: çutz

4: mayul nima çakboch: cabraɛan: caɛulha [1330]ri

5: quibinibal quichacabal: ta roquic cut labal

6: cumal vuɛamaɛ tlecpan xa ɜut poy ahamche

7: ri xquilabalih xɜiz na quichuɛab [1340]ɜate ɜut

8: xhakatah çocob cumal xoɛohauab rixoɛil ba

9: lam ɜitze balam aɛab mahucotah yqui balam

10: are ɜut ta xhakatah çocob ta xhaɛatah vonon

11: çital [1350]ɛavonon: Are ɜut xkaçan quech vuɛamaɛ

12: ahlabal chuach vleu are ɜut e ɜo chuach vleu

13: ta xɛol canoɛ quitzol ɜuigununche xaki quiɜhab

14: quipocob ɜo xcam canoɛ [1360]ɜo xanumah chi chiquch

15: vukama_ tlecpan chi maui ɜo ta labal xquiba

16: no xa loɛ xquibana labal = quehe ɜut vni

17: maric quiche vae e ɛaɛ e tepeu xevs chiquibi

18: vae vuɛamaɛ = [1370]vae ɜute quibi vuɛamaɛ

19: rah xelabalinic chila haɛauitz ¶ rothayib:

20: ɜibaha: vxab: bacah: quebatzunha ri ta xeba

21: nou labal vtiqueric labalin rib [1380]vtiqueric

22: puch ɜhab pocob ɛi vxe quehe ɜut vɜutu

23: nic ɛaɛal tepeɜual rumal ɜiche uinaɛ

24: chuach ronohel rahlabal xel ui ɜu apanoɛ

25: cuinimal = [1390]Roxmal chi ɜut labal Rah

Folio 12v

1: xqui4uxlah chic vukamaɛ tlecpan ta xqui
2: camiçah chi quitzih chirech qui4haquic chic e
3: kamam e kakahau balam 4itze balam aɛab
4: ¹⁴⁰⁰Mahucotah yqui balam = rumal vɛutaɛ
5: ɛih queatin ui ri ahcah ah4uix e kamam
6: kakahau = ta xecha chi 4ut vuɛamaɛ
7: xa ta quebeka4haca ¹⁴¹⁰chi miɛina chi catinabal
8: ma pa xa rumal maui caquil vuach yxoɛ
9: are 4u rumal ɛitzih e ɛaɛ e tepe xa ta 4ut que
10: kauik quekacauj vbic oxib hozɛilah alitō
11: ¹⁴²⁰vue ta pu chibe qui4ux chiquech chet4elax ta
12: 4ut v4ux tohil. auilis haɛauitz. chiquech
13: xa 4u cha vtz 4uicamiçaxic chux ɛumal
14: xecha 4ut ta xbanatah quitzih x4hiquitah 4ut:
15: vɛihil qui4haquic kamam ¹⁴³⁰kakahau cumal
16: vuɛamaɛ ahlabal = hutzu 4ut chi anim x
17: quetamah balam 4itze: ta quibic e atinel
18: pa miɛina: e chi 4u co chic oxib ¹⁴⁴⁰hozɛilah
19: ɛilah alitom pa miɛina ta xeopanic = hutzu
20: 4ut xepe ri alitom caniman allaɛ allaɛ ahauab
21: mi xujpe v4 allaɛ vj 4uitaɛon kakahau ohix cu4
22: ahauab Balam 4itze ¹⁴⁵⁰balam aɛab mahucotah
23: yqui balam: hey4habej vae naki chicah chi
24: ya chiquech vue pu chicah 4uix4ule cu4 quecha
25: e kakahau Rotzhayib: ¹⁴⁶⁰vxab: 4ibaha: bacah

Folio 13r

13

1: quebatzunha: xecha ϟut ɛapohib chiqueh ba

2: lam ϟitze: ta xechoɛobex ϟut vtz ba la yx ka

3: mial [1470]mi ba xekaϟhabeh ri ahauab mi puch

4: ɛil quivach quixcha ba apanoɛ chiquech yka

5: hau yx kamial xecha balam ϟitze Are ba ri

6: kataɛiquil [1480]Alak ahavab[869] chiϟama vloɛ retal

7: chi kitzih xeychabeh vue maui co retal

8: chul yvumal quixkacamiçah quixchoy chu

9: vach ha chuach çiuan [1490]quecha kakahau

10: chiɛech allaɛ ahauab toɛob ϟu kauach chiya ta allaɛ

11: retal chiɛe xecha ϟut ɛapohib = ta xquiϟulu

12: ba ϟut balam ϟitze [1500]chiueyebeh na chika

13: ya retal chiuech xevchax ϟut ɛapohib

14: ta quibic ϟut balam ϟitze chuach tohil: [1510]a

15: hilis: haɛauitz. at tohil auilis nakipa

16: retal vae tzih chikaya chiquech vae

17: ɛapohib quimial vuɛamaɛ xecha ϟut

18: tohil auilis chitzibah oxib ɛal [1520]chiya

19: chiquech: hun çital vpam hun ϟut ba

20: lam vpam: hun ϟut cot upan chiqui

21: ɛuvuh apanoɛ quikahau loɛobal que

22: xcha ϟut tohil: auilis. haɛauitz chique

23: [1530]balam ϟitze quehe cut vgibaxic oxbu

---

[869] This word appears to have been written with a different hand.

Folio 13v

1: oxbuçah chi ɛal cumal balam ɟitze xqui

2: ya vbic chiquech oxib ɛapohib quimial

3: vuɛamaɛ vae quibi [1540]ɛapohib: hun puch

4: hun tax. hũ ɟibatzunha: ta xcuɟaah

5: oxib tzibam ɟu lloɛobal rech quikahau

6: quequicot chic xebec — ta copanic ruɟ

7: quikahau nim xequicot ahauab chi

8: rech quiloɛxic [1550]rahaual vuɛamaɛ—

9: are ba vae cul huhun quech ykahau

10: quecha ahauab balam ɟitze xecha

11: chiquech quikahau = hutzu ɟut xu

12: ɟam vɛu [1560]ri hun chiquech are ri çital

13: vpam xucoh chirih hutzu ɟut xɟaztah

14: quivach chi çital xuti vtiohil ahau

15: xaui quehe ri cot vpam xɟaztah quivach

16: cot balam xeti cut ahauab rahaual

17: amaɛ [1570]makipa chi ɟaxɟol vae xbey

18: ɟama vloɛ vloɛ yx ɟaxtocanel xecha

19: chiquech quimial quehe ɟut vɛili

20: tahic labal ri cumal amaɛ [1580]chila ha

21: ɛauitz ɟhipaɛ vnimal vɛaɛal qui

Folio 14r

1: che quehe ƻut vƻutunic vɛaɛal vtepe
2: val ƻiche uinaɛ chuvach ronohel Rah
3: labal xel ui ƻu apanoɛ quinimal [1590]e kamā
4: kakahau Balam ƻitzɛ: balam aɛab. Mahu
5: cotah. yqui balam varal ƻut cheta
6: maz ui ɛaɛal tepeval xban haɛauitz ƻhipaɛ
7: [1600]chi vƻial may xquiban chiri haɛauitz————
8: ¶vae ƻut vnaohixic ahauarem cumal
9: balam ƻitze chui quiƻhacatahic vuɛamaɛ
10: Ta xecha xa ta ba chibe kaçamahel chi
11: la chuach ahau nacxic chi relebal ɛih
12: [1610]ma ta cohquiƻhac ri vakamaɛ ahlabal
13: ma ta pu cohquiçacho cohquimayh ma
14: ta pu chikah ɛaɛih kalaxic kabi kavach
15: ta ui chux apanoɛ xecha [1620]quehe ƻut qui
16: takic vbic e cayb vƻahol Balam ƻitze
17: vae ƻut quibi e cayb vƻahol balam ƻitze
18: ta xya quitakiquil vae ƻocayb. ƻoɛauib
19: ta xebe chi relibal ɛih e ƻama ahauarem
20: chi relibal ɛih [1630]hun xbe chiqueh chi reli
21: bal ɛih hun ƻut xbe chukahibal ɛih ƻocaib
22: xbe chi relibal ɛih = ƻoɛauib xbe chuk hibal
23: ɛih are ƻu ri ƻocayb huçu çuƻulic xbe chi re
24: libal ɛih are ƻu ri ƻoɛauib [1640]xa xtzalih vlo

Folio 14v

1: chi palo maui xɛax palo ta xtzalih vloɛ
2: xico ta xuȝhutinah vȝux ta xhoxou canoɛ
3: ruȝ rixnam rixokil ȝocayb ta xȝaholan ca
4: na ri balam ȝoɛauib = ȝola chi ȝu aȝal chi cu
5: çul [1650] ta xȝulun vtzihoxic cocayb ta xbeuȝa
6: ma muj ɛalibal: tziquil coj tziquil balam
7: ta xul puch: titil ɛan abah xbanatah xbe
8: ubana ȝocayb [1660] ta xul puch cogihabal puaɛ
9: . . . chi puach rech mama ahgalam rah
10: pop ahgalam utzam chinamital ȝate
11: . . . xcha chi ȝut ȝoɛauib ɛitzih ba chiyan mi xin
12: ban canoc xa ta quibehigaxoɛ chupam ri
13: ba [1670] xitzalih ui vloɛ rumal mi xpe ri aha
14: ȝocayb nakipa xchihachah ri aȝal xcha
15: ta xumalih vȝux are ȝu xquiban ri are
16: pu uheȝhbal rib cahauarem ri ri ȝute
17: retal [1680] rahauarem ȝocayb kitzih ui muh
18: ɛalibal coj balam vacachibal cotziha
19: bal puaɛ ȝut rech rahpop ahtzalam
20: utzam chinamital nabe chapel [1690] ta
21: ol vpe vuinaɛ chi vȝahol vchaɛ ka
22: çam ahȝhatam vlee nin ha çoc ba la vi
23: are ximonel are Rapanel tihoy [1700] vȝahol
24: vchaɛ ri mama ahgalam nabe xpe
25: ri queɛalem rumal ȝocayb vae ȝut x
26: ban chi chi haɛauitz xaui ba chiɛalajin apa
27: noɛ

Folio 15r

15

1: oxmul oxlahu vinaɛ xculun ui 4ocayb

2: ta xpe chi relibal ɛih [1710]4ola chi 4ut a4al chi

3: cuçul ta xulic Apachina ri a4al xcha

4: 4ut ahau 4ocayb chirech xoɛohau he xaui

5: ba tiohil la tzumal la xaui pu atz la

6: chaɛ la [1720]ahchoɛe xcha 4ut yxoɛ noj ba

7: ba la maba xchivixovah tah ma pu

8: xchivitzelbih tah xaui ba chinya rahaua

9: rem xaui pu chinya vɛaɛal vtepeval

10: xcha 4ut 4ocayb ta xu4ono4a vuach [1730]cu

11: çul are ba vae alla balam 4onache chu

12: chaxic chibe ɛih chibe çak xcha 4ut 4o

13: cayb quehe 4ut rulic nabe ahauarem

14: ri rumal [1740]4ocayb ta x4aholā canoɛ 4oɛa

15: uib chirih rixnam quehe 4ut vuinaɛi

16: Ric bi ri chi 4onache riztayul ahau cu

17: chax vacamic quehe puch vuinakiric

18: ahpo 4amhayil ri vcab ahauarem ahau

19: ztaiul chuchaxic are cu ri nabe ahau

20: [1750]4ocayb v4ahol balam 4itze ri ajau

21: ahpop cauɛɛ——xchita chi 4u allaɛ vçu

22: 4uliquil xchicholotahic xchinloɛbij 4ut

23: qui4oheic xchingibaj cut [1760]yn Die4o rey

24: noso popol uinaɛ ¶ v4ahol lahu noj

25: ARe chi 4ut xchikatiquiba chic vbixic

Folio 15v

1: vae quibic chic e oxib naval uinaɛ chuca

2: mul chic ta xebe chic chi relibal ɛih vae

3: ^{1770}quibi: ɜocaib. ɜoɛauib. ɜoacul acutaɛ —

4: Ri xebec chi relibal ɛih chuach ahau nacxic

5: e ɜamol rech ahauarem ^{1780}ɛalibal coh ɛali

6: bal balam: çucbaɛ cham cham rahauarem

7: ahau ahpop ahpo ɜamha: ɛalel atzih uinaɛ

8: ta xbe ri nim ɜhoɛoh caueɛ ^{1790}xa ɜhocohil tem

9: xuxic maui xubih tzoɜotz nimaɛ ahme

10: va ɜaxcol maui cahauarem tah xbequiɜa

11: ma quitaɛiquil rumal ahau balan ɜitze

12: ta xepam chuach ahau naɛxic ^{1800}xquitzonoh

13: ɜut quitakiquil chirech ahau naɛxic

14: ta xmolobax ɜu vloɛ ahauarem chiquech

15: rumal ahau nacxic ta xetzalih vloɛ ri ɜo

16: cayb ɜoɛauib. ruɜ nim ɜhocoh caueɛ ^{1810}ta cu

17: lic ɜut xquimoloba ɜut quitakiquil xba

18: natah xkabano xpe vae ahauarem

19: retal xpetic xecha ta xquimoloba ^{1820}quita

20: kiquil maui xquibiih tzoɜotz nimaɛ

21: ahgiçomcha. ahcuɜumam ɜaam

22: beleh uinaɛ oxlahu vinaɛ chi meva

23: chi ɜaxɜol ^{1830}vɜaxɜol ahauarem ta x

24: quimoloba chirech balam ɜonache vae

25: muhiɛuɛ muhiraxon ɛalibal coh ɛali

Folio 16r

16

1: bal balam çubaɛ cham cham [1840]tatil ɛan abah

2: holom pich queh tziquil vil cot tziquil balā

3: ttoot mattacuz chiyom ahtapulul [1850]he ꝗuch

4: macutax: malili nacatabah retal a

5: hauarem chila xnuꝗ ui vloɛ chi relibal ɛih

6: chiquech çamahel are ta quechapoɛ aha

7: vab quehe retal [1860]va xevchax çamahel

8: Aare ri ahau ahpop cahib muh pa vui hū

9: vɛalibal: ꝗo vraxon ri ahçubaɛ ahcham chā

10: [1870]Are ꝗu ri ahpo ꝗamha oxib[870] vmuh pa vui

11: Are ꝗu ri nima Rahop achih: cayb vmuh

12: pa vui Are ꝗu ri ꝗhuti Rajpop achih [1880]hū

13: vmuh pa vui pa xicaha chi chap ui ma na

14: ꝗo ta vçubaɛ ucham chan rumal ꝗal

15: ꝗaholaxel ri ꝗute cahauarem ahauab

16: ta xulic [1890]xpe chi relibal ɛih xa hunulic

17: ahauarem ta xulic. ɛalelai tem atzih ui

18: nakil tem nim ꝗhocohil tem ɛale ꝗam

19: jayl tem nima ꝗamhayil tem cahib

20: ahtohil oxib ꝗhocohib oxib vtzā pop

21: [1900]oxib yacol ha ꝗi ꝗut pop ꝗamha chirih ꝗiche

22: // quehe ꝗut rech ahau ꝗiche ta rulic

---

[870] It appears that the scribe originally wrote *cajib* ("four") and changed it to *oxib* ("three").

Folio 16v

1: atzih uinakil tem e lolmed ahau // nim

2: 4hocoh ahau // ahau haεauitz Rech ahau

3: 4iche xa oxib chi nimaε 4hocohib [1910]alay

4: tem xaui rach chapic vpop v4amha a

5: hauab xaui chi relibal εih xpe ui vbina

6: tiçaxic 4iche ahauarem 4iche pop 4i

7: che 4amha [1920]ahaual vinaε ————

8: mi 4ut. xcube v4ux balam 4itze Balā

9: aεab Mahucotah yqui balam mi xviki

10: tah ahauarem cumal [1930]e qui4ahol chui

11: huyub haεauitz 4hipaε — vacamic 4ut

12: xchita chi allaε vae qui4ax4ol kamā

13: kakahau chi meva chi 4ax4ol xe4ohe chui

14: juyu [1940]haεauitz Balam 4itze vae kamā

15: oh caueεib varal 4ut mi xtiquel ui v4aho

16: lanic balam 4itze = balam aεab Mahu

17: cotah: [1950]are 4u yqui ballam xcam chupā v4a

18: holal vae 4ute v4ahol balam 4itze vae

19: vnabe 4ahol = 4o4oha: 4oraxonamaε qui

20: bi e cayb v4ahol balam 4itze = xe4aholan

21: chi 4u ri 4o4oha: 4oraxonamaε = [1960]e tzin

22: chi 4ut xqui4aholah = xe4aholan chi 4u ri tzi

23: quin

Folio 17r

1: ahcan chi4ut quibi xqui4aholah = [1970]vcah
2: le vuinaɛ = 5 Role uinaɛ 4ut vae 4ocayb
3: 4oɛauib // xqui4aholah goca ahcan Role
4: uinaɛ = ¶ hoob 4vtt xu4ahola 4ocayb
5: [1980]quehnay. 4oyoy // xmaiqueh // chocoy ——
6: r laɛamal ri xu4aholah 4ocayb ———
7: // are 4ut 4oɛauib 4onache xu4aholah
8: [1990]hosbal al tzipitavar vbi rixokil
9: xvaɛleok 4aholax. ta xic ta xbe4amoɛ
10: ahauarem chi relibal ɛih
11: vae 4ut quipixabaxic Balam 4itze [2000]balam
12: aɛab cumal tohil auiliz haɛauitz yx aha
13: vacob xa z4akin chic maui chiçakiric chi
14: na 4u yuib cuhyueleçah ta varal [2010]ru
15: mal toɛob yvach chux apanoɛ cohyia
16: ta chupam evam 4echelah chiri 4ut coh
17: ychabej ui rumal cape nima çaɛ cape
18: pu ɛih y4 4humil [2020]vh ta 4uteuachim chic
19: yvumal xcha ri tohil chiquech Bala
20: lam 4itze balam aɛab majucotaj

Folio 17v

1: yqui balam ta xunimah ꜱut balam ꜱitze

2: [2030]xbe ri tohil chupam hun nima ꜱechelaj

3: jutzu xubinaj ri ꜱechelaj patohil e ꜱo ui

4: 6 ꜱula ui cot ꜱula ui balam ꜱula ui çochoh

5: ꜱula ui ꜱanti xcohe ui vꜱabauil Balam

6: ꜱitze = [2040]Are ꜱut rech balam aꜱab xbe

7: pa auilis pa evam ꜱachelah = are ꜱu rech

8: Mahucotah xaui chiri xꜱohe ui chui huyub

9: haꜱauitz xaui ꜱo chiri ta xçakiric —— [2050]quehe

10: ꜱut xequiçot ui xaki xqueyebeh chi vçaki

11: ric chila chui huyub haꜱauitz hunelic x

12: xꜱi xe chvach chi relibal ꜱih chireyebe

13: xic vçakiric —— ta vçakiric ꜱu — nabe

14: xel vloꜱ ri nima ꜱhumil ꜱamol vbe ꜱih

15: [2060]ꜱate ꜱut relic vla ꜱih xçakir ꜱut ta xe

16: oꜱ ꜱut giꜱuin are nabe ri ahpop ꜱeletza ꜱa

17: chiri ꜱut xquil ui ꜱih çaꜱ chui huyub haꜱa

18: vitz = ꜱate ꜱu ri ta xequicotic xeꜱamo

19: vanic [2070]xebixanic ꜱate pu ri ta xquiquir

20: quipam xare ui xquixim vloꜱ quipam chi

21: relibal ꜱih ta xepetic ral maylo qui

Folio 18r

1: petic ta xeɜamovan ɜut ta xquihaɛ ɜut

2: quipom quicamovabal Balam ɜitze: caçiuaz

3: tan [2080]vpom // Balam aɛab: miztan pon re

4: mahucotah ɜabauil pom rech — ta xquipo

5: roh camul ɜamo oxmul ɜamo at gakol at bi

6: to [2090]at ɜu vniɜahal cah vleu at cah tzuc

7: cah xuɜut ɜamo mi xɛih ri vçakiric upa

8: catahic mi xɛil ɛih mi xɛil ɜhumil = at

9: ɜut at kahuyubal [2100]tulan çeuan ɛanallaj

10: huyub raxalah huyub xecha ta xquiporoh ri

11: quipom are ɜu ri vçibel quipom çuɜulic

12: xbe chicah nabe ta xçuɜmayh ɜu vuach

13: [2110]xbe chi relibal ɛih rumal aretal xopā

14: chupam quihuyubal xopam puch roɛeh

15: quiɜux chuach ahau naɛxic rumal xe

16: cha xa ta hū mi xɛil ui ɛih çak yvuɜ yx ɛuɜ

17: katzab [2120]katz kachaɛ tlecpā yx ɜo cana chi ɛa

18: huyubal chi kataɛahal xecha roɛeh

19: quiɜux e ɛamā kak.hau ta xquil vçaki

20: ric ta xeɜamovā [2130]cot çak ɜut xquiça

21: quib chui tak che huyub vae ɜut vça

22: kiric quicaxcol e kamam ɛakahau——

Folio 18v

1: vae ɜute quipixab chiquech quiɜahol chui
2: vcakiric[871][2140]yx kaɜahol mi xixgakatic mi
3: pu xixpoɛotahic chiɜama ɜu vae piçon ɜa
4: ɜal ɜolo ui na chi choconic maha cakariɛ
5: kahuyubal chiban ui ɛaɛal tepeual [2150]ɜa
6: chiri ɜut chihakatah ui ri retal ahauarē
7: xpe chi relibal ɛih chiɜaholah chi na ri ah
8: pop ahpo ɜamha ɛalel atzih uinaɛ chiba
9: nou ɛaɛal tepeɜual chux apanoɛ rumal
10: cohcamic [2160]cojçachic cohbec cohtzalilic
11: mi xixkaya canoɛ pa vtzil mahi chic labal
12: cumal vuɛamaɛ ahlabal mixbiçon ɜut
13: chiuila ychuch xecha maui e yavab tah ta x
14: xepixabic [2170]vtz quivach ta xoɛ aɛab = are
15: chi ɜut ta xçakiric e chi ɜut ~~yava~~ Mahi chic
16: xa ɜa et xeçachic = ma ta ɜu chiçach vɜux
17: chitaou vae tzih xaui ki are balan ɜitze yqui
18: binah quiɜahol: balam aɛab [2180]mahucotah yqui
19: balam xevchax chic chupam vcaɛiric e ɜu ɜi
20: chic quimam quiɜahol chi caveɛ chi nihayi . . .
21: chi ahau ɜiche ta xbinah ri huyub [2190]çaɛiri
22: bal tohil rech cauɛɛ çakiribal auilis
23: ta roɛotaxic nabe tinamit ɛaɛaui . . .

---

[871] The manuscript reads *vcakirik*, scribal error for vçakiric. The same error appears in line 19.

Folio 19r

1: rech nihayib: çakiribal haɛauitz rech ahau
2: ꝗiche———quech tamub çakiribal maɛtan
3: quech caɛoh eɛomaɛ———caɛiribal ahu
4: ꝗin [2200]quech ylocab çiꝗaab Juaniha———
5: // xa ꝗu hun xeꝗohe chi ui patohil cuꝗ niha
6: yib ɛi xubinaah ꝗhaka ha cauɛɛ chaɛa ha
7: nihayib xecha retvach quitzih hunam
8: xquiban quitzaɛ———[2210]nabe çakiri
9: 2 xcoɛotah chi ꝗu ri tohil vcab tinamit ta xe
10: opan chi ꝗu çibakiha nah quiban chiri xaui
11: queɛam ri piçō ꝗaꝗal retal ahauarem xpe
12: chi relibal ɛih chi maui va chi maui ha ta
13: xeopan chi cac [2220]chivayh
14: 3 = ros tinamit chivayh nima cabal xqui
15: bā chiri xquicotoh vcok vuach taɛ che
16: abah chivaya chicakih chi———
17: 4 vcah tinamit [2230]pa caha xehoyan xaɛan chi
18: ui quigak chiri nah xquiban chiri———
19: 5. ro tinamit———
20: 6: vuaɛaɛ tinamit barabic chun bokota
21: hinaɛ çanay lo—nah chi ui xquiban chiri
22: [2240]7 vuɛ tinamit panhilil pangocon nah
23: xquiban chiri xa ral vonon çital xquechah
24: xquiloo xa vꝗatibal che xc . . .
25: vahuij ui caɛix alRah

Folio 19v

1: 8 vuahxaɛ ttinamit vae ticah ꝗhalib [2250]xaɛã

2: chi ui quitzaɛ chiri xa ui cuꝗam ri retal aha

3: varem xpe chi relibal ɛih chi meva chi ꝗaxcol

4: 9. vbelej tinamit tibatzi rahauiche xaɛan

5: chi ui quigak chir [2260]chiri xtiquer ui caɛiɛ ta x

6: quicayih vui çoɛoh vꝗin lae lae xecha

7: 10 vlahuh tinamit hobalam ɛana vleu

8: vbi huyub xeyꝗou vi xaui xemayin chiri

9: [2270]11 vhulah tinamit chi vaan chi ɛaɛ qui

10: vbi huyub xeꝗohe chi ui xaui xemayin chiri

11: 12 ucablah tinamit vae xeꝗhayab ximba

12: xuc xaui quekam ri retal ahauarem xpe

13: chi relibal ɛih [2280]chivayh chichakih chi xeꝗohe

14: 13 roxlah tinamit vae ta xopan gutuha

15: ꝗa chiri ꝗute xquicanabeq ui jũ ahau gu

16: tuha ta xriɛitah payo pabaɛoh cuban

17: roɛibal çaɛcorovach [2290]ta xquita balã

18: aɛab balam ꝗi mahucotah ta xoc cu pa

19: xuc ta xcanabexic ta xꝗhau ꝗut ma ta

20: quinivuchah yx ahauab ma ta quini

21: camiçah [2300]xcha xuchax ꝗut apa catuxic yn

22: ba tzutuha quinuchaxic xcha ꝗut xa ta ba

23: yn yvahil ytzakat chuxic xcha ꝗut ki

24: tzih pa la cabih vtz ba la quehe chuxic

25: at ta [2310]vlaɛel nuach nutzij puch chuxic xecha

26: balam ꝗitze chirech gutuha at vuꝗaxel

27: kahau yqui balam chuxic xuchax

Folio 20r

20

1: 4ut quehe 4ut riɛitahic [2320]ahau tzutuha ri
2: ri çakic v4aaut 4ut mahucotaj xuxic v4a
3: xel yɛui balam xuxic ri xcam chupam v4aho
4: lal quehe 4ut vgakatic cahib nabe ui u ri
5: xpe [2330]chi relibal ɛih quehe 4ut vbinatiça
6: xic chiçakic ahau 4iche 4a chiri xcam ui pa
7: gutuha ma ta chiçach v4uxlal cumal ka
8: 4ahol kaman xaui chiri xquiçiqui hun abah
9: [2340]xqui4abauilah 4ual abah vcab 4u ri xpe
10: chi relibal ɛih xgakat 4ut cayb 4ual chiri
11: gutuha nah xquiban chir
12: 14 vcahlah tinamit vae 4ut ube chiv4abal
13: xaui xaɛan cochoch chiri xemayn chi ui
14: chiri xaui cu4am ri retal ahauaren [2350]xpe relibal ɛih
15: 15 Rolah tinamit vae yamucutu raxah
16: mah xquiban chiri xa tum xa ral vonō
17: xa ral çital caquechaah e kamā kakahau
18: [2360]16 vuaklah tinamit vae chitsaɛeb chiya
19: qui xeyaluj chi 4u chiri xquiban chi chiri
20: quigak quicoxtun chi nima 4ax4ol xe4ohe
21: ui huvuɛ ɛih chiquiɛumeh yxim chicube 4u
22: qui4ux chiri [2370]xaki hun quivach cauɛɛ nihayib
23: 17 vuɛlah tinamit vae ɛalemial cucurabah
24: xaui xeyaluh chi chiri xemolomanic xe4hiho
25: manic pa çiuan pa 4echelah [2380]chi vayh chi cha
26: ɛih chi ——

Folio 20v

1: 18 vuahxaklah tinamit vae pa che chi ɛohom
2: vbi huyab xe4ohe ui nah chi 4u xquiban chiri
3: e ɛamam e kaɛahau balam aɛab balam 4itze
4: [2390]mahutah Bi e ahquix e ahcah ——————
5: 19 vbelelah tinamit vae chi4abauilanic 4a chiri
6: 4ut xqui4abauilah ui ri abah cual xpe chi re
7: libal ɛih ta xeheke chi 4u chiri xquiban chi ui qui
8: gak chiri xaui cu4am quib chi cauɛɛ [2400]chi nihayib

9: chi ahau 4iche ri Balam 4itze balam aɛab ma

10: hucotah xaui 4u cachbilam chi ri tzutuha v4e

11: xevach chi yqui balam = chiri 4ut xquitiqui

12: ba ui [2410]tzucun maçat are 4u ri vqui4el xqui

13: ya chuach 4abauil tohil 4a chiri 4ut xquiti

14: quiba ui 4abauilanic chi 4ix chi 4hat quetahin

15: 4ut e pilol rech ri maçat chua ha ta xey

16: 4ou cayb 4echelahil uinaɛ [2420]xaui are cu4 vuɛ

17: amaɛ hutzu 4ut xecha nakipa ri quipilo vue xa

18: ɛu4 katzab queypilo xecha 4u canoɛ vuɛamaɛ

19: quehe chi 4ut vnu4ic chiri labal cumal amaɛ

20: 4u varal chic xquicut ui quib xare ui xquitih

21: tobeh labal chila haɛauitz hutzu 4ut xqui4ux

22: lah labal vae ah4alaɛā [2430]ahtibilcat xul chi

23: 4u hun chic vɛuvm vxiquin 4a toɛol vxiquin

24: chuɛul rakan nicvachinel 4u ri chirech quica

25: miçaxic e ɛamam e ɛakahau hutzu 4u xnatah

Folio 21r

21

1: chiquech kamā kakahau are e 4o chiri chi 4ix [2440]chi 4hat

2: 4a chiri 4ut xril ui labal ri ahau gutuha çakic

3: mahi xril labal haɛauitz hutzu 4ut xetereni

4: bex vbic ri çamahel vtz ba la cohcamoɛ xe

5: cha ɛaman [2450]ɛaɛahau ta quibic 4ut oyeu achih

6: e ylol quech ri ahlabal apa 4o ui 4ochoch ta xil 4ut

7: chui huyub are xubinah ui muɛbaçib ta tobob

8: quiçib tahquil apanoɛ oyeu achih e çonolic

9: [2460]e 4hanalic ahmeva ah4ax4ol xa 4ut xquicut

10: quipuz quipuz quinaval chui ri huyub muɛbaçib

11: xquiçi4ih cakiɛ caɛ çut cumcaboch [2470]caɛulha

12: ɛeteb pubayx chir paquivui vuɛamaɛ ahla

13: bal xa xma 4o ui labal xquibano xa loɛ xqui4ux

14: laah labal ri: ah4alakan ahtibilcat xa quehe xux

15: e vuɛamaɛ [2480]ahlabal ——————————————

16: 20 vhuinaɛ tinamit vae ta xeopan chic humet

17: taha vtuquel humet cochoch xquibano

18: xaui 4abauilanic xquibano çaɛul xa yahom

19: 4ox xa ral giquin [2490]xquiya chuach 4abauil xaui

20: nima 4ax4ol xe4ohe ui xemolomanic xe4hi

21: homanic pa taɛ quechelah xaui cu4aam ri

22: tohil auilis [2500]haɛauitz ru4 ri piçon 4a4al ri Re

23: tal ahauarem xpe chi relibal ɛih ——————

24: 21 vhuinaɛ hun tinamit vae [2510]4ulba cauinal

25: xaɛan chi ui quitzaɛ chiri 4ulba cauinal

26: chiri 4ute xqui4ul ui quib ru4 aɛaab lal ɛa

Folio 21v

1: mam lal kakahau lal kaui lal kaholom xcha

2: ahaɛaab chiquech e kamam e kakahau balam

3: ʒitze [2520]balam aɛab mahucotah ruʒ ahau çakic

4: gutuha vʒexevach yqui balam xquiya qui

5: çip quimayh chuach quiʒabauil xa ral tolob

6: xa ral cuyuʒh xquiya chuach quiʒabauil chi

7: ri culba cauinal —————

8: [2530]22 vhuinaɛ cayb tinamit vae ta culic varal

9: chi yzmachi ʒa varal ʒut xɛah ui hu le chun

10: chiri chi yzmachi ʒiarinaɛ chi ʒut ʒahola

11: xel vʒahol ahau vmā ahau atz chaɛ [2540]chi

12: rih ahau Balam ʒitze ʒiarinaɛ chic ral vʒa

13: hol caueɛib = xaui quehe balam aɛab xaui

14: ʒiarinaka ri ral vʒahol nihayib = xaui ma

15: . . . cotah xaui e ʒiarinaɛ chi [2550]vʒahol ri ahau ʒi

16: che ʒa varal ʒut xchivachin ui zʒakin aha

17: uarem —————

18: ¶ ʒate ʒut vbanic chapanic chiri chi yzmachi

19: nabe chaponic ta xchap ahau ʒotuha chi ahaua

20: rem ahpop xuxic vʒahol balam ʒikab —— [2560]xaui.

21: quehe chic ahpo ʒamha: ztayul hū chi ahau

22: vʒahol ʒonache ri xoc chi ahpo ʒamhayil vae

23: ʒute xchiɛacholo quiʒaholaxic cakimos ztayul

24: ¶ vae chi ʒute vcholic ahauarem pa ʒiche chi y-

25: machi: vae vcholic ahauarem eɛalen puch

Folio 22r

1: ²⁵⁷⁰¶ahpop ꝝikabi uinaꜩ ¶ ahpop ꝝamha zta
2: yul ꝝonache = ¶ Nima Rahop achih ¶ ꝝhuti
3: Rahop achih ¶ chiꜩauach oh caueꜩib
4: ¶ ahau vtzam pop ¶ ahau laꜩpop ²⁵⁸⁰¶ ahau
5: ahau vchuch ꝝamha ¶ ahau nima lolmet
6: = Rahaual ꝝikabil vinaꜩ cauekibab hui vae
7: ¶ ahauab pop ꝝamha: e alay tem ꝝut vae
8: ꝝute quibi ahpop alomab alay tem caue
9: ꜩib alay tem chiquih ahauab

10a: ─────────────

10: ²⁵⁹⁰vꜩalel alomab nihayib = nim ꝝhocoh alomab
11: ahau ꝝiche = vuachibalal = xa oxib ninha xuxic

11b: ─────────────

12: ¶ Da xoc ꝝut ahau ꜩalel nihayib ¶ ahau atzih uinaꜩ
13: ¶ahau ꜩale ꝝamha ¶ nima ꝝanha ²⁶⁰⁰¶vchuch ꝝamha
14: ¶ hulahuh tem ¶ahauilis ¶ metaçanic ¶ çaꜩlatol
15: e nihayibab = ¶ ahau ꝝiche ꝝu vae ¶ atzih uinaꜩ ahau
16: ¶ nim ꝝhocoh ahau ¶ ahau lolmet ²⁶¹⁰¶ ahau haꜩa

17: uitz ─────────────────

18: Ri ꝝute quichapobal xpe relibal ꜩih xpe
19: puch ꝝhaka cho chaka palo # buz ꜩaxeō
20: rixcaꜩ cot rixcaꜩ balam # holop ²⁶²⁰pix
21: queh # çubaꜩ cham cham # nima tzu

Folio 22v

1: tziquil cot tziquil balam # ttott mata cuz # he
2: queh: macutax # [2630]chiiom aztapulul # malili
3: tatil ɛan abah retal ahauarem voric ɟakic
4: xpe [2640]relebal ɛih: nanacat abah: beleheb chu
5: ɟoheyc rech ahpop ahpo ɟamhail cahib muh
6: oxib muh: cayb muh: hun muh chi ɛuɛ [2650]chi
7: raxon: chi ɟubul: chi chalDit: heque cama
8: chal: tubɛaɛ tauizcal: camul beleh cal: ox
9: mul beleh ɟal: chi ɛecha chi tunūcha———
10: ¶ ARe ɟu ri cahib [2660]alomiab: yboy ɟharab vuachi
11: bal quiɟhamiy ta quechapanic: ¶ Ri ɟute xbā
12: chi ysmachi ta xban chaponic ta xban chuti
13: ɛaɛal tepeual taɛqui chuxe [2670]xa oxib nimha xa[872]
14: xic xare yɟu xchap ri xɛob puch xa ɟa chutinoɛ
15: ɟa varal chi ysmachi haɛatah ui vae retal
16: ahauarem ri xbevɟama [2680]ɟocayb ɟa e ɟola chi
17: la haɛauitz nabe tinamit xaui pu ma na que
18: he xban chi ɟix chi ɟhat xa ki labal xban oher
19: haɛauitz nabe labal [2690]vcamul labal chi ɟix chi
20: ɟhat xare ui huyub ri xban vi puz naual
21: chi rox ɟut vae chi ysmachi—varal
22: ɟut xeɟamovan ui [2700]chi ysmachi at cah
23: vleu at pu gakol bitol chaya ta ka
24: mial kaɟahol chaya vxer vebal

---

[872] The manuscript reads *xaxic*, scribal error for *xuxic*.

Folio 23r

1: vꜫabal chiꜫe at pa chaꜫa cho [2710]chaꜫa palo at vpã
2: cah at relibal ꜫih at raꜫanibal ꜫih cha
3: ya`ta kaꜫih ꜫaçack xecha at nima chumil ꜫꜫo
4: ꜫih xecha # xquiya quipom [2720]tziquin ral aꜫ
5: xquiya ri uinaꜫ chuach tohil varal chiyzma
6: chi varal xquixah ui hunahpu ꜫoy vuꜫub
7: cakix ta xquitiquiba ruꜫaxic che quicab qui xe
8: ꜫabaric xeekaxic xquiçipah quimial chiqui
9: bil quib quimial [2730]eꜫabal quech e vꜫal qui xqui
10: çipah chirech meba ahꜫakoval xa xbeyaoꜫ
11: chi rochoch mi xuhloꜫonic mi xuhmayhanic
12: xecha xa hū ꜫebal chi çaka xa hū tol chi matuh
13: oh xa pu hu tiꜫab chi tzucurüm vuꜫ [2740]puch hun
14: peral chi ra huyubal aꜫ hū tol cu chi ua çuban
15: pa xaꜫ ꜫanaꜫ pa xaꜫ cub rahil quimial xqui
16: bano chiri xban ui chi ysmachi ———
17: ¶ xaüi ꜫut cachbilam quib oxib amaꜫ chi ꜫiche
18: tamub [2750]ylocab cakahib xa zꜫataꜫ quixol
19: xaui hunam xepꜫ chi relibal ꜫih tulan çeuã
20: ri ꜫute xban chi ysmachi maha bioꜫ pom
21: [2760]quiꜫ alaçi pō alaçi quiꜫ holomax raxtunim
22: ꜫatoh maha bioꜫ canab teleche maha bioꜫ vchuch
23: giquin [2770]xco cakix mahaha bioꜫ ¶ nima ꜫatoh
24: mahaha bioꜫ poꜫob chanal xa ꜫa vꜫhutinal
25: oꜫ ꜫolic ———

Folio 23v

1: ɜolic xa ɜal xam xeɜaxtoɜaxic chuçiɜixic che
2: abah e nabe uinaɛ [2780]huinaɛ cayb chi tinamit chi
3: huyub xeyɜo ui vloɛ ————
4: vae ɜut quichapic ahtzalamib vue puch ɛana
5: mama ɛana tata quekalen ri ta xmolobax chi
6: queh ri queɛalen ri xbevɜama ɜocayb nabe
7: ri cotzihabal puach çochi puaɛ [2790]ruɜ ri vachi
8: bal ɜhamiy ri yboy ɜharab quichapabal chi
9: chirech ahpop ahpo ɜamha ɛalel atzih uinaɛ
10: xa zɜakina chic xaui xmobax rech rahpop
11: ahɜalam reɛalen ivachibal cotzihabal
12: puaɛ ɜut rech rahpop ahgalam [2800]vtzam chi
13: namital nabe chapel nabe vlel rahauarē
14: chila haɛauitz xkabih canoɛ taol vpe vuinaɛ
15: chi vɜahol vchaɛ kaçam ɜhatam vleu nim
16: ha [2810]çocbaqui are Rapanel ximonel tihoy
17: vɜahol vchaɛ çakitoɛ çak vɜa queh ɜaz
18: tabal vuach ɜahol ɛapoj [2820]cah ɜalah chi tuh
19: chi xiɜay cahim muchum tih xaui cut horo
20: nalah ha lemo ɛebun muchuchen atiniba
21: çel atinibal cucub [2830]ɜaztabal vuach ɛa
22: hol tzih quehe vtzih ahau naɛxic chire
23: ahau ɜocayb xaui ɜut are quebanou tzih
24: chirij ɛalel ahpop vɛalechih [2840]rahpop achi
25: maui xa et chiya ahauarem chiquech are
    26: xcha cocayb

Folio 24r

1: ¶ Are 4ut cahauar ahau 4otuha chi ysmachi
2: yzmachi xa xevtaε cayb çamahel chila chu
3: pam quihuyubal malah uinaε oxhix chila
4: pa malah chivu4aah vmul [2850]çakcorovach chi
5: ya chiri chui mul ba cul ui oyeu achih rech malah
6: xcha ahau 4otuha = chiueuah 4u yuib mi4ut yuib
7: xevchax çamahel rumal 4otuha v4exvach
8: tzonoh [2860]are 4u ri vmul giquin 4amom chic ta
9: xeopanic = εuε chi 4o canoε v4axel ri vmul
10: giquin] chi cahmul xquiban [2870]quibanno quehe vae
11: chucahmul 4ut ta xeylou quivach çamahel
12: ¶ xcha 4ut vçamahel malaj naεipa at uxic ma
13: at on vçamahel εucumatz 4otuha xcha 4ut
14: [2880]¶ yn yba l|a vçamahel εucumatz 4otuha xcha
15: 4ut ta xachbilax 4u vbic vçamahel quiche —
16: ta xopan 4ut chuach malah uinaε ¶ ta xpe 4ut
17: ru4ia çamahel [2890]huti4ab cakvuach huti4ab ça
18: εi εutum: xcha 4ut ahau malah naεipa carah
19: εuεumatz xitao xcha // xa ba 4ulalem carah
20: xcha 4ut çamahel ¶ mi ba xinta ri vtzih εucu
21: matz 4otuha xcha 4u ahau malah = [2900]ta vya
22: yc uloε çaki εutum rax ho4on Retal nutzih
23: chul4ama ri alit chipe 4amol re xcha malah
24: ta vbic 4ut cahib pop 4amha 4amol re vmi
25: al malah uinaε xcu4ah 4u vbi vae

Folio 24v

1: ɛanaab: [2910]cakapop: patachion val xahab

2: xcuȝaah ta xebec ta vpetic quimial ma

3: lah vinaɛ ta rulic ȝut [2920]chiri pa quiche

4: chi ysmachi xlem vbi yxoɛ ta xulic // moca

5: ni chi cut xubinaah poz chi xubinaah:

6: cayb vtut rachbel ahpata chirih [2930]quehe

7: ȝu vpetic vae ta xpeti – quimial ma

8: lah vinaɛ quehe ȝu roquibexic ri ma

9: vi chi labal tah tah xa xhiax apanoɛ

10: ahau ɛucumatz ȝohtuha chila ta v

11: petic ȝut xamal ton peɛ xamal ton caco

12: çaki pacay çaki boxom [2940]rixȝak ba çakton

13: yc çehebam chom canteel ȝiquin caby i

14: bote xȝulun ruȝ ɛucumatz ȝotuha————

15: quehe ȝut vȝuleyc ɛucumatz ȝotuja ri

16: ruȝ quimial malah uinac gutuhil————

17: [2950]¶ x ȝu quehe coponic ahxetulul ri ruȝ ah

18: yatza ¶ ahȝuque ¶ lakamcuc ¶ mama cot

19: mama çaquipat ¶ vancoh yabacot————

20: ¶ ahȝakol queh # ri ȝute hoob chi uinaɛ

21: [2960]nabe uinaɛ xoquiben huyub taɛah malah

22: gutuh ta xȝhacatah malah gutuhil uinaɛ

23: ta xȝiah vȝut al [2970]ȝahol chiquih chiquihuhunal

24: ¶ ta vbanic ȝut labal cumal oliah chi ȝiche

25: vinaɛ ral vȝahol ɛucumatz

Folio 25r

1: ꜩotuha ta xquiꜩulelaah aqui vinaε ahgiqui

2: naha xa vhe cuc ^{2980}xquilaεamih xquikaçabeh

3: quech yaqui ahgiquinaha ¶ ta vximitahic

4: ꜩu vloε cayb cachihilal yaqui = velpan vbi

5: xucutzin vbi = ta vpetic ꜩut chuach ahau εu

6: cumatz ꜩotuha = ta culic ꜩut oyeu achih ^{2990}chiyz

7: machi mi xuhꜩulunic mi xεaεaçah quiεih cala

8: xic ahvua cho ahvua palo vae mi xεaxim v

9: loε vue ꜩut ꜩo chupatanih chiech la lal ahau

10: ^{3000}εucumatz cotuha xecha ꜩut oyiu achih ta xe

11: vlic: vtz mi xibano yx koyeval yx kachihilal

12: et ba la vyayc chiuech yεaεal ytepeval xcha

13: ꜩut ahau εucumatz ꜩotuha chiquech———

14: ¶ ta vꜩuxlaxic ꜩut ^{3010}cumal ahauab εucumatz

15: ꜩotuha ruꜩ ahau ztayul ta xquiban quitzih

16: xa ta ba chiban kahauarem chila pa malah

17: cumal kachibal kavachibal chibe tah εaça

18: mahel ^{3020}quebe ta chapoε chibe tah hubotah chi

19: guvm balam hubotah chi cha chibe pu quitzo

20: ꜩotz quilakam chicamiçabex quech ri ahvua

21: cho palo vua palo chikaçabex pu quemerib

22: ahgiquinaha quehe ꜩu roquic quiεalelal ^{3030}cah

23: popol ri varal xel ui quekalen ri ahxetu

24: lul ri ah xsan min cuchax vacamic

25: vcamul chi ꜩut ta xechap ri: vanacoh yaba

26: coh εinom . . . unati iiz ^{3040}oliaah orem ahxe

27: raεan peε caco obotaj cha

Folio 25v

1: are uquilaɛam obotah xya rumal ahau ɛucu

2: matz ɟotuha rachbil quitzol quigununche ³⁰⁵⁰qui

3: chab quipocob quehe ɟut vbanic chaponic ri

4: utiqueric varal xel ui pa ɟiche chi ysmachi rū

5: ahau ɟotuha ɛucumatz rumal puch ztayul

6: ahau ahpop ahpo ɟamha ³⁰⁶⁰quehe ɟu relic vbic ɛale

7: lal ahpopol ri: hob ɛalel hob ahpop hob vɛa

8: le chila hoob rahpop achih = xa ɟu quehe vtique

9: ric chaponic ri allaɛ ɛamam ɛahol ³⁰⁷⁰ta xeb ahpo

10: alomab e chaponel alay tem ruɟ mama ahgalam

11: ri ɟute xban chizmachi ɟia may xquiban chiri

12: chi ysmachi oxib nimaɛ chū ɛaɛcab ³⁰⁸⁰xquiban chi

13: ri chi ysmachi rah ɟut vinaɛir quiɟhaoh aha

14: uab chiri pa ɟiche chiizmachi cumal cayb pop

15: ɟamha xculiçah xquibaneçaj tzih chiquech

16: ahauab ³⁰⁹⁰cayoɛ ri vɟia la lal ɛucumatz xa vpulu

17: tzoy caruɟah cuchax la rū ahau ztayul xecha

18: ri taom tuma cah neh ma pa vech xchaah chique

19: ³¹⁰⁰xaui ɟut quehe caquibih chirech ztayul naɛi

20: pa vpatan ri xa yxim xa vpen xa pu rachaɛ

21: hoɟha amolo carechaah cacha ahau ɛumaɛ chie la

22: lal ahau ³¹¹⁰quecha chirech ztayul ma pa que

23: he ta ri vech rax car rax chom cauecah cacha

24: ɛucumatz chiech la xecha quehe ɟut vhunum

25: quitzih auab ri chiquih

Folio 26r

26

1: ^{3120}ta xzθahiçax quivach = xhalθatix vuach qui

2: metabal cumal ahauab |_hun yac hun çaɛbin

3: chirech vuach quimetabal xbanic = rumal e tzih

4: talom — quehe θu vuinakiriɛ vɛaɛanibal θux ri

5: ^{3130}cumah roɛche cahib ah ri ta vθuxlaxic chi quica

6: miçaxic ahau θotuha ɛucumatz ruθ ahau zta

7: yul ri xbequiθama ylocab camiçay quech tah

8: ta xeobex θut cumal e cab oyeu achih ^{3140}chiri

9: voronic çiuan queatin θu ri e cayb oyeu achih

10: ta xeθulun θut ri taom tuma cah e θamol qui

11: be ylocab e ahlabal = ta xquiquir cut quipam

12: ri oyeu achih ta xeycaɛix cu ^{3150}ri taom tuma -

13: cah chi ycaɛ cumal e royeual rachihilal

14: θiche ri θut xban chi ysmachi are θu ri huyub

15: chi ysmachi xa cahib chi zgul vnaual xa θu cha

16: maui kixuθam θū vach ^{3160}quehe chi θu roɛotaxic

17: chi ysmachi ri cumal ahauab = ta xeθaholax

18: θut vuɛlahuh chi achih rumal ahau ɛucumaɛ

19: uθahol θotuha ɛiɛabil uinaɛ Decum ztayul

20: vinaɛ depepul θiɛabil vinaɛ Depepul caui

21: çimah ^{3170}vae e vmam balan θitze nabe uinaɛ

22: uca le θoθoha ¶ rox le tziquin vcah le ahcā

23: ro le cocayb coɛauib hob cut xuθaholah

Folio 26v

1: ɜocauib 1. quehnay [3180]2. ɜoyoy. 3 xmayqueh
2: 4 lakamal rochoɜoy. 5. hob xuɜaholah vɜahol
3: chi ɜut xmayqueh vae ahau ɜotuha —
4: vak le ahauarem vae ɜotuha εucumatz
5: ri ahpop = [3190]are ɜu ri ahpo ɜamha vɜahol εauib
6: ɜonache hoxbal al gipitavar vbi rixokil
7: chi vaε le ɜo ui vae ɜotuha————
8: vahxaε le chi ɜu vae εucumatz xuɜaholah
9: chi ɜotuha = εucumatz ɜut xchiɜaholā
10: 17. lahuh chi ɜaholaxel [3200]varal ɜut xchiεa
11: lahin ui ɜia bi varal ɜut xɜaholax ui ɜika
12: cauiçimah vuε al chiquech Decū depepul
13: Tepepul ɜauiçimah ɜikab Depepul [3210]mi xe
14: ɜaholax chi yxmachi xaui ɜotuha vɜahol
15: εucumaε ¶ vacamic chi ɜut x chikatiqui
16: ba chic ubixic utzihoxic pach vae loεolah
17: tinamit mayhalah tinamit [3220]pa ɜichi chi εu
18: marcaah chi ysmachi tlecpan ɜiche mi x
19: εoεotah canoε vbixic ri chi ysmachi oher tina
20: mit cuchax vacamic xa chi ui ɜut x chirakani
21: beh vloε [3230]εatzih ma ta chiçach yɜux chirech yx
22: kamam kaɜahol chiri ta chiɜam ui ynaoh chux
23: apanoε xa vçuɜuliquil xa pu vnataxic qui
24: banoh kamam kakahau

Folio 27r

1: ³²⁴⁰¶vcab 4u hunab vcamil 4otuha ta xbā
2: nima labal rumal 4ikab 4auiçimah 4iç
3: xecanabexic xetelechexic conohel caha
4: val amaɛ ri ³²⁵⁰xecamiçanic rech 4otuha
5: ri amaɛ 4ohayil vxahayil quevchaxic
6: ta xebec 4ikab 4auiçimah Decum Depepul
7: ta xebatelechexoɛ amaɛ 4ohayil vxaha
8: yil ³²⁶⁰oxlahuh rahaual 4iz 4ut xepetic
9: ru4 cal quicahol xemunixic xeḡiyxic
10: xeul pa 4iche chiri xelotz ui xe4ak ui
11: ³²⁷⁰xquizyc quivach varal maui xa kiyabil
12: xoc chiquech xa vpaɛuriçaxic baɛ holom
13: rumal 4ikab 4auiçimah rumal quexel
14: vachix canoɛ ra ahau 4otuha ralaxic 4ikab
15: chalaxic ³²⁸⁰poroy vpa cah poroy vpa vleu xcha
16: 4otuha ¶ quehe 4ut vbanic nima pokob vpo
17: ɛob tohil ta xban choloh ḡiquin ɛih xul oxlahuh
18: chi vuɛamaɛ varal pa 4iche xul v4abauil tamub
19: ylocab varal 4iche ³²⁹⁰¶ tohil v4abauil ɛale
20: tam ahpotam ɛale cakoh atzih uinaɛ cakoh
21: yeol ahtunala xpe chi tamub ¶ are 4u tohil
22: xpe chi ylocab ³³⁰⁰ɛale roɛche atzih uinaɛ roɛ
23: che ɛalel cahib ahatzih uinaɛ çi4a lolmɛt j
24: juv ylocab ¶ xul 4u ahau cakah ¶ 4ate 4u
25: rabinaleb Dalmalin ³³¹⁰ahpop ahbom atzi
26: uinaɛ habhalaveh nin 4hocoh xevl lotzo

Folio 27v

24

1: voɛ xevl ꝣakvoh ¶ xul nay pu ahau ahpo
2: çogil ahpo xahil baꝣaholab ɛekaꝣuch [3320]¶ xul ꝣu
3: vchubaha ahau ꝣhumilaha ¶ aɛaab balamiha
4: ꝣubul caal cumatz ¶ xul nay puch nahtiha ahꝣi
5: baha ¶ahɛuha ꝣiçiha [3330]# ahꝣabauil # ahpotzo
6: lola # ahpovaiz # ahpobuluxa # ahporunam
7: # ahpoçakiachaɛ balam vtiu # ahhaɛɛoche #
8: # ahpo balaha [3340]# ahpocon # ahpotuctum #
9: ahpohun ahpuale # ahoçanay #lolmet ca
10: vinay are ꝣu xepe chi ahgiquinaha ri ronohel
11: ri ——————————————
12: Ri ꝣute quivach vuɛamaɛ [3350]xeul lotzovoɛ xeul
13: ꝣakovoɛ xul quiɛuvuh tzuvm chomam tzuṽ
14: quitzumal oxlahuh rahaual amaɛ ri xe
15: camiçan ꝣotuha # xaui oxlahuh chi nimaɛ
16: ahauab xeɛunic # ta xban pochoh [3360]xbā çu
17: tinem xbin ronohel cabauil xekexaheic
18: cumal ahauab = hū ꝣu ahpo ꝣahol xna
19: beyehic e ɛo vɛab tohil ronohel xitam
20: puakim vuachibal humah cohbal humah
21: [3370]cutum pamam lamaxintzi mayat tzatz
22: chi ꝣhabi ɛaɛ cak tihax caɛulha vꝣux cah
23. cah ekam ahetaɛ [3380]xpoɛobaxic vpokoba
24: puaɛ ɛoɛol xtecoc ɛuɛ raron ronohel
25: hanic xchabih xchikacholo vꝣulū

Folio 28r

28

1: ⁴u quivach conohel ahauab ——

2: ³³⁹⁰vae ⁴ut varal xvor ui ⁴ikab cauiçimah

3: Decuṁ tepepul e ⁴ikabil vinaɛ ——

4: ¶ahpop cahib muh pa vui hū vɛalibal ³⁴⁰⁰⁴o vRa

5: jon ahçubac ¶ ahpo ⁴amha oxib muh pa

6: vui ¶ Nima rahop achih caib muh pa vui

7: chuti hahop achih hū muh pa vui xchap

8: pa xicaha ³⁴¹⁰xare y cu ahauab ri ca muh

9: pa quiui xevoric xe⁴akic chi tatil ɛan a

10: bah lotz qui⁴ kaɛche he queh macuDaj

11: ³⁴²⁰tziquil cot tziquil balam ttot matacuz

12: chiom aztapulul ɛoɛol xtecoc chi⁴ual v

13: vzapil tzam ³⁴³⁰chiquech ahpop ahpo ⁴anha

14: ri xecakic xeuoric varal pa ⁴iche

15: chi ɛumarcah tlecpan ⁴iche

16: ¶ Are ⁴u ri beheb nim ha ³⁴⁴⁰chiri xpaxin vi ri

17: pa rochoch ahau ⁴ocayb beleheb nim ha

18: rech cauaɛib ⁴ikabil uinaɛ ¶ beleheb

19: ⁴u nim ha rech nihayib ahau ¶cahib nim

20: ha rech ahau ⁴iche: 2 ⁴ut nin ha rech

21: ahgib çakic tzutuha ³⁴⁵⁰qu he ⁴u vgaka

22: tic 24 rahaual ⁴iche ri ri caha

23: var tlecpā ⁴iche chi ɛumarcah

Folio 28v

1: vae ϩut quibi e beleheb nin ha 4-
2: ahauarerem ϩo chupam ri nabeal
3: ahpop ϩikabil uinaε ahpo ϩamha
4: ³⁴⁶⁰nima Rahob achih chutō rajup a
5: chih e ϩikabil uinaε e chi ui vϩahol
6: vman e leε baε lahu noh e rach chapic
7: ϩikab cauiçimah: ³⁴⁷⁰roεche ah vbi yxoε
8: xealanic xoεohau ma na xa halum
9: ahauarem ϩo ui huhun chique Ri ah
10: tohil ah εucumatz chituy quehnay
11: ³⁴⁸⁰nim ϩhocoh cauee xocotzil———
12: xel ϩu vbi quivachibal quitem qui
13: ϩhacat pa huhun chi huyub ri be
14: leheb chi achihab ahauab vae ϩute
15: nabe xxya bic reεaleñ cumal aha
16: uab ³⁴⁹⁰ahgalam rahpop ahgalam vtzā
17: chinamital 9. ahgalam. 9. rahpop ah
18: galam 9 vtzā chinamital nabe
19: xquichap pa nin ha xa hū xel ui xa
20: pu hun xban ui cabilto
21: ³⁵⁰⁰ta xechapic e mamayb ta xquipaxi
22: h quib pa huhun chi huyub

Folio 29r

+ 30

1: vae ꝗute quelic vbic e ɛalel e ahpop ri. 13. ɛula

2: ha cablahuh: tzihbachah # ruc vahxakib ɠalam ꝗoxtun

3: Ri çiha raxꝗim e oxchob chi quiꝗoheyc ³⁵¹⁰hunam ꝗut

4: xeel vbic ta xebɛc ta xepixabax vbic ———

5: ¶ vuahxaɛ le tzih co ui vcholic quibanoh ahauab: ta xe

6: taɛ ꝗu vbic e ahauab: catz quichaɛ: ³⁵²⁰uꝗahol ahau vmam

7: ahau: ri xetzucuxic ꝗate ꝗut ta xepixābaxic are ꝗut qui

8: pixab xquibano allaɛ katz alaɛ kachaɛ: nim nabeɛ ꝗoɛ ka

9: ꝗux chiech allaɛ: are cakataɛ ui allaɛ vbic: ³⁵³⁰allaɛ koyeval

10: kachihilal = cabeꝗulelaah allaɛ vuɛamaɛ ah

11: chibeyeɛuh alaɛ ronohel huyub taɛah: chibeꝗuyeꝗuh to

12: loɛ mazquell allaɛ xevchaxic ta xepixabaxic ³⁵⁴⁰xcoɛeh qui . . .

13: quivach xquicuba quiꝗux xquimez quiui chiquiwach

14: e ahtzol e ahɠununche e rih chun çaɛcab xevxic maui xa

15: quiraym quiɛalelal cahpopol e Royeval ³⁵⁵⁰rachihilal

16: tlecpan ꝗiche = elenaɛ ui quitem quiꝗhacat= catbec at

17: vatz at nuchaɛ matbiçonic matoɛic mavuchah aꝗux

18: ³⁵⁶⁰xaui catulic xaui pu catꝗulunic ruc acanab ateleche que

19: he xcatbe ui at ꝗulelay rech vuɛamaɛ tlecpā ———

20: ¶ Ri ahpoçotzil ahpoxahil: ³⁵⁷⁰baꝗaholab ɛekaꝗuch ¶ ruꝗ

21: ahpocoon: buluxa # ahporuman hunahpuale ———

22: chibana yuoyeual yvachihilal xevchaxic ————

23: vae ꝗut quelic vbic pa ꝗiche chi ysmachi ³⁵⁸⁰xeopon yquiyac

24: xeopon tzam chinɛah: xeaɛan hocol: ɛana pec: xeaɛan

25: apanoɛ chi pagan chi cakꝗix # xeaɛan apanoɛ ꝗhay

26: bamɛt cakiquil ———

Folio 29v

1: 4a chiri 4ute xehachou uib cu4 ɛulaha [3590]vlaɛobexic
2: huyub taɛah xaui 4u chiri xquiba ui quitzaɛ qui
3: 4oxtun cakiquil hoyam ɛanaɛ——— e 4u 4ola chiri
4: ta xechapic chi ahauarem chi ɛalelah chi ahpopol [3600]vae
5: oxlahuh ɛalel oxlahuh ahpop ahɛulaha———
6: ¶vae chi 4ute cablahuh tzihbachah cablahuh
7: ɛulel cablahuh ahpop cablahuh vɛalechih rah
8: pop achih xechapic chiri chua hoyam ɛanaɛ [3610]xe4iar na
9: xetzatzar na chiri ta xechapic 4iarinaka chic cal qui4a
10: hol ta xechapic xeyaylah chiri are xbinah ui
11: huyub taɛah cumal: Ta xquicuch quilaɛam chiri
12: chui cuchulakam [3620]xecha chire oxib chi laɛam———
13: hũ quech 4ikabil uinaɛ ɛquiɛab nima yas ruc tepe
14: pul 4ikabil uinaɛ = xaui hun rech ɛale nihayib
15: atzih uinaɛ nihayib hun 4ut rech ahau 4iche [3630]chi
16: oxib chi laɛam yaxic Are chi 4u ri vahxakib çiha
17: vahxaɛib chi tzalam 4oxtum are chi 4u ri ahvxe
18: yohovt ral4im çababache yacalic xeaɛan pa
19: raxtum pec vti4ilibexic 4ut ri chiçubit [3640]hu
20: çu xquiban quitzaɛ chiri xcohe 4u canoɛ quiçemiento
21: chiri 4a chiri chi 4ut xehacho ui quib çabache 4hu
22: ti çabache nima çabache chuchaxic 4ate chi 4ut vɛo
23: bic xeyohovt quehe 4u ri quibic 4ut ri ahxeyo
24: hovt yacalic [3650]xebɛc ta xqui4am quibe ahcakçay ah
25: ahçamayac cuchax vacamic cachbilam 4u quib
26: cu4 tamub ylocab vuɛmil çi4a Ju° nihayib

Folio 30r

1: 4a chiri 4ut xechap chi ui chi εalelal [3660]chi ahpopol

2: a quehe chi 4u 4hahcar ri xeel pa balax abah lemo ha ———

3: ARe 4u vae cablahuh ~~εulaha~~ tzihbachah xe

4: hach canoε hoyam εanaε cumal εulaha ruc çiha

5: rax4im xa 4u vεobic huyub cumal ta xqui4am vloε

6: quibe [3670]quihoc ———Vae 4ute 4ute quibe quihoc

7: vae cablahuh tzihbachah are caMol be vae

8: 4ikabil uinaε ahau ahpop 4ikab nima yas vcab

9: 4ut ahau εalel nihahayib: ros 4ut [3680]ahau

10: atzih uinaε ahau 4iche quicamom vbe vhoε

11: cal quicahol ————————

12: Ta xeaεan raxchuh # xeopam mu4hulic baε # omu4h

13: 4aholab yiε 4hopi çiuan # εaxion # [3690]4a4amabal

14: xeoc xe huyub: ri 4u taε navalaε ta xekah na

15: vala # xeaεan chutanabal huyub # xeaεan

16: pa vuaal xucuεab # ta xey4ou pan4ix # xolta

17: car abah # xey4ou gulgul pec # [3700]chihul # cha

18: εih cho ta culic chui huyub tzihbachah tzaε tina

19: mit ————————

20: Vae 4ut quibi nabe ahyiε 4ikab nima yas yaxō

21: balam e hu4içic etamanel cauεε 4ikabil uinaε

22: [3710]Ru4 εalel nihayib atzih uinaε ahau 4iche nabe ui

23: naε xepe pa 4iche chi ysmachi ta culic miεina

24: giquiche pa vuaal sahoε ta quimayhanic

Folio 30v

1: chui çakmal ahau # [3720]xeaɛan ɛuxliquel # chu
2: ha giquin
3: Vae ɟute vɟahol ɟikab hoob xuɟaholah vae nabe
4: vɟahol xitapul. 2 çun . 3. yzɟuat. 4 yamu
5: 50 vbi ɛanil # are ɟu ri xitapul xquihach quib [3730]qui
6: chaɛ quib ri e hoob chi ɟu ɟaholaxic rumal ɟi
7: kab chiri ɟo ui hob chi chi gak chuixtoca chi ɟua
8: chiri e ɟo ui ta xul vtzihoxic bō p° alvarado
9: [3740]Donatii xaui hun chiyiɛ chipulput uiha = pa
10: xcaktunum vyiɛ ɟikab——
11: // vae ɟut xelic vbic ɟikab ɟauiçimah paɟiche chiɛu
12: marcah ta xerachbilah oxlajuj ɛulaha [3750]cablahuh
13: tzihbachaj ta xuinaɛir nima ɛaɛal te val rū ɟikab
14: cauiçimah kamā oh cauɛeib ta xuçut vchi vleu
15: ɟiche vleu ɟiche huyub [3760]taɛah ta xeel pa ɟiche
16: xeyɟou chuchi cho ☐ lemoa chiri xulemovah
17: vi rib chi cotal chi ɛuɛil ta xeyɟou cakixcan xe
18: aɛan pabal abah: chahaxaɛ: [3770]chi ɛapoh tzam
19: tzolola pec balam abah niɟah cho ta xuhach ri
20: cho nicah nicah re ahpotzogil nicah rech ɟiɛab
21: ta xoc ɟhoy huyub ta xoc chi hucba ycah pa
22: meçebal [3780]xeyɟou chi ruɟabala ɛuɛ chi ɛohom
23: tzam ɛana vleu chua naranjos ta xkah apanoɛ
24: muɛulic xicat ta xbevya canoɛ vchi huyub

Folio 31r

1: ... chi quivach [3790]yaquiab
2: a vtiquic cayb ynup rũ 4ikab 4auiçimah
3: laɛalic ynup laɛalic mumuz chuchaxic hũ 25
4: rech yaqui vinaɛ ayutlecat macatlecat xu
5: xic vae chi 4ut [3800]vchi huyub quech çakulevab
6: yoc ɛanchibix = ɛaɛalix oxlah uinaɛ xuban ri ahau
7: 4iɛab chiri ri kitzih kama kakahau oh [3810]caue
8: ɛibaɛ // oxlah uinaɛ xu4ut vpuz vnaval chi
9: 4habi ɛaɛ cat tihax çutz mayul raxa kaɛulha
10: 4hipa caɛulha ta xevpaxih [3820]ronohel amaɛ ——
11: ɛae chi 4ute vchi vleu rech 4iche uinaɛ
12: ɛaɛaab 4oxom xak = chuach vçiatic chuach
13: abal tzam 4i quiche # chua laɛā abah # tzā
14: yaqui // aɛa yoka [3830]4ut cut balā colob ——

Folio 31v

1: uacam . . . año 155 . . .

2: 4ikab ξ———

3: ————————alte ahau nand . . .

4: Dō diego carcia ξ 4iche — yib———

5: chituy———Dō cptoual de belasco

6: Dō Jorje nihayib ξ nim 4hocoh cauee

7: Dō diego peres Juº lugas ahtohil

8: aheucumatz r Dō pº xiquitzal tepe ξ

9: dō cpual escrŭ cabilto ξ

10: vae kafirma oh ³⁸⁴⁰nabe 4iche cauekib niha

11: yib ahau 4iche ahtohil aheucumae

12: tituy quehnay————————

13: yn dō Joseph cordes yn dō Juº de Ro . . .

14: 4ikab canuya nufir 4ikab cakaya va . . .

15: ma ³⁸⁵⁰chirih vae auto auto rech apop

16: rech 4ikab nima yas chui mieina

Maps

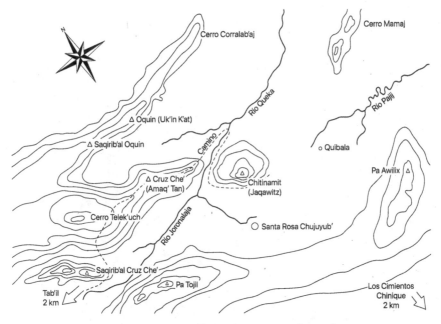

Map 1. Map of Early K'iche' sites. Modified with permission from John Fox 1978.

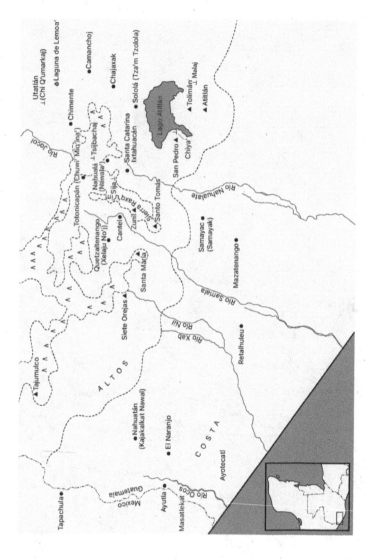

Map 2. Map of Late Postclassic sites in central Guatemala. Modified with permission from John Fox 1978.

Map 3. Map of southwestern Guatemala with sites mentioned in the *Title of Totonicapán*. Modified with permission from Carmack and Mondloch 1983, 277.

25 km

△ Pueblo Viejo
San Sebastián Huehuetenango

△ Zaculeu (Saqulew)

△ Nebaj

△ Tenam (B'alamja')   ● Cunen

Chultinamit (Tuja)   △ Lamak (Lamakib')

Chuixtiox (Kumatz)△ ● Sacapulas

△ Agua Colorado (Uspantán)

△ Pueblo Viejo (K'ulb'a Kawinal)

△ Pueblo Viejo
Malacatancito
(Malacatán)

△ Pueblo Viejo Momostenango
(Chwa Tz'aq)

Tzakabala (Tzakib'alja)△
Pugertinamit (Tz'oloj'che')

△ Chi Pixab'   △ Los Cimientos (Chi Xpa'ch)

Saqirib'al Ilokab'△ Oquin (Uk'in K'at)△Xab'aj △ Pueblo Viejo Canilla (Joyab'aj)
Cruzche (Amaq' Tan)△ △ Chitinamit (Jaqawitz)   (Saqirib'al-Sajkab'aja)
Saqirib'al△   △Pa Awilix
Tamub'   △Pa Tojil

△Chisalin   △Los Cimientos – Chinique
Chi Ismachi'△△Utatlán (Chi Q'umarkaj)   △El Cementerio – Zacualpa

△Los Cimientos – Joyab'aj (Pa Maka)

△Los Cimientos–Pachalum

△Mixco Viejo

△Pueblo Viejo Salamaa
(Tzalamja-Kilaja)

Laguna Lemoa'

●Chichicastenango (Chuwila)
△Patzak (Chiawar)

△Totonicapán
(Chuwi' Mig'ina')

△Nahualá (Nawala')

△Quetzaltenango
(Xelaju No'j)
△Chultinamit (Zunil)

Soloia
(Tza'm Tzolola)

Laguna Chicabal

△San Martín Zapotitlán
(Xetulul)

△Samayac
(Samayak)

Jiilotepeque Viejo

△Pueblo Viejo Jilotepeque (Jolom)

△Chuitinamit — Comalapa (Chi-Xot)

△Ikimche'

△ Cerro de Oro
Chuitinamit (Chiya')△ ●Chukumuk
△Santiago Atitlán

Malaj

△Chinautla (Mixku)

Lake Amatitlán

Lake Atitlán

Río Negro

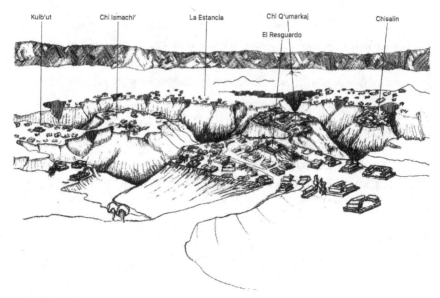

Map 4. Plateaus of the Central K'iche' region. Drawing by Humberto Ak'abal and Robert M. Carmack.

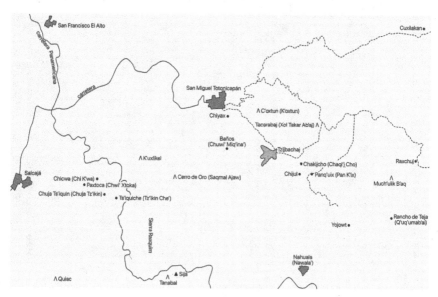

Map 5. Map of the valley of Totonicapán. Modified with permission from Carmack and Mondloch 1983, 278.

References

Acuña, René, ed. 1982. *Relaciones geográficas del siglo xvi: Guatemala*. Cd. de México: Universidad Nacional Autónoma de México.

Acuña, René, ed. 1984. *Relaciones geográficas del siglo xvi: Tlaxcala*. Vol. 1. Cd. de México: Universidad Nacional Autónoma de México.

Ajpacaja Tum, Florentino Pedro. 2001. *K'ichee' Choltziij*. Guatemala City: Cholsamaj.

Akkeren, Ruud W. van. 2000. *Place of the Lord's Daughter*. Leiden: Research School CNWS, Leiden University.

Akkeren, Ruud W. van. 2003. "Authors of the Popol Wuj." *Ancient Mesoamerica* 14, no. 2 (October): 237–256.

Akkeren, Ruud W. van. 2011. "Fray Domingo de Vico: Maestro de autores indígenas, *Theologia Indorum*." In *Cosmovisión Mesoamericana*. Ed. Horacio Cabezas Carcache. Guatemala City: Publicaciones Mesoamericanas, 83–117.

Alvarado, Pedro de. 1924. *An Account of the Conquest of Guatemala in 1524 by Pedro de Alvarado*. Ed. Sedley J. Mackie. New York: Cortes Society.

Alvarado, Pedro de. 1946. *Relación hecha por Pedro de Alvarado a Hernando Cortes (1524)*. Biblioteca de Autores Españoles, vol. 22. Madrid: Real Academia Española.

Alvarado, Pedro de. 1979. *Muerte de Pedro de Alvarado: Cartas de Relación de Alvarado a Hernán Cortés*. Biblioteca de Cultura Popular, vol. 4. Guatemala City: Editorial "José de Pineda Ibarra."

Alvarado López, Miguel. 1975. *Léxico médico quiché-español*. Guatemala City: Instituto Indigenista Nacional.

https://doi.org/10.5876/9781646422647.c005

Álvarez Sánchez, Adriana. 2014. "La Orden de San Francisco y el conocimiento de las lenguas indígenas del Reino de Guatemala Siglo XVI." Sémata 26: 471–489.

Ángel, Fr. ca. 1775. *Arte de la lengua cakchiquel*. Manuscrit Américain 41 in the Bibliothèque nationale de France, Paris.

Anleo, Fr. Bartolomé de. ca. 1660. *Arte de lengua k'iche*. Manuscript in Princeton University Library, Princeton, NJ.

Anonymous. 1935 [ca. 1700]. *Isagoge histórica apologética de las Indias Occidentales*. Vol. 8. Guatemala City: Biblioteca "Goathemala."

Anonymous. 1952 [1571]. "Relación de los caciques y principales del pueblo de Atitlán." *Anales de la Sociedad de Geografía e Historia de Guatemala* 26: 435–438.

Aquinas, St. Thomas. 1952. *The Summa Theologica*. Vol. 1. Tr. Daniel J. Sullivan. Chicago: Encyclopaedia Britannica, Inc.

Barrera Vásquez, Alfredo. 1995. *Diccionario Maya*. Cd. de México: Editorial Porrúa.

Basseta, Fr. Domingo de. 1921 [1698]. *Vocabulario en lengua quiché*. Typescript by William Gates of the original in the Bibliothèque nationale de France, Paris. In the W. E. Gates Collection, Special Collections and Manuscript Archives, Harold B. Lee Library, Brigham Young University, Provo, UT.

The Book of Enoch. 1917. Tr. Robert Henry Charles. London: Society for Promoting Christian Knowledge.

Boone, Elizabeth H. 2000. *Stories in Red and Black: Pictorial Histories of the Aztecs and Mixtecs*. Austin: University of Texas Press.

Brasseur de Bourbourg, Charles Étienne. 1961. *Gramática de la lengua quiché*. Guatemala City: Editorial del Ministerio de Educación Pública "Jose de Pineda Ibarra."

Bunzel, Ruth Leah. 1952. *Chichicastenango*. American Ethnological Society 22. Seattle: University of Washington Press.

Campbell, Lyle R. 1970. "Nahua Loan Words in Quichean Languages." *Chicago Linguistics Society* 6: 3–11.

Campbell, Lyle R. 1971. *Historical Linguistics and Quichean Linguistic Prehistory*. Los Angeles: University of California Press.

Campbell, Lyle R. 1983. "Préstamos lingüísticos en el Popol Vuh." In *Nuevas perspectivas sobre el Popol Vuh*. Ed. Robert M. Carmack and Francisco Morales Santos, 81–86. Guatemala City: Piedra Santa.

Carlsen, Robert S. 1997. *The War for the Heart and Soul of a Highland Maya Town*. Austin: University of Texas Press.

Carmack, Robert M. 1973. *Quichean Civilization*. Berkeley: University of California Press.

Carmack, Robert M. 1979. *Evolución del Reino Quiché*. Guatemala City: Editorial Piedra Santa.

Carmack, Robert M. 1981. *The Quiché Mayas of Utatlán: The Evolution of a Highland Guatemala Kingdom*. Norman: University of Oklahoma Press.

Carmack, Robert M., and James L. Mondloch. 1983. *Título de Totonicapán*. Cd. de México: Universidad Nacional Autónoma de México.

Carmack, Robert M., and James L. Mondloch. 1989. *Título de Yax, y otros documentos quichés de Totonicapán, Guatemala*. Cd. de México: Centro de Estudios Mayas, Universidad Nacional Autónoma de México.

Carmack, Robert M., and James L. Mondloch. 2007. *Uwujil Kulewal aj Chwi Miq'ina': El Título de Totonicapán*. Guatemala City: Cholsamaj.

Carrasco, Pedro. 1967. "Don Juan Cortés, Cacique de Santa Cruz Quiché." *Estudios de Cultura Maya* 6: 251–266.

Charencey, Charles-Félix-Hyacinthe Gouhier, comte de. 1885. *Título de los señores de Totonicapán/Titre généalogique des seigneurs de Totonicapán*. Alençon, France: E. Renaut-De Broise, Imprimeur.

Chimalpahin Quahtlehuanitzin, Don Domingo de San Antón Muñon. 1997. *Codex Chimalpahin: Society and Politics in Mexico Tenochtitlan, Tlatelolco, Texcoco, Culhuacan, and Other Nahua Altepetl in Central Mexico*. Vol. 1. Norman: University of Oklahoma Press.

Chinchilla Mazariegos, Oswaldo. 2013. "Tecum, the Fallen Sun: Mesoamerican Cosmogony and the Spanish Conquest of Guatemala." *Ethnohistory* 60, no. 4 (Fall): 693–719.

Chinchilla Mazariegos, Oswaldo, and Rosa Helena, eds. 1993. *Arte de las tres lenguas, kaqchikel k'iche' y tz'utujil, por Fr. Francisco Ximénez*. Biblioteca "Goathemala," vol. 31. Guatemala City: Academia de Geografía e Historia de Guatemala, ix–xxxii.

Christensen, Mark Z. 2016. *The Teabo Manuscript: Maya Christian Copybooks, Chilam Balams, and Native Text Production in Yucatán*. Austin: University of Texas Press.

Christenson, Allen J. 1985. *Quiché-English Dictionary*. FAMSI.org.

Christenson, Allen J. 2001. *Art and Society in a Highland Maya Community*. Austin: University of Texas Press.

Christenson, Allen J. 2003. *Popol Vuh: Literal Poetic Version*. Winchester, UK: O Books.

Christenson, Allen J. 2006. "Sacred Bundle Cults in Highland Guatemala." In *Sacred Bundles: Ritual Acts of Wrapping and Bundling in Mesoamerica*. Ed. Julia Guernsey and F. Kent Reilly III. Barnardsville, NC: Boundary End Archaeology Research Center, 226–246.

Christenson, Allen J. 2007. *Popol Vuh: The Sacred Book of the Maya*. Norman: University of Oklahoma Press.

Christenson, Allen J. 2010. "Maize Was Their Flesh: Ritual Feasting in the Maya Highlands." In *Pre-Columbian Foodways: Interdisciplinary Approaches to Food, Culture, and Markets in Ancient Mesoamerica*. Ed. John Edward Staller and Michael Carrasco. New York: Springer, 577-600.

Christenson, Allen J. 2012. "The Use of Chiasmus by the Ancient K'iche' Maya." In *Parallel Worlds: Genre, Discourse, and Poetics in Contemporary, Colonial, and Classic Maya Literature*. Ed. Kerry M. Hull and Michael D. Carrasco. Boulder: University Press of Colorado, 311–336.

Christenson, Allen J. 2016. *The Burden of the Ancients*. Austin: University of Texas Press.

Ciudad Real, Fr. Antonio de. 1929 [1590]. *Diccionario de Motul: Maya Español*. Ed. Juan Martínez Hernández. Mérida: Talleres de la Compañía tipográfica Yucateca.

Cojti Ren, Iyaxel. 2021. "The Saqarik (Dawn) and Foundation Rituals among the Ancient K'iche'an Peoples from the Guatemalan Highlands." In *The Myths of the Popol Vuh in Cosmology, Art, and Ritual*. Ed. Holly Moyes, Allen J. Christenson, and Frauke Sachse, 77–90. Boulder: University Press of Colorado.

Cortés, Hernán. 1986. *Hernán Cortés, Letters from Mexico*. Tr. Anthony Pagden. New Haven, CT: Yale University Press.

Coto, Fr. Thomás de. 1983 [ca. 1656]. *Thesaurus Verboru: Vocabulario de la lengua cakchiquel v[el] Guatemalteca*. Ed. René Acuña. Cd. de México: Universidad Nacional Autónoma de México.

Craine, Eugene R., and Reginald C. Reindorp. 1979. *The Codex Pérez and the Book of Chilam Balam of Maní*. Norman: University of Oklahoma Press.

Davies, Nigel. 1977. *The Toltecs, until the Fall of Tula*. Norman: University of Oklahoma Press.

Dezso, Genevieve Alexandra. 2015. "The Use of Honey in Maya Construction." MA thesis, Department of Anthropology, Stanford University, Stanford, CA.

Dürr, Michael, and Frauke Sachse, eds. 2017. *Diccionario k'iche' de Berlín: El Vocabulario en lengua 4iche otlatecas: edición crítica*. Berlin: Ibero-Amerikanisches Institut Preußischer Kulturbesitz, Gebr. Mann Verlag.

Early, John D. 2006. *The Maya and Catholicism: An Encounter of Worldviews*. Gainesville: University Press of Florida.

Edmonson, Munro S. 1965. *Quiché-English Dictionary*. Middle American Research Institute Publication 30. New Orleans: Tulane University Press.

Edmonson, Munro S. 1971. *The Book of Counsel: The Popol Vuh of the Quiche Maya of Guatemala*. Middle American Research Institute Publication 35. New Orleans: Tulane University Press.

Edmonson, Munro S. 1982. *The Ancient Future of the Itza: The Book of Chilam Balam of Tizimin*. Austin: University of Texas Press.

Edmonson, Munro S. 1986. *Heaven Born Mérida and Its Destiny: The Book of Chilam Balam of Chumayel*. Austin: University of Texas Press.

Flegontov, Pavel, N. Ezgi Altınışik, Piya Changmai, Nadin Rohland, Swapan Mallick, et al. 2019. "Palaeo Eskimo Genetic Ancestry and the Peopling of Chukotka and North America." *Nature* 570: 236–240.

Fox, John W. 1978. *Quiché Conquest: Centralism and Regionalism in Highland Guatemalan State Development.* Albuquerque: University of New Mexico Press.

Fox, John W. 1987. *Maya Postclassic State Formation: Segmentary Lineage Migration in Advancing Frontiers.* Cambridge: Cambridge University Press.

Freidel, David, Linda Schele, and Joy Parker. 1993. *Maya Cosmos.* New York: W. W. Morrow.

García Elgueta, Manuel. 1892. *Etimologías kiche.* Manuscript in the Harold B. Lee Library Manuscript Archives, Brigham Young University, Provo, UT.

García Elgueta, Manuel. ca. 1900. *Mam i Español.* Manuscript in the Harold B. Lee Library Manuscript Archives, Brigham Young University, Provo, UT.

García Hernández, Abraham, and Santiago Yac Sam. 1980. *Diccionario Quiché-Español.* Ed. David Henne Pontious. Guatemala City: Instituto Lingüístico de Verano.

Ginzberg, Louis. 1939. *The Legends of the Jews*, vol. 3 (revised edition): *Moses in the Wilderness.* Philadelphia: Jewish Publication Society of America.

Ginzberg, Louis. 1948. *The Legends of the Jews*, vol. 2 (revised edition): *From Joseph to the Exodus.* Philadelphia: Jewish Publication Society of America.

Guzmán, Fr. Pantaleón de. 1984 [1704]. *Compendio de Nombres en la Lengva Cakchiqvel.* Ed. René Acuña. Cd. de México: Universidad Nacional Autónoma de México.

Helmke, Christophe, Julie A. Hoggarth, and Jaime J. Awe. 2018. *A Reading of the Komkom Vase Discovered at Baking Pot, Belize.* San Francisco: Precolumbia Mesoweb Press.

Herrera, Fr. Francisco. 1745. *Vocabulario de la lengua castellana y quiché.* Manuscrit Américain 7 in the Bibliothèque nationale de France, Paris.

Hill, Robert M., II. 1992. *Colonial Cakchiquels: Highland Maya Adaptation to Spanish Rule 1600–1700.* Fort Worth: Holt, Rinehart, and Winston.

Hill, Robert M., II. 1996. "Eastern Chajoma (Çakchiquel) Political Geography: Ethnohistorical and Archaeological Contributions to the Study of a Late Postclassic Highland Maya Polity." *Ancient Mesoamerica* 7 (1): 63–87.

Hill, Robert M., II, and John Monaghan. 1987. *Continuities in Highland Maya Social Organization: Ethnohistory in Sacapulas, Guatemala.* Philadelphia: University of Pennsylvania Press.

Houston, Stephen. 2013. "Run, Don't Walk: Sacred Movement among the Classic Maya." Paper presented at the Los Angeles Mesoamerican Symposium, California State University, April 13.

Houston, Stephen, David Stuart, and Karl Taube. 2006. *The Memory of Bones: Body, Being, and Experience among the Classic Maya.* Austin: University of Texas Press.

Landa, Fr. Diego de. 1941. *Landa's Relación de las Cosas de Yucatan*. Ed. Alfred M. Tozzer. Peabody Museum of American Archaeology and Ethnology Paper 28. Cambridge: Harvard University.

Las Casas, Fr. Bartolomé de. 1958 [ca. 1550]. *Apologética historia*. Ed. Juan Pérez de Tudela Bueso. Madrid: Real Academia Española.

Las Casas, Fr. Bartolomé de. 1967 [ca. 1550]. *Apologética Historia Sumaria*. 2 vols. Cd. de México: Universidad Nacional Autónoma de México, Instituto de Investigaciones Históricas.

Las Casas, Fr. Bartolomé de. 1992 [1552]. *In Defense of the Indians*. Tr. Stafford Poole. DeKalb: Northern Illinois University Press.

León, Juan de. 1954. *Diccionario quiché-español*. Guatemala City: Universidad Rafael Landivar.

León-Portilla, Miguel. 1969. *Pre-Columbian Literatures of Mexico*. Trans. Grace Lobanov and Miguel León-Portilla. Norman: University of Oklahoma Press.

Lindo, John, Alessandro Achilli, Ugo A. Perego, David Archer, Cristina Valdiosera, Barbara Petzelt, et al. 2017. "Ancient Individuals from the North American Northwest Coast Reveal 10,000 Years of Regional Genetic Continuity." *Proceedings of the National Academy of Sciences* 114, no. 16: 4093–4098.

López de Cogolludo, Diego. 1957 [1688]. *Historia de Yucatán*. 2 vols. Introduction and notes by J. Ignacio Rubio Mañé. Colección de Grandes Crónicas Mexicanas, no. 3. Cd. de México: Editorial Academia Literaria.

López Ixcoy, Candelaria Dominga. 1997. *Ri Ukemiik ri K'ichee' Chii': Gramática K'ichee'*. Guatemala City: Editorial Cholsamaj.

Lucie-Smith, Edward. 1972. *Symbolist Art*. London: Thames and Hudson.

Lutz, Christopher H. 1994. *Santiago de Guatemala, 1541–1773: City, Caste, and the Colonial Experience*. Norman: University of Oklahoma Press.

MacNutt, Francis Augustus. 1909. *Bartholomew de Las Casas: His Life, His Apostolate, and His Writings*. New York: G. P. Putnam's Sons, Knickerbocker Press.

Martínez, Fr. Marcos. 1575. *Arte de la lengua utlateca o k'iché, vulgarmente llamado el arte de Totonicapan*. Manuscrit Américain 62 in the Bibliothèque nationale de France, Paris.

Matsumoto, Mallory. 2017. *Land, Politics, and Memory in Five Nija'ib' K'iche' Títulos: "The Title and Proof of Our Ancestors."* Boulder: University Press of Colorado.

Maxwell, Judith M., and Robert M. Hill II. 2006. *Kaqchikel Chronicles*. Austin: University of Texas Press.

Mendelson, E. Michael. 1957. *Religion and World-View in a Guatemalan Village*. Microfilm Collection of Manuscripts on Middle American Cultural Anthropology 52. Chicago: University of Chicago Library.

Mendelson, E. Michael. 1958. "A Guatemalan Sacred Bundle." *Man* 58 (August): 121–126.

Mendieta, Fr. Gerónimo de. 1993 [1597]. *Historia Ecclesiástica Indiana*. Cd. de México: Editorial Porrua.

Miller, Mary, and Karl Taube. 1993. *The Gods and Symbols of Ancient Mexico and the Maya*. London: Thames and Hudson.

Molina, Fr. Alonso de. 2001 [1571]. *Vocabulario en lengua castellana y mexicana y mexicana y castellana*. Cd. de México: Editorial Porrúa.

Mondloch, James L., and Eugene P. Hruska. 1975. *Basic Quiché Grammar*. Guatemala City: Centro Indígena.

Morley, Sylvanus G., George W. Brainerd, and Robert J. Sharer. 1983. *The Ancient Maya*. Stanford: Stanford University Press.

Nabokov, Peter. 1981. *Indian Running*. Santa Barbara: Capra.

Nicholson, Henry B. 2001. *Topiltzin Quetzalcoatl*. Boulder: University Press of Colorado.

Olivier, Guilhem. 2007. "Sacred Bundles, Arrows, and New Fire: Foundation and Power in the *Mapa de Cuauhtinchan no. 2*." In *Cave, City, and Eagle's Nest: An Interpretive Journey through the* Mapa de Cuauhtinchan no. 2. Ed. Davíd Carrasco and Scott Sessions. Albuquerque: University of New Mexico Press, 281–313.

Oudijk, Michel R. 2002. "La toma de posesión: Un tema mesoamericano para la legitimación del poder." *Relaciones* 23, no. 91: 95–131.

Orellana, Sandra. 1984. *The Tzutujil Mayas: Continuity and Change, 1250–1630*. Norman: University of Oklahoma Press.

Par Sapón, María Beatriz, and Telma Angelina Can Pixabaj. 2000. *Ujunamaxiik ri K'ichee' Ch'ab'al: Variación dialectal en K'ichee'*. Guatemala City: Cholsamaj.

Pérez Mendoza, Francisco, and Miguel Hernández Mendoza. 1996. *Diccionario Tz'utujil*. Antigua, Guatemala: Proyecto Lingüístico Francisco Marroquín.

Platt, Rutherford H., ed. 1976. *The Lost Books of the Bible and the Forgotten Books of Eden*. New York: Collins.

Posth, Cosimo, Nathan Nakatsuka, Iosif Lazaridis, Pontus Skoglund, Swapan Mallick, Thiseas C. Lamnidis, et al. 2018. "Reconstructing the Deep Population History of Central and South America." *Cell* 175, no. 5: 1185–1197.

Pope, Hugh. 1907. "Angels." In *The Catholic Encyclopedia*, Vol. 1. New York: Robert Appleton Company.

Preucel, Robert W., and Samuel Duwe. 2019. "Introduction: Engaging with Pueblo Movement." In *The Continuous Path: Pueblo Movement and the Archaeology of Becoming*. Ed. Samuel Duwe and Robert W. Preucel. Tucson: University of Arizona Press, 1–33.

Pseudo-Dionysius. 1987. *Pseudo-Dionysius: The Complete Works*. Tr. Colm Luibheid. Mahwah, NJ: Paulist.

Rands, Robert L., and Robert E. Smith. 1965. "Pottery of the Guatemalan Highlands." In *Handbook of Middle American Indians*, vol. 2. Ed. Gordon R. Willey. Austin: University of Texas Press, 95–114.

Recinos, Adrián. 1950. *Anales de los Cakchiqueles y el Título de los señores de Totonicapán*. Cd. de México: Fondo de Cultura Económica.

Recinos, Adrián. 1957. *Crónicas indígenas de Guatemala*. Guatemala City: Editorial Universitaria.

Recinos, Adrián, and Delia Goetz. 1950. *Popol Vuh: The Sacred Book of the Ancient Quiche Maya*. Tr. Delia Goetz and Sylvanus G. Morley. Norman: University of Oklahoma Press.

Recinos, Adrián, and Delia Goetz. 1953. *The Annals of the Cakchiquels and the Title of the Lords of Totonicapán*. Norman: University of Oklahoma Press.

Relación de los caciques y principales del pueblo de Atitlán. 1952 [1571]. *Anales de la Sociedad de Geografía e Historia de Guatemala* 26: 435–438.

Remesal, Fr. Antonio de. 1966. *Historia general de las Indias Occidentales*. 2 vols. Ed. P. Carmelo Sáenz de Santa María. Madrid: Real Academia Española.

Roys, Ralph L. 1965. *Ritual of the Bacabs: A Book of Maya Incantations*. Norman: University of Oklahoma Press.

Roys, Ralph L. 1967. *The Book of Chilam Balam of Chumayel*. Norman: University of Oklahoma Press.

Sachse, Frauke. 2008. "Over Distant Waters: Places of Origin and Creation in Colonial K'iche'an Sources." In *Pre-Columbian Landscapes of Origin*. Ed. John Edward Staller. New York: Springer, 123–160.

Sachse, Frauke. 2016. "The Expression of Christian Concepts in Colonial K'iche' Missionary Texts." In *La transmisión de conceptos cristianos a las lenguas amerindias*. Ed. Sabine Dedenbach-Salazar Sáenz. Sankt Augustin, Germany: Academia Verlag, 93–116.

Sachse, Frauke, and Allen J. Christenson. 2005. *Tulan and the Other Side of the Sea: Unraveling a Metaphorical Concept from Colonial Guatemalan Highland Sources*. www.mesoweb.com/articles/tulan/Tulan.pdf.

Sáenz de Santa María, Carmelo. 1940. *Diccionario Cakchiquel-Español*. Guatemala City: La Sociedad de Geografía e Historia de Guatemala.

Sahagún, Fr. Bernardino de. 1950–1963. *Florentine Codex: General History of the Things of New Spain*. Trans. Charles E. Dibble and Arthur J.O. Anderson. Monographs of the School of American Research and the Museum of New Mexico. 13 vols. Salt Lake City: University of Utah and School of American Research.

Sam Colop, Luis Enrique. 2008. *Popol Wuj*. Guatemala City: Cholsamaj.

Santo Domingo, Fr. Tomás de. ca. 1690. *Vocabulario en la lengua cakchiquel [y española]*. Manuscrit Américain 47 in the Bibliothèque nationale de France, Paris.

Saturno, William A., Karl A. Taube, and David Stuart. 2005. "The Murals of San Bartolo, El Petén, Guatemala, Part 1: The North Wall." *Ancient America* 7 (February): 1–56.

Schele, Linda, and Peter Mathews. 1998. *The Code of Kings: The Language of Seven Sacred Maya Temples and Tombs.* New York: Scribner.

Schultze-Jena, Leonhard. 1954. *La vida y las creencias de los indígenas quichés de Guatemala.* Guatemala City: Ministerio de Educación Pública.

Sharer, Robert J. 1994. *The Ancient Maya.* Stanford: Stanford University Press.

Siméon, Rémi. 1977. *Diccionario de la lengua nahuatl o mexicana.* Cd. de México: Siglo Veintiuno.

Skoglund Pontus, Swapan Mallick, Maria Cátira Bortolini, Niru Chennagiri, Tábita Hünemeier, Maria Luiza Petzl-Erler, Francisco Mauro Salzano, Nick Patterson, and David Reich. 2015. "Genetic Evidence for Two Founding Populations of the Americas." *Nature* 525, no. 7567: 104–108.

Smith, Michael E. 2003. *The Aztecs.* 2nd ed. Oxford: Blackwell.

Sparks, Garry. 2017. *The Americas' First Theologies: Early Sources of Post-Contact Indigenous Religion.* New York: Oxford University Press.

Sparks, Garry. 2019. *Rewriting Maya Religion: Domingo de Vico, K'iche' Maya Intellectuals, and the* Theologia Indorum. Louisville: University Press of Colorado.

Sperling, Harry, and Maurice Simon, tr. 1984. *The Zohar.* 5 vols. London: Soncino.

Steiner, George. 1998. *Errata: An Examined Life.* New Haven, CT: Yale University Press.

Tarn, Nathaniel, and Martin Prechtel. 1990. "Comiéndose la fruta; Metáforos sexuales e iniciaciones en Santiago Atitlán." *Mesoamérica* 19: 73–82.

Tarn, Nathaniel, and Martin Prechtel. 1997. *Scandals in the House of Birds: Shamans and Priests on Lake Atitlán.* New York: Marsilio.

Taube, Karl. 1994. *The Maya Vase Book*, vol. 4: *The Birth Vase: Natal Imagery in Ancient Maya Myth and Ritual.* Ed. Justin Kerr. New York: Kerr and Associates.

Tedlock, Barbara. 1982. *Time and the Highland Maya.* Albuquerque: University of New Mexico Press.

Tedlock, Barbara. 1992. *Time and the Highland Maya.* Revised ed. Albuquerque: University of New Mexico Press.

Tedlock, Dennis E. 1983. *The Spoken Word and the Work of Interpretation.* Philadelphia: University of Pennsylvania Press.

Tedlock, Dennis E. 1985. *Popol Vuh.* New York: Simon and Schuster.

Tedlock, Dennis E. 1996. *Popol Vuh.* Revised ed. New York: Simon and Schuster.

Tezozomoc, Fernando Alvarado. 1975. *Crónica mexicáyotl.* Cd. de México: Universidad Nacional Autónoma de México, Instituto de Investigaciones Históricas.

Tokovinine, Alexandre. 2013. *Place and Identity in Classic Maya Narratives*. Studies in Pre-Columbian Art and Archaeology 37. Washington, DC: Dumbarton Oaks Research Library and Collection.

Torre, Tomás de la. 1985. *Diario de viaje de Salamanca a Chiapa, 1544–45*. Burgos, Spain: Editorial OPE Caleruega.

Torquemada, Juan de. 1969. *Monarquía Indiana*. Cd. de México: Editorial Porrúa.

Vare[I]a, Fr. Francisco de. 1929 [1699]. *Calepino en lengua cakchiquel*. Typescript by William Gates. Gates Collection, Manuscript Archives, Harold B. Lee Library, Brigham Young University, Provo, UT.

Vázquez de Espinosa, Antonio. 1969. *Compendio y descripción de las Indias Occidentales*. Biblioteca de Autores Españoles 231. Madrid: Real Academia Española.

Vico, Fr. Domingo de. 1605 [1553]. *Theologia Indorum: Vae nima vuh rii theologia indorum ubinaam*. Mss. 497.4.Ua13. Philadelphia: American Philosophical Society.

Villacañas, Fr. Benito de. 1692. *Arte y vocabulario en lengua cakchiquel*. Manuscript in the University Museum Library, University of Pennsylvania, Philadelphia.

Villaseñor Alonso, Isabel. 2010. *Building Materials of the Ancient Maya: A Study of Archaeological Plasters*. Saarbrucken, Germany: Lambert Academic Publishing.

Vitoria, Francisco de. 1991 [1539]. *Francisco de Vitoria: Political Writings*. Ed. Anthony Pagden and Jeremy Lawrance. Cambridge: Cambridge University Press.

Watanabe, John M. 1992. *Maya Saints and Souls in a Changing World*. Austin: University of Texas Press.

Weeks, John M., Frauke Sachse, and Christian M. Prager. 2009. *Maya Daykeeping: Three Calendars from Highland Guatemala*. Boulder: University Press of Colorado.

Ximénez, Fr. Francisco. 1701. *Arte de las tres lenguas 3a3chiquel, quiche y 4'utuhil*. Manuscript in the Ayer Collection, Newberry Library, Chicago, IL.

Ximénez, Fr. Francisco. 1929–1931. *Historia de la provincia de San Vicente de Chiapa y Guatemala*. Vols. 1–3. Guatemala City: Biblioteca "Goathemala."

Ximénez, Fr. Francisco. 1967. *Escolios a las historias del origen de los indios*. Sociedad de Geografía e Historia de Guatemala Special Publication 13. Guatemala City: Sociedad de Geografía e Historia de Guatemala.

Ximénez, Fr. Francisco. 1985 [1701]. *Primera parte del tesoro de las lenguas cakchiquel, quiche y zutuhil, en que las dichas lenguas se traducen a la nuestra española*. Special Publication 30. Guatemala City: Academia de Geografía e Historia.

Ximénez, Fr. Francisco. 1999. *Historia de la provincia de San Vicente de Chiapa y Guatemala de la orden de predicadores*. Ed. Carmelo Sáenz de Santa María. 2 vols. Cd. de México: Consejo Estatal para la Cultura y las Artes de Chiapas.

Zorita, Alonso de. 1963. *Life and Labor in Ancient Mexico: The Brief and Summary Relation of the Lords of New Spain*. Tr. Benjamin Keen. New Brunswick, NJ: Rutgers University Press.

Zorita, Alonso de. 1999. *Relación de la Nueva España II: Relación de algunas de las muchas cosas notables que hay en la Nueva España y de su conquista y pacificación y de la conversión de los naturales de ella*. Ed. Ethelia Ruiz Medrano and José Mariano Leyva. Cd. de México: Conaculta.

Index

40, 112–17; origins of, 90–96; settlements, 129–35; symbols of authority, 164–65
Kik' Re', 39
Kik' Rixk'aq, 39
K'iq'ab', Lord, 18, 56–57*n10*, 145*n477*, 155, 154–55*n540*, 164, 169–70*n626*, 183, 184; conquest by fire, 177–78; Great Houses of, 166; sons of, 176; warfare, 157–58
K'iq'ab'il, 135, 154, 172, 173
K'iq'ab' Kawisimaj, 180, 182
K'iq'ab' Nima Yax, 4, 6, 172, 173, 175, 186*n707*
K'isija, 160
Knowledge Zapote Tree, 73*n73*, 75, 76
K'o Ajaw, 117–18*n324*
K'o'akul Akutaq', 25; journey of, 117–21
K'o Akutek, 117–18*n324*
K'ochojlan, 95, 101
K'oja, 157; destruction of, 158–59*n560*
K'oka'ib' (Co Caib), 24, 25, 103, 123, 134*n414*, 140, 144, 145, 154; Great Houses of, 166; journey of, 117–22; lordship of, 115–17
K'okawib' (Co Caiuim/Caibim), 24, 25, 103, 123, 154; adultery of, 115–16; journey of, 117–22
Kokoa K'iq'ab', José, 185
K'ok'oja, 122, 154
K'onache, 134*n414*, 135
K'onache Ristayul, 116–17
K'opichoch, 95, 101
K'oq'anawil, 95, 101
K'oraxonamaq', 122
K'otuja, 134*n414*, 135, 146, 154, 155
K'otuja Q'ukumatz, 152–53, 154, 183*n692*; death of, 157*n550*; marriage negotiations of, 145–49; warfare, 150, 151
K'oxom Xaq, 184
K'oyoy, 123, 154
K'ub'ul Ka'al, 160
K'uch Ulaq'am, 172
Kukulcan, 14
K'ulaja, 168*n616*, 180
K'ulb'a Kawinal, 133
K'ulel, 39–40
Kumatz, 157–58*n554*, 160
K'wal Ab'aj, 10

Lajuj No'j, 23, 25, 117, 166
lamentation, 77
Landa, Diego de, 57*n11*
Land of Abundance, 62

land rights, 3, 4, 6, 29, 178, 179
languages: K'iche', 96; changing of, 79–80, 88
Laq'alik Mumus, 183*n693*
Laq'am Ab'aj, 184
Laq'amal, 123, 154
Laqam Kuk, 149
Laq' Pop, 135
Las Casas, Bartolomé de, 35–36; marriage alliances, 147–48*n487*
Last Judgment, 31
Latin alphabet: K'iche' in, 49–50; Maya languages in, 36–37
legitimacy, K'iche' rulers, 14, 24
Lemo'a', Laguna, *178f*
Leq' B'aq, 166
Lesser Ajpop of Valiant Men, 120*n343*, 135, 137*n436*, 151, 165, 166, 171
Levi, 80
life cycle, human, 62*n21*
Life Zapote Tree, 73*n73*, 75
lightning deities, 164*n584*
lip plugs, 106*n256*
Little Sab'ache', 172
Lolmet, 121, 136, 160
Lolmet Ajaw, 121
Lolmet Kawinay, 161
López de Cerrato, Alonso, 22, 185*n702*
lords, 3, 6, 122; K'iche', 112–17; military sentinels, 168–70; symbols of, 118, 119–20, 137–45, 151, 164–65. *See also* nobility
Los Achiotes, 99*n222*
Los Cimientos, 99*n220*
Lucas Ajtojil, Juan, 186
Lucifer, 70

maidens, sent by Seven Nations, 109–12
maize, maize dough, 71, 77; as abundance, 62*n20*, 62*n21*; humans created of, 81*n118*, 84*n129*, 89*n172*; origins of, 99*n223*
Majk'inalom, 95, 101
Majukotaj, 12, 56*n5*, 83*n124*, 94, 95, 100, 101, 103, 105, 122, 124, 128, 130, 131, 133, 135; first dawn, 123, 125; migrations, 96, 99; and Seven Nations wars, 106, 107, 108, 110, 112
Makol Ab'aj-Tab'alamin, 180
Malaj, *146f*
Malaj Tz'utujil, 150; marriage negotiations, 145–49
malice of heart, 153